CW00820771

I first became acquainted with the name of John Ross, the Highland-born, Gaelic-speaking missionary to Korea, when I was working on a new edition of the Gaelic Bible for the National Bible Society of Scotland in 1986–87. I was anxious to learn more about him and his translation of the New Testament into Korean, but I failed to find a suitable biography. Ross's namesake, the Rev. Dr John Ross, Drumnadrochit, has now filled this gap admirably. Meticulously researched and written, this book unites the various strands in the other John Ross's life. I learned an immense amount about Ross himself, his Gaelic background, his decision to go to Manchuria (rather than Portree), his later arrival in Korea, his remarkable acquisition of the Korean language, the nature and significance of the translation, and wider Christian missionary strategies in China. This is a thrilling story, taking the reader through the God-given successes of Ross's labours, as well as the immense challenges he faced, including the Boxer Rising. It is a thoroughly worthy memorial to Ross, the missionary and translator, but supremely a timeless and inspiring testimony to the fruit which follows the faithful sowing of Gospel seed.

DONALD E. MEEK
formerly Professor of Scottish and Gaelic Studies,
University of Edinburgh

This biography of the Scottish missionary to China, John Ross, is the most thorough discussion of his life, missionary work, and writings available in English. It breaks new ground in many areas, giving us a much more thorough description of Ross and his endeavours, and therefore insight into why Ross was such a successful missionary. The book goes well beyond a simple biographical statement of his life, but thoroughly sets him and his missionary work in the church, social, and cultural context of his time, both in the Scotland, and in China. This book is to be warmly welcomed because of Ross's seminal influence on the establishment and growth of the Christian Church in Manchuria, Northeast China, and in Korea, through his translation of the New Testament into Korean. This is a must read for anyone interested in missions and Christianity in East Asia.

JAMES H. GRAYSON
Professor Emeritus,
School of East Asian Studies,
The University of Sheffield

John Ross has produced an inspiring, engaging and realistic portrait of a missionary namesake who left a profound legacy in the Chinese and Korean churches. Ross does not shy away from challenging issues and yet recounts the wonderful work of God through a Gaelic speaking Highlander who would go on to remarkable missionary service, including translation of the Bible into Korean.

Donald John MacLean
Adjunct Professor of Historical Theology,
Westminster Presbyterian Theological Seminary, Newcastle

We are indebted to the author for a work of extensive and seriously thorough research and scholarly writing, not just into the life and work of his namesake, John Ross, but in his portrayal of the Gospel partnership of missionary pioneers and the growth of the Church in Manchuria and Korea. All this set against a backcloth of the mid-nineteenth century Presbyterian world of Scotland and written out in a clear and accessible style. Alongside the more familiar names of William Chalmers Burns and James Hudson Taylor, nineteenth century pioneers of mission in China, we are introduced to many other men and women whose life and ministry was material to the growth of the work of God in Asia – a set of well documented mini-biopics of these missionary pioneers appear in the appendix. The far sighted strategies of evangelism adopted by Ross early on in his ministry and the sovereign work of the Spirit of God in the growth of the Church in Manchuria give cause for praise as they bring glory to God. In exciting and remarkable ways, we learn how a God given vision for seminal Gospel work in Korea, practically surmounting serious obstacles, materialises. For students of Cross Cultural mission the book is food for thought and an invaluable and rich resource of cultural and historical material. The implications of gospel ministry in hostile political situations such as the martyrdom of so many missionaries in China during the Boxer uprisings, a reminder that discipleship is costly. The level of sacrificial commitment, breadth of education and learning, willingness to face hardship and danger of John Ross and those nineteenth century pioneers seriously challenges the level of our twenty first century commitment to missions. Packed solid with carefully documented information, the author has written in a narrative style which draws you to read on. With its many helpful theological and cultural insights, it is a book set to become a classic.

David W. Ellis
Former National Director OMF International UK

One of Scotland's great exports to the world was missionaries who have changed countries – perhaps none more so than John Ross, a United Presbyterian minister who is regarded as the founding father of the ten million strong Korean Presbyterian church. As someone who lived as a boy in Ross's home parish of Nigg in Easter Ross in the Scottish

Highlands, I had always wanted to write a biography of this extraordinary unsung hero of the faith. Now I don't have to. Because John Ross (also a Highland Presbyterian minister, but no relation!) has given us this excellent biography. *The Power and the Glory* has both historical and spiritual depth. It is a fascinating account of life and ministry in Scotland, Manchuria and Korea. Just as the Korean Church is greatly indebted to John Ross the missionary, so we are indebted to John Ross his biographer for a work that should have a lasting impact.

DAVID ROBERTSON
Well-known pastor and apologist

With the eye for detail of a careful historian and the facility with words of a skilled storyteller, Dr John Ross has provided a fascinating account of a remarkable aspect of the story of the Christian church in East Asia. While John Ross of Balintore is the primary subject of the narrative, Dr Ross introduces the reader to a wide range of characters and matters of context with clarity, a fine turn of phrase, and, in particular, an eye to the bigger story of God's providential and missional purposes. The role of indigenous believers in the progress of Christian witness is given due prominence. Dr Ross offers a compelling account of how God has worked out (and continues to work out) his purposes through the lives and testimonies of his people in various parts of the world. This book is essential reading for the serious student of mission and the general reader alike.

ALISTAIR WILSON
Lecturer, Mission and New Testament,
Edinburgh Theological Seminary, Edinburgh, Scotland

For the first time in the English language, we finally have a comprehensive retelling of the life and work of John Ross, the important Scottish missionary to Manchuria (Northeast China) and Korea (then, the 'Hermit Kingdom'). This is a meticulously researched and immensely readable book that weaves together the fascinating biography of the man John Ross with the social, religious, and imperial history and context which shaped him and his mission. We are told of the ways he relied on and empowered local Chinese and Korean coworkers in the work of the Gospel, the intellectual contributions he and his collaborators made – not least in one of the first Korean Bibles – and the enduring legacy which has been left behind. This is such a wonderfully captivating read.

ALEXANDER CHOW
Senior Lecturer of Theology and World Christianity,
School of Divinity, University of Edinburgh,
Editor of Scottish Missions to China (Brill 2022)

The Power and the Glory

John Ross and the Evangelisation of Manchuria and Korea

John Stuart Ross

Hardback ISBN 978-1-5271-0891-2
Ebook ISBN 978-1-5271-0981-0

10 9 8 7 6 5 4 3 2 1

Published in 2022
by
Christian Focus Publications Ltd,
Geanies House, Fearn, Ross-shire,
IV20 1TW, Great Britain.

www.christianfocus.com

Cover design by
Daniel van Straaten

Printed and bound by Bell & Bain, Glasgow

CONTENTS

This book is dedicated to the
Free Church of Scotland congregations
around Scotland's Great Glen in which
I have been privileged to serve:

Greyfriars and Stratherrick,
Glenurquhart and Fort Augustus,
Kilmallie and Ardnamurchan.

Preface

'The missionary should be as learned as his university can make him; he should have as thorough a knowledge of theology as his professors can bestow upon him; he may be as religious as the most extreme pietist; yet he may be wanting in the essentials of a Church-building apostle. The man who is to plant Churches must be himself on fire of the Holy Ghost. Men of learning and diligence, though cold and unsympathetic, may be very useful in a Church already formed; but such men will not found a Church. A breeze, even a cold breeze, will fan into brighter blaze a fire already lit; but only by fire can fire be engendered. Fire alone can introduce fire into material previously dead.'

JOHN ROSS, 'The Most Difficult Missionary Problem.'

THE first thing I need to say is that this book is not an autobiography. The fact that both subject and author share the same name is fortuitous; there is no reason to believe we are blood relations. North and east of Scotland's Great Glen, Rosses are run-of-the-mill, and John Rosses two-a-penny. The more famous Rosses have been soldiers and Arctic explorers, one even a Cherokee chief. The less famous were and still are butchers, bakers and, doubtless, candlestick makers. Not a few have been Presbyterian ministers. At least three were missionaries. The subject of this biography, John Ross of Balintore, Manchuria and Korea, was, however, singular.

It is a truism to say that I could not have written this book without help, but it must be said for all that. Even the idea came from someone else. As I was contemplating retirement – or was that re-tyre-ment? – William Mackenzie of Christian Focus Publications approached me to say that he had a project up his sleeve that might enjoyably and profitably occupy my time after pastoral ministry, but he wouldn't tell me what it was. The disclosure was only made after my formal retiral, just when we were in the throes of moving home to Fort William to care for the Kilmallie and Ardnamurchan Free Church of Scotland congregation. To them I owe a very great debt, not least for their gracious tolerance when they had so much on their minds and quite rightly expected the undistracted attention of their interim moderator.

The task of research and writing has been a roller-coaster, successively a thrill and a daunting challenge. The lockdowns connected with the Covid 19 pandemic meant that libraries closed. Simultaneously, the hugely important New College Library in Edinburgh temporarily moved its collection to 40 George Square during building improvements at The Mound. Once more, the imperturbable staff, including Lauren McKay, Karen Bonthron and Linda Blackwood, went further than the second mile in assisting me electronically, but even they couldn't do the impossible when some important material I wished to consult was stored even beyond their long reach. It was then that the indomitable Maureen Ross of The John Ross Visitor Centre at Hilton came to the rescue, loaning me Dr Hyung Shin Park's two volumes: *The Rev. John Ross: A Primary Source Book*, published in 2019 by the Institute of the History of Christianity in Korea. These contained scanned images of almost all the documents I wished to consult.

I also record my gratitude to the staff of the National Library of Scotland, Edinburgh; Iver Martin, Principal, and Ruth Smith, Assistant Librarian, for access to the Edinburgh Theological Seminary library; Hector Morrison, Principal, and Geordie Cryle, Librarian, for access to the library at the Highland Theological College; Mhairi Jarvie, Archive Assistant at the Highland Archive Centre, in Inverness; and Craig Brough, the Information Services Librarian at the Royal Botanic Gardens, Kew, who illuminated Ross the botanist and the plants named after him. Donald E. Meek, previously Professor of Celtic at the University of Aberdeen, and James Grayson, Emeritus Professor of the School of East Asian Studies at Sheffield University, read the manuscript and spared my blushes with helpful corrections and suggested improvements. James Skinner of

Tain cast light on education in Ross-shire's seaboard villages in the mid-nineteenth century, and supplied a copy of John Ross' will, thus clarifying details regarding the properties he came to own in Balintore. Another Easter Ross resident, Hugh Mackenzie, very kindly chauffeured us around the area pointing out places connected with the Ross story, while his wife Mary sustained us with gracious hospitality. Kim Watt helped me track down one of Ross' daughter's movements. Malcolm Maclean, Rosanna Burton, Irene Roberts, Alex MacAskill and Willie Mackenzie of Christian Focus Publications have all corrected me, prodded me, assisted and chivvied me, and altogether encouraged me to keep going.

My wife Elizabeth has, once again, been a tower of strength supporting and encouraging me, and sometimes applying the brakes when the project became obsessive. The publication of this volume marks not only the one hundred and fiftieth anniversary of John Ross' arrival in Manchuria, but also our Golden Wedding anniversary, when together we look back on fifty rich and blessed years of Christian ministry together in Nigeria, Belfast, globally with Christian Witness to Israel, at Greyfriars Free Church of Scotland in Inverness, at Dumisani Theological Institute in South Africa, and at Glenurquhart and Fort Augustus, and Kilmallie and Ardnamurchan Free Church congregations. I hope she feels that this book in some way compensates for, or at least explains, my frequent distraction, preoccupation and inattention.

Many Chinese place names have changed since John Ross' time: I have used modern names of places better known to westerners, but otherwise retained the forms used in contemporary missionary accounts, although these vary; for example, the town of Mukden, which features so prominently in this narrative, is sometimes spelled 'Moukden' and sometimes 'Mookden'. I have retained Mukden throughout. When I am quoting verbatim, I have adhered to the spelling as given by the source. South Korean place names are generally given in their contemporary form. North Korean place names are unaltered. There is a table at the back of the book that lists many of the names occurring in this account with their modern equivalents.

Of course, any misinterpretation of events and other errors are mine. I regret any failure to acknowledge the work of others. This is not a comprehensive biography; there are many facets of Ross' character and work left unexplored, and my hope is that my deficiencies may stimulate someone else to do better.

This book leaves my desk with the prayer that what God did in Manchuria and Korea through John Ross and his colleagues, he might do here in Ross' homeland, and everywhere where this book is read. To him alone belongs the power and the glory!

Drumnadrochit,
Easter 2022

1

William Burns: 'The Spiritual Father'

'Make the desolate of heart to sing.'
HENRY GRATTAN GUINNESS

THE vigour with which the dying William Burns spoke was so startling that his biographer, his brother Islay, felt he had to render the words in block capitals: FOR THINE IS THE POWER, AND THE GLORY. As he lay on his bed in Newchwang, Manchuria, his last lucid thoughts were spoken with 'extraordinary power and decision.' Indeed, there was something about them of the old passion that had marked out the best of his preaching, 'an almost preternatural terribleness and grandeur.'[1]

For a month or more, Burns' life had been ebbing away and he was reconciled to it. He was ready for rest and eager for what his Lord had promised and prayed for, that he might be with him and see his glory (John 17:24). He might be dying, but God's work in Manchuria was not yet finished. Of that he had no doubts. 'God will carry on the good work; I have no fears for that,' he had said. Still, a question burned in his mind. If he couldn't continue the work, who would? He had had his own thoughts on that too. He had told his colleague Carstairs Douglas that he hoped the Irish Presbyterians might come up to Newchwang and take over. But when he died on 4th April, 1868, and was buried in the foreigners' graveyard, the matter remained unresolved.

William Chalmers Burns was one of the most remarkable figures in Scottish Church history. He was born in 1815 in the manse of Dun, near Brechin, Angus, where his father was minister. The family relocated to Kilsyth, Lanarkshire, in 1821. Here he enjoyed the countryside and entertained a notion of being a farmer. His plans were disrupted when his uncle Alexander Burns, a lawyer, seeing his intellectual potential, took him under his wing and put him through Aberdeen Grammar School. In 1829 Burns entered Marischal College. Two years later he left to work in his uncle's office in Edinburgh. The next year he was converted. He recommenced his studies, this time at Aberdeen University, graduating in 1834. Believing himself called to be a minister, he took a divinity course at Glasgow University, where he felt drawn to consecrate himself to God's will with a premonition that this might mean overseas missionary work.

Burns was acutely sensitive to the lostness of humanity. Once, overwrought by the crowds thronging Glasgow's bustling Argyle Street, he sought respite in the Argyle Arcade and completely failed to notice his mother who, entering from the other end, had walked right up to him. Apologising, he explained, 'I was so overcome with the sight of the countless crowds of immortal beings eagerly hustling hither and thither, but all posting onwards towards the eternal world, that I could bear it no longer, and turned in here to seek relief in quiet thought.'[2]

In 1839 Burns was licensed to preach by the Presbytery of Glasgow, the same year that Robert Murray M'Cheyne, the twenty-six-year-old minister of St. Peter's, Dundee, departed with three other ministers to conduct a survey of Jewish communities in Europe and Palestine to inform the strategy of the Jewish Committee of the Church of Scotland. Although St. Peter's was a new congregation, established barely two and half years earlier, and despite Burns having no pastoral experience, M'Cheyne nevertheless invited him to be his locum for the duration of his absence. Burns was overawed by the responsibility. After walking around the parish with one of the elders on his first Saturday afternoon in Dundee he went straight to his room and was later found 'lying on his face in an agony of prayer'.[3] What struck those who listened to him preach next morning, however, was not panic, but a deep calm that he had been given.

Hardly settled in Dundee, Burns impulsively wrote to the Jewish committee offering his services as a missionary in Aden. Then he just as hurriedly withdrew his offer, citing 'peculiar circumstances'. Two revivals had broken out almost simultaneously, one at his father's parish in Kilsyth and the other at St. Peter's. The story of these revivals is well known. Both William's brother Islay and his friend Andrew Bonar recounted them in detail. As did others. The local Dundee press made much of the emotional drama: the large crowds, and the groanings, faintings, uncontrolled weeping and screaming that accompanied Burns' preaching. But when John MacDonald, the 'Apostle of North', arrived in Dundee and the revival accelerated, these emotional outbursts subsided. This cannot be explained by any difference of theology between Burns and MacDonald. There was none. The explanation lies in the differences of temperament and the levels of maturity of the two men. Under MacDonald's influence, Burns' ministry at Dundee matured and blossomed. The godliness of his life so endeared him to the congregation of St. Peter's that one group, somewhat disloyally to M'Cheyne, wanted him to stay on as their minister. A party spirit threatened the work of revival. But when M'Cheyne returned in early November 1839, the Christian love between him and Burns was so evident that all unhelpful competition melted away.

Burns next embarked upon an unpaid itinerant ministry in northern England and Scotland, leaving in his wake a number of local revivals. An evangelistic tour of Ireland, however, met with little success. Then, in 1844, after joining the newly formed Free Church of Scotland, Burns went to Canada where he was warmly received by Scottish immigrants, but without any great results. In 1846 he became a missionary of the English Presbyterian Church and the following year arrived in Hong Kong. His first seven years of missionary service were endured with scant encouragement and no obvious outcome. His ministry at Amoy, however, saw young Chinese people coming to faith and enthusiastically establishing new congregations. Burns learned to entrust the nurture of these new converts to the Holy Spirit and the ministry of others, as he, travelling lightly, with a small selection of Bibles and tracts to distribute, went on his way. The pioneer was always keen to see what lay on the other side of the hill. In 1854 a brief furlough in Scotland led to a final decade of unbroken missionary service.

As a foreigner in China, Burns was both conspicuous and vulnerable. He suffered arrest and imprisonment, and was despised, ridiculed, robbed and victimised. Meeting the English missionary, James Hudson Taylor, newly arrived in China, he was persuaded to follow Taylor's example, and though ridiculed by westerners and Chinese of higher status, wore the dress of ordinary people and carefully followed local customs to avoid offence. Strategy apart, a close bond developed between the two men. Taylor looked to Burns as his mentor and found his stories of blessing in revivals and God's care of him in difficulties a source of sound instruction and rich inspiration. For his part, Burns was refreshed by Taylor's enthusiasm. Taylor later wrote, 'Never had I had such a spiritual father as Mr Burns.'

In 1867, now fifty-three years old, Burns travelled to the port of Newchwang, with the intention of commencing missionary work in Manchuria. Here he succumbed to fever, brought on by a chill and exacerbated by fatigue. Aside from converts and congregations, Burn's tangible legacy was a translation of Bunyan's *The Pilgrim's Progress,* some English hymns and a partially completed translation of the Psalms in the Scottish metrical style, but such British Christian classics proved too foreign for Chinese tastes.

In 1869, in response to Burns' overtures, the Presbyterian Church in Ireland sent a medical doctor, Dr Joseph Hunter, and a minister, Rev. Hugh Waddell, as their first missionaries to Manchuria. But others too were showing an interest. Alexander Williamson, a missionary of the Scottish United Presbyterian Church and agent of the National Bible Society of Scotland, sought to prevail upon his denomination to commence work in Manchuria. The United Presbyterians sent John Ross and his wife to Chefoo in Shantung province in 1872, with Williamson entertaining the hope that they might end up in Manchuria.

What follows is the strangely neglected, but remarkable story of John Ross' missionary work in Scotland, Manchuria and Korea. Ross left behind an amazing legacy of culturally sensitive evangelism, soundly established Presbyterian-pattern churches, innovative missionary principles, valuable publications, and a rich vein of translations, including the first version of the New Testament in Korean.

With justification, Ross has not only been called the Maker of the Manchurian Mission, but also the Father of Presbyterianism in Korea. Evidence of the latter claim is the fact that half of the twenty million South Korean Christians and two thirds of South Korean Protestants are Presbyterians. But the most intriguing and as yet untellable story concerns what may remain of evangelical Presbyterianism in North Korea. Pyongyang, a centre of American Presbyterian missionary activity, was once regarded as the 'Jerusalem of the East'. Today the city is dominated by landmarks of the North Korean regime, from where the country is administered according to the atheistic philosophy of *Juche* and the diktat of Kim Jong-un. Nowhere in the world is Christian persecution so fierce. Bible-owning North Koreans face banishment to labour camps or even execution. Christian parents share their faith with their children only when they feel they are old enough to count the cost. Yet, tantalising, but unverifiable, reports of church growth are also heard. The Lord knows.

In North Korea, as elsewhere, the truth of Tertullian's famous saying, that the blood of martyrs is seed, is irrefutable. Persecution invariably proves counter-productive. Who can forget the moving testimony of eighteen-year-old Gyeong Ju Son, the young North Korean student who, at the 2010 Third Lausanne Congress in Cape Town, shared her dream that one day she would return to North Korea and there witness to her Saviour? And so, she may, for his is indeed THE POWER, AND THE GLORY. The following lines from Henry Grattan Guinness' sonnet commemorating William Burns, so appropriate in the light of John Ross' work, enunciate the principle so clearly.

And now, Lord, let thy servant's mantle fall
Upon another! Since thy solemn call
To preach the truth in China has been heard,
Grant that a double portion be conferred
Of the same spirit on the gentler head
Of some Elisha who may raise the dead,
And fill the widow's cruse, and heal the spring,
And make the desolate of heart to sing.

2

Heir to a Goodly Heritage

A fine looking set of men [though] not remarkable for any personal qualities.

REV. LEWIS ROSE, MINISTER OF NIGG.

IN the rich Easter Ross farmland, close to the seaboard villages of Shandwick, Balintore and Hilton, there rises an ancient spring known in Gaelic as *Sùil na bà*, the 'cow's eye', said to have medicinal properties. A mile or so south-east, near the coast, is another spring, *Tobar na Slàinte*, the 'well of health', or salvation. By the 1840s, both wells were neglected. But so too were the Christian wells of salvation, or so complained Rev. Lewis Rose, the parish minister of Nigg and contributor to the *New Statistical Account* of 1845.[1] Not far from these reputedly salubrious sites, in a place called Rarichie, stood the home of twenty-nine-year-old master tailor Hugh Ross and his teacher wife Catherine Sutherland. Here on Wednesday, 6th July, 1842, a son, John, was born. Hugh Ross was one of perhaps a dozen tailors in the general neighbourhood who counted themselves fortunate to be able to make a living from making up men's workwear from homespun or women's dresses from shop-bought cloth. A tailor's income was modest, though a master tailor, having one or more apprentices under his instruction, fared better than average.[2]

John's birthplace was in the Church of Scotland parish of Nigg. Twelve days after his birth, his parents brought him to be baptised in Nigg Old Parish Church, which indicates that at the time Hugh and Catherine adhered to the Church of Scotland. John's siblings were all baptised at the United Succession Church at Chapelhill, a few miles to the east, suggesting a change in the family's church allegiance took place soon after John's birth. Why, we can only conjecture.

Nigg parish is situated on a peninsula of approximately seven thousand and sixty-one acres in extent, six miles long, by a little over two broad, jutting into the Cromarty Firth in a southern direction. The Hill of Nigg, the parish's main topographical feature, takes up about a third of the area. The population at the time was around one thousand four hundred souls, most of whom were native Gaelic speakers, though many also spoke English. According to the *New Statistical Account*, written by the admittedly biased minister, the parish was honest, upright and God-fearing; not one case of crime had been reported for twenty years. The parish records, however, don't share such a rosy view. The kirk session had cause to deal with occasional moral lapses, but their discipline was neither harsh nor resented, and most culprits were restored to full communicant membership.

A generation or so before the time of Hugh Ross the countryside had been convulsed by the infamous Highland Clearances, when landlords, such as the Duke of Sutherland, eager for a larger income than the rents of their tenants could sustain, took from the people their traditional hill grazing, and let it to large scale commercial graziers who ran large flocks of improved Cheviots and Southdowns. Some of the lairds instructed their managers, known as factors, to evict sitting tenants on the flimsiest of excuses and deny them the possibility of return by leaving their homes inhabitable. Such callousness condemned the poorest to distress, destitution, and even death, and indelibly stained the reputation of those who had hitherto been the guardians of the clans.[3]

By the 1830s, agriculture on the Nigg peninsula had settled down. The poorer people found employment on the larger improved farms, each with a patchwork of enclosed fields, grazed by mixed flocks of sturdy Cheviot sheep and the smaller local breed. Cattle were also reared, mostly the traditional black variety, supplying local people with milk and butter, and beef for the export market.

On the rough ground goats browsed what cattle and sheep couldn't or wouldn't eat. Well-tilled arable ground produced crops of wheat, the recently introduced brewing barley, Swedish turnips (swedes), as well as the traditional crop of oats. A small quantity of hay for local consumption was made. In a cottar's home acre or a tailor's garden, fertilised by manure and seaweed, grew potatoes, beans and cabbages. On his table could be found oatmeal brose (oatmeal mixed with hot water), as well as oatcakes and bannocks, along with crowdie cheese, meat, mainly mutton, and fish. Buttermilk and sweet milk, water, beer and whisky were his beverages. He lived simply, but well.

The post-Clearance years in Sutherland, so brilliantly described by Neil Gunn in his masterpiece, *The Silver Darlings,* had their equivalent in Ross-shire. Those who had once tilled the land demonstrated remarkable versatility by turning to fishing. To stimulate this redeployment and overcome the financial challenge of buying a fishing boat, some landowners made the capital investment and provided a new boat every seven years, in return for a fifth of the catch. Some people, however, preferred to maintain their independence by taking out loans for boats and gear, and repaying them – or not – from the profits of the catch, after each member of the crew had taken a share.

The most profitable fishing was in summer when, between late July and mid-September, large shoals of herring could be caught at night up to fifty miles offshore. For the rest of the year, long-line fishing for white fish, such as turbot, cod, haddock, whiting, cuddies and sole, made up the bulk of the catch, supplemented with salmon. Over a few good seasons the catch might fund the building of new stone cottages and furnish them comfortably. But in other years the herring were scarce, and the repayment of debts led to hardship.

About sixteen local crews from the seaboard villages of Shandwick, Balintore and Hilton took part in this precarious business, subject not only to fluctuations of the fish stocks and the buoyancy of the market, but also to the vagaries of weather and a treacherous coast. The Moray Firth was especially susceptible to north-easterly storms. It took considerable skill – or luck – to negotiate Balintore harbour in stormy conditions in an open fishing skiff. Even larger boats were not safe. 1843, the year after John Ross' birth, was not marked in the seaboard villages, as it was elsewhere, as the year of the Disruption of the Church of Scotland and the formation of the Free Church, but as the year the schooner *Linnet* was dashed upon the rocks below Cadboll, with the loss of all the crew. The disaster was epoch making. In the seaboard villages, events were referred to as before or after the *Linnet*.

Terrible as it was, the *Linnet* disaster was eclipsed by the catastrophe of August, 1848. The weather of 18th August promised good fishing, and around eight hundred Moray Firth boats put out from harbours between Wick in the north and Stonehaven in the south. By midnight, strengthening winds and heavy seas led many skippers to haul their nets and run for shelter. In the course of the following storm, one hundred and twenty-four boats were lost or seriously damaged, many while trying to enter harbour, within sight of anxious friends and relatives. Around one hundred fishermen lost their lives.

Fishing has always bred men: hard, courageous men. Seven years after Ross' birth, in his *The Value and Importance of Scottish Fisheries*, James Thomson observed that the Moray Firth fishermen on the coasts of Ross and Sutherland were strong-bodied, strong-minded and staunch traditionalists, the habits of one generation falling naturally upon the next. 'The man who ventures from day to day on the briny deep must have mental courage combined with physical strength ... a thoroughbred fisherman is distinguished by attributes – moral, mental, physical.'[4] Rose, the minister, concurred, considering the men of Nigg 'a fine looking set of men', though he acidly commented that they were 'not remarkable for any personal qualities'.[5]

The *New Statistical Account* reported that the population of the Nigg peninsula, maritime and agrarian, enjoyed good health, listing only rheumatism and scrofula (cervical tuberculosis) as common diseases. Apparently, there were no blind, deaf and dumb persons in the parish and only one who suffered from serious mental illness. Nor does Rose mention the cholera outbreak of 1832 which hit the fishing communities hard. Having made its way from the south, the infection was rumoured to have arrived in Easter Ross during the herring season by a boat from Prestonpans. Hugh Miller reported how locally it was being said that when the infected vessel was offshore a little yellow cloud detached itself and flew along the ground, which was cleverly intercepted by man with a large linen bag in which the miasma was caught, and safely buried in the church yard, under a stone near to which the sexton will never open a new grave.[6] To this day there is a plot marked with the sign, 'cholera grave.'

By the beginning of August, one fisherman in Shandwick had died, a week later several cases were found in Hilton, though few proved fatal. By 20th August, however, Hilton had suffered twenty-one deaths with another twenty sufferers given scant hope of survival. At Balintore, fifteen died, and many were infected. *The Inverness Courier* reported that a *cordon sanitaire* had been thrown around the area, policed by Chelsea Pensioners, who had been sworn in as constables. Unscathed families nervously isolated themselves, living in the fields in makeshift tents. The only available doctors were in Tain, and had not the Nigg Board of Health and the Kirk Session responded promptly, many more deaths might have occurred.

The provision of education in the community was barely adequate, but it was not altogether popular either because parents were too poor or the benefits of education were undervalued. John Ross' mother was a teacher but at which school we cannot be sure. Whatever their attitude to formal education, the people of Nigg were not ignorant of the wider world and its different peoples. Black pupils, the children either of Scottish owners of plantations in the West Indies, or their servants, attended schools in Cromarty, Fortrose and Tain. The lurid story of the murder in 1806 of twenty-seven-year-old Arabella Phipps, married to Hugh Rose of Bayfield, allegedly by Rose's unnamed black mistress and housekeeper, remained a staple of the local gossip. The community's knowledge was gathered not only by personal observation and hearsay, but through the circulation of national and local newspapers. The Edinburgh *Evening Courant,* the *Caledonian Mercury* and the *Glasgow Herald,* Scotland's first daily, found their way northwards to Tain's public reading room, the laird's library, the manse study, the doctor's home, and perhaps the tailor's cottage.

There were also local papers: *The Inverness Courier* and *The Nairnshire Mirror*. Then there was *The Witness.*

Founded in 1840 as the organ of those who would form the Free Church of Scotland, *The Witness* enjoyed a healthy circulation in Easter Ross, not least because its editor, Hugh Miller, was a local man from Cromarty, just across the water from Nigg. *The Witness* assiduously reported and astutely commented on current national and international affairs, especially from those parts of the world to which Scottish exiles had emigrated or where Scottish missionaries were active. He scathingly remonstrated with political opponents or unscrupulous lairds, and castigated his adversaries, especially Church of Scotland Moderates – those who distrusted emotion in religion, disliked theological dogmatism, and, fatally, supported patronage, the controversial right of landowners to appoint ministers to a congregation over the heads of its members. The people of Nigg had sufficient intelligence – in both senses of the word – to form opinions and to take sides, especially where religion was concerned.

Across the Highlands, the Church was the most powerful single influence in the community. In Easter Ross, Christianity had been present since Pictish times, as evidenced by a very fine eight-century cross-slab believed to depict two of the desert fathers, St. Paul of Thebes and St. Anthony, receiving bread in the desert from a raven sent by God. Nearby Fearn Abbey, one of Scotland's oldest pre-Reformation church buildings, had a link to the country's first Reformation martyr, Patrick Hamilton, who in 1571, at the age of thirteen had been appointed its titular abbot. With no ecclesiastical obligations, he was able to use the stipend to study in Paris, where he was introduced to Reformed thought. Returning to St Andrews in 1524, he preached Lutheran doctrine, was arrested, tried and burned at the stake on 29th February 1528. Such stories were well known in the community and in the Ross household. So too were the exploits of Donald Ruadh, one of the most remarkable Christians to live in Nigg.

To distinguish him from others of the same name, his red hair earned him the Gaelic nickname Domhnall Ruadh, Red Donald, or Donald Roy. Born in 1665, Donald gained a reputation for strength and wildness. He attended church on Sunday mornings out of duty, but spent the afternoons playing shinty. When, on three consecutive Sunday evenings, he returned home to find a cow from his small herd of black cattle lying dead, he took it to be God's judgement on him and immediately took seriously his spiritual responsibilities. Still in his early twenties he was ordained an elder and by visiting homes and drawing neighbours together for Bible reading, prayer and fellowship, he diligently supplemented the ineffective work of his indifferent parish minister, James Mackenzie, by establishing a small group of faithful Christians in Nigg.

Regarded for his Scriptural knowledge, wisdom and deep piety, Donald Ruadh was reputed to be gifted with spiritual second sight, or 'the secret of the Lord', as Kennedy of Dingwall called this much prized sign of otherworldliness. Hugh Miller was a great, great grandson of Donald Ruadh, but was as sceptical of the paranormal as he was fascinated by it. He believed Donald was one who had lived 'as it were on the extreme verge of the natural world ... seeing far into the world of spirits ... the extreme bounds of the distant and the future.' But he thought Donald no more had 'the secret of the Lord' than had Kenneth Mackenzie, the clairvoyant Brahan Seer, whose spurious claims he dismissed.[7]

Donald Ruadh's first minister, Rev. James Mackenzie, died in 1701 and was succeeded as the Nigg parish minister by George Munro in 1706. By repute Munro was a good preacher, but despite Donald Ruadh's diligence, he suffered from an apathetic congregation, described by Donald Sage as in 'grossest ignorance'.[8] In 1729 Munro was succeeded by John Balfour, whose incumbency coincided with that of other evangelicals in the wider area: Fraser at Alness, Porteous at Kilmuir, Beaton at Rosskeen, and across the Cromarty Firth, MacPhail of Resolis and Wood of Rosemarkie. Their influence resulted in an evangelical resurgence in Easter Ross.

According to Kennedy of Dingwall, and corroborated by John Noble, this revival arrived almost imperceptibly, was promoted through ordinary preaching by ordinary ministers, was outwardly undemonstrative, and did not proliferate special meetings.[9] Kennedy thought that it had produced a generation of thoughtful, concerned and consistent Christians, distrustful alike of religious superficiality, innovation and formalism.[10] The movement reached its zenith in 1782 at a communion at Kiltearn attended by hundreds from the surrounding districts, all of whom had, according to Kennedy, 'as much of the comforting presence of the Lord as they were able to endure.'[11] Noble reported that Dr Alexander Fraser of Kirkhill's open air Gaelic sermon on the Monday produced an 'extraordinary manifestation of the Lord's gracious presence in the congregation'.[12] From this highpoint the revival tapered off until, in 1792, its last flickering embers were extinguished, so it was said, by disregard for the Fourth Commandment.[13]

1792 is known in Gaelic as *Bliadhna nan Caorach,* (Year of the Sheep), a time formative in the history of the Highlands, when an exasperated population pushed back at their overbearing lairds whose heartless ways had brought about the Clearances. A non-violent plan was made to gather thousands of the intruded sheep from the counties of Sutherland and Ross and drive them out of the north across the River Conon. The gathering went well, and the drive commenced successfully, until, with the authority of Donald Macleod of Geanies, Sheriff Depute of Ross, soldiers of the 42nd Regiment from Fort George and some of the landlords' men attacked the herders near Boath, just north of Alness. No resistance was offered and most of the shepherds scattered, though some were arrested and appeared in court in Inverness. Seven were found guilty and harshly sentenced: one punitively fined, some sentenced to seven years' transportation, and others banished from Scotland for life.

To landowners, such as Macleod of Geanies, these people were insurgents, incited by radicals bent on violent revolution. The Press was fickle. The *Edinburgh Evening Courant* at first sympathised with the protesters, but turned against them on hearing unfounded rumours of violence. The *Caledonian Mercury* saw the protest as an outrage, but excoriated the landlords whose oppression had given rise to it.[14] The sympathies of the majority, including the most influential evangelical ministers, were with the protesters. Never again would landed proprietors enjoy the trust of the people, nor would those unprotesting ministers who showed obsequious allegiance to their wealthy patrons.

Forty years earlier, in 1752, John Balfour, minister of Nigg, had been succeeded by Rev. Patrick Grant. Grant was not a popular choice, having been imposed upon the parish by the General Assembly, against the will of the congregation. On the day of the induction, the presbytery delegation found the church empty apart from a solitary individual, Donald Ruadh. Stern of face, he warned that if they dared to induct Grant, God would require it at their hands. Baulked, the presbytery reported to the Assembly. The Assembly was adamant. One Sunday, Grant's wife, looking out from the manse window, saw a long line of people wending their way across the Sands of Nigg, and asked her husband what he made of it. He knew only too well. The people were crossing Nigg Bay to hear Rev. John Porteous at Kilmuir. Unperturbed by what he saw, Grant mockingly asked his wife if she could see if they were taking his stipend with them. Their absence didn't trouble him so long as his income was secure and his workload light. It was said that the grass grew under disused pews in the largely abandoned Old Parish Church.

Porteous had a reputation as a winsome pastor. Fond of his garden, but worried lest it distract from his duties, he developed the habit of identifying the members of his congregation with specific plants and flowers that reminded him of them, and prayed for them as he tended the plant with which they were associated. Although his preaching was gentle and nurturing, his neighbour and first cousin, James Fraser of Alness, was more abrasive. From time to time, some of Fraser's battered people would slip across to hear the gentler Porteous. Once, Porteous and Fraser met at a funeral. Porteous apologised for accommodating those of Fraser's congregation who came to hear him. Big-hearted Fraser would hear no apology: hadn't he been given arrows to wound the Lord's enemies, and hadn't Porteous been given balm to soothe and make whole? Their ministries were complementary and they the closest of friends. Porteous' earlier neighbour in Nigg had been Balfour. When asked how he and the Porteous got on, Balfour said it had been like two thatchers working on the same roof; though they started far apart, the higher they rose the closer they got.

Fraser also proved a good friend of the Nigg people.[15] On the understanding that when an acceptable minister took Grant's place they would return to the parish church, he arranged for a Gaelic-speaking preacher from the Secession Church at Inverness to provide services. This anonymous but colourful character had left Inverness owing a debt to his landlady, who, when she discovered his whereabouts, sent a messenger-at-arms to arrest him. The men of Nigg were away that day cutting peats at Logie, but the preacher's popularity was such that the women of the congregation confronted the agent, chased him up the road, and pelted him with stones to within two miles of Tain.

Much to Fraser's annoyance the arrangement so suited the Nigg people that they permanently severed their link with the Church of Scotland, rented a site at Ankerville, built for themselves a little heather-thatched stone meetinghouse, and formed a congregation of the Secession Church. Fraser's fear of fragmentation, however, proved well founded. The Secession Church at Nigg was but another example of Scottish Presbyterianism's friability over an ever-narrowing search for ecclesiastical purity.

Separatist churches often carry within them the seeds of their own dissolution. Having detached itself from the Kirk in 1733, twelve years later the Secession Church fell out over the oaths that burgesses were required to take before assuming office, and so was born the Burgher and Antiburgher branches of the Secession. Another cleavage resulted in 1773 when the Relief Church promoted the unpopular but generous view that it was agreeable to sit at the Lord's Supper with Episcopalians, Baptists or Independents so long as they were 'visible saints', that is, Christians of a credible profession of faith. Fifty years later, another division in the Secession wreaked havoc when the traditionalist Auld Lichts found fault with the more forbearing New Lichts, though both were essentially evangelical.

As can be imagined, a congregation formed by Donald Ruadh and his friends belonged to the more conservative faction, joining the Antiburgher Secession Presbytery of Dunfermline and Perth (there being no nearer). The Rev. Roderick Mackenzie, though never inducted as their minister, preached to them and established the congregation. Their first true minister was Patrick Buchanan from Callander, inducted in June, 1765. In the previous winter Donald

Ruadh passed away, aged one hundred and nine years, having served eighty-four years as an elder, ten in the Secession.

In 1798, as Buchanan's ministry entered its final phase, the Ankerville site, for which no formal contract had been agreed, was repossessed by the landowner. Determined to end the Secession witness he decided to pull down their church, but no local, man or boy, could be found willing to lift a hand. A squad had to be brought in from Logie to dismantle the church and cart away the stones for reuse in a private house. Outraged by this provocation, a Secession member, around whose shoulders the mantle of Donald Ruadh seems to have fallen, roundly pronounced a solemn curse on both mansion and owner. Reputedly, the house was never completed, and the unused Old Red Sandstone blocks of the Secession Church were conspicuous among the dereliction.

A new church was erected in 1802 for the sum of £600 and by 1842, the year of John Ross' birth, the congregation was in good health. As well as the regular Lord's Day services, there had been for the past two years prayer meetings for men and women together on Thursday evenings, and for men only on Saturdays. Many had been admitted to communicant membership, and elders added to the Kirk Session. Sound spiritual health had practical benefits: the pulpit and the precentor's desk in the church were furnished with crimson cloth, the cost defrayed by a subscription raised by the women of the congregation, improvements were made to the manse and garden, and a productive and well-cared-for glebe supplemented the minister's stipend. The parish population was now almost equally split between the two denominations: one hundred and sixty families attended the Church of Scotland, and one hundred and twenty were loyal to the Secession.

The Rev. John Munro, a cousin of Hugh Miller's mother, had been inducted in 1799 and it was under his ministry, and that of his son who succeeded him, that John Ross learned the psalms and paraphrases, and the Shorter Catechism, was received into communicant membership, nurtured in the Christian faith, and guided through his youth. When John was just four, an event took place that was to shape the rest of his life: the Relief Church and the United Secession Church came together to form Scotland's third largest Presbyterian denomination, the United Presbyterian

Church, of which the Chapelhill congregation was a part. The United Presbyterians would run some of the most progressive foreign missions' ventures of any Scottish church and Ross would in time have more than his share in forwarding their aims and shaping their strategy. In 1867 Archibald MacMartin, a Free Church probationer, was ordained and inducted to the Chapelhill. He was Ross' minister until he departed for China. As old families moved away and incoming families largely took up membership in the burgeoning Free Church or the Church of Scotland, MacMartin found himself presiding over a declining congregation, which, nevertheless, in 1871 commenced building a much grander church at Chapelhill, designed by renowned Inverness architect Alexander Ross.

In the absence of personal letters, a journal or other contemporary records it is hard to say to what extent it was nature or nurture, heredity or environment, that most shaped John Ross. Doubtless, inherited traits and life experiences played a large part, as did community characteristics such as courage, industriousness, loyalty and versatility, especially when combined with an innate conservatism of a close-knit community. Perhaps Ross' intelligence, curiosity and insatiable appetite for knowledge were passed on through his teacher mother, who nurtured them. Maybe his diligence and industriousness came from his father. Who knows? The Church he attended, with its orthodox Christian teaching, evangelical preaching and piety, and warm fellowship, laid the spiritual foundation upon which he built his life. Ross' identity, then, was formed partly by heritage, partly by his genes and upbringing, partly by the choices he made for himself, but wholly by God. The sovereign Lord had set his man in a specific environment and had placed within him a genetic and cultural heritage which, refined and supplemented by grace, he would use for his greater glory in Manchuria and Korea.

3

Student and Home Missionary

Remember that life is very short and …
the opportunity of China is overwhelming.
Hamilton MacGill

THERE appears to be no documentary evidence directly relating to John Ross' early youth and so tracing the course of his education is difficult. We know from family records that his mother was a teacher, though it is not at all clear at which school she taught, whether she continued to teach after her marriage, or if John attended the same school. By the time he went to school, the Rosses resided either at Rarichie or Broomton. The first was in the Church of Scotland parish of Nigg, the other in Fearn. The Fearn parochial school was situated at Hill of Fearn, and offered for boys – girls had a separate curriculum – English, reading, writing, arithmetic, bookkeeping and Latin, as well as an introduction to geometry and classical Greek. There was a similar school for the parish of Nigg. Because of their denominational affiliation, however, neither school was generally supported by those belonging to the Chapelhill United Presbyterian Church, who preferred to send their children to the Balintore school operated by the Society in Scotland for Propagating Christian Knowledge (SSPCK), despite the irony that neither a United Presbyterian nor a Free Church of Scotland teacher would have been permitted to teach there. The constitution of the SSPCK required its teachers to be attached to the Church of Scotland, a stipulation reinforced by an 1846 judgment of the Court of Session.[1]

It is also unclear what part Gaelic, the language of Ross' home and community, played in John's education. *The New Statistical Account* records that by 1837, 'Gaelic [in the nearby town of Tain] has of late rapidly lost ground. … In the country the change has not been quite so marked.'[2] In the parish of Nigg, 'the Gaelic language is that generally spoken; but the English has made rapid progress of late.'[3] It is likely that further challenges to the primacy of Gaelic occurred during Ross' childhood. By 1851 a Gaelic School had been established in Hilton under the auspices of The Edinburgh Society for the Support of Gaelic Schools, whose sole teacher was thirty-three-year-old John Maclean from Lochbroom, on the west coast. The school offered little more than very basic Gaelic literacy, teaching 'the inhabitants of the Highlands and Islands to read the sacred scriptures in their own tongue'.[4]

It is equally uncertain where Ross completed his local education. Only the better parish schools offered a higher-grade level of instruction, and it is not at all clear that Fearn or Nigg did. The obvious choice would have been Tain Royal Academy, eight miles away, but there is no suggestion Ross attended. This blank in his educational record – he entered the University of Glasgow in 1862, at the somewhat advanced age of twenty – suggests that he may have entered paid employment for a number of years to help the family economy, though there is no evidence to this effect.[5]

The period during which Ross was growing up was a momentous time in Scottish Presbyterianism, not least in the Highlands. The Disruption of the Church of Scotland in 1843 had resulted in the formation of the Free Church of Scotland. Four years later the United Secession and Relief Churches came together to form Scotland's third largest Presbyterian denomination, the United Presbyterian Church. Though adhering to the Westminster Confession of Faith and sharing a common approach to worship and church government, at a national level the Free Church and the United Presbyterians were unable to join forces owing to an irreconcilable difference of opinion in regard to the relation of church and state.

The Free Church held to the doctrine of ecclesiastical establishment, but the United Presbyterian Church was constitutionally opposed to the idea of a national church, insisting on the complete separation of church and state, rejecting both state interference and support. United Presbyterians were 'voluntaries', insisting that it was the sole responsibility of its members to voluntarily support the ministry of the church and not benefit from state endowment. The Free Church held that it was the duty of the state to support national Presbyterianism, though it never itself received a penny of state aid. The Free Church's opinion was embraced by most Presbyterians in the Highlands, which largely explains why the United Presbyterian Church struggled to advance in the region. In the Lowlands and Borders, however, the United Presbyterian Church was of a similar size to both the Free Church and the Church of Scotland. It was very well represented in Edinburgh and in the latter years of the nineteenth century became dominant in Glasgow. It also had congregations in England and Ireland. The few it had in the Highlands were precarious.

At a local level, however, there was often good cooperation between United Presbyterians and the Free Church. In Easter Ross, Archibald MacMartin, a Free Church probationer, made a smooth transition to become a United Presbyterian minister. The same accommodating spirit prevailed in foreign missions; for example, in South Africa, the United Presbyterian missionary James Laing celebrated the fact that all the missionaries, regardless of their denominational allegiance, were determined 'to pursue our work as if the [Disruption] had never occurred'.[6] Indeed, it was often missionaries who were the keenest on union, seeking to avoid unhelpful competition in establishing the church where the gospel was unknown. When advocates of Scottish church union took a further step in 1900, uniting the United Presbyterian Church with the Free Church of Scotland to form the United Free Church, all missionaries of both denominations joined the new church. As was demonstrated in his conciliating work in Manchuria, John Ross possessed this same spirit.

In 1847, however, there appeared to be no further possibility of Presbyterian realignment and so the United Presbyterian Church established its own Divinity Hall. Funded by the Synod and under the oversight of the Committee on Theological Education, it was located at 5 Queen Street, Edinburgh. Whilst primarily educating Scottish candidates for the United Presbyterian ministry, students of other backgrounds and nationalities were accepted. For example, around 1852 the Xhosa-speaking Tiyo Soga from South Africa attended the Hall, as did, round the same time, the Lithuanian Jewish Christian, Isaac Salkinson, who gained fame as the translator of the Salkinson-Ginsburg Hebrew New Testament. Training could also be arranged for women, though not at the Divinity Hall. When twenty-eight-year-old Mary Slessor, a contemporary of John Ross, applied to the United Presbyterian Foreign Mission Board, Hamilton MacGill arranged for her a brief period of training at Moray House, the Free Church of Scotland's teacher training institution in Edinburgh.[7]

All of this helped Ross to discover, if he had not known earlier, that the United Presbyterians were the most sensitive of all Scottish Presbyterians towards cultural diversity and the most progressive regarding racial equality. This generosity of spirit was epitomised in the story of Tiyo Soga, whose work in establishing congregations in South Africa was, during Ross' time as a student, regularly featured in the pages of the *United Presbyterian Missionary Record*, and avidly followed by students in the Divinity Hall, as in the wider denomination. On 23rd December 1856, the United Presbyterian Presbytery of Glasgow became the first Presbyterian body to ordain a black African. Soga's ordination was officiated over by the presbytery's senior cleric, Rev. William Anderson, minister of Glasgow's John Street congregation. Anderson's prayer was remarkable. With his hand resting on Soga's head, he prayed earnestly for God's blessing on his young African friend, passionately begged God to make the British government change its oppressive South African colonial policy, and sought divine protection for 'the noble chieftain Sandile', who at that very moment was being hunted by the British authorities in South Africa as a rebel and fugitive from justice. Similarly, a few weeks later, Anderson, the John Street congregation and Soga's very many United Presbyterian friends welcomed his interracial marriage to Janet Burnside at Ibrox United Presbyterian Church, Glasgow, on 27th February, 1857. The newly married couple suffered no embarrassment or criticism during their time together in Scotland, though that changed when they arrived in South Africa.

Rev. Dr John Brown (1784–1858), formerly the Divinity Hall's Professor of Exegetical Theology, was one of the denomination's most influential champions of racial equality. Brown had expressed himself very clearly on the matter in his acclaimed 1857 commentary on Romans, with which it is inconceivable that Ross was unfamiliar. Brown wrote:

> Christianity does not unhinge the relations formed by nature; it draws them closer. It does not extinguish the affections which grow out of these relations; it regulates and sanctifies them, and, connecting them with religious duty, secures a healthful strength and a steady operation. Paul, when he became a Christian ... did not cease to be a Jew. He ... continued a patriot. Before his conversion, his patriotism manifested itself in his wishes and exertions to promote the worldly prosperity and glory of his race. It is their salvation now that he is chiefly anxious about. For this he lives; for this he is willing to die.[8]

When Ross believed himself to be called to Christian ministry, he probably followed the usual route by first informing his minister, through whom he then applied to the local presbytery. The presbytery's duty was to rigorously test his sense of vocation, suitability, piety, motives, talents, and academic attainments. As was customary, before commencing at the Divinity Hall, a student was expected to complete four or five sessions at university, studying Latin, Greek, logic and moral philosophy at undergraduate level. Between 1862 and 1867, Ross took his four sessions at Glasgow University.[9] In addition to the required subjects, students were expected to keep up with contemporary thought and learning through a grasp of the natural sciences. Presbyteries reserved the right to examine their students at any time during their course. Having been accepted as a candidate for the ministry, Ross, on completion of a written test, was eligible for a small Synod bursary of between £10 and £15 a year.

In his autobiography, Thomas Guthrie casts light on how frugally theological students subsisted in the city. Their spartan fare might have included a cup of tea once a day, oatmeal porridge twice a day, and for dinner, maybe a fried herring and potatoes, with butcher's meat enjoyed no more than twice a term. Guthrie tells of a student who took with him to his bare room in poor lodgings, a large box, which in view of the fact that his landlady claimed all she ever served her lodger was hot water, led to the logical and correct conclusion that the box contained a session's supply of oatmeal and the student had lived on a diet of brose, suited best to the tough digestion of a ploughman or shepherd.

Ross entered the Divinity Hall in 1867, as one of thirty or so students. He completed his studies in 1870. During this period his professors included James Harper (systematic and pastoral theology), Neil McMichael (historical theology), William Lindsay (Greek and Hebrew and Biblical criticism), and John Eadie (hermeneutics and Christian evidences). Lindsay died in 1866 and John Cairns was appointed in his place. The course consisted of the Synod's syllabus, including Calvin's *Institutes* in Latin, John Dick's *Lectures on Theology* (1840), the controversial Samuel Davidson's hermeneutical study, *A Treatise on Biblical Criticism* (1852), and George Waddington's *A History of the Church from the Earliest Ages to the Reformation* (1835), supplemented by J. H. Merle d'Aubigne's, *The History of the Reformation in the Sixteenth Century* (1835–1853). Biblical Hebrew was studied by exegesis of selected chapters of Genesis, Isaiah, the Psalms and Daniel, and the Greek text by reading Romans, Timothy, Galatians, and Hebrews. Apart from Calvin's *Institutes* the set texts were all contemporary, scholarly, diverse, but not necessarily the most conservative; indeed Davidson's liberal tendencies led to accusations of unsound views.

Hall lectures were confined to eight weeks of the year. For the remaining ten months, students were under the direction of their presbyteries who set written discourses on the Greek and Hebrew Bible, readings in denominational history and distinctives, practical theology, and the study of the Confession of Faith. For Ross, direct experience of ministry and the development of his preaching, pastoral and evangelistic skills came largely through short-term placements in mission churches or vacant congregations. His Gaelic fluency meant he was recruited by the Home Missions Board for preaching in Highland churches. The Board usually drew upon the Synod's accredited list of preachers, but exceptionally it could engage senior students. In its 1870 report to Synod, the Board explained why they had asked Ross to assist both in a two-week evangelistic mission in Glasgow, organised by the Cathcart Street Mission in November and December 1869, and as preaching supply on the Isle of Lismore, in Argyllshire over the New Year period from December 19th, 1869, to January 6th, 1870.[10]

> The Committee have availed themselves of the permission given by the third rule to employ in evangelistic work not only ministers and preachers, but also other persons of whose qualifications they might approve, – as to secure the services of Mr John Ross, student of the fifth year, in connection with meetings in Glasgow and at Lismore; and they recommend as one means of increasing the interest of the rising ministry in evangelistic work, and of imparting greater readiness for its performance, that advanced students should be invited and encouraged to assist in such evangelistic services as may be conducted in the districts where they reside, or in connection with the congregations of which they are members.[11]

The strength of the Free Church and the support it enjoyed from the majority of Gaelic-speaking Christians in the Highlands posed a great challenge for the United Presbyterian Church. The Free Church had, in only forty years, doubled the number of its Highland ministers. By contrast the United Presbyterian Church languished with a handful of struggling groups and tiny congregations. Secession services at Evanton in Easter Ross were unable to continue beyond 1841, and after the establishment of the Free Church in 1843 those on the south side of the Moray Firth, at Petty and Dulsie Bridge, also terminated.

After the formation of the United Presbyterian Church in 1847, the Presbytery of Inverness sought to revive the Gaelic mission by petitioning the Synod to make a grant to encourage Gaelic-speaking students to offer for ministry in the Highlands. The next year, however, the Presbytery of Elgin persuaded Synod to do no such thing, arguing that Gaelic was in steep decline and Free Church dominance doomed any such scheme to oblivion. Some people thought that the only justification for a United Presbyterian ministry in the Highlands was to establish congregations in the few pockets without evangelical witness. For a denomination which held mission and church extension to be highly important, such a challenge proved irresistible, and the Gaelic-speaking Nigg congregation of Easter Ross was to play a significant role in this scheme, not least through John Ross.

It is possible that the members of the United Presbyterian Home Mission did not fully realise the strength of Highland prejudice against their predominantly Lowland denomination. Though there were a few ecclesiastical and doctrinal differences, real antipathy in the *Gàidhealtachd* was also attributable to the more temporal but still critically important matter of land reform. This was explained in 1873, in an early edition of the Inverness-based newspaper, *The Highlander,* by its radical editor, John Murdoch. 'The land question,' wrote Murdoch, 'has very properly and naturally a great deal more to do [with opposition to the United Presbyterians and Free Church union with them] than most people take the trouble to think.'

> It is worthy of being given as a morsel for their consideration that, without the fault on the part of present members and ministers of the U. P. Church, the originals of it were associated in an unfortunate way in the minds of Highlanders, with clearances and consolidations of farms. Rightly or wrongly, Highlanders in many cases looked upon the Relief Churches as, in some measure, the churches of those who came into their country to take the land from under their feet, and the houses from over their heads.'[12]

It is all the more remarkable that the youthful John Ross made as much progress as he did, little though it was, for the United Presbyterian cause among Highlanders. This speaks highly not only of his religious orthodoxy and Gaelic skills, but also of his tact and maturity, and the warmth of his pulpit ministry, especially considering that the legacy he inherited was largely one of failure and decline.

In 1841 a United Secession preaching station had been established in Stornoway, but by 1845, with a thriving Free Church now in the town, there came a slump in attendance. The Board withdrew its support and the minister. As Robert Small quaintly put it, 'the station had been abandoned ere the year was half out, and, as there were no belongings, and the adherents had never been congregated, it was easy to lift the anchor and sail away.'[13] In 1858 a group of English-speakers attending the Free Church in the town saw an opportunity which the Gaelic-speaking Free Church and the Church of Scotland congregations were unable, or unwilling, to exploit. During the herring fishing season, a huge influx of some six thousand English-speaking fishermen, herring lassies (the girls who gutted and packed the fish), merchants and fish factors descended on the town. United Presbyterian services were restarted in the old Secession preaching station. A congregation under the distant care of the Glasgow Presbytery was formed with sixteen members and a much larger number of adherents. Rev. George Graham was inducted in 1861, the year after an attractive church had been built in James Street, but after only two years, he resigned and departed for Australia. During the ensuing vacancy the congregation was served by Home Mission preachers, including John Ross. Although Ross' Gaelic skills would not have been called upon in Stornoway, they doubtless added to the reputation of the church in the eyes of the local community.

The next location for Ross' ministry was the Isle of Lismore. From the windy, treeless, acid heather moorland of Lewis to the sheltered, balmy fertile island of Lismore seems further than the mere one hundred and twenty miles the seagull flies. Situated at the southern end of Loch Linnhe, Lismore is twelve miles long by two wide, enjoys a mild climate, is low lying, with limestone-based soil of high fertility, excellent grazing, and a rich habitat for grasses and wildflowers; it has hardly any heather. The island had not suffered from clearances as its enlightened laird's instruction to his factor had been 'improvement not clearance', nor did it suffer hunger when the potato crop failed in the 1840s, as it had little dependence upon the vegetable.[14]

Christianity is said to have been introduced to Lismore when in the sixth century Moluag arrived from Ireland with his twelve companions to establish a centre for the development of piety and outreach. Moluag is also associated with the west coast islands of Skye, Raasay, Mull, Tiree and Lewis, and on the east coast, with Rosemarkie on the Black Isle and Mortlach near Elgin. What is reputed to be his pastoral staff (*Bachuil Mòr*) remains on Lismore, in the keeping of the Baron of Bachuil. Between the twelfth and sixteenth centuries, when the island was a significant centre of Christianity, a small stone cathedral was built. After the Reformation, when its outbuildings fell into dereliction and their stones were recycled into other building projects on the island, the remains of the cathedral were incorporated into the parish church.

In 1836, the patron of the Lismore Church of Scotland congregation, the Duke of Argyll, presented to the parish Rev. Gregor MacGregor, who continued minister until 1885. Although he worked sedulously to keep the islanders within the Established Church, in the 1830s a small anti-patronage group in the south of Lismore associated themselves with the United Secession Church. In 1840, a Gaelic-speaking probationer for the Secession ministry, John Brown, settled the group on a solid basis, renovated a derelict Roman Catholic chapel, which he rented for £8 a year, and built up the congregation to twenty-nine members. Brown remained until 1842, when William Wood arrived as an unordained missionary. There being no manse, Wood demonstrated his dedication to the congregation by uncomplainingly lodging at one end of a small farmhouse with the cattle at the other, and the farmer and his family in between.

Ordained as a missionary in 1847, Wood was not inducted as minister until 1861, and died the following year. In November 1862, Donald Ross, a vernacular Gaelic-speaker from Nigg, was ordained, but, owing to the financial incapacity of the congregation – it contributed barely £20 of the minister's £100 stipend, he was not inducted until end of 1865. By this time there were around twenty members, with Sunday attendance of four times that number. The congregation also possessed a small manse. Leadership was also provided by John McDougall, a weaver, who ran the only Sabbath School on the island. McDougall was held in such high regard by the parish minister and others, both on the island and the mainland, that they willingly contributed to a 'purse' presented to him at an event in Oban to mark thirty years of service in the congregation.[15]

On 19th December, 1869, John Ross, now a senior at the Divinity Hall, came to Lismore. Though he only stayed for two weeks, his Christmas and New Year ministry stimulated a local revival, according to his modestly worded account for the Board.

> Meetings were held in Lismore and Appin from 19th December up till Thursday, 6th January, when I had to leave for Glasgow, to attend the

> presbytery on the succeeding Tuesday. The people generally seemed greatly interested in these meetings, and many were deeply impressed; there was a very manifest earnestness and seriousness on the part of the hearers, which, I trust, shall not be like the 'morning cloud.'[16] The attendance was such as has not been witnessed for years, on week-days, in Lismore – not since a previous revival in 1848. The children of God there were sorry the nightly meetings were to be given up; but I believe two or three meetings per week will be continued by our excellent missionary there and the Free Church minister of Appin [Duncan C. Ross], who is greatly interested by the aspect of affairs on the island. Several professed anxiety for their soul's salvation; but only the two before mentioned have professed to have found peace. I believe the good work is only begun, however, for the believers on the island have been stirred up to earnest prayer, and to expect blessings from above.[17]

Ross' final period of student ministry was exercised at Portree on the Isle of Skye, a congregation to which he became so attached that he was open to a call to settle among them as their minister. It would appear from the cordiality of their correspondence that a warm friendship had developed between Ross and Hamilton MacGill, the secretary of the United Presbyterian Home Missions Board, who had oversight of his work in the Gaelic-speaking churches. They got to know each other during Ross' time as a student in the Divinity Hall. MacGill saw great potential in Ross and believed in him. Then in 1868, MacGill resigned as Home Secretary to become the secretary of the Foreign Missions Board, taking with him his knowledge of Ross whom he now wished to influence for missionary service in China. The United Presbyterians encouraged a competitive spirit between the Home and the Foreign Mission Boards, not only in regard to Ross, but also for the attention, prayers and financial support of the Church. This friendly rivalry was articulated in the 1873 Synod in the report of Robert Scott, then the Home Secretary:

> While the Synod and the Church are ... presenting their prayers and consecrating their substance and sending forth their missionaries to ... win back Africa and China and Japan to the service and love of Christ, let them not be forgetful of those at home, who have too often had to say that no man cared for their souls.[18]

The Gaelic-speaking congregation in Portree had come into being through a fact-finding mission to Skye undertaken in 1840 by Rev. David M'Rae, the Secession minister of Oban. But with so few Gaelic preachers available it was a difficult congregation to sustain. In 1855, Alexander Adam (also from Nigg) commenced mission service in the town and in 1860 a church capable of holding two hundred and fifty people was built at a cost of £780, though all but £8 came from outside the island. The group grew until two years later it was formed into a properly constituted congregation able to call and induct a minister. Early in 1868 Adam's health failed and he left the area. After a delay of some months, the presbytery arranged for an unnamed student to take the services for nine months between Divinity Hall sessions, with ordained ministers travelling to take the services during July, August, and September. This unnamed student, who arrived in Portree on 1st April 1870, was John Ross.

Ross went to Skye with his mind already on the possibility of missionary service in China. In the Divinity Hall, he had heard Hamilton MacGill's missionary addresses and while we can't be sure what exactly impressed Ross, we get an idea of their persuasiveness from published extracts of his speeches in *Memories of the Rev. Dr Hamilton M. MacGill*. In one address, MacGill reflected upon a situation in rural Scotland as common in his day as it is in ours. In any single village, he said, there might be a number of evangelical ministers each preaching 'the same glorious message, amidst a limited population.' Each minister 'faithfully instructs the young, and each is reverenced by the aged … as he visits in their homes in joy and sorrow.' On the day such a minister is buried, everyone will agree 'that *there* a noble and a happy life is ended.' He then imagined the vacant congregation searching for a new minister, but raised the question as to the propriety of bringing another minister to such a small village. The congregation would be within its rights to have one, but MacGill challenged them to think carefully in the light of hard facts arising from international challenges:

> Since your former pastor was ordained over you, six hundred millions [the combined populations of China and India in c.1850] … have become accessible to the gospel who were then shut out from it. True you *have* a right, but these six hundred millions have a right

> to *missionaries,* as many as the Church can send, and the twenty-five millions around Newchwang have a right, among whom there are but three [missionaries] ... and to all these millions the Great Master points as distinctly as to any city or village in the world in his sweeping command, 'Preach the gospel to every creature.'[19]

MacGill left an inescapable conclusion: Newchwang in Manchuria had as much right to hear the gospel as the people of Portree in Skye.

These competing and conflicting voices perplexed Ross. Should he stay to serve a suffering community in the venal grip of a cartel of heartless proprietors? Men, who, in the four decades following 1840, had served one thousand seven hundred and forty writs of removal, involving nearly forty thousand people, all of whom, whether they were removed or not, had to pay the substantial sum of ten shillings for the writs to be served against them. Ross must often have witnessed sad farewells as family and friends escaped the pitiless gentry by embarking on white-sailed ships bound for the colonies. Had he not a duty to bring the consolations of the gospel to these who were as hungry for the Word of God as they were for a good meal? On the other hand, dare he consider China a distraction, dismiss it as a temptation, and shut his mind to its claims? What was God's will in all this and where could guidance be found? Part of the answer came from the wise, kind, yet persuasive correspondence of Hamilton MacGill. China wouldn't go away.

In one of his addresses MacGill had pressed home an old biblical lesson that ought never to be forgotten: Jonah who shrank from his mission to Nineveh, and took ship for Tarshish, was not long in learning the danger of debating the point between duty and inclination. There is no suggestion that MacGill ever thought of John Ross as a Jonah, an escapist, following an inclination to run away to Skye, rather than go to China, because he thought Portree a more comfortable place to serve. Nevertheless, MacGill's words did not allow Ross the luxury of confusing a passing impulse with duty, a temporary opportunity with a life's call, no matter how good and useful his presence in Portree might be for the present.

MacGill's letters to Ross start on 2nd October, 1868. Regrettably we have none from Ross to MacGill. In his first letter MacGill responded to the difficulties Ross felt as he considered the claims of China. He took them seriously, interested in Ross' inhibitions and alive to the force of his concerns, not least that God might have called him to minister in the Gaelic-speaking community at a time when even the Free Church was struggling to provide ministers fluent in the language. Nonetheless, MacGill believed that all of Ross' concerns would be resolved if only he would understand that the only openings for Gaelic ministry would be either at Lismore or Portree, but were either of these places really where Ross believed God wanted to use his considerable talents?

There was also an incentive at the back of MacGill's mind. Ross could not settle in Skye if he were not called by the congregation, and he could not be called until he had completed his studies in the Divinity Hall and had been licensed. But, he wondered, how might Ross respond to service overseas if instead of having to volunteer, as was the custom, he was invited – called – as if to a home congregation, but by the Foreign Mission Board to serve in China? Of course, MacGill knew it would be improper for the board to issue such an invitation until Ross had completed his course, but, thinking hypothetically, he wondered, how he might respond if he were to receive such an invitation?

Ross in fact was slow to respond. In his mind far more was at stake than the resolution of some hypothesis. Unhurriedly, he took himself to thinking, praying and agonising over the question. Not one to be easily deflected, MacGill wrote again, keeping the question open, affirming Ross' linguistic ability and general aptitude, and following up with the news that 'a medical friend' was also considering China.

There appears to have been no further correspondence from Ross until April 1869, when MacGill sent a confidential letter to five members of the Foreign Missions Board proposing the innovation he had suggested to Ross. The main paragraph reads:

> I think you know Mr John Ross well. I am aware he has acquitted himself with much satisfaction as a student and preacher. If at our meeting on Tuesday next I had in my hand one or two decided testimonies in favour of his piety, scholarship, prudence and linguistic aptitude, I think the Missions Board would do the unusual thing of

> giving him a call to go to China. He is not aware that I am consulting in this way, and I do so confidentially, and shall be glad [of] your testimony in whatever way it leads.[20]

In the meantime, on 21st March, MacGill had written to Ross an understanding, undemanding, understated and very diplomatic letter saying how glad he was that Ross was taking very seriously the possibility of service in China, and frankly admitting that there was, of course, substance in what others were saying about the claims of the Gaelic-speaking people. He understood perfectly well why the Home Mission Board wanted to keep Ross in touch with the Gaelic ministry, rather than see him go to China, for he understood how keen they were to have Ross to serve with them.

And so the tug of war went on. In July 1869, Ross was in Edinburgh. On the 25th he happened to be in the same building as that in which MacGill had his office, but the two did not meet. Ross was about to take the train north for Inverness, when MacGill, who was busily gathering together a team for China, was keen to see him, so he wrote him a note:

> The moment I heard you were in the office today I thought (as a one just deliberating about China) that it was very providential. I would like much to see you. Can you not delay going to Inverness a day and see me? If not when can you return at our expense? I feel I am pressing [on you a claim] as truly of the nature of a call to go over and help those millions in China, as if it had been signed by as many China men as would outnumber the signatures of any call that could be put into your hands in any conceivable circumstances .... [I hope you will be] our first ordained missionary to China .... We have now besides Dr Parker, a Chinaman native preacher and a Scotchman ... who has been preaching in Chinese for five years. Do nothing from my pressure but ... consider whether or not it is the Great Master who says to you 'go'. Your affectionate friend, etc.[21]

There is no suggestion that Ross delayed his journey north to wait on MacGill, and there then follows another long silence filled only by a reiteration, in their report to the Synod of 1870, of the Home Board's desire to employ Ross.

> In addition to the services of these evangelistic labourers, meetings have been held in various districts of the Highlands by Mr John Ross,

> probationer, at which he has preached the gospel of the grace of God to those who have assembled to hear him, and has endeavoured to direct them .... It was hoped that by these more occasional services the way might have been opened for the permanent location of Mr Ross in some district in which there might be a lack of the ordinary means of grace, and where a settled congregation might be formed, in connection with which Mr Ross's knowledge of the Gaelic language might be turned to practical account .... Still there have not been wanting among the people whom Mr Ross has visited those who have heard him gladly; and the good seed which he has scattered may hereafter spring up in unlooked-for places, and yield fruit unto life eternal.[22]

The next official letter in the Foreign Missions Board's letterbook is dated 2nd February, 1872. It appears that Ross was still in Portree, but had, perhaps with mixed feelings, decided in favour of China, although he had neither concluded the matter with his own presbytery, nor the Foreign Missions Board. MacGill was sympathetic and supportive, but relentless:

> Had you remained at Portree as the minister of a congregation the instruction of which though the membership had been quadrupled (which it might have been) would have proved in my opinion a failure in contrast with the opportunities of China. Portree is very small ... we must remember that life is very short and admits not of [repetition] and the opportunity of China is overwhelming. You have seen the remarkable statements by Dr Williamson. I assume [you know] that your call is still in force and as soon as I have time to [report] to our subcommittee I shall communicate with you .... Let me congratulate you from the bottom of my heart for being so shut up to China in a way so honourable.[23]

MacGill wrote on 8th February, 1872, to discuss settling the matter with the presbytery, which was due to meet on the 13th, to satisfy himself and the board that Ross was in robust health, and that nothing unforeseen stood in the way of his living in China. Finally, there was the small matter of what are known in Presbyterian circles as presbytery trials, concluding examinations which must be completed to the presbytery's satisfaction before a student could be ordained. Evidently, perhaps predictably, all went well at the presbytery because the next we hear from MacGill is in a letter clarifying the date for Ross' ordination at Chapelhill on 20th or 21st March and hoping that either of those dates would suit others too. Ross was now quite ready, as the jargon goes, to 'close with the call' from the Foreign Board. The date for his ordination at Chapelhill was settled as 20th March, 1872, the very same day as the newly completed Chapelhill church was to be inaugurated.

That was a great day for the Rosses! There was John Ross, his father Hugh and his mother Catherine, as well as his brothers and sisters. There were numerous other Rosses of Easter Ross, some from the Chapelhill congregation, other neighbours and friends, all glad that one of theirs was setting out for missionary service on the other side of the world. There too was Alexander Ross of Inverness, the esteemed architect of the impressive new church, whose elegant Italianate tracery and sturdy tower came from the same drawing board that had produced designs for Inverness' Free North and Free East churches, St. Andrew's Episcopal Cathedral, and many other Highland meeting places. Keen to exploit the occasion as fully as possible, MacGill and the presbytery prevailed upon the denomination's most notable preacher and keenest advocate of foreign missions, Dr Thomas Finlayson of Rose Street, Edinburgh, to lead and preach at the service of dedication. The ordination charge to the congregation was preached by Rev. J. M. Erskine who spoke from Christ's words in Matthew 8:11: 'And I say unto you, That many shall come from the east and west, and shall sit down with Abraham, and Isaac, and Jacob, in the kingdom of heaven' (AV). Rev. John Whyte from Moyness, near Brodie, in Nairnshire, delivered the charge to the missionary, and Dr MacGill and Rev. Adam Campbell of Petty also contributed.

After his ordination and the opening of the new church, Ross made haste to travel to Edinburgh, where on 26th March he married his fiancée Mary Ann Stewart at Larkfield, Ferry Road, Leith.[24] The house, a substantial villa of architectural significance, is now long gone, but was then Mary Ann's residence and presumably also that of her parents.[25] The marriage registration document describes Mary Ann's father, Robert Stewart, as a house proprietor and spirit merchant.[26] How, when and where John and Mary Ann met is unclear. The Stewarts appear to have had a connection with St Andrews Free Church, Newhaven, situated at Pier Place, a short distance from their home, as the minister of the congregation, Rev. James Fairbairn, conducted the marriage. Fairbairn was considered 'at once quaint and noble, with a character and idiosyncrasy quite original.' He spoke in strongly accented broad Berwickshire Scots, which, like Lord Cockburn, he considered classic, 'befitting the gentleman and the scholar.'[27] In 1838 he was inducted to Newhaven Church of Scotland, but at the Disruption of 1843, aged thirty-nine, he led most of his congregation into the Free Church.[28]

Ross may well have felt a special affinity with the minister of Newhaven's 'Fishermen's Kirk', not only on account of sharing a Seceder heritage, but, coming himself from a fishing community, he would have empathised with Fairbairn who, deeply moved by too often having to take funerals of drowned fishermen, had been instrumental in raising funds to provide Newhaven fishermen with the safer decked boats as replacements for their open boats, as recommended by the enquiry following the 1848 Moray Firth fishing disaster.[29] There is an evocative photograph, c.1843, by the Free Church portraitists, David Octavius Hill and Robert Adamson, of Fairbairn reading to a group of Newhaven fishwives with whom he reputedly enjoyed a special rapport.[30] At the time of Ross' marriage, the 'portly and imposing' Fairbairn was seventy-five years old and single.

In May, Ross was present at the United Presbyterian Synod, where he is recorded as a 'Missionary to China', and with other missionaries present was invited to contribute to the discussions. Whether he did or not we don't know. Then, as John and Mary Ann were organising themselves for departure to China, there came a final lighthearted letter from MacGill dealing with the travel arrangements which the Foreign Board had put in place for them, taking fully into consideration Mary Ann's fears of being subjected to the fierce heat of the Middle East. 'I think providence will speed your way to China,' writes MacGill, 'without you seeing the Red Sea, and enduring its terrible heat, till perhaps you return with your sheaves rejoicing .... With your present prospects I fancy you will both feel rather satisfied than otherwise with the new proposal.'[31] Present prospects? New proposal? What had the kindly designing MacGill got in mind for the newly married couple?

4

Go West, Young Man!

After dinner we repaired to our drawing-room car, and,
as it was Sabbath eve, intoned some of the grand old hymns…
while our train… rushed into the night and the Wild.

MARK TWAIN

WHOEVER coined the expression, 'Go West, young man, go West,' expressed precisely what Hamilton MacGill had in mind for John and Mary Ann Ross. But the observant reader might ask, isn't China in the East? MacGill's letter light-heartedly continues, 'Well, my proposal is that Mrs Ross – the lady first – and then yourself… shall go by America to Shanghai… And of course, we shall try to put you as comfortably across the American continent as possible… I fancy you will both feel rather satisfied than otherwise with the new proposal.' In that brief paragraph, in a playful, if matter-of-fact style, MacGill encompasses three of the most exciting travel revolutions of the second half of the nineteenth century: the opening of the Suez Canal, the completion of the American Transcontinental Railroad, and steam-powered ocean navigation.

John and Mary Ross would get to their promised land without having to negotiate the torrid Arabian desert. They would travel west, not east via de Lesseps' Suez Canal, opened to navigation a bare three years earlier with a great extravaganza organised by the Khedive of Egypt. The Khedive's invitation list included Queen Victoria, Franz Josef (the Austrian Emperor), Henry of the

Netherlands, Prince Frederick William of Prussia, and the French Empress, Eugenie. Queen Victoria, still mourning Albert, declined to attend, but sent in her place the Prince of Wales. Her Majesty opened the Holborn Viaduct instead.

The high point of the Suez ceremonies was the first transit of the canal. For this Britain stood in imminent danger of being upstaged by the Empress Eugenie, aboard the very smart French Imperial yacht, *L'Aigle,* leading, in Victoria's absence, the first flotilla. Not for the first nor the last time, the Royal Navy saved the honour of the nation; the night before, as the flotilla lined up in readiness at the entrance to the canal, in total darkness and without showing any light, Commander George Nares, acting on a nod and wink from his superiors, insolently but very skilfully navigated HMS *Newport* into pole position. Much to the chagrin of Eugenie and the French, the flotilla was forced meekly to follow the British gunboat through the canal.

The *Illustrated London News* reported on the celebrations. A multi-faith, or as it was described at the time, pan-religious, ceremony included the 'blessing' of the canal, with Latin and Greek priests and Muslim mullahs officiating. Among exotic pavilions and beneath billowing pennants and fluttering flags, on a gorgeously draped grandstand, the great and the good paraded. A mullah mounted an Islamic *minbar* (pulpit) and intoned a Koranic blessing over this international crowd decked out in cocked hats, top hats, tarbooshes and turbans. As much as they might otherwise have been religiously and politically at odds with each other, all were confident that the canal was a passage to prosperity and a channel of wealth. Perhaps a truer portent of its troubled future was the near demolition of part of Port Said by the accidental ignition of the stored fireworks. But aside from its commercial and strategic significance, the opening of the Suez Canal greatly benefitted missions in the East, making redundant the long and hazardous voyage round the Cape, through treacherous southern seas and in often atrocious weather.

The canal opening celebrations were, however, long past when John and Mary Ann Ross, with their aversion to heat, made their way to the Orient, not through the canal or round the Cape, but westwards by steam-powered ships and railway trains. Judging from what it had spent the year before on Alexander and Isabelle Williamson's passage to China, the United Presbyterian Foreign Mission Board budgeted £100 each for the Rosses. The sum itself, combined with MacGill's promise that they would travel as comfortably as possible, and a generous half-price discount negotiated through the American Presbyterian Board of Foreign Missions with the railway companies, indicates first class travel, both by steamer and by train.[1]

Most North Atlantic passenger shipping lines offered first and second-class cabins, as well as steerage or, as it was sometimes called, emigrant class. In each cabin class there were optional extras depending upon which deck (promenade, upper or main) one's cabin was located, whether it was an outside or inside room, and whether it had a private bath or not. Until the early 1860s most voyages to the United States took around thirty-five days, but steamships slashed the time to between seven and ten days. By the time the Rosses travelled, a first-class passage from Glasgow to New York cost around thirty guineas, 'wines included.' The Glasgow departures list suggest that they may well have sailed on the S.S. *Trinacria*, departing Glasgow on 14th June, 1872, arriving in New York on 27th June. The *Trinacria* was one of the new iron-built, screw propelled, three-masted, sail-assisted steamers, built the previous year at Robert Duncan & Co's Port Glasgow yard.

At New York, passengers for China boarded the San Francisco train, advertised as running 'from ocean to ocean', along the transcontinental railroad which had been opened on 10th May 1869, when the Central Pacific Railroad Company's President Leland Stanford drove in the last golden spike with a silver hammer at Promontory Summit, Utah. What had once been an arduous six-month trek across America by Conestoga wagon, now by rail took a mere six days, or to be precise – and it was an age of timetable precision – six days, seventeen and a half hours, actual time, by a traveller's watch, or, with due allowance made for crossing the different time zones, six days and fourteen hours for a total distance of three thousand, three hundred and fifty-three miles. Thus was achieved the goal of lobbyists like Asa Whitney, who sought to shorten the one hundred and fifty-three days he had endured in his 1842 journey from New York to China, via the Cape of Good Hope.

Driven by Christian faith and sound commercial judgement, seeking a goal far greater than financial profit, Whitney sought to annihilate distance with steam and speed. Like Livingstone in Africa, his hope was that, in the wake of successful trade, ignorance and poverty would be banished and worldwide Christian mission furthered. Had he known, he doubtless would have rejoiced that his brainchild was already rapidly carrying at half price the Scottish missionaries, John and Mary Ann Ross, to their destination in China.

Each train included restaurant cars appropriate to each class, and comfortable carriages, some of which were furnished with little balconies where passengers could get fresh air. Book and news vendors, sellers of snacks, drinks and cigars, passed repeatedly along the train, doing brisk business replenishing travellers' needs. In first class, at eight o'clock in the evening, a steward turned your plush velvet seat into a snug sleeping berth, complete with crisp clean sheets and cosy pillows. As passengers slept in comfort, the train sped through the night, negotiating curves, winding round mountains and crossing high trestle bridges spanning swiftly flowing rivers. The locomotive, with its pot-bellied funnel, belched a plume of sparks and black smoke skywards, its iron cowcatcher thrusting aggressively into the darkness, and its high-toned bell announcing the train's relentless progress across the great continent.

Again, we regret that no letters or reports recounting the Rosses' journey have survived, but we can reasonably accurately reconstruct their journey through the accounts of others, such as the American humourist Mark Twain who crossed America by rail that same year. In typical style, he recounted the luxuries of first-class travel in his tongue-in-cheek semi-autobiographical book, *Roughing It* (1872). Here are a couple of paragraphs:

> It was a revelation to us, that first dinner on Sunday. And though we continued to dine for four days, and had as many breakfasts and suppers, our whole party never ceased to admire the perfection of the arrangements, and the marvellous results achieved. Upon tables covered with snowy linen, and garnished with services of solid silver, Ethiop waiters, flitting about in spotless white, placed as by magic a repast at

> which Delmonico himself could have had no occasion to blush; and, indeed, in some respects it would be hard for that distinguished *chef* to match our *menu*; for, in addition to all that ordinarily makes up a first-chop dinner, had we not our antelope steak (the gourmand who has not experienced this – bah! what does he know of the feast of fat things?), our delicious mountain-brook trout, and choice fruits and berries, and (sauce piquant and unpurchasable!) our sweet-scented, appetite-compelling air of the prairies?
>
> You may depend upon it, we all did justice to the good things, and as we washed them down with bumpers of sparkling Krug, whilst we sped along at the rate of thirty miles an hour, agreed it was the *fastest* living we had ever experienced. (We beat that, however, two days afterward when we made *twenty-seven miles in twenty-seven minutes*, while our Champagne glasses filled to the brim spilled not a drop!) After dinner we repaired to our drawing-room car, and, as it was Sabbath eve, intoned some of the grand old hymns … the voices of the men singers and of the women singers blending sweetly in the evening air, while our train, with its great, glaring Polyphemus eye, lighting up long vistas of prairie, rushed into the night and the Wild. Then to bed in luxurious couches, where we slept the sleep of the just and only awoke the next morning (Monday) at eight o'clock, to find ourselves at the crossing of the North Platte, three hundred miles from Omaha – *fifteen hours and forty minutes out.*[2]

Lest we be tempted to think the missionaries were being indulged by the United Presbyterian Foreign Mission Board, we need to remember that such luxury was affordable owing to the health of the British economy. The strength of sterling and the weakness of the dollar combined to give excellent value for money. In any case, there is surely more than a grain of truth in the story which has C. H. Spurgeon, the Prince of Preachers, standing on a railway platform about to board a first-class carriage, when a priggish fellow minister, with whom he had been conversing, told him that he was travelling third class, 'to save the Lord's money.' To which Spurgeon retorted, 'You save the Lord's money. I'll save the Lord's servant!'

Besides Twain, another early traveller on the route was Sarah Chauncy Woolsey, whose pseudonym as a children's author was Susan Coolidge. With her friend Helen Hunt Jackson, Woolsey set out in the same year as the Rosses, but travelled less luxuriously than those in first class. In an article called 'A Few Hints on the California Journey', published in *Scribner's Monthly* in May 1873, she advised women travellers, such as Mary Ann Ross, to provide themselves with a warm, substantial travelling dress, and also a silk or cashmere suit suitable for the hotel dinner-table. With trunks stowed away, she also advised taking 'a large bag or small valise .... In this bag should be put, beside night-dress, change of linen, etc., plenty of clean collars, cuffs, pocket-handkerchiefs and stockings, a bottle of cologne, a phial of powdered borax to soften the hard water of the alkali district, a warm flannel sack for the chilly nights, – which even in midsummer must, in those high altitudes, be provided against – soap, brushes, combs, a whisk-broom, a pocket pincushion, a brandy flask, and small quantities of two or three of the simplest medicines. Old and easy boots should be chosen for the journey. I should advise everybody to be provided with two linen dusters [coats].' Though not dining, like the Rosses, *a la carte,* in the opulent first-class dining cars, Wolsey's opinion was that the food was 'fairly good'. Though she added that it was so monotonous that it was necessary to look at one's watch to tell whether it was breakfast, dinner or supper, as all meals offered the same beefsteak, fried eggs, and fried potato.

Wolsey and Jackson did the journey for fun, but we ask, did they find it so? Wolsey answers: 'The discomforts, the heat and dust, the weariness by the way, the trifling vexations, are soon forgotten; while the novelty and freshness, the beautiful sights, the wider horizon, the increased compass and comprehension, remain to refresh us always.' Alas, we are left to our imagination to complete the details of John and Mary Ross' journey and must draw on the colourful accounts of travellers such as these. Yet for sheer excitement, nothing upstages Jules Verne's account of travel on the Transcontinental Railroad, in his classic, *Around the World in Eighty Days.* Verne's story is set in the very same year as John and Mary Ann's trip, and tells how a few months later, in December 1872, Mr Phileas Fogg, an English gentleman, Aouda, an Indian lady, and Fogg's servant, Passepartout, hurriedly traversed the United States, but in the opposite direction. Although the Rosses' journey was less dramatic than Fogg's, the men shared something in common: they were both gamblers. Fogg in the conventional sense, and Ross in that he had willingly staked his life to spread the gospel of Christ in the Orient.

Helen Jackson's account concludes with an amusing description of an English gentleman standing on one leg in the aisle, putting on his boots, adding that life on the train was like that, nobody seemed to mind, 'and, now that the thing is over with, you laugh to think how droll it all was.'[3] Who might that Englishman have been? John Ross? After all, Americans habitually confuse Scotsmen with Englishmen.

At San Francisco the railroad terminated and passengers for China embarked on one of the many steam ships crossing the Pacific. During the 1870s, Trans-Pacific shipping reached a zenith of busyness, conveying goods and passengers in all directions, including missionaries to China. We don't know which ship John and Mary Ann Ross boarded, but we do know that after some days steaming, they arrived at the United Presbyterian mission station of Chefoo on the Shantung Peninsula.

5

Opium and Missionaries

Take away your opium, and your missionaries, and you will be welcome.
CHINA'S YIXIN (PRINCE GONG)

ON 9th November 2010, British Prime Minister David Cameron and his entourage arrived at the Great Hall of the People in Beijing, displaying red remembrance poppies in the buttonholes of their dark suits. Allegedly unfamiliar with the poppy's symbolism as a remembrance of the sacrifice of those who gave their lives in defence of British freedoms, Chinese officials asked that they be removed. Poppies reminded them of their humiliation at the hands of Britain during the Opium Wars of the nineteenth century. Cameron refused.[1] Five years later, on 21st November, 2015, once more sporting a red poppy, rarely worn after Remembrance Sunday, Mr Cameron entertained China's President Xi Jinping at Chequers.[2] It was widely felt in the United Kingdom that such a display of deliberate cultural insensitivity was not only provocative but inappropriate, especially if you wanted to lecture Chinese leaders about political freedoms, the rule of law and a free press. If embraced by Christians such assertiveness and cultural insensitivity would prove terminal to effective mission.

No one expressed the importance of cultural graciousness better than Dutch missions' thinker, Johan Herman Bavinck (1895–1964), who in 1960 warned that Christian mission would be wrecked if its advocates were inconsiderate to those with whom they speak. 'I must,' said Bavinck, 'bring the gospel of God's grace in Jesus Christ to the whole man, in his concrete existence, in his everyday environment. It is obviously then a great error on my part if I do not take a person's culture and history seriously.'[3]

The logic is clear. Christ took us very seriously indeed, accommodating himself to us, not superficially, by speaking our language, eating our food and wearing our clothes, but at the deepest level. By assuming human nature in indissoluble union with his divine person, he experienced our temptations, carried our sorrows and bore our sins. He did not require us to adapt to him, but taking us as we are, he adapted himself to us. We, in turn, therefore, can make no prior demands on those with whom we wish to share the Christian message. We must take people as we find them and adjust to their cultural and historical reality. For that reason, before continuing the story of John and Mary Ross, we need to note aspects of the cultural and historical heritage that shaped the lives and attitudes of the Chinese people to whom they bore witness, and which in turn made their ministry what it was.

For centuries China – or the Middle Kingdom, as it referred to itself – was a virtually unknown land. Highly suspicious of foreign contact, it prized its seclusion, which allowed the development of a distinctive, highly sophisticated and culturally rich heritage. Chinese isolation, however, would be intruded upon as European nations, not least Great Britain, exploited trading possibilities in the East. In 1600 Queen Elizabeth I chartered a new trading company, known as the East India Company, nicknamed John Company or just The Company. From early times, The Company traded in high quality Indian opium for medicinal purposes. From 1756, when the British seized Calcutta, the trade became very big business indeed.

Opium is derived from the sap of the opium poppy (*Papaver somniferum*). The father of medicine, Hippocrates, celebrated its ability to induce the sleep hinted at in its Latin name. In 1680, Britain's most respected physician, Thomas Sydenham, praised God for this wonder drug: 'Of all the remedies it has pleased Almighty God to give man to relieve his suffering, none is so universal and so efficacious as opium.' By the eighteenth century, dilute opium mixtures were the 'go to' children's medication of the period, despite the fact they caused many deaths. Adults took laudanum, a mixture of opium and other herbs in red wine or sherry, to regulate their bowels and as an analgesic. In 1803, Frederich Sertürner, a twenty-year-old German pharmacist, purified opium's most active ingredient. Six times more powerful than opium, he called it 'morphium' after Morpheus, the god of dreams. William Osler (1849–1919), founder of Johns Hopkins Hospital, considered opium as 'God's own medicine'.

By the nineteenth century opium's mind-influencing properties were celebrated. Oliver Wendell Holmes, the American physician, poet and academic, sang the drug's praises.[4] John Keats was addicted after heavily dosing himself with opium for a sore throat. He enjoyed the way it opened up a world of fantastic imagination: to 'fade far away, dissolve, and quite forget,' as he put it in his *Ode to a Nightingale.* Samuel Taylor Coleridge's *Kubla Khan*, some of the works of Percy Bysshe Shelley, and novelist Wilkie Collins' *The Moonstone* were written under the effects of opium. Charles Dickens was a user, and so was George Eliot.

As was early apparent, opium was dangerous and highly addictive. In 1821, in his *Confessions of an English Opium-Eater,* Thomas de Quincey described the drug's alleged benefits, but offset them against its perils, especially the great difficulty of kicking the habit. The artist Henry Wallis portrayed the ultimate end of addiction. His *Chatterton* depicts the seventeen-year-old, penniless poet, Thomas Chatterton, lying dead on his bed as a result of the effects of a lethal cocktail of arsenic, thought to be a cure for syphilis, and the opium to which he was addicted. When first exhibited at the Royal Academy in 1856, the painting was accompanied by the following poignant quotation from Marlowe: 'Cut is the branch that might have grown full straight.'[5]

Opium was mainly grown in Afghanistan and on India's northwest frontier, giving Britain a monopoly on the narcotic, which was marketed exclusively by the East India Company. In 1830 the trade peaked, with twenty-two thousand pounds weight brought into Britain, before a growing awareness of the drug's dangers led to a decline in demand. In 1868 the British Parliament passed the

Pharmacy Act, controlling the sale of poisons and dangerous drugs, including opium and its derivatives.

As the British use of Indian opium ebbed, so the use of another herbal product was in the ascendent: tea. In 1700 Britain imported ninety-two thousand pounds weight, which rose to more than two and half million pounds by 1751, and twenty-three million pounds in 1800. Tea overtook beer as the nation's favoured beverage, creating a large balance of payments deficit as the Chinese wanted little from Britain apart from the settling of its bill, in silver. The shrewd operators at The Company proposed rebalancing the deficit by exporting something they knew appealed to ordinary Chinese consumers: opium.

Smoked in pipes, opium had been introduced to the Chinese by the Dutch, who traded it not for any medicinal benefit, but purely as an addictive narcotic which they would supply and from which they would profit. The Chinese authorities deeply resented their people becoming opium addicts, with all that it meant socially and economically, especially if the process of their degradation made Europeans wealthy. By 1729, the British had so flooded the market with cheap opium that addiction reached epidemic proportions, triggering an Imperial edict banning the drug for all except medical use. But the edict was ignored, as was a more stringent one in 1799. The East India Company treated Chinese law with contempt. Auctioning opium to smugglers and private traders, such as the Scottish merchants William Jardine and James Matheson, by 1840 the British were shipping forty thousand opium chests to China each year. The result was millions of smokers, and at least two million addicts.[6]

The Americans, coveting a share of this ruinously antisocial but lucrative market, bought up cheap Turkish opium, flooded the market with it and increased the number of addicts. As the trade reached a new zenith, Chinese leaders considered accepting it and taxing it, but the Daoguang Emperor resisted this approach. He despatched to the southern provinces Imperial Commissioner, Lin Zexu, to treat directly with representatives of foreign governments and make decisions without prior reference to Beijing.[7]

Reaching Canton, the only port officially open to foreign traders, Lin tackled the issue head on. In March 1839 he issued an edict requiring British traders to surrender their stocks of opium within three days, on pain of death. Captain Charles Elliot, the Chief Superintendent of British trade in Canton, attempted to negotiate, but Lin suspended all foreign trade, taking hostage the British merchants. With no other option, they surrendered their stocks of opium, some twenty-one thousand, three hundred and six chests, which were burned in public. Chinese troops boarded British ships in the harbour, confiscating and destroying all additional opium found.

Elliot was in a moral quandary. Responsible as he was for the protection of British trading interests in Canton, he utterly deplored the opium trade. Writing to Lord Palmerston, the Foreign Secretary, Elliot was frank:

> If my private feelings were of the least consequence upon questions of a public and important nature, assuredly I might justly say, that no man entertains a deeper detestation of the disgrace and sin of this forced traffic on the coast of China than the humble individual who signs this despatch. I see little to choose between it and piracy; and in my place, as a public officer, I have steadily discountenanced it by all the lawful means in my power. and at the total sacrifice of my private comfort in the society in which I have lived for some years past.[8]

When the news of the Chinese action at Canton reached Britain, the belligerent Lord Macaulay, Secretary of State for War, proposed prompt military action. The public were less decided: some backed the government; others opposed the trade. An important contribution to a debate in the House of Commons was made by the thirty-one-year-old William Ewart Gladstone, whose sister was addicted to laudanum. Gladstone roundly blamed British opium dealers for inflaming the Chinese by their arrogance. Seeking to exonerate Elliot, he argued that 'we ... Christians, are pursuing objects at variance both with justice and with religion ... a war more unjust in its origin, a war calculated in its progress to cover this country with a permanent disgrace, I do not know and have not read of.'[9] Notwithstanding such moral indignation, the government, angered by the loss of trade and the destruction of British property, in November 1839 declared war on China.

British forces arrived in China in June 1840 and were placed under the direction of Charles Elliot, together with his cousin, Rear-Admiral George Elliot. The Rear-Admiral rapidly got out of his depth, became ill and was invalided back home. In January 1841, Charles Elliot, with the Chinese Imperial Commissioner, Qishan, who had replaced Lin Zexu, drafted the Convention of Chuenpi, which both parties hoped would end the war.

The terms imposed by the British included the cession of Hong Kong Island and harbour to Britain, the release of detained British citizens, and reopening of trade at Canton. The Chinese refused to obey the terms and hostilities recommenced. With its technologically superior forces the British crushed the Chinese army. Charles Elliot, out of favour with the government in London, was replaced by Sir Henry Pottinger, who was instructed by the Foreign Secretary, Lord Palmerston, to replace the Convention of Chuenpi by a treaty which would more effectively open China to British trade. The war ended on 29th August 1842, with the signing of the Treaty of Nanking, known later to the Chinese as the first of the unequal treaties. Under its terms the old Canton System, which had focused all trade with China on the Port of Canton, was abolished. Instead, five so-called treaty ports – Canton, Amoy, Foochow, Ningpo, and Shanghai – were opened to British traders. China was required to pay an indemnity of twenty-one million silver dollars, and Hong Kong Island remained ceded to Britain.

Although confined at first to the five treaty ports, the war and the treaties opened up the Chinese Empire to Christian missions. They were also responsible for Christianity being treated with deep resentment and suspicion. Travel to the interior and the propagation of Christianity there remained prohibited, but by 1845 an understanding was reached that so long as missionaries acted inoffensively and cautiously their presence might be tolerated. Among the first societies to respond to this opportunity was the London Missionary Society (LMS) under the leadership of James Legge. The LMS established three autonomous missions: the South China Mission (Canton, Hong Kong, and Fukien); the Central China Mission (Shanghai, Hankow and Wuchang); and the North China Mission (Tientsin and Beijing), moved its

Chinese College from Malacca to Hong Kong, and transferred its missionaries to China.

For the LMS, as for other missionary societies, the thought of mission in China was daunting. Learning the language was the work of years, not months. The country was vast and travel difficult. The sophisticated Chinese were highly resistant to foreigners and their religion. Educated Chinese egged on officials to make life difficult for missionaries. Property disputes were rife. Relations with British authorities were fraught as the missionaries openly denounced the opium trade.

Unsatisfied with the Treaty of Nanking, Britain, supported by France, was eager to wring further concessions from the Chinese, who felt they had already conceded far too much. With breath-taking high-handedness, Britain demanded trading access to all China, the legalisation of the opium trade, the exemption of foreign imports to duties, permission for a British ambassador to reside in Beijing, and for the English language translations of the treaties to take legal precedence over the Chinese. Beijing resisted. On 8th October 1856, Britain found the *casus belli* it sought and went to war once more.

Chinese marines, suppressing piracy, had boarded a merchant ship called *Arrow* in Canton harbour. Whilst the *Arrow* had previously been implicated in piracy, it now flew the British flag. Alleging an insult to the flag, the governor of Hong Kong, Sir John Bowring, demanded the release of the detained Chinese crew. The Imperial Commissioner at Canton liberated nine of the twelve prisoners, retaining three in jail. Two weeks later British forces under Admiral Sir Michael Seymour attacked Canton, destroying four defensive forts and shortly after bombarding the city itself.

The response by the British government to the *Arrow* incident met heavy criticism. In early March 1857 the House of Commons passed, with a majority of twenty-six, a resolution critical of the 'violent measures resorted to at Canton' and considered that the evidence produced by the government had failed 'to establish satisfactory grounds for the violent measures resorted to at Canton'. A Select Committee inquiry was ordered. The war couldn't have been worse timed. In May tensions between the East India Company and the Indians they ruled had flared up, first as a military mutiny, and then, supported by Indian rulers and their people, as a rebellion that threatened British colonial power on the subcontinent.

The French, just as eager to recommence hostilities against China, found their excuse in 1856 in the torture and execution of a French priest, Father Auguste Chapdelaine. Having made enemies in the Chinese community, Chapdelaine was accused of fomenting insurrection and arrested in Yaoshan. The mandarin, Zhang Mingfeng, condemned him to death. He was tortured, beaten and suspended by his neck in a small cage. Four days later he died of his injuries. A brutal war ensued. China's virtually mediaeval military was overwhelmed by the modern arms and tactics of the Anglo-French forces, resulting in such devastating losses that China's armies were almost annihilated.

The Qing dynasty now found itself fighting on two fronts. In 1851, rebels under a young man called Hong Xiuquan renounced the emperor and fought to usher in The Heavenly Kingdom of Great Peace. Hong and his followers were motivated by a heady mix of syncretistic Christianity and indigenous Confucianism. Hong was believed to be the younger brother of Jesus, called to cleanse China of the Manchus and all who stood in the way of the kingdom of the true God. The effect on southern China of the anarchic thirteen-year campaign, the world's bloodiest civil war, was horrific, resulting in the deaths of twenty million people, more than the entire population of the United Kingdom at the time.

Not only was the Taiping (or Great Peace) movement ideologically wedded to a garbled version of Christianity, but some of its leaders had worked for western missions. Hong Rengan, the Prince Gan, or Prime Minister, had had close links with American Southern Baptist missionary Issachar Jacox Roberts, the London Missionary Society's James Legge, and the Swedish missionary Theodore Hamberg of the Basel Mission in Hong Kong. This further prejudiced China's Qing rulers, their followers and advocates against Christianity, making it difficult for missionaries to enter the country and for an indigenous church to prosper.

Then in 1860, British, French and Indian troops poured into Beijing, looting the Summer Palaces in the Garden of Perfect

Brightness of their priceless porcelains, silks, ancient books and personal possessions, destroying all they couldn't carry away. News emerged of the deaths of twenty European and Indian prisoners, including two British envoys and a journalist for *The Times* called Thomas Bowlby. Accounts of their agonising deaths varied. Some said they died by *lingchi,* in which their limbs and body parts had been sliced off. Others claimed they were swathed with bandages soaked with water designed to shrink and so constrict breathing and circulation. However they died, their bodies were said to be unrecognisable. Moreover, the punishments inflicted were seen as expressions of Chinese contempt for Europeans.

Faced with this gruesome intelligence, the British Commander Lord Elgin was vengeful. He was afraid to be lenient, worried about his reputation at the hands of the influential *Times* newspaper and British popular opinion if he did not avenge the death of Bowlby and the other nineteen. He contemplated the complete destruction of the Forbidden City, the palace complex in southern Beijing that had been home to China's emperors, and the ceremonial and political centre of Chinese government for five hundred years. On October 14th 1800, from his camp near Beijing, he justified himself, writing that the army was there 'not to pillage, but to mark, by a solemn act of retribution, the horror and indignation with which we were inspired by the perpetration of a great crime.'[10]

Persuaded by French and Russian diplomats to desist from razing the Forbidden City, Elgin chose instead to destroy the Old Summer Palace, the Yuanmingyuan, the Garden of Perfect Brightness, burning it to the ground in a three-day orgy of arson and death, involving over four thousand British and Indian troops. Despite the prospect of loot, some of the soldiers found their duties distasteful. Military chaplain James M'Ghee felt the action was justified, but nevertheless lamented such a 'sacrifice of all that was most ancient and most beautiful'. It is said that when the Emperor, XianFeng, heard the news he vomited blood and was dead in less than a year.

The destruction of the Yuanmingyuan emphatically confirmed the Chinese opinion that Europeans were a ferocious people devoid of any cultural values and worse than barbarians. Barbarians might be redeemed by long exposure to culture and education, but Christians destroyed civilisation and outraged all standards of decency. Ever since, Elgin's destruction of the Yuanmingyuan has coloured Anglo-Chinese relations and evokes in the Chinese anger, grief and desolation at an act of unparalleled cultural barbarism.

The second Opium War ended in 1860 with the imposition on the Chinese of the punitive terms of the Convention of Peking, forcing a humiliated nation to sign further unequal treaties, imposing heavy monetary reparations, ceding to Britain the harbour of Kowloon, opening up free trade, including the unrestricted sale of opium, and the granting of full civil rights to all Christians, allowing them to own property and propagate their religion. For the Chinese the convention was ratified by Yixin, known to Europeans as Prince Gong, on 18th October 1860. On the death of the Xianfeng Emperor, Yixin went on to become Regent.

Lord Palmerston, the serving British Prime Minister, may have felt satisfied with his intervention, but not all British statesmen agreed. Gladstone was appalled, confiding to his diary that he was 'in dread of the judgments of God upon England for our national iniquity towards China'. Many ordinary British people abhorred war against an essentially friendly country, in the interests of drug traffickers, and which seriously compromised Christian missions in China.[11] Five years later, a remark to the British Minister in Beijing, Sir Rutherford Alcock, revealed how opium dealing and Christian missions were equally despised by the Chinese. Yixin's comment was, 'Take away your opium, and your missionaries, and you will be welcome.' In the eyes of Beijing, both had to be purged if relations between the two nations were to flourish, and if anything, Christianity was considered the greater threat to China.

When John Ross arrived in the port of Newchwang, Manchuria, he found the opium trade was being conducted with vigour by Baghdadi Jewish entrepreneurs. In the *United Presbyterian Missionary Record* of January 1874, he reported, without a trace of antisemitism, the facts as he found them:

> I forgot to say that the opium traffic in this place is fearful. Two warehouses, in connection with Sassoons of London and Bombay, are devoted to its sale. The Sassoons and their employees are Jews .... Sometimes upwards of £100,000 worth of opium is laid up for sale

> during the winter months. This drains the place of silver, and ... cripples trade in foreign goods, as there is little or no spare silver with which to purchase clothes, etc. This loss is small, however, compared with the awful ravages, morally and physically, of this dreadful poison. Yuen [the catechist] tells me many are applying to him for foreign medicines to get rid of the evil.[12]

The presence of Christianity in China may possibly date from the fourth century. The North African (Berber) Christian apologist, Arnobius of Sicca, who died c.330 AD, wrote that the proclamation of the Gospel had 'caused races, and peoples, and nations most diverse in character to hasten with one accord to accept the same faith. For the deeds can be reckoned up and numbered which have been done in India, among the Seres, Persians, and Medes ....'[13] The Seres were the people of Serica, the inhabitants of what is now northern China, the land of silk – its name is said to derive from 'si,' a Chinese word for silk. More confidently, scholars consider that the earliest recorded advent of Christianity in China was by the Nestorians during the Tang dynasty, in the early years of the seventh century, as corroborated by an eighth century, bilingual Chinese-Syriac stele, now located in Xi'an's Beilin Museum.

The religious persecution instigated by the Taoist Tang Emperor, Wuzong, c.845, banned Christianity along with Buddhism and other non-indigenous religions. What remained of Christian witness went underground. In 986, a monk reported to his superiors in the West that Christianity had become extinct in China and only one Christian had survived. But Chinese Christianity did survive to flourish again in the thirteenth century during the Kublai Khan's open-minded Yuan dynasty. The Khan welcomed Nestorian Christian doctors from present-day Kyrgyzstan and Kazakhstan, who contributed to the development of the already highly sophisticated Chinese pharmacology.[14] In 1271, the Khan wrote to Pope Gregory X requesting one hundred educated people to teach science and religion throughout his realm.[15] The arrival of the letter, however, coincided with a papal interregnum which, combined with fears of travelling to China and doubts of the authenticity of the invitation, resulted in inertia and created one of history's most significant 'what if' moments.

Twenty-three years later, Pope Nicholas IV belatedly sent the Franciscan John of Montecorvino as his legate to China, but Kublai Khan died that year and the opportunity was squandered, though not immediately. Befriended by the new Khan, Timur, John built the first Catholic church in China, learned Mongolian and translated the Psalms into the language. He was joined in 1303 by Arnold of Cologne, and together they baptised thousands of Mongol converts in Cambaluc (Khanbaliq, Beijing). John was appointed archbishop of Cambaluc in 1307 by Clement V, who also supplied missionary bishops to expanded Catholic missions a thousand miles south-east into Fujian Province.

In 1368 the Yuan dynasty collapsed and was replaced by the Ming, which resumed an isolationist foreign policy intolerant of Christianity, whether Nestorian or Catholic. In 1453, with Muslim dominance in Central Asia and Western China, a boycott by the Ottoman Empire of trade with China closed the hitherto safe northern trade routes, commonly known as the Silk Road, ending access by Christian traders.

There is no evidence that Christian congregations of the Mongol period survived into the Ming and early Qing dynasties. Two hundred years would pass before the arrival of Father Matteo Ricci and the Jesuit missionaries. Ricci reached China by sea in 1583, and by the time of his death in 1610, had established Catholic missions in Canton, Nanking and Kiansi. In 1605 Bento de Góis, the intrepid Portuguese missionary, after a gruelling two-year journey, travelling overland from India, via Afghanistan, the Pamirs and the Gobi Desert, reached Suchow, the first Chinese city inside the Great Wall. Here he died, possibly poisoned, but not before he sent word to Ricci in Beijing. Over the years other missionaries followed, including Ferdinand Verbiest (1623–1688). By the time of his death in 1688 it was estimated that three hundred thousand Chinese adhered to the Roman Catholic Church, but such gains were infinitesimal when compared against the vastness of the Chinese population.

Confucian scholars already thought Christian doctrines egotistical and unethical, and when Rome forbad its converts from taking part in Confucian ancestral rites, it demonstrated conclusively that Christianity threatened the integrity of society. It caused no surprise among Chinese when, in 1724, the Yongzheng Emperor, distrusting Jesuit priests, passed an edict expelling foreign missionaries and requiring Chinese Christians to renounce the Faith. Persecution ensued, buildings were confiscated, and the number of Christians dwindled.

Fifty years later, the position of surviving Chinese Catholics was made even more precarious by being once more suppressed as members of a foreign cult. For one hundred and twenty years, a few brave priests operated clandestinely. Most congregations, however, were unsupported, being left for decades to their own devices. Utilising the knowledge derived from printed catechisms and hymns, and orally transmitted Bible stories, often mixed with elements of folk religion, indigenous lay catechists and congregational leaders maintained as best they could Catholic worship traditions. The true pillars of Catholicism were the unmarried Christian women known as *virgins,* who dedicated themselves to the transmission of the gospel by teaching it as best they could to women and children.[16]

The unequal treaties of 1858–60 had gained important concessions for the protection of Christians and the propagation of Christianity. Protected by the French government, Catholics could now purchase land, erect buildings, and establish schools and churches. This inevitably created a conflict of interest, resulting in disputes between missionaries, converts and local people. John Ross also considered Catholics subversive, not only of Chinese traditions, but also of the Christian gospel. His excoriating condemnation of the behaviour of the Catholic Church ought not to be dismissed as a result of an innate Scottish Presbyterian anti-Catholic prejudice. Ross went out of his way to be scrupulously honest, substantiating his misgivings by reference to reliable sources, both at the Chinese Foreign Office and the British House of Commons parliamentary papers (Blue Books). Ross has been justifiably described as 'a careful and perceptive analyst of the conundrums facing the Chinese government', who, better than many, understood the Chinese fear of the encroachment of western trade and missionary activity on their scholarship, culture and sovereignty. [17]

Only when he had accumulated significant evidence did Ross feel justified to argue in his 1877 pamphlet *Chinese Foreign Policy* that, whilst the more lurid allegations against Roman Catholics, such as the kidnapping and trafficking of children – the alleged causes of the Tientsin Massacre of 1861 – may have been exaggerated or even fabricated, the Catholic Church's many dubious property transactions and its general moral laxity in regard to its converts, justified Chinese resentment. The claims made in a British government circular of 9th February 1871 were, Ross believed, perfectly justified: the 'indiscriminating enlistment of proselytes has gone so far that rebels and criminals of China ... take refuge in the profession of Christianity .... This has deeply dissatisfied the people, and their dissatisfaction long felt grows into animosity, and their animosity into deadly hostility.'[18]

So much then for Chinese grievances over Roman Catholic behaviour, but was it really very different in regard to Protestant missions? Protestant Christianity entered China around 1800, but not without difficulty. At first, missionaries were allowed to operate in only a few localities on the coast, but to operate at all they were forced to depend upon the cooperation of the opium traders. Robert Morrison of the London Missionary Society learned Chinese in London and upon arrival in the country speedily produced a Chinese-English dictionary and became the East India Company's chief translator. This provided him with a rationale for residence in the country but compromised him in Chinese eyes. Morrison's successor, the German Lutheran missionary, Karl Gützlaff, sullied his reputation by acceding to William Jardine's request to be the translator for the captain of the Jardine, Matheson and Co. opium clipper, *Slyph,* despite the fact that Jardine had been at pains to point out to him that 'our principle reliance is on opium ... by many considered an immoral traffic.'[19] Gützlaff also served as an interpreter to the British authorities during the war of 1839–42. For Gützlaff, the trade-off was that good personal relations with such powerful men gave him opportunities to promote the gospel, win converts and change lives. The effect of this compromise was witnessed at first hand by the American medical doctor Charles Taylor. When he arrived in Hong Kong in 1848 he spent time with Gützlaff and in his published account portrayed him 'as bold, intrepid and valiant a soldier of the cross as ever set foot on Pagan shores,' but added that he had by then 'almost entirely laid aside his missionary character, having become Chinese secretary, and interpreter of the British government, with a large salary.' Gützlaff died shortly after this meeting. Taylor, hearing of his passing, wrote appreciatively but couldn't hide a hint of doubt: 'we cannot help thinking that he must have accomplished great good, and that he is saved through the mercy of the Redeemer.'[20]

Almost all the earliest missionaries, Protestant and Catholic alike, were troubled by a connection to the opium trade. They may well have deplored both it and its effects; certainly they often spoke sternly of them, and worked tirelessly to relieve their victims; but few were not to some extent implicated in and compromised by this evil trade, carried on against the express wishes of a Chinese government powerless to stop it. Much light would have to be shed to banish the long shadow cast by the opium trade, and that light would have to shine through and not be dimmed by the character of the missionary as light bearer.

6

In Chefoo

Whoever holds Shantung grips China
like a man grips the throat of his victim.
CHINESE PROVERB

I did not stay, nor linger long.
PSALM 119.60. SCOTTISH METRICAL VERSION

THE Scottish Metrical Version of Psalm 119:60, often sung by John and Mary Ann Ross, expresses prompt obedience to God's will. The words, 'I did not stay, nor linger long,' articulates a sentiment which was certainly true of their brief time in Chefoo and early decision to relocate to Manchuria.

As a Treaty Port, Chefoo boasted a European community drawn from eight or nine different nationalities. For much of the year the region was blessed with an attractively mild climate, though it had a short and sharp winter, often cold enough to freeze the sea, and a hot, enervating July and August, with a likelihood of a typhoon. Spring was delightful. The autumn, with its succession of warm days, tempered by cool breezes, was an ideal climate for a holiday. Contemporary photographs show a prosperous little town, backed by hills, fringed by a beach traversed by the bund, or promenade, and dominated by faux European-style buildings, which were the churches, homes, offices and warehouses of its foreign residents.

According to Frances Wood, the poor state of its harbour, exposed as it was to northerly winds and having no facilities, other than lighters, to load and unload cargoes, meant, that, all in all, 'Chefoo was never much of a trading port, with only four foreign trading firms (three of them British) active ... shipping [soya] bean-cake, vermicelli, peanuts, silks, hairnets, lace and fruits.'[1]

The oldest foreign trading company in town was H. Sietas & Co. (1861), a general merchant and import and export business, which also ran the local printing press. Sietas may have been the oldest, but the most influential firm was reputed to be Wilson, Cornabé & Co. who exported straw-braid for hat making, luxury woven silk cloth – the famous Shantung silk – as well as silk hairnets for the New York market. The company imported food stuffs, coal and indigo, and ran first-class shipping and insurance agencies.

Chefoo's social amenities were enhanced by a two-storied waterfront club, built some ten years earlier by William Alexander Cornabé, boasting 'two billiard-rooms, a card-room, a bar, a reading-room, and a library, which for so small a Club is well stocked.'[2] Adding spice to the gossip at the club was the tale of the Revd Dr Thomas Tierney Fergusson, the unlikely founder of Fergusson & Co. It was a strange story indeed. At the age of eighteen, Fergusson found himself before a court of law in Sydney, Australia, to answer a charge of fraud. The evidence against him did not eclipse a glowing character testimony by Revd. Henry Gregory, a Benedictine monk working in Australia as a Catholic catechist. Fergusson was found not guilty; nevertheless, he departed hastily for England in January 1837. This was not his last brush with the law.[3]

A convert to Roman Catholicism, probably through Gregory's influence, Fergusson, believing he had a vocation to the priesthood, studied at the Vatican's missionary training college, the Pontificio Collegio Urbano de Propaganda Fide, before returning to England in 1848 with the degree of Doctor of Divinity. He was appointed as the first priest of the Catholic church of St Thomas of Canterbury in Fulham, London. In November 1854, he found himself at the Old Bailey charged with solemnising a marriage without the required special license.[4] The judge directed he be found guilty on a technicality. Shortly afterwards he demitted clerical status, whether willingly or under duress is unclear, and still only thirty-six years of age, left England. By 1861 he was established in business in Chefoo, where as well as his commercial activities he was a supporter of St Mary's Roman Catholic Church and of Catholic missions generally in China.[5]

Further colour was added to the Chefoo scene when, around the time the Rosses arrived, the Chinese entrepreneur Cheong Fatt Tze (1840–1916), known as 'the Rockefeller of the East', planted two hundred acres of vines for wine and brandy production under the direction of Austrian viticulturist Baron August von Babo, who was rewarded handsomely on the strict condition that he spoke to no-one outside the company about the quality, or otherwise, of its products.[6]

Very likely most of the missionaries had neither the time nor the inclination to frequent the club and probably took little enough interest in the town's commercial activities. They were probably more familiar with the old Chinese town which, far from salubrious, was archaic, but not romantically so. A British Consul's description of the place in 1903 would have fitted the facts as they were in 1872, when the Rosses arrived: 'the present condition of the streets, drains, etc., is probably little changed since early mediaeval days. The roads are only passable for mules, donkeys and ponies which are fitted with pack saddles. Most travellers are, of necessity, pedestrians, donkeys being reserved for ladies and the aged, whilst the wealthy alone are able to indulge in the luxury of a mule litter.'[7]

Compared to other ports, Chefoo was a relative backwater; nevertheless, it was, with the whole of the populous Shantung province, considered strategic. The veteran China missionary Mildred Cable once cited an old Chinese proverb: 'Whoever holds Shantung grips China like a man grips the throat of his victim.'[8] Her opinion is corroborated by the fact that, between 1860 and 1986, membership in the officially recognised churches in Shantung grew from around two thousand to over a quarter of a million and in the following thirty years that number quadrupled.[9] It is unlikely that such growth would surprise the nineteenth-century pioneers; it would rather have justified their conviction that the place held rich spiritual potential which called forth the investment and energy of churches and missionary agencies. Who then were the missionary pioneers of Shantung province?

Even before William Chalmers Burns arrived in Manchuria in August 1867, interest in China was being stirred up among the people of the United Presbyterian Church through the work of Dr Alexander Williamson and Dr William Parker. Williamson had gone to Shanghai in 1855 under the auspices of the London Missionary Society, but falling ill, after only two years' service, he had to return to Scotland. Whilst at home he established a book and tract society that became the Christian Literature Society for China. In 1863 he returned to Chefoo to take up itinerant preaching and literary work, with the goal of reaching the higher, more educated, class of Chinese society in the hope that their influence would somehow trickle down to society at large. His extensive travels took him not only to Mongolia and Manchuria, but also to the border between China and Korea at a place then known to foreigners as Corean Gate. Here he had hoped to extend his missionary activity into Korea, which under the Chosŏn Dynasty's strict seclusion policies had gained the reputation of a Hermit Kingdom. In Chefoo, Williamson not only represented the United Presbyterian Church but also the National Bible Society of Scotland.

Dr William Parker had sailed to China in 1854 to serve in Shanghai with the Chinese Evangelization Society, but being poorly organised, the society let him down and failed adequately to support him and his family. In 1855 it was agreed that he should accept an invitation to serve as the physician to the foreign community in the treaty port of Ningpo, where he also sought to evangelise the Chinese population. In 1857 the twenty-five-year-old James Hudson Taylor joined him and that, for many, is more or less where Parker's story ends. In 1859 Parker's wife succumbed to cholera. Leaving Hudson Taylor to run the little hospital, the grief-stricken man returned to Scotland to put his five motherless children in the hands of their grandparents.

Parker's work had largely been supported by a small committee of friends whose chairman was the merchant and philanthropist, John Henderson of Park in Renfrewshire. A stalwart of the United Presbyterian Church, Henderson was an enthusiastic champion of many evangelical causes. Under his chairmanship the committee felt that they may have been encroaching upon the church's prerogatives, and so asked the United Presbyterian Foreign Mission Board, subject to the approval of the Synod, to take on the responsibility of managing the Chinese work. In May 1862, the Synod, fearful of diverting funds from its other missionary work, gave limited sanction to the request, undertaking to help only for the three years for which funds were available, unless continuing financial support permitted them to extend the deadline.[10]

By the time of the Synod's decision, Parker had married again and returned to Ningpo to find the city and the surrounding countryside convulsed by the Taiping reign of terror, with the little hospital full of its victims. The unrest had shaken Chinese confidence in traditional religion, which had been ineffective in supporting them through troubled times, and many were willing to hear what Parker had to say. Then, one afternoon in late January 1863, riding home from the hospital, Parker was crossing a bridge when a stone slab gave way precipitating him into the canal below, where he sustained fatal injuries. He died within a few days, in great agony and gasping for breath, with his wife holding his hand. In 1864, his brother John, also a medical doctor, arrived in Ningpo to keep the work functioning.

Five years later, in the face of severe financial recession, the church at home appealed for further support. The United Presbyterian members rose to the occasion, and contributed generously. Added to their donations was a large legacy of £4,000 from the estate of Henderson of Park, who had died two years earlier. With sufficient funds to meet all the costs, the Foreign Mission Board took on the contentious Lewis Nicol as an unordained evangelist at Ningbo – he had to be dismissed when he accused Hudson Taylor of tyranny by insisting missionaries wear Chinese dress – and a few months later made an offer to Dr Williamson that the church would share his services with the Bible Society. And so, the United Presbyterians came to Chefoo.

By 1870 a number of other missions were active there. In 1860 the American Southern Baptist North China Mission established a brief but tragic presence in Chefoo. That year Rev. and Mrs J. L. Holmes arrived from Shanghai, but in less than a year Mr Holmes was murdered, and Mrs Holmes moved to Tengchow to join Dr and

Mrs J. B. Hartwell. In 1871, Dr Hartwell re-opened the mission station in Chefoo, residing there with his wife from 1872. At first Hartwell was permitted to use the Baptist Missionary Society chapel, but shortly afterwards built his own at the cost of $4000 sent from America, as well as a residence at the same cost. In the following years the Southern Baptists also built and ran two schools, the Williams' Memorial Girls' School and a boy's school.[11]

Two years before the arrival of John and Mary Ann Ross, a Welshman called Timothy Richard of the Baptist Missionary Society also came to Chefoo. Converted during the Welsh revival of 1858–60, Richard studied at Haverfordwest Baptist College, and there felt God leading him to join the China Inland Mission, whose founder, James Hudson Taylor, he greatly admired. In the event, however, he was persuaded to join the Baptist Missionary Society. Shortly after arrival in Chefoo, he thought there were too many missionaries clustered in the town, and so with a strong urge to reach further inland, set out in 1875 for the walled city of Ch'ing-Chou-Fu. In this burgeoning administrative, educational, business and religious centre, with its population of 30,000, he found great scope for evangelistic activity, tract distribution and rudimentary health care. Influenced by the cultural sensitivity of William Chalmers Burns and Hudson Taylor, he immersed himself in Chinese language and traditions, wore local clothing, adopted an indigenous way of life, and took a Chinese name.[12]

American Presbyterians arrived in Chefoo in 1871, when Dr John Livingstone Nevius relocated there from Ningbo, and where, twenty-two years later, he died. Of him and of his important views on indigenous church growth, and their relation to John Ross' own thought, we will have more to say later. In 1874 two Anglicans came to Chefoo: Rev. (later Bishop) Charles Perry Scott and Rev. Miles Greenwood, nominally of the North China and Shantung Missionary Association, but actually of the Church of England's Society for the Propagation of the Gospel. During that first winter Scott and Greenwood were guests of Dr Nevius and his wife. Among its other provisions, the signing of the 1876 Chefoo Convention between Britain and China, permitted missionary activity in inland China, which brought the China Inland Mission to the town in

1880. The Plymouth Brethren arrived eight years later. Both had designs on penetrating deeper into the country.

Within two months of arriving in Chefoo, John Ross wrote to Hamilton MacGill, sharing his first impressions of Christian work in the area. He wrote appreciatively, even if unenthusiastically, of the general activities of the missionaries. He was warmer about Dr Williamson and his work, but became most animated when describing the character and work of Williamson's Chinese catechist and assistant, Li Ki-yeun. Ross thought Li to be 'an excellent man, of noble appearance, thorough gentlemanly deportment, and earnest Christian tone.' Adding, that if he had been a Saul in opposition to the truth, he was now a Paul in favour of it: 'Were there a hundred such men in China, it would be an immense blessing of the Lord; I should hope of good things of even the immediate future of this immense empire ...'[13] Even in those first days of his missionary experience, we see Ross forming a key component of his future strategy, that of identifying, training and equipping gifted Chinese people to promote the gospel of Christ.

Another aspect of Ross' character is seen in these first notes, namely, a disinclination to invest heavily in mission station infrastructure and property. He was troubled by the tendency to build large, prestigious, well-equipped mission stations that encompassed comfortable homes for missionaries, sometimes residences for converts, as well as churches and hospitals. That was not the way he wished to go: 'It would be a pity to devote time to house-building, with all its harassing affairs, after being able to preach and go about the country.'[14]

With such a plethora of missionary activity in the area, in anticipation of the Rosses' arrival, Dr Williamson had suggested to the local missionary committee that the Rosses should go soon to the port town of Newchwang in Manchuria, the scene of Burns' labours. The case was put to John Ross, and he wholeheartedly concurred. The decision had to be made speedily and without prior approval by the Foreign Mission Board as there was only a small window of opportunity before the river would become iced-up in November and remain unnavigable until April. In August, before the Rosses arrived in Chefoo, Williamson wrote to MacGill asking him to present the case for Newchwang to the Foreign Mission Board, arguing that a missionary presence in Manchuria was strategic not only for that region, but for Korea too. He had no doubt that Ross was a suitable person, with the ability and initiative to exploit the situation. In any case, he maintained that the plan was not irreversible; if it didn't work out, the Rosses could easily and at small expense return to Chefoo in the spring.

At its 26th November meeting the Board deferred to Williamson's superior knowledge and accepted the cogency of his arguments, approving the Rosses' settlement in Newchwang.[15] Unfortunately, Dr Hunter, the only missionary of the Presbyterian Church in Ireland in Manchuria, shaken by the loss of his wife Elizabeth to tuberculosis and the departure in ill health of his colleague, Rev. Hugh Waddell, resented what he saw as the United Presbyterian intrusion into Newchwang.[16] This required the Board to correspond with the Irish church to resolve the matter.[17] In the meantime, the Board justified the Rosses' presence in the port city on the grounds that there was no ordained minister in Manchuria to serve the needs of the expatriate community, to baptise Chinese converts and organise them into a church. The Rosses, therefore, should remain in Newchwang, at least temporarily, even if the Presbyterian Church of Ireland were to send a replacement for Waddell. What Williamson had not said in his letter, probably because he did not know, or was, perhaps, too reticent to mention, was that Mary Ann was now pregnant and also suffering from an annoying chest complaint.

7

The Valley of the Shadow

Yea, though I walk through the valley of the shadow of death, I will fear no evil: for thou art with me.

PSALM 23.4 (AV)

Truly the harvest here is great, and *one* labourer.

JOHN ROSS

MARY Ann Ross passed away, only a few weeks after giving birth to the son they named Drummond Stewart, in the icy winter at Newchwang, and less than a week after their first wedding anniversary. The news took three months to travel across the world and was announced to the supporters of the United Presbyterian mission in North China in a brief note in the June edition of the *Missionary Record*. No explanation was offered as to the cause of death, nor any mention made of the birth of the baby. The single hastily inserted paragraph matter-of-factly stated:

> We have to announce with deep regret that intelligence has just arrived (16th June) of the death of Mrs Ross on 31st March at Newchwang, where, on 2nd of April, her interment took place, by the side of the grave of William Burns. The British, American, and German flags were lowered at the respective consulates, in expression of the universal respect in which she was held.[1]

Before the final blow fell, thirty-one-year-old John could write of pressing on with resolution and commitment to God's call, though his words might strike some modern readers as perhaps somewhat too resigned:

> I am told that the past winter has been the most favourable for many years. I am both glad and sorry to hear this: glad, inasmuch as if it has been severe as last winter, I should despair of the recovery of my wife; and sorry to think it possible that she may again be attacked this winter, if she can remain here. The greatest cold during winter was in January and February, when the thermometer frequently touched 5 deg. Farh. [-15° C] at night. And sometimes not more than 8 or 9 deg. at midday in the shade .... To one of robust health this matters little, because of the extraordinary dryness of the climate, the skies being blue very much longer than the far-famed Italian .... I don't dislike the climate myself. I have come so far, and the same reason which urged me to come holds good. I believe also that the welfare of those immortal souls is to be regarded more than private comfort and pleasure. I shall be deeply grieved if Mrs Ross has to go, and I believe I shall feel far worse than if I had never married; but though the worst come to the worst, I have not now the shadow of a thought of retreating from this position without more serious reasons for it that either comfort or pleasure.

Although he was submissive to Providence, he nevertheless felt frustrated that Mary Ann's illness was affecting his plans:

> I thought I would have been preaching by this time in Chinese, and might, but for Mrs Ross's serious illness. I shall soon be able to resume, and intend to prosecute with vigour my neglected studies.[2]

On 25th March, days before Mary Ann's death, Ross wrote a longish note about opening a new church and appointing a Chinese teacher, as well as describing general progress, but, with characteristic reticence, he made no mention of his young wife's deteriorating condition. Publishing this report in the August 1873 edition of the *Missionary Record*, McGill added a note that reads rather like a disclaimer, stating that Mary Ann Ross' death had nothing to do with any Mission Board decision, either in regard of relocating the Rosses from Chefoo to Newchwang, despite the onset of bitter winter weather, or as a result of their long and arduous journey to China.

> Mrs Ross died unexpectedly on March 31, six days after the preceding sentences were written. She had given birth to a son a few weeks before;

> and the severe cold seems to have accelerated a chest complaint, the origin of which was in no way connected with her brief residence in China, or which the fatigue of her land journey across the American continent, or her voyage across the Atlantic and Pacific. By Mrs Ross's death, her husband has lost a partner singularly fitted for the position of a missionary's wife; and our Chinese mission has been bereaved of a wise, able and devoted fellow-helper.[3]

Leaving aside McGill's attempt to exonerate himself and exculpate the board, it would be wrong to rush to judgement on Ross himself. Those who knew Highlanders best knew that reticence did not mean that he felt lightly, but rather the contrary, that he very deeply felt his loss. Those closest to him, able best to empathise with him, made speedy arrangements for his sister Catherine to set sail for China to care for baby Drummond and bring comfort to the desolate home. Catherine would arrive in Newchwang the following year. In due course she would marry John Ross' colleague, John Macintyre.

In the weeks before Mary's death, when there was little he or anyone else could do to help her, and having arranged for every possible comfort for the ailing mother and baby son, Ross threw himself into establishing a lasting gospel presence in Newchwang. Rather than seeing this as callousness, we might better understand it as a necessary response to the emotional trauma he was suffering through inability to do more than he had for his wife and son.[4]

Instead of doing as many another new missionary might, indiscriminatingly standing on street corners preaching and distributing tracts, Ross, whose awareness of and sensitivity to Chinese culture was already shaping his ministry, decided to follow the ancient Chinese practice of establishing a discussion hall where people were invited to come to hear Christianity explained and discussed. With some difficulty he found a shop suitable for use as a chapel, but the owner refused to rent it to him. This hostility wryly reminded Ross of how, during student days in Scotland, in his missionary forays into the Gaelic-speaking parts of the Highlands, he had faced similar rebuffs from the more reactionary elements in the Free Church of Scotland. The opposition in Newchwang, he wrote, evoked memories 'of … my attempts to get into anti-union schoolhouses to preach; only the anti-unionists were more bitter.'[5] But as he had persevered in Scotland, so now did he in China. Another, more obliging, shop owner was found, who, claiming to have heard the Christian message and considering it to be inoffensive, settled on a fair rent, though the more plausible reason was that a murder had taken place on the premises and no Chinese would rent it for fear of it being haunted.[6]

On the Sunday before Mary Ann's death, in company with the local European doctor and the British consul, Ross commenced Christian services. Around twenty people had gathered early, including six enthusiastic young enquirers who respectfully stood up when he entered. The building had been well prepared and was clean and bright. Three walls and the ceiling had been newly papered in the Chinese style; the fourth wall was a door wide open to the street. By the time the meeting was due to commence a hundred people had gathered, all with serious intention and not to mock.

The audience included Confucian scholars, a wealthy merchant, a young man stylishly enjoying his long tobacco pipe, coolies in their traditional blue wadded cotton clothes, and another thirty or forty people with whom Ross had become acquainted through his language teacher. He was encouraged by their good humour, inherent politeness and serious intent. He noted uncritically a gentle buzz of conversation during the sermon, which, however, readily stopped when the speaker (not himself) indicated a wish for quietness. Although he did not on that occasion speak himself, he had suggested the text that the Chinese speaker should expound, and had constructed most of the sermon, including an explanation of why daily meetings were to be held and what other events might take place on the premises. Ross could not refrain making comparisons between his new congregation in Newchwang and the congregation in Portree, yet not in Portree's favour: Newchwang, he felt eclipsed the Scottish congregation not only in size but in attentiveness too.

It was not until 12th May, six weeks after Mary Ann's death, that Ross felt inclined to resume adding personal observations to his regular reports to MacGill. Despite an apparent stoicism, the loss of his wife had affected him very deeply; yet he still made no allusions to his feelings, apart from a desire that a companion missionary be sent out to join him. There were, he noted, a dozen or more Roman Catholic priests in the area, and he feared their numbers were increasing; but, he added, it was not numbers of missionaries that were required, so much as the right kind of missionaries: 'One good man is far better than a dozen middling ones.' But in that too he thought he had perceived a danger. Maybe the board was being too fastidious or too passive in relying only on volunteers. Why not, he urged, do as they had done with him, actively recruit young men of known ability and piety, and let the responsibility of refusal be upon their own souls. In defence of this more proactive policy he cited a French friend who had not gone to China, but would have done had he been directly appealed to; he simply could not imagine how he could have possibly refused. In the face of such great need, with so few missionaries, in a region with a population equal to that of Britain's, might now not be the time for the board to energetically recruit missionaries?

In the August 1873 edition of the *Missionary Record*, MacGill wrote briefly but very sympathetically of Ross' bereavement and Mary Ann's character, piety and many accomplishments.[7] Now, five months after her death, McGill felt that he could provide further insight into the emotional cost to John Ross. He did this by an address to the students of the United Presbyterian Divinity Hall. They ought, he said, look further east, beyond India, see the plight of one of their fellow-students and feel the force of the appeal of one 'smitten, solitary and bereaved' but still 'resolute and unwavering'. Ross, said McGill, was heroic, his situation 'truly awful and sublime'. He himself 'sorrowful, but not hopeless, amidst a population exceeding that of these three kingdoms – himself the only ordained missionary among all these millions.' Coming to the peroration of his address, McGill implored the students to consider missionary service. Maybe his words were not as direct as Ross' might have liked them to have been, yet what he said was both powerful and persuasive. 'Consider the fact that any of you, who may desire to have your ministerial lot cast among…the hardy worldly men of Northern China … we can satisfy your choice. We can point you to where you could have a million in your parish, instead of sitting down … in some little Scottish town, where two or three ministers are labouring among a limited population, where the strange word "over-churched" is sometimes heard, and where Christian work might be better done if the three churches were in all respects *one*, and if two ministers were to say to their people, "Be content and united under one pastor … that we should preach among the Gentiles the unsearchable riches of Christ."'

There was no further report from Newchwang in the *Missionary Record* until the November edition, when we learn of the situation as it prevailed in July that year. Ross had been busily, though reluctantly, erecting 'indispensable' buildings, but that was by the way. He was much more interested in the opportunity the building project provided for getting to know culturally, religiously and personally the fifty or more Chinese stonemasons, joiners, bricklayers and coolie labourers on the site. Most of these, he had learned, were not Manchus, as he had thought, but Han Chinese, or as he called them 'Chinese proper'. Compared to the Chinese of the south, these were a 'giant race', taller than men in Scotland, many over six feet, and 'by no means slimly made'. These powerful men, with well-developed limbs and strong muscles, were quite equal to any labouring challenge that might arise. He wrote glowingly of two young bricklayers whose physique so impressed him that he described them as having 'a beauty of form that cannot possibly be surpassed … even from a limner's [portrait painter's] hand.'[8] But what struck him most was their innate intelligence which, he thought, could not be equalled, let alone surpassed, in the West.

Reticent to comment on the impression Chinese women made upon him, Ross understatedly remarked that from what he had seen, 'beauty is granted here as well as Britain.' All in all, he was greatly impressed with these gifted, handsome, composed and self-possessed inheritors of a proud heritage; a people who rightly demanded the respect of Westerners. Evidently, he was not only feeling a God-given burden to reach these people for Christ, but he had also a growing regard, indeed a love, for them.

With his great aptitude for languages, Ross was by this time using his limited but growing familiarity with Mandarin Chinese to preach to around thirty people gathered daily in his little meeting place in Newchwang. Here they could also hear the catechist, Yuen, whom Ross described as 'a regular orator', though he nevertheless still felt it incumbent upon himself sometimes publicly to correct Yuan's errors, and to keep to himself the responsibility of teaching the growing number of converts.

Strategically, Newchwang was the gateway to Manchuria, and through it went Ross to travel widely throughout the southern part of the province, visiting many towns and villages. Although encouraged by the general friendliness of people towards him, he was under no illusions that unaided he could do much to spread the gospel in so vast an area, other than to make infinitesimal gestures in exploiting the curiosity, intellectual power and energy of the people. He badly needed help. His last report for that sad and challenging year carried the poignant line, 'Truly the harvest here is great, and *one* labourer.'[9]

8

Wang Ching-ming: The Chinese Agent

What then of the future? How without natives able to preach will the Chinese Church ever become any other than a rickety child always carried about by a nurse?

John Ross

Let the foreigner depart, we have the Bible,
and we know the truth,
and we will teach and repeat it if there are
no foreigners in the land.

Wang Ching-ming

JOHN Ross was one of those rare souls able to see beyond their immediate circumstances to embrace the opportunities of a wider sphere. He was, in that sense, a strategic thinker; which made it inevitable that, as his knowledge grew, his vision broadened and his influence increased. His own thoughts doubtless gained impetus from conversations with his fellow missionaries at Chefoo, perhaps with that other strategic thinker, Nevius, certainly with Williamson, whose urging had led him to Newchwang. The tragic consequences that flowed from this seemingly impetuous decision had brought sadness, but it had also opened up Ross' heart and imagination to the prospect of building the Kingdom of God in wider Manchuria, and, perhaps, Korea too. Not that there was insufficient work to occupy his energy and attention in Newchwang itself. Indeed, far from it. He found plenty to do, but his involvement locally always drew him on to usefulness elsewhere.

Thinking and praying through the immediate challenges he faced, Ross came to see the way forward in three steps. First, there ought to be a sound and active Christian community in the Manchurian capital of Mukden. Second, the Mukden church should be linked to Newchwang by a chain of smaller Christian communities at points along the connecting road. These would serve not only as a line of supply for the Mukden community, but as points from which the gospel would radiate into the surrounding countryside. Third, Ross was by now unshakeably convinced that foreign missionaries were wholly inadequate, both numerically and in other respects, to evangelise Manchuria, or, for that matter, wider China: the only way was through properly trained Chinese Christians.

By 1874, the use of local Christians to evangelise and plant churches was by no means an innovation, although it was something of a novelty in China. For over a century the idea of 'native agency', as it was then termed, had been recognised and implemented in many parts of the world. Thirty years earlier, the Free Church of Scotland's Jewish Mission in Budapest, Hungary, had utilised lay missionaries recruited from among the Hungarian Jewish Christians. Simultaneously with what was developing in Ross' mind, though entirely independent of him, James Stewart, the Principal of the Free Church of Scotland's Lovedale Missionary Institute in South Africa, was preparing to take with him, into what is now Malawi, a group of black student missionaries to give impetus to the already established but troubled work at Livingstonia.[1]

Native agency, however, was not a Scottish Presbyterian idea. Rather it owed its genesis to the Anglican, Henry Venn. In his capacity as secretary of the Church Missionary Society, he had pioneered indigenous ministry, as well as self-governing, self-supporting and self-propagating churches. Venn saw the supreme usefulness of suitable local Christians serving as evangelists, maybe initially under the supervision of European clergy, but later as equal members of the ordained ministry of the church.

Unlike Livingstone and others who advocated the importance of establishing churches within a colonial ethos of European Christian civilisation, Venn believed that the gospel ought to be preached and churches established in a manner that respected and authentically reflected the local cultural heritage. Ten years before Ross contemplated the possibility of enlisting Chinese evangelists, the Anglicans, under Venn's influence, had not only ordained to the ministry, but consecrated to the episcopate, a Nigerian, Samuel Ajayi Crowther, as bishop of Western Africa whose diocese was the churches along the River Niger. Regrettably, Venn's ideal of indigenous independent churches, separate from but in communion with the Church of England, foundered on the racial prejudice of European missionaries who shamefully refused to accept Crowther's episcopal authority or follow his lead.

Venn was not alone in advancing the claims of indigenous ministry. Rufus Anderson, his American counterpart in The American Board of Commissioners for Foreign Missions, thought along broadly similar lines. Together they created what J. Pierce Beaver has referred to as the 'Venn-Anderson tradition', which according to Max Warren influenced church planting in Africa, India, Sri Lanka, the Middle East and China, adding that it 'had an importance for the missionary movement that can hardly be exaggerated'.[2]

How, when or where the theory of indigenous ministry – of native agency – had entered Ross' mind is unclear, though some of its ideas were latent in his United Presbyterian voluntary tradition and also in his denomination's remarkable openness to cultural equality and respect for racial diversity. As time passed, and his understanding of missionary theory and practice matured, locally sustainable indigenous ministry emerged as its single central element. As Ross was developing and implementing his ideas, American mission circles were opening their minds to similar policies promoted by John Livingstone Nevius. Crucial to the practical outworking of Ross' ideas, however, and what placed him in the forefront of such thinking, turning theory into practice, was his collaboration with Wang Ching-ming, the first Chinese man he baptised, the first elder he ordained, and the first preacher he commissioned.[3]

Wang Ching-ming was born near Beijing, the son of a small landowner who despite his poverty managed to secure for his son a rudimentary education in order to spur him to seek better prospects than could be found slaving, as his father had done, over a small and unproductive plot of land. Wang may not have made the fortune of his dreams, but he did learn important life skills. For example, when working for a mandarin, with neither wages nor perks, he learned how to dress himself respectably and keep a good table. Similarly, when following the tough life of a gold miner he learned how to live in a decent law-abiding manner in a lawless environment. Moving to the port of Newchwang, he entered the soya bean trade, the crop being at that time the most lucrative of the port's exports. Wang was successful and remained in this business for several years, and through it made his first contacts with Europeans. At the time it was customary to seal a business deal between a trader and his client by smoking opium together. Inevitably Wang became addicted, and although at the end of each year he had made a reasonable profit, there was little left after the payment of his opium bill. Consequently, Wang failed to meet traditional Confucian responsibilities, such as supporting his old mother, or his wife and children, all of whom were living far away in deep poverty.

In 1873, around the time the Rosses arrived in Newchwang, Wang came across a copy of one of the Gospels. How we do not know. At any rate, he read the small volume, becoming increasingly perplexed as he did so. As Ross put it, 'this book was a riddle to him.' But a riddle that had to be resolved, and so Wang sought an explanation. With two others, he sat for hours daily, for several months, as Ross in his broken Chinese sought to make clear the Good News from a close reading of the books of Romans and Galatians. Gripped by this intriguing new teaching, Wang suspended his business activities and became wholly engrossed in studying the Bible. At this time, he could not, however, abstain from opium, to which he was addicted, but from which he sincerely wanted to break free.

On learning of God's supreme power, and even more of his unconditional love, Wang spent three days and nights in prayer, seeking strength to break the habit. What he sought, he found. From that time the craving lessened and, before the year was out, he had put opium behind him and was an enthusiastic professing Christian, his fervour readily finding verbal expression.

When Wang thought he was ready for baptism, Ross was cautious. Always setting high standards for admission to the membership of the church, Ross examined Wang and five others, but doubting the sincerity of four, he refused to baptise them for the time being. One of the two admitted was Wang. Ross had entertained doubts about Wang's readiness, but these had been removed when Wang, having noticed that on one occasion Ross seemed reluctant to witness to the Good News as clearly as he might have liked, stepped in himself, and according to Ross 'spoke so earnestly, clearly, forcibly and enthusiastically' that all uncertainty evaporated. It was clear to Ross that it was his duty to admit Wang to the little Newchwang church as promptly as possible.

Doubtless, in Newchwang as elsewhere, conversions could be nominal, a mere realignment of religious affiliation, sometimes motivated by the prospect of material advantage. Wang, however, was not one to whom the derogatory term 'rice Christian' might be applied. Though it ought to be said that, more often than not, the blame for the creation of dependent converts lay on the missionaries themselves and the inducements they offered. Wang, however, was offered no inducement and needed no inducement; it was incentive enough to have seen for himself the love of God in Jesus Christ. This revelation utterly transformed him, giving him that renewed mind which leads to a change of heart and results in a change of behaviour which indicates authentic Christian conversion. As Ross put it himself, 'The love of the Father manifested in the loving Son is that which makes men here break their idols and cast their chanted prayers into the flames.'

Drawing on his experience of how Wang and others came to faith, Ross strongly inveighed against missionary work which was, in his opinion, badly and insensitively done. It was crucial, he held, for the missionary to conduct himself with the utmost patience, gentleness and humility of spirit and never allow even a vestige of racial, moral or spiritual superiority to put on his dignity and lead him to berate new converts over that confused melange of ideas and opinions which are inevitably jumbled together in the early stages of Christian experience. Had Wang been so treated, Ross was sure that, responding with his naturally fiery and impetuous nature, he would have turned away from Christianity. But patience had her perfect work, and Wang Ching-ming grew in dependence upon the Holy Spirit, rather than leaning on the transient foreign missionary. It greatly pleased Ross to hear Wang say, as over the years he so often did, that he was no 'running dog' of the foreigner, but rather a follower of the truth of Heaven, the doctrine of which the foreigner was but a messenger. 'Let the foreigner depart,' he once said to a group of listening Chinese, 'we have the Bible, and we know the truth, and we will teach and repeat it if there are no foreigners in the land.'

In the same year that Wang came to Ross for instruction, the grain harvest around Newchwang failed. Famine gripped the land and as winter closed in many were reduced to choosing whether or not to eat the roots of grass they had gathered or burn them as fuel. To alleviate suffering Ross had received a sum of money donated by the local European population, which had been matched by a sum sent from the United Presbyterian Church in Scotland. This enabled him to buy several cart-loads of millet for famine relief. A free supply of grain was made available for any children who would study Chinese literature at a village school to be established at Dapingshan, some few miles from Newchwang. Ross also put it about that no one coming to the mission house at Newchwang, and giving evidence of need, would ever be turned away. Aid was usually given in the form of an allowance of thirty pounds of millet, per person, per month, until spring arrived.

Wang was appointed to open and run the Dapingshan school, but struggled to get it going. Fearing that the foreigners were seeking to take advantage of people's suffering, fully two months passed before a single child could be persuaded to attend the school or, for that matter, before any adult would go to the mission house at Newchwang for help. Those who did, did so only when death stared them in the face. In Dapingshan, a wary eye was kept on the few children who appeared at the school and suspicions were only allayed when it became obvious that not only did they not suffer harm, but they positively thrived, both physically and mentally. Others were allowed to join them and soon anyone passing on the street could hear a full complement of children chanting their Chinese characters.

As part of the school day, Wang held a short service of worship, with hymns, prayers and Scripture readings to which adult neighbours were invited to join. Many did so, coming first out of curiosity, then out of genuine interest. In order to allay fear of foreigners,

Ross only visited the school every few months; though, when the villagers' confidence was won, he visited each week, riding out on Wednesdays. Finally, when he had come to be seen as a friend rather than a threat, he stayed overnight, marvelling at Wang's times of worship, his competent delivery of education to the children, and the solid Christian instruction he provided for the adults.

Ross was delighted by the enthusiasm with which the children sang the hymns, and greatly amused that the tunes bore absolutely no resemblance whatsoever to any European or Chinese tune. After a hymn, a chapter of the Bible was read, each child reading a verse in turn, followed by Wang explaining and applying it appropriately to his audience before the worship concluded with another hymn. After breakfast the next day, the service was repeated, with the children who prayed doing so in their own words and not by rote, except in the case of the youngest.

As the long winter came in, Christian conversations in Dapingshan took place in a more relaxed atmosphere than during the busier times of the year, so that by the time spring came around the gospel had taken hold in the community. As is so often the case, it was the less conservative young people who led the way, not only in accepting the Good News for themselves, but also drawing the necessary conclusion that it could not coexist with idolatry. Some daringly destroyed their family idols. The villagers witnessed this, but took it calmly, recognising that even at a material level, Christianity had brought to them far more than had Taoism's Jade Emperor, the Eight Immortals or the Three Pure Ones. Whether or not their profession of Christianity was always credible, the people had at any rate renounced idolatry, and even in the families of important landowners many were reading the Bible for themselves.

It was at Dapingshan that an appealing, but for Ross, exasperating characteristic of Wang's Christian life revealed itself. Many famine victims were qualified to take advantage of the relief offered by the missionary, and did so; but there were others who were not actually starving and so did not qualify, though they were genuinely needy. Wang provided help for such people at a cost to himself of three months' wages. Not wanting to demean people with unconditional charity, Wang employed them in improving the appalling roads in the village. His generosity deprived him of warm clothing necessary to combat the intense cold of winter.

Wang was impulsively generous to a fault: he could never sit down to a meal if a hungry man was nearby, or keep his second coat if there was a ragged or semi-naked person in sight. Ross recognised the sensitivity of the situation, Wang was many years his senior, but he nevertheless felt impelled to say something, as even Wang himself, when viewing his impulsive enthusiasm rationally, had to admit that he was inclined to be imprudent.

Ross had no desire to judge Wang's seemingly rash actions by cold reason alone, and no intention of inhibiting a Christ-like generous and empathetic heart which made Wang respond in Christ-like practical action. In any case, there was no doubt that it was his generosity of spirit that had so endeared him to the hearts of the Dapingshan people. The problem was never really resolved, and there was no change of mind or behaviour in Wang, so Ross, as well as dutifully and graciously chiding him, compensated for his self-inflicted impecunity by increasing his winter allowance in the hope it would keep him warm and offset his often-injudicious financial investments in others.

What Ross did not know, when he first invited Wang to undertake the duties of the school in Dapingshan, was that, motivated by the love of God, Wang agreed to do so despite the allowance Ross offered being less than half of what he had earned as a soya trader. As he no longer spent large sums on opium, Ross may have miscalculated that Wang was better off than he in fact was. Although his expensive habit no longer drained his income, he now voluntarily spent heavily on the needs of others, and also sought to correct his earlier neglect of his elderly mother and his wife and children.

The Confucian teaching of filial responsibility, deeply ingrained in Wang, as it was in most other Chinese, had long lain dormant within him. After his conversion it was reawakened and energised by the new life of the Holy Spirit, leading him to reestablish contact with his mother and his wife and family. Now, from time to time, he sent small sums of money, accompanied by affectionate letters. A younger brother in business in a remote town in Mongolia heard of this, and curious to know what kind of religion it was which had not only delivered his brother from opium but had revived in him a sense of duty towards his family, travelled all the way to Newchwang to find out. He too was converted and never did return to Mongolia, but became an effective evangelist. To distinguish him from his older brother he became known as Wang Number Two, and Wang, himself, though hardly elderly, became known as Old Wang or Wang the Illustrious.

Wang's concern for his family extended far beyond material considerations and led him to visit his old home, near Beijing, to share with them all, but especially his old mother now drawing to the close of her life, the saving truth of Jesus. He returned with a joyful request that Ross would go to the family to baptise his mother and wife, but before he could go, Wang's eager mother travelled to Newchwang.

By 1875, Wang was encouraged by Ross to delegate responsibility to others whom he had trained up to share the work. Wang now found himself at the centre of a prospering church at Dapingshan, over which little direct supervision was necessary other than that provided by its Chinese church leaders and office bearers. It now became clear that Ross' theory – that in Chinese Christians such as Wang lay the true means of reaching into the vastness of China – was a practical reality. Confident that Wang's ability, character and motivation had been well proved in Dapingshan, Ross invited Wang to consider a new and greater challenge, that of establishing a toehold for the gospel in the capital of Manchuria, the large and thriving city of Mukden.

The Dapingshan experiment convinced Ross of the soundness of his strategy. Aware that the United Presbyterian Church Mission Board had sanctioned the use of native agents in Jamaica, in an article in the *Missionary Record* he claimed that what was useful in Jamaica was essential in China, and stated his intention henceforth to use it not hesitantly or nervously, as an adjunct to his work, but 'as much as possible'.[4] His goal would be to encourage and train Chinese Christians such as Wang and his brother, Wang Number Two, Yuen his catechist in Newchwang, Tang the schoolmaster and others to assume responsibility in the church, quite unalarmed that if in finding their feet they would make mistakes. As he pointed out in the final chapter of his sketch of the life of Old Wang, progress couldn't be made unless calculated risks were taken. The exigencies of the situation required it. The missionary was not omnipresent; he must trust others to reach those living in places he couldn't visit. Not only so, but he saw it was incumbent upon him to look to a future when he would no longer be present. Ross pressed the point:

> Then what of the future? Is the Chinese Church to be always dependent on foreign Churches? If foreigners had to leave China, is it not desirable that the converts should be able ... to carry on the work? Can this ever be if the natives are not trained to preach independently of the foreigner? How without natives able to preach and employed in public preaching will the Chinese Church ever become any other than a rickety child always carried about by a nurse? No infant ever took to running on its feet by unceasing careful nursing on his mother's knee. And what though in the act of learning to walk he fall occasionally? He must be encouraged and taught to walk more steadily.[5]

In the same place Ross answers the question of the criteria by which such leaders ought to be selected. Those who naively argued that a mere profession of faith was adequate in itself could never have grasped the often-overwhelming nature of Christian ministry, a formidable reality that even had the Apostle Paul crying out in desperation, 'Who is sufficient for these things?' For Ross, the inescapably impressive argument in favour of a rigorous selection of Chinese leaders was the conviction that if 'very few foreigners are fully qualified to be missionaries to the Chinese', then how could he believe 'that more than a fractional proportion of Chinese converts are qualified to be public preachers?' Whilst acknowledging that every Christian was called to bear witness to the faith he possessed, his particular task was to identify those within the Chinese Christian community who were especially qualified by the grace of true Christian character and the work of the 'many-gift-bestowing Spirit' to be preachers to their own people, those best able to give intelligent and convincing reasons 'for the hope that is in him'. Or to put it contextually, Ross argued that 'warmth of heart and clearness of the intellect are the *yang* and *yin* of the Chinese preacher – the positive and negative spiritual electricity, without both of which a powerful battery is not to be hoped for. The first is the most important, but you must have both.'[6]

Potential candidates needed to be trained, supported financially, and provided with adequate oversight. Ross saw three possible sources of financial support: first, the worker might provide for himself and his dependent family by maintaining a trade or business. Second, he might already possess sufficient private wealth to maintain himself. Third, he might be supported by some external source of income. The first, Ross argued, was at best precarious; too often the demand of making a living distracted the preacher from his main work. The second and third reasons gave him the necessary liberty to devote his main energy and most of his time to the work of preaching, to the exclusion of other cares, but if the man in the second category was rare, even in the wealthy West, how much rarer was he likely to be in China? The most viable option was to support him through money raised elsewhere until such time as a self-supporting church came into existence. Initially the funds came from Ross' own pocket.

Ross pressed upon his United Presbyterian supporters the implications of one of the fundamental principles of their doctrine of the church, the belief that national churches were unbiblical. The tendency to think territorially had, he argued, dangerously narrowing consequences for missionary work, because the Church of Christ ought never to be seen as national, but always as cosmopolitan. Moreover, he disliked the alienating tendency inherent in the term 'foreign' missions. The Church of Christ was one, and therefore 'it is no less right for London or New York to supply the deficiency of Peking, than it was for the Churches of Philippi or Corinth to collect for the needs of Jerusalem.'

Having settled in the affirmative the fraught question of whether money donated by the United Presbyterian mission's supporters in Scotland ought to be invested in Chinese leaders, rather than exclusively in their foreign missionaries, he went on to minimise the importance of the question, by claiming that money was always relatively easy to come by, but suitable men were not. Everything possible, therefore, should be done to recruit and retain them in useful ministry. The time would come when Ross would adjust this ideal of mutual interdependence, putting a greater emphasis on locally sustainable ministry, arguing that Chinese churches should be self-supporting, self-governing and self-propagating. But he wasn't quite at that point yet. First, he had to establish a body of properly trained, equipped and adequately supported Chinese evangelists.

To clinch his arguments in favour of local ministry, Ross demonstrated the effectiveness of Chinese-to-Chinese witness. Speaking modestly from his limited experience – though an experience already wider than that of even his senior colleagues – he claimed that the number of converts won by foreigners to the church with which he was connected was little more than a dozen. Yet the actual number of those that had been baptised and received into communicant membership on a credible profession of faith amounted to more than a thousand. To be sure, the foreign missionary had an important role in the instruction and preparation for baptism of such converts, but that in no way detracted from the fact that most converts were the fruit of Chinese Christians such as Yuan and Wang. Moreover, their witness had broken down barriers and helped remove prejudice against Christianity, so that many Chinese now thought well of it, and some had the root of it in their hearts, even if they were unable as yet publicly to profess it in baptism.

If ordinary Chinese Christians were so effective in their witness, Ross believed that even more effective would be trained preachers, who, relieved from mundane concerns, could dedicate most of their time and energy to preaching. This was borne out by his own experience. He was not aware of any foreigner in China, no matter how long they had been there, who could trace to his direct and immediate agency half as many converts as Old Wang had been enabled to win.

Even then his argument was not concluded. Anticipating the objection that the true cause of all conversions was not men, whether foreign or local, but the Holy Spirit, and well aware that this argument had been used to justify indifferent human agents, Ross asserted that although in Old Testament times effective preachers were indeed sometimes weak in their characters, yet they were never weak in their intellects. And when we come to the New Testament, do we not discover that by far the most effective of the Apostles were those who were both intellectually and spiritually the strongest of men? The same was true of both mediaeval and modern missions. God, says Ross, has always demanded the choicest men for his work, and he claims them still. Wang Ching-ming was one such.

9

Advance to Mukden

Mukden is the heart of all that is active and thoughtful throughout this land, and is therefore of the greatest importance from a missionary point of view, as everything done here is speedily known throughout, and influences more or less the entire province.
JOHN ROSS

FOR some men grief is confusing, isolating and paralysing. Not a day passes without depressing waves of heartache. Often the darkness of loss eclipses the ability to keep up a normal routine of duties and little pleasures. Such might have been the reaction of a young husband like John Ross after the loss of his wife, especially in a new and alien environment, and in the midst of a bitter winter. But such was not John's response. This was doubtless partly due to the fact that he knew he was supported by the prayers of a wide circle of friends and colleagues at home in Scotland, among the Chefoo missionaries, and in the Newchwang European community. He was especially encouraged by the thoughtfulness of his warm-hearted medical missionary neighbour, Dr Joseph Hunter of the Irish Presbyterian mission, now completely reconciled to Ross' presence in Manchuria. He and his wife Elizabeth Jayne had arrived in Newchwang four years earlier in April 1869, but in 1871 Elizabeth died of tuberculosis, leaving their infant son John to be brought back to Ireland by Hunter's colleague, Rev. Hugh Waddell, who had to return for the sake of his own health. Having thus passed through his own valley of deep darkness, Hunter was well placed to support and encourage his Scottish neighbour.[1]

Beyond and behind the support of his neighbours and colleagues, Ross was upheld by the grace of God and the blessings of a resilient temperament able to turn grief into a force for good. As there is no surviving record of Ross' own feelings, we can only conjecture how such forces, divine and human, fused together in his experience, but it is surely not fanciful to believe that they brought to him an assurance that he was not alone; his heavenly Father was always at hand. It is also probable that his loss served as a sharp reminder of his own mortality, which itself gave fresh impetus to the task he was called to undertake, and which he now saw in the light of eternity and the brevity of time. Ross' grief was a transformative force that moved him beyond any inclination to depression, or to succumb to the temptation to bask inert in the thoughts and prayers of others. Rather, affliction seems to have led him more deeply into a sphere of active energy, driving real change, spiritual change, missionary change.

Conjecture apart, it is a fact that within months of Mary Ann's death Ross had acquired reasonable proficiency in spoken Mandarin, a basic knowledge of Chinese characters that allowed him to begin reading classic Confucian texts, and had gained a working grasp of the local Manchu language. Gone was the frustration of having always to communicate via a translator. He was now free to speak directly, and even to preach haltingly in his little chapel. He also travelled. His journeys, exploring the Manchurian countryside, gave him familiarity with its vast range of plants and wildflowers – he was a keen amateur botanist and plant collector – as well as opening his eyes to its vast human population with almost limitless missionary opportunities. One of his early expeditions, undertaken in the spring of 1873, was a four-hundred-mile round trip to Mukden, the capital of Manchuria, which had an immediate impact on his plans. Another itinerary in October 1874 took Ross to the frontier between Korea and Manchuria. That journey too would have great future significance.

After visiting Mukden, Ross reported to the United Presbyterian Foreign Mission Board that it was an impressive city, not only in size, nor because of its status as the Manchu capital, nor because it enjoyed a relatively clean and orderly environment, or even that it was teeming with people and all around it were industrious peasants diligently cultivating the surrounding fields.[2] What caught his keen missionary eye was the fact that the city was simultaneously a commercial hub, administrative centre and provincial capital; its web of links and connections radiated out in all directions. It was also the revered heart of Manchuria, from which had come the Manchu founders of China's Later Jin dynasty (1616–1636) and the Qing (1636–1912), the country's last imperial dynasty, and here was replicated the imperial capital of Beijing, with its philosophical, cultural and religious significance. As Ross put it: 'It is the heart of all that is active and thoughtful throughout this land, and is therefore of the greatest importance from a missionary point of view, as everything done here is speedily known throughout, and influences more or less the entire province.'[3]

Mukden was an ideal base from which to reach out to Manchuria, though it was not an easy place for a foreign missionary to become established. Ross, however, made light of what others thought were the risks inherent in travelling to such locations: 'it does not appear in the least dangerous to travel, though the unbounded curiosity of the people makes it somewhat uncomfortable.' He likewise dismissed worries about discomfort, that foreigners, especially women, could not live comfortably in such places. The grain of truth in the argument had certainly inhibited the board in Scotland from sanctioning missionary work in the interior. But it did not inhibit Ross. What troubled him was that because of lingering official resistance to European residence in inland China, the city could only be visited occasionally. What foreigners might do only with difficulty, Ross believed a Chinese could do with ease. He would send one of his Chinese helpers to Mukden.

The first chosen was a Muslim convert, whose name we do not know. We do know, however, that he didn't stay in Mukden long. Sent to distribute Bibles and Christian literature he failed to rise to expectations. There was no proof of mismanagement, neglect or anything untoward on his part. He simply couldn't make a go of it. But there were others ready to step into the gap: one was Old Wang, another was Tang.

Sketching out the history of the work in Mukden, Mrs M'Laren in her official account *The Story of the Manchurian Mission* early introduces us to Wang's partner Tang, but says no more about him other that he and Wang were sent by Ross to Mukden in 1876.[4] Ross' missionary report, however, informs us that it was the famine of the winter of 1873/4 that brought Tang to Ross.[5] One freezing winter's day a tall young man, clad in rags, presented himself at Ross' house with such an air of dignity and manners of a gentleman that Ross was quite disconcerted. He came seeking help, but not with the fawning attitude adopted by so many. Indeed, he conveyed the distinct impression that if he was refused, he wouldn't demean himself by asking a second time. Of course, he wasn't turned away. He was invited in and made welcome. In the conversation that ensued the young man claimed to have passed the second stage of traditional Chinese education, holding the equivalent of what might be regarded today as a Master of Arts degree.

Interested to test the authenticity of this modestly stated claim, Ross handed to him a book that he had been working through with his teacher, both of whom had found it difficult going. Not so for this young man. Running his eye down the columns of Chinese characters, he read them as easily as if they were a child's reading book. But what impressed Ross most of all was that this was accomplished with none of the swagger adopted by many Chinese scholars.

It transpired that Tang had been a teacher in one of the large towns to the south, but because of the famine had been made redundant. Unable to sustain himself or his family, he had wandered northwards with his wife, her father and mother, his three young brothers and a sister-in-law, eventually arriving in Newchwang. After pawning or selling all their furniture and most of their clothing, and affording only the smallest room able to accommodate them all, and barely any food, he had come to hear of the missionary and the promise of relief. He had risen off his bed where he was trying to stave off the pangs of hunger and the pains of illness, and braving a bitingly cold north-easterly wind with the temperature hovering around minus twenty-three degrees centigrade, destitute and hopeless, he arrived on Ross' doorstep to seek a small supply of millet to keep body and soul together for just a little longer. Never one to allow himself to be cheated, and intrigued at the thought of gaining the help of such an obviously gifted young man, and, as always, seeking an opportunity to speak to him and his family about Jesus, Ross set off with him to verify his story. He was appalled at what he discovered.

As they neared the hovel in which the family's single room was, they saw a wild-eyed, starved and half-naked child run across the icy road with a tattered piece of straw matting. Tang, for that was the young teacher's name, called her back, informing Ross that this was his sister-in-law who was taking away the last possession they had to exchange it for a mouthful of food. Entering the house, Ross found himself in a scene of abject squalor and utter destitution. The room was fireless, freezing cold, bare, dirty, damp and entirely cheerless; its four occupants dangerously ill from malnourishment. Ross told the child to put down the mat, and, calling on Tang to follow him, returned to the mission house to make ready a supply of millet. Tang, still dignified, but deeply grateful, bowed and thanked Ross for this 'abundance' of food, though Ross considered it little enough for so many hungry mouths.

Soon afterwards, Ross employed Tang as schoolmaster at Newchwang. His wages included his meals. His family were housed about a mile away, subsisting on a portion of Tang's wages and whatever help they could get. Curiously, Ross seems to have neglected their long term needs and felt guilty about it. In a report to the Board, published in the *Missionary Record,* Ross stated that he reproached himself for not giving Tang more money, over and above his wages, to meet the pressing needs of his family, including the debts they had run up with unscrupulous lenders to tide them over the worst of the winter famine, but which were even then being called in at exorbitant rates of interest. Ross excused his neglect on the grounds that Tang, unlike his compatriots, never reminded him of his need.

In time Tang said he wished to be baptised, but Ross was resistant, thinking that he had mistaken something that he, Ross, had said about the importance of baptism and believed that 'those who do not receive baptism cannot be saved'. Tang wrote to Ross a long letter, beseeching him to baptise him, or as he put it, give him the Great Water. Whether Ross was able to correct this misunderstanding, if indeed there ever was one, we shall never know, but Ross soon saw the reality of Tang's faith, notwithstanding any alleged doctrinal muddle in his mind. The clinching argument came when Ross heard of Tang's arrest by some soldiers, who tied him up, beat him, and holding a sword to his throat, demanded to know if he was a believer in Jesus. 'Yes,' came Tang's unhesitating succinct but clear reply, 'I am a Christian.' Returning home the following Sunday, the preacher at Newchwang, quite possibly Yuen, asked Tang how was it that he, a Christian of so brief a time, had the courage to say what he had said. Tang simply told him how the story of Peter's denial of his Master, and his subsequent remorse and bitter tears, had brought him to the conclusion that he would never deny his Lord. To which the preacher's confident answer came, 'Tang will not again have to ask in vain for baptism!'[6] To these two remarkable disciples, Wang and Tang, Ross entrusted the initial evangelisation of the city of Mukden.

10

Progress in Mukden and Beyond

How pleasant … to find those who love and serve our Master – the precious fruit of a brother's toil is a sight full of bright hope and cheer to us in our labours.

THOMAS WELLESLEY PIGGOT, CIM

DESPITE Ross' caution in admitting converts to baptism, and considerable local opposition to Christianity, membership of the Mukden congregation grew. By 1878 it numbered some twenty-six loyal communicants. One, a seventy-year-old convert, was a courageous and outspoken witness, defiantly stating: 'Though they drag me with cart ropes, they shall not pull me away from my Saviour Jesus.' In that church, there was not one, Ross believed, unready to give a reason for the hope that inspired him.

Although the Christians of Mukden stood solid, the physical building in which they met was ramshackle. It was time to move. A more suitable property was found in one of the main streets of the city, and this gave great impetus to the work. The daily patient and clear explanation of the gospel, from three o'clock in the afternoon to eight o'clock in evening, resulted in many showing their enthusiasm to be considered Christians. That number was whittled down, however, by the probationary period Ross required, leaving the solid believers to be baptised and brought into the membership of the church.

In March 1879, Ross took leave and returned to Scotland. Three years earlier, John Macintyre had married Ross' sister Catherine;

they had decided to remain in China and promised to keep an eye on Mukden. Eager to relieve his brother-in-law of the arduous duty of travelling back and forth the one hundred and twenty miles from Newchwang to Mukden, and having every confidence in Wang's ability, Ross decided to test both Wang and his own increasing conviction of the viability of an authentically Chinese, broadly Presbyterian church, by leaving Wang in sole charge at Mukden. The experiment was a complete success. Wang reported that during that year not only had a further sixteen baptisms taken place, but he, following Ross' example, had recruited the more promising members of the congregation to assist him in preaching. During this period some missionaries of the China Inland Mission happened to arrive in Mukden. They were thrilled to meet Wang and the faithful members of the little church. One of their number, Thomas Pigott, wrote home, well-meaningly enthusing over his experience, but really missing the point. 'How pleasant,' he wrote, 'to find those who love and serve our Master, —the precious fruit of a brother's toil. It is a sight full of bright hope and cheer to us in our labours.'[1] Ross would have deflected the plaudit and drawn attention to Wang.

Shortly after this, Macintyre came over from Newchwang to visit Wang and found another eight converts waiting for examination prior to being admitted to baptism. Two were the wives of men who had been converted earlier and who had in turn won their spouses for Christ. He was greatly encouraged by all he saw. Knowing that elsewhere in China similar growth might have taken considerably longer to achieve, he recognised in the speed of growth under Chinese leadership the promise of a bright future.

In reviewing Wang's character and ministry in those early days at Mukden, Ross singled out his patient teaching and gentle demeanour whereby he overcame fierce opposition and won the respect, albeit sometimes grudging, of many who heard him. This, thought Ross, was all the more impressive to any, who, like himself, knew Wang's natural disposition towards impetuosity and short-temperedness.[2] Before his conversion Wang had been a respected trader. Now, he was living in a prosperous city surrounded by many of his former class who ostentatiously flaunted their wealth and status, yet he remained free of all vanity, demonstrating great

Christian humility. Not for a moment did he ever consider himself above visiting the poor, whom he assisted as sedulously in Mukden as he had in Dapingshan. Indeed, his desire to alleviate poverty intensified during the coming three years when famine gripped northern China, driving many from the rural hinterland into towns and cities in search for food. Many starving people came to Mukden and found their way to Wang's chapel. Only after exhausting all his own resources, to the extent of even giving away his own food to the hungry and clothing to the naked, did Wang seek the help of others. Ross once movingly said of him: 'To the last this trait ... never abandoned him, and his generous impulses ceased only when his heart had ceased to beat.'[3]

Meanwhile, back in Scotland, Ross was busy raising financial support for the printing of the Gospels of his translation of the Korean New Testament, and advocating the claims of Manchuria and Korea. The United Presbyterian response was to send out two pairs of missionaries, each consisting of a minister and a medical doctor: Rev. Alexander Westwater and Dr A. Macdonald Westwater were sent first to Chefoo, and then some five years later to Manchuria; and Rev. James Webster and Dr Dugald Christie went to Mukden.

During this furlough, on 24th February 1881, Ross married thirty-two-year-old Isabella Strapp Macfadyen, and with them would travel a further important addition to the missionary staff, Miss Barbara M. Pritty. Miss Pritty went out under the auspices of the United Presbyterian Church's newly founded zenana mission to Chinese women. Named after a Persian and Urdu word that could be roughly translated as 'pertaining to women', the term *zenana* had been adopted by the Muslim Mughal rulers of India to be more or less synonymous with the Arabic *harem,* meaning *sanctuary.* A zenana mission, therefore, was a mission to secluded women of whatever religion who were inaccessible to male missionaries. Following a pattern recently established in India, the United Presbyterian zenana mission was intended, in part, to channel the growing number of single ladies, often trained teachers, who felt themselves called to work in women-to-women evangelism.

Of all the new missionaries it was Dr Dugald Christie who was to make in the medical field as great a contribution to the overall success of the mission in Manchuria as Ross did in establishing the Church.[4] Christie was born at Kingshouse Inn, Glencoe, in the Scottish Highlands, in 1855. In those days the inn was what was known as a change house, where those on government business and others on long-distance journeys, such as the Fort William to Glasgow stagecoach, could get fresh horses for the next section of the journey. Dugald's father Malcolm was both the innkeeper and a reasonably prosperous sheep farmer. He died shortly after Dugald's birth, but his wife continued to keep the inn and the farm, and it was here that Christie spent the first seven years of his life. Glencoe was a small and scattered community with an ancient history, in which Gaelic was the primary language and where the Celtic culture remained strong. At the age of six Dugald started school at Ballachulish, thirteen miles distant. To accommodate his children whilst at school, his father had, before his death, rented a house, over which he set a servant to care for them during the school week. The family were loyal supporters of the Free Church of Scotland, each Sunday travelling in their horse-drawn wagonette the twenty-six miles round trip from Kingshouse to attend the morning Gaelic and the afternoon English services at Ballachulish.

In 1862, Dugald's mother moved the family to a farm at Invergarry, Inverness-shire, which she had taken on a five-year lease. The lease also included running an inn, but unlike the Kingshouse, which rarely had visitors over the winter period, when at times not even the stagecoach could run, Invergarry was busy throughout the year. For Dugald, these years were carefree and happy, but for his mother they brought financial ruin. Within a year of the expiry of the lease, Mrs Christie died, a broken and ill woman. She had been unable to work due to recurring illness, and her children were either too small or too inexperienced to do more than attend to a few of the basic tasks on the farm. Homeless and motherless, the family was now dispersed. The younger ones – Dugald, his brother James and sister Agnes – were sent to a farm ninety miles away at Portsonachan on the south side of Loch Awe, in Argyllshire.

It was at the small school there that Dugald came under the invaluable influence of Donald Stewart, then a teacher, though later a distinguished medical doctor. Stewart's instruction and kindly nurture laid the foundation for Dugald's future university education. But what might have been a direct course into an academic career was, however, frustrated by a shortage of money which forced the fifteen-year-old Dugald and his siblings to move again, this time to Glasgow. Leaving behind the uncomplicated life of the Highlands, with his beloved hills and moors, lochs and rivers, to live in a dingy flat in a teeming city, was a violent shock to Dugald's system. The shock was somewhat mitigated by a growing awareness of his personal responsibility to supplement as best as he could the family income, giving him a somewhat romantic prospect of eventual financial success.

Early in 1874, Dwight L. Moody and Ira D. Sankey, the American evangelists, visited Glasgow. Having been brought up in the Highland tradition of the Free Church of Scotland we might have expected nineteen-year-old Christie to have looked askance, as many Highlanders did. Indeed, the great stalwart of the conservative northern tradition, John Kennedy of Dingwall, railed against Moody and Sankey's campaign, denouncing it as hyper-evangelism. Likewise, Kennedy's associates in Glasgow, the influential Free Church Gaelic ministers, including the Christies' minister, also declaimed against Sankey and his hymns and organs, and Moody and his novel anecdotes and casual speech. They instructed their people to give the Americans a wide berth, despite the fact that it had been a Free Church minister, James Hood Wilson, supported by other southern Free Church leaders, such as Horatius and Andrew Bonar, who had invited Moody to come to Scotland. Such ministerial wrangles, with all their highfalutin rhetoric, did not hinder huge crowds flocking to hear Sankey sing and Moody preach.

What rankled with the conservatives was what they saw as Moody's naive approach to the ministry. They admitted that he was a Bible Christian alright, and that he held an orthodox view of the inspiration of Scripture, but his theology, such as it was, was considered amateurish and implicit, rather than scholarly and direct. Worst of all he discarded the doctrines of confessional Calvinism. Consequently, in the eyes of his detractors, the results of his ministry were suspect. Schooled in Highland reticence, they doubted that authentic Christian experience lay behind the confidence with which new converts so openly professed their faith, or the rapidity with which they engaged in Christian work, including speaking in public.

Doubtless many of Moody's audience attended the meetings out of idle curiosity, but there were higher forces at work too, not least in the case of Dugald Christie. For him, these influences were connected to his earlier home life in the Highlands and the encouragement and prayers of his sister Jessie in Glasgow. But the main influence over Dugald was, he later considered, that of the Holy Spirit, creating within him a deep sense of discontent. One night, dropping to his knees in his room, he asked God to fill the emptiness of his life, of which he was painfully aware. It appears that then and there that emptiness was replaced with a deep sense of satisfaction and fulfilment. His biographer, his second wife Iza, says that from that night in May 1874, 'Christ was his Master and his Saviour, there was neither doubt nor turning back, the service of God became his passion, the leading of others to know him his chief aim and joy.'

Constricted by the narrowness of the traditionalist Gaelic-speaking congregation in which he worshipped, Christie joined the Finnieston congregation of Dr Andrew Bonar, one of Moody's most ardent Free Church supporters. Under Bonar's encouragement, Christie matured rapidly and was sometimes asked to take occasional evangelistic meetings in Glasgow's Saltmarket slums, while at the same time attending tutorial classes for aspiring Free Church ministers. One of these classes was led by the veteran India missionary, Dr Alexander Duff, who, much to Christie's consternation, called upon him to pray. There was also a life-changing meeting with a young Highlander called Morrison who was preparing to go to India as a medical missionary. Morrison both encouraged and inspired Christie to follow the same path of service. Without once looking back Christie, sensing that this was indeed God's will for his life, set his mind to study for university entrance in order to commence a medical course in Edinburgh in 1877.

Upon moving to the Scottish capital, Christie joined Barclay Free Church at Bruntsfield Place. Under Dr James Hood Wilson, Barclay was a vibrant centre of evangelistic activity and church planting, stimulating and equipping Christie for future usefulness. Busy as he was with both his medical studies and church life, Christie did not allow either to hinder him from undertaking divinity classes in both the Free Church College and the United Presbyterian Divinity Hall, as well as following a short course at the Navigation School in Leith. As his university career was undertaken in connection with the Edinburgh Medical Missionary Society, he was also expected to invest time in the society's Cowgate Dispensary and Medical Mission, with the result that in 1881, immediately upon his graduation, he was appointed resident physician.

Christie's natural expectation was to serve as a missionary with his denomination. Just where, however, was the question that needed to be resolved. His friend Morrison suggested India. A meeting with Robert Moffat raised the possibility of Africa. His inclination to be a medical missionary ran into a brick wall. The Free Church Foreign Missionary Committee's attitude to medical missions was, to say the least, ambivalent. Repeated impassioned appeals from Dr James Stewart at Lovedale for a medical mission to be established in South Africa, upon the foundation laid by Dr Jane Waterston's three years voluntary service, had fallen on deaf ears. He was therefore little surprised to receive a discouraging letter from a friend who had gone to Africa as a Free Church medical missionary but had neither hospital nor dispensary and was deeply frustrated.

Attempting to resolve his confused thoughts, Christie attended an interview with a representative of the Free Church Foreign Missions Committee, a crusty, old, retired colonel. Christie, naturally, made no secret of his wish to serve as a medical missionary, upon which the colonel stuffily and imperiously insisted that a soldier must go where he was told to go and do what his commanding officer required of him. The situation rapidly moved beyond retrieval when Christie retorted that that may indeed be so, but it begged the question as to the identity of his commanding officer. Learning of Christie's readiness to serve and that the Free Church Committee was dragging its heels, the Mission Board of the United Presbyterian Church moved with alacrity to invite Christie to be become their medical missionary in Manchuria, offering him a free hand in establishing and developing a well-supported medical work according to his own plans. Christie leapt at the offer, and hearing that another opening existed for a minister in Manchuria, contacted his friend James Webster, who was shortly afterwards ordained and appointed.

In August 1882, Christie married Elizabeth Hastie Smith, a daughter of a leading light in the anti-Calvinist 'Morisonion' Evangelical Union Church of Muirkirk, Ayrshire.[5] The question now arises as to whether his transfer to the United Presbyterians and his marriage to Elizabeth Smith suggest that Christie had loosened his ties to the confessional Calvinism of the Free Church and had embraced the less constrained evangelical theology of the United Presbyterians, or even the barely evangelical Morisonion doctrine of the universal love of God. It might also be supposed that Christie's doctrinal realignment is also reflected in the somewhat denigrating references of his second wife, Iza Inglis, to the Free Church. Whilst that may seem plausible, it would be dangerous to exaggerate the degree of Christie's disaffection with Calvinism. Certainly, there is no evidence that his commitment to an orthodox, evangelical and evangelistic theology had slackened.

Within a few days of their marriages, the Christies and the Websters joined up with John Ross and his new bride, Isabella, and Miss Pritty to travel to Manchuria. About a year later Dugald and Elizabeth Christie settled in Mukden, where Dugald opened his dispensary and immediately found his services in great demand. The Mukden patients received from him not only medical care for the ailments of their bodies, but also spiritual care for their souls. It was Christie's invariable practice not only to share the Good News briefly with each patient, but also to send them home with a printed tract and an encouragement to buy for themselves a part of the Bible or a Christian book. This holistic approach proved both attractive to the Chinese and very effective. In a short time five men professed faith and despite Ross' high demands were accepted for baptism and church membership. A class for enquirers was commenced and through it even more were added to the church.

In 1886, with funds raised by the children in Scotland, a hospital was erected on an excellent site close to the mission house. Christie had the good sense and the cultural sensitivity to have the buildings constructed in the vernacular Chinese architectural style. These were officially opened in 1887 by a high Chinese government official, the President of the Board of War, accompanied by a number of important mandarins.[6] As a matter of policy the hospital made no charge for treatment, though inpatients were required to pay for their food. Christie was greatly aided in his spiritual work by the appointment of Chang Lin as the hospital evangelist, whose retentive mind acquired a sound knowledge of the Bible, and his empathetic spirit made him an effective worker with anxious and ill patients.

It was, however, another Chang, known as Blind Chang, whose story so wonderfully captures the essence of the sacrificial commitment to Christ of the early Chinese Christians in Manchuria. Someone once remarked that you could no more omit Blind Chang from the history of the Manchurian church than the story of the New Testament could dispense with St. Paul.[7]

On a cold winter's night in 1886, a blind man knocked at the door of hospital.[8] He was worn out, very ill, and appeared to be old, although he was in fact only thirty-seven years of age. Having heard it said that in Mukden there was a doctor able to open the eyes of the blind, he, against all advice of family and friends, had set out on a one-hundred-and-twenty-mile journey. On the way he had been robbed and assaulted, but was not in the least deterred. On his arrival he found that the hospital was full. He was nearly turned away, but his obvious need appealed to the hearts of Christie and his staff, and a corner was found for him.

For a month Chang lived in the hospital. His dysentery was cured and his sight slightly improved, but the real change that came over him was not physical but spiritual. The light of the gospel of Christ dawned upon his soul. In conversations with Christie he revealed himself to be a man of exceptional character: proud, self-willed and very determined, but nevertheless of an open mind. Before his sight had failed, he had been a scholar of Confucian and Taoist philosophy and an ardent member of a Buddhist sect. He had also been an inveterate gambler. But none of these things had satisfied him as much as the Christian message, to which he now avidly listened, promised to do.

Blind Chang, as he became known, to differentiate him from other Changs, responded to the compassion he was shown. His heart opened to the gospel as a flower to the sun. Later he described his experience with a simile: it was as if he had been crossing a river by a weakened bridge which suddenly gave way, plunging him into the muddy water below, from which he could not extricate himself. Along came Buddha, Laotze and Confucius, each telling him that he should not be there and ought immediately to get out of the mud that threatened to engulf him. Each passed, offering only words but no hand to help, leaving him to drown. But then Jesus came along and went down into the mud and mire of Blind Chang's sin, lifted him out, and placed his feet upon a rock.

During his convalescence at Mukden, Chang listened with rapt attention to the words of Chang Lin, the hospital evangelist, the instruction of Webster and the counsel of Christie, who, when he could snatch the odd half hour, sat with Chang elucidating the message of Christ. Inevitably, the day dawned when Chang was to be discharged. Much to his great disappointment, but in line with Ross' caution in these matters, it was thought imprudent to baptise him after so short a time under Christian teaching. In this state he returned to his home in the picturesquely named Tai-ping-kou, the Valley of Peace.

For some time, nothing more was heard of him, until one day in October 1886, when Webster found himself close to the Valley of Peace, and decided to make a short detour to try to meet Chang. After a trying journey on foot through deep mud, Webster arrived at the village, and was immediately directed to a schoolteacher called Li, who was said to be of the same religion as Chang. This, Webster took to be a reference to Chang's former adherence to Buddhism rather than the Taoism more prevalent in the community. But to his delight he learned that Li was but one of a number of villagers who had followed Chang's example and become a Christian.

When Chang had returned from hospital in Mukden he had, with almost sightless eyes, groped his way around neighbouring villages sharing what he had learned of the gospel, singing the solitary hymn he had memorised at Mukden, and praying for God's blessing on his hearers. Sometimes he preached to hundreds. At first people were amused by the novelty of what they heard, but soon opinion polarised. Some blessed him, but others cursed him for abandoning the old ways. Yet those who resisted his teaching could not deny his changed life, and this proved to be the undeniable and convincing apologetic not only for Li, but also for the other fifteen who had turned to Christ.

Chang, however, was away from home when Webster arrived, but news was sent to him and he returned as speedily as he could, delighted to meet his teacher. Webster remained in the village for a few days and interviewed Chang, Li and all who wanted to be baptised, agreeing to baptise nine candidates, including both Chang and Li.

This was but the beginning of Chang's very fruitful ministry of evangelism in the Valley of Peace. As he went from home to home, village to village, Chang was fiercely protective of his independence. Just like Wang the Illustrious, Chang was unwilling to be thought of as a lackey of foreigners. Whilst maintaining the warmest personal relations with the missionaries, for the sake of the gospel he insisted upon his independence, adamantly refusing to take either instructions or remuneration from them. His guide was, he said, the teaching of Matthew 10, which had never failed him. Now a respected religious teacher, Chang found that village people willingly supplied his food, local women cheerfully made his clothes, and village boys gladly guided him from place to place.

As time passed, the little sight he had was lost. During these trying times, Chang would withdraw into a secluded place to pray, fasting for days on end, to emerge with reports of experiencing visions of his Lord.[9] One dream given to Chang was of Christ, who came towards him with a book in his hand. Smiling, he passed the book to Chang and immediately vanished. Confiding to a friend his account of this experience, Chang was stunned to learn that a blind man might indeed learn to read, as a way had now been found to make it possible.

What in fact had occurred is that a one-armed Scottish missionary with the National Bible Society of Scotland, William Hill Murray, had not only remarkably invented the first numeral tactile reading system for the Chinese language, but also founded at

Beijing the first school for blind people in China, and established in Scotland the Hill Murray Mission to the Blind and Illiterate Sighted in Northern China. In retirement Webster became chairman of the Scottish society and Mrs Duncan M'Laren, who wrote the official United Presbyterian account of the Manchurian mission, was also a member.

Murray too had had a dream. Unable to utilise braille, which was based on the Latin alphabet, he was frustrated that Chinese had no alphabet, and baffled to know how best to reduce the thousands of Chinese characters into a tactile system. It came to Murray in a dream that numbers could be used to represent four-hundred and eight characters in a system that could be learned in a few months.

Chang had great reservations about his ability to learn to read in so unusual a manner, yet he assured his friends he would try his best. Accompanied by a blind lad, who also wanted to acquire this wonderful ability, Chang started on the long and difficult journey. From the Valley of Peace they crossed one hundred miles of mountainous terrain to Mukden, where they boarded a river boat to Newchwang, then on by sea to the mouth of a river, another two or three days by boat upriver, before finally taking a cart to Beijing.

With Murray's warm welcome, kind hospitality and every encouragement, Chang was able to master the skill of tactile reading and writing in as little as three months. He also learned to write and read music. Much as Murray wanted Chang to remain to teach others, he knew he could not stand in his way. Chang had made it very clear that his new abilities were God-given, that he held them in trust, and that they must be used to advance the gospel among his own countrymen. Supplied with the latest Bible sheets and a tactile writing frame, he and his young companion retraced their steps, eventually arriving in the Valley of Peace to astound their neighbours by reading to them from God's Word with their fingertips. One day, one of Chang's Christian friends commented that 'Had Chang not become blind, there might have been no Christians here yet.'[10]

Not only so, but Ross noted the quality of the converts that came to faith, from a wide disparity of backgrounds, through Chang's witness. One had been an opium addicted highway robber. Another a seventy-year-old Chinese doctor. Chao had been a profound-thinking ascetic, earnestly seeking for 'the True' with a following of over a thousand disciples. Another, the son of a wealthy landowner, had, like others, followed Chao and with him found Christ. Then there was a blind man, a former schoolteacher, who coming to faith won others. In Chang's inner circle of disciples was a band of twenty-four who met twice daily for prayer and instruction.[11]

A further one hundred miles beyond the Valley of Peace is the Valley of Victory, and it was here, whilst visiting a friend, that Chang opened up the community to the gospel, gathering around him another group of loyal followers. He sent word to the missionaries at Mukden to come and examine them and baptise all who made a credible profession of faith. John Ross, accompanied by the newly appointed Rev. James W. Inglis, made the journey in 1891, receiving new members into the fellowship of the Church. Over a period of some fourteen years, hundreds became Christians in these remote valleys, and some were valued Christian leaders.

Many years later, Christie was asked what the most worthwhile incident in his entire missionary experience was. Without hesitation, he responded with the story of Chang, saying that if the only result of his long years in Mukden had been the conversion of Blind Chang, 'The Apostle of Manchuria,' as he called him, it was all thoroughly worthwhile. We will later return later to the Valley of Victory to witness Chang's greatest triumph and his most fruitful sowing of the Christian seed.

Christie's friend, James Webster, concurred, drawing out the essential strategic lesson:

> One thing of which I am well assured is this: Blind Chang, of Tai-ping-kow, with little knowledge, but with a heart thrilled to the core with the truth which he knew, had in these months done more work and better work for the kingdom of heaven than half-a-dozen foreign missionaries could have done in as many years. And this is only one of many proofs that China must be evangelised by the Chinese.[12]

It is evident that Christie, like Ross, developed a systematic approach to his work. In some regards he followed the approach adopted by pioneers like William Chalmers Burns, Williamson and Parker, but in many other respects they broke radically new ground. Ross and Christie recognised the importance of fluency in Mandarin Chinese, and so immediately on arrival in the country they accepted the challenge of acquiring the language, despite its three formidable difficulties. The first was that Mandarin is a tonal language, and this requires the learner to have a good ear able to hear subtle differences of tone, an ability to reproduce them, and the discipline to shake off familiar English intonation patterns. The second difficulty was the Chinese writing system which doesn't use twenty-six or so alphabetic letters, but over 50,000 characters, of which an educated person is supposed to know about 8,000. The acquisition of sufficient characters to read even the simplest of texts can take years of memorisation. And the third problem is that the characters are not phonetic, but logograms giving few clues of how to pronounce a word. Christie and Ross found that being bilingual helped them in learning an additional language, and they both agreed that having Gaelic was especially helpful.

As we have noted in passing, Ross and Christie carefully cultivated a sensitivity towards Chinese culture. Christie, recognising the strategic importance of establishing good relations with the highly influential Mandarins, carefully adopted the intricate etiquette of these officials, as well as their particular use of language. He understood that if a Mandarin approved of foreigners, others would too. But if he opposed you it would be difficult to gain any acceptance in the community. Good relations with the Mandarins mattered. In this Christie was greatly helped by his friendship with a *Tao-ting*, a magistrate of importance, who had spent some time abroad. This man offered advice freely, informing Christie of how Westerners' ignorance of Chinese culture was offensive and prejudicial to friendly relations. He taught Christie how the Mandarin and official classes looked with utter disdain on the short jackets commonly worn by foreigners, considering them loutish and uncouth. Even worse was the tendency of going about in shirt sleeves in the hotter summer months. It was likewise considered extremely impolite to receive even the messengers of officials when dressed like this, much worse to receive the officials themselves. Disregard of Chinese propriety did not serve the gospel; it was a blessing to have this information and so avoid blunders.

An equal irritant, but in the opposite direction, said the adviser, was the misguided attempt adopted both by Burns and Hudson Taylor, and by some other foreigners, of wearing Chinese clothes. He acknowledged that by so doing foreigners might be less conspicuous when travelling, and therefore more comfortable, but they were invariably ridiculed for trying too hard, unless their choice of clothing was accompanied by all the other subtleties of speech and cultural etiquette that few non-Chinese ever managed to acquire. He therefore advised Christie to wear a plain long robe of Chinese silk in which to receive visitors and see patients. Christie accepted the advice, and from that time forward, he and all the missionaries under his direction never left home unless wearing a robe or at least a long coat of some kind.

Familiarisation with language and etiquette and appropriate dress were but two aspects of cultural respectfulness, which extended also to the architectural style which the missionaries adopted for their homes and hospital buildings. In Christie's case such punctiliousness paid off. With the passage of time he came to be greatly respected and consulted by many in positions of influence; as a result, the once prevalent contempt for foreigners ceased, with approval, sometimes even affection, taking its place.

In line with John Ross' policy of training indigenous Christian evangelists to spread the gospel, make converts and establish new congregations, Christie developed an advanced scheme for training Chinese medical assistants. It would have been completely impossible for him to have run a hospital of any standard depending only on the few westerners available to him. Chinese help was indispensable. The question Christie asked himself was to what level should these assistants be trained. Should he be content to train them to the level of, say, a second-rate doctor, or should he aim to turn out highly skilled members of the medical profession? Christie had no doubts. Impressed as he had been with the remarkable ability of his first Chinese assistants, he opted for the highest training achievable. Of course, not all would rise so high, but even those who did not would be useful both in the hospital and the wider community.

And, he acknowledged, there would be disappointments too, as some might grasp the rudiments of medicine and then set up in a lucrative private practice.

Despite wars, revolutions, epidemics, and financial and staffing challenges, Christie eventually saw his vision become a reality when, in March 1912, the Mukden Medical College was opened with fifty students.[13] The curriculum, teaching methods and the standards at which it aimed, were all based on those of the Scottish university medical schools, but the teaching was all in Chinese and the college was integrated into the Chinese educational system. Rev. James Webster, Dugald Christie's friend and colleague, once said of him that he had great faith, and great hope, and great love, but the greatest of these was his love, and that, he believed, was the true secret of great missionary achievement.

We must now step back thirty or so years to 1881 when John and Isabella Ross returned to China from Scotland with the Christies and the Websters. Because no suitable property could be found for them in Mukden, the Rosses went into temporary lodgings in Newchwang, but this was irksome, requiring him regularly to undertake the arduous one-hundred-and-twenty-miles journey to Mukden in order to support the three proven and effective Chinese evangelists, Liu, Chun and Hsü, who in turn were seeking to stiffen the resolve of the new Christians who needed all the encouragement they could get. Local prejudices towards foreigners and their religion remained strong, and those who associated with the missionaries might still experience ostracism and hostility. For showing interest in the gospel, three printers had lost their jobs; so had four shoemakers, and many others suffered for Christ's sake. Few, however, had wavered in their faith.

Despite difficulties, accommodation was eventually located and the Rosses, accompanied by Miss Pritty, moved from Newchwang to settle for the rest of their missionary career in Mukden. Once again tragedy intruded upon Ross' family, exacting the high price so many nineteenth-century missionaries were required to pay. Isabella survived the birth of their first child Hugh, who died shortly afterwards. In the next eight years, three more of their children died in infancy: Findlay in 1884, John (Jackie) in 1888, and Catherine (Cathy Jane) in 1889. All were buried with Mary Ann in Newchwang. A further four survived: Margaret (1884), John Herbert (1891), Findlay (1893) and Elizabeth (1902). Three years after John Ross' own death his youngest son, Findlay, who had signed up at the outbreak of war in 1914 and, serving as a lieutenant with 9th (Highlander) Royal Scots, was killed in action in France on 1st August, 1918.

Notwithstanding the prevalence of opposition at Mukden, the growing number of able Chinese preachers meant there was every prospect of the cause of Christ flourishing, both numerically and spiritually, in the city. The chapel in the west suburb, where Old Wang had preached, was well attended, and it was therefore considered opportune to open a new meeting hall in the main street of the city, and behind that a smaller chapel where Sunday worship could be held with only the church members in attendance. From the outset it was impressed upon the converts that in the church they should manage their own affairs and not defer to the foreign missionaries. It was, therefore, decided to hold an election for the appointment of deacons. Perhaps predictably, the members chose the faithful Liu, Chun and Hsü, who were then set apart for their task. This was for all an emotional occasion. Liu, who was to go on to become the first ordained pastor of the Mukden church, was too overcome to say anything, but offered a deeply moving prayer. Hsü managed to blurt out thanks to the members for their confidence in him and earnestly asked for their prayers. Chun was so overcome that he was unable to say anything at all.

With such competent Chinese Christians leading the work in Mukden, it was now possible for the missionaries to consider reaching out to hitherto unevangelised places with a view to establishing new churches. For Ross, the time seemed ripe to commence work in the city of Liaoyong, some forty miles southwest of Mukden, and the earlier capital of Manchuria, before Mukden had supplanted it. Smaller than Mukden and less influential it may have been, but it was nevertheless prosperous, being situated in the heart of fertile cereal-producing country. Ross decided to send Wang to rent a chapel, and with him a junior colleague to assist in opening up work in the city.

It would not be easy. Those determined to resist the encroachments of Western influence, especially Christianity, erected every kind of barrier in the way. As leader, Wang attracted most of the opprobrium. Ridiculed, insulted and accused of being in the pocket of the foreigners, he nevertheless remained unintimidated. He would respond spiritedly to the allegations of his opponents by asking if any self-respecting Chinese would sell his soul for the pittance he received from the missionary, only to stand day after day before his critics and be vilified as a traitor to his country and a slave to a demon. He fiercely asserted his Chinese identity, insisting he was no foreigner, though he readily admitted to following the teaching which the foreigner had brought. Gladly acknowledging his indebtedness to the missionary, but recognising he was by no means indispensable, Wang would assert that they had the Bible, they knew the truth, and they could and would teach it whether there were foreigners in the land or not. Such expressions of dependence upon God alone were music to Ross' ears.

It was as well that Wang was blessed with a resilient spirit because the hostility in Liaoyong continued for many years, caused many difficulties and much discouragement. Although it was relatively easy to find vacant premises suitable for a small meeting place, they all invariably and mysteriously became unavailable to Wang to rent. He prayed much about this concern, and one day his prayers were answered. Some months previously, he had shared the Good News with a man he had met at a wayside inn, a person well known and greatly respected in Liaoyong. This man had responded to what he heard with faith, receiving Christ as his Saviour and Lord. When he heard of Wang's frustrations he sought to help, and a house was soon found in the main street where Wang could preach. This did not, however, lessen in any way the general opposition, which became so trying that Wang felt obliged to appeal to the magistrate. Much to Wang's great surprise the magistrate immediately issued a favourable proclamation, which greatly improved matters. In the year that followed, Wang had the joy of several inquirers coming to him secretly, two of whom were afterwards baptised. Over the succeeding six years, the number of baptised communicants grew steadily to around fifty, despite unremitting bitterness being directed towards Christians at every possible opportunity. As most of the first believers were financially independent businessmen, the old canard, that people became Christians only because they were bribed by the foreigners, was readily scotched.

Both Ross and Christie had early on grasped the fact that new converts were, from the very moment of regeneration, indwelt, gifted and empowered by the Holy Spirit, and even as young converts not as incapable of leadership as might be supposed. Up to this time it was the received wisdom that the missionary should do everything for the new converts who were considered to be but children, although it was acknowledged that there might come a time when through a prolonged process of education and training they might become mature enough to take responsibility for ministry. Ross and Christie repudiated this outlook; they considered it patronising, pernicious and stultifying.

Key to Ross' and Christie's conviction was their reading of the biblical record of the withdrawal of the physical presence of Christ at the ascension and the subsequent residence of the Holy Spirit permanently in the Church at Pentecost. In this they saw our Lord's supreme confidence that the Spirit would bring to perfection his work in the Church. They also noted how St. Paul had trusted the Holy Spirit by spending only a brief time, often less than a few weeks, with even the newest converts and youngest churches. Furthermore, they understood that the apostles dealt with the problems of young churches not by micromanaging their day-to-day life, which would have stifled Chinese initiative and hindered the effectiveness of their own ministry, but by teaching the Word and embedding its principles in the hearts and minds of the believers.

Whilst understandably, and rightly, taking great pleasure in the maturity and ministry of their own proteges, neither Ross nor Christie saw Wang or Chang as extensions of themselves, but as Christian evangelists and missionaries in their own right. As John the Baptist had modestly withdrawn from the limelight to allow it to fall on his successor, so too did both missionaries. Christie acknowledged Chang as the Apostle of Manchuria, and Ross described Wang was the founder of Protestant Christianity in Manchuria.

All this was entirely in keeping with the strategy the Scottish missionaries chose to adopt, the evangelisation of China primary through the ministry of local Christians and by establishing churches with a truly Chinese ethos. This strategy would reach its zenith in the evangelisation of Korea, despite Ross only visiting the country briefly on a single occasion, but it was in Manchuria that Wang Ching-ming, the evangelists Liu, Chun and Hsü, the hospital evangelist Li, Blind Chang and others, gave clear and early evidence of its wonderful potential.

11

Korea: Reconnaissance

A stormy wind fulfilling his word.
PSALM 148.8

IT is not clear whether Korea was originally in Hamilton MacGill's mind as a sphere of the Rosses' missionary activity, at least not until he received Alexander Williamson's letter urging their prompt relocation from Chefoo to Newchwang in Manchuria. But such a plan had been percolating in Williamson's mind for some time. He saw the new missionaries' presence in Newchwang as urgent and strategic not only for that region, but also because it put them in closer proximity to Korea.

Despite poor health, Williamson had at least once visited the China/Korea border at the Yalu River, at a place known to expatriates as Corean Gate. There he learned that it was one thing to visit the border, but altogether another to cross into Korea. Nonetheless, he had met Koreans, including merchants taking advantage of the occasional openings of the border, and members of the sporadic delegation from Korea to Beijing, bearing tribute to the Chinese emperor. He had also come into contact with a few who had made their way to Chefoo. Through interviews with such acquaintances, Williamson gathered information which he published in his, *Journeys in North China, Manchuria, and Eastern Mongolia: With Some Account of Corea*, published in London in 1870.

Williamson's account of Korea was wide-ranging, but necessarily superficial. It consisted of snippets of information on the geography, ethnology, linguistics, economy, architecture, sociology and religion of Korea. He wrote glowingly of the good harbours on the peninsula's eastern coast, referred to the Korean climate as 'magnificent', and expressed his admiration for the enterprise, ingenuity and diligence of the people, qualities which were, in his mind at least, second only to their courage. Korean bravery, Williamson wryly noted, made them excellent friends, but dangerous foes. He understood why they relished their reputation as the Hermit Nation and was not unsympathetic. He wrote approvingly of their repulsion of the 1866 French punitive expedition, and appreciated their spirited and successful attacks on intrusive Russian gunboats. He wrote, 'Judging from what I have seen of them, I like them, admire their pluck.'[1] Yet, what he gave with one hand, Williamson took with the other. He was much less complimentary about the successful Korean action against the American-built paddle-steamer *General Sherman,* which was destroyed in 1866. However, his second-hand account was confused.

In overbearing language, likely to enflame the ire of any Korean, as well as prejudicing any attempt to share with them the gospel, Williamson took it upon himself to lecture the Korean government. He advised opening its borders to trade with Britain and America and allowing the free flow of western goods and ideas. If it did not do so voluntarily, then, he believed, the western nations were entitled to open up the country forcibly, by the military power that he argued had been given to them by God. War was, he thought, undoubtedly terrible, in every aspect, but, as he saw it, it was 'a condition of progress in this fallen world'. With breathtaking callousness, Williamson believed war's costs, both economic and human, though high at the time, might with hindsight appear slight when weighed against the advantages of an open border and free trade. Thankfully, he reined-in his bellicosity by hoping that 'the opening up of the country might be effected without war'.[2]

Williamson learned of three annual cross-border trading fairs. These allowed the 'pernicious [Korean] laws and regulations', designed to hamper international trade, to be legally circumvented.[3] The most important was held at Fenghuang; the others, he thought less important, took place at Hun-chun, and at an unnamed military station. By personally distributing tracts and selling books and Bibles at one or more of these fairs held in 1867, Williamson considered them as providing strategic opportunities for evangelising Koreans.

He was, however, not the first Protestant to consider the evangelisation of Korea. Karl Gützlaff, whom we earlier met, made a number of voyages along the coast of China, and in 1833 landed at various points on the Korean peninsula, though it is not known if he made any meaningful contact with local people. Gützlaff's expeditions were emulated by the Welsh missionary Robert Jermain Thomas. Thomas, born in Rhayader, Radnorshire, in 1840, joined the London Missionary Society in June 1863, sailing for China in July the same year. His wife, whom he had married just before embarking for the East, died within months of their arrival. Maybe because of this personal tragedy, twenty-three-year-old Thomas, who had already learned something of the Chinese language, found it hard to settle at his work. The following December he resigned, taking up a job as a translator at the customs post in Chefoo. This, however, proved to be even more unsatisfactory than his missionary career, and so he reapplied to the London Missionary Society, was reaccepted, and resumed missionary work. In autumn 1865 a fortuitous meeting with two Korean traders, who happened to be secret Catholics, led Thomas to embark with them on a Chinese junk bound for Korea. During the two-and-a-half-months voyage he landed at various ports, distributed Bibles he had obtained from Williamson, and picked-up a smattering of the Korean language. On his return to China, he made his way to Beijing, where he took up an appointment at the Chinese government's Anglo-Chinese school.

On learning of the planned French retaliatory expedition to Korea, the erratic Thomas, against advice, returned to Chefoo with the reckless hope of joining the expedition as a translator and thereby reaching Korea. But before the matter was settled with the French, the American-owned but Chinese-crewed S.S. *General Sherman* sailed into Chefoo *en route* for Korea to test the strength of its resistance to foreign trade. Preferring Protestant to Catholic company, Thomas offered to translate for Captain Page. This offer was gladly taken up, and with high hopes of evangelising in

Korea, and having obtained a fresh supply of Chinese Bibles from Williamson, Thomas embarked on the *General Sherman*. In the event, however, matters went badly awry. The Americans ran into opposition, the ship was set on fire by the Koreans, and the crew, including Thomas, were all put to death.

Over the years considerable muddle has arisen in the various accounts of this incident. Williamson, and others following him, are guilty of conflating two entirely separate incidents involving the American-owned ships *General Sherman* and *Surprise*. The *Surprise* was wrecked on the coast near Chulsan, Pyongyang Province, in June 1866. Its crew disembarked unharmed and was allowed by Korean Governor Park Gyu-suto to return safely to China. It was different in the case of the *General Sherman*. This vessel arrived on the Korean coast on 16th August 1866 bound for Pyongyang. By entering the Taedong River, it violated Korean sovereignty and ran into hostility. In the panic that ensued, Page grounded the vessel upon a sandbank, where, after an exchange of gunfire, it was set alight. The escaping crew was massacred by the enraged crowd. Why, we may ask, was there such a very different response, by the same person, Governor Park Gyu-su, to two similarly endangered American vessels? The answer may be found in the suspicion that arose from the provocative high-handedness of the *General Sherman's* captain.

Although ostensibly on a peaceful mission, the *General Sherman* was in reality probing the Koreans' capability of resisting foreign trade. The nature of the vessel itself roused suspicion. Why should an innocent trading vessel, which was what the *General Sherman* claimed to be, be an armed ironclad (a steam-propelled ship protected by iron or steel armour plates)? The behaviour of the crew also justified Korean concern when, after mild resistance was shown, they retaliated by holding hostage Adjutant-General Yi Hong-ik and his two deputies. Finally, when the rowing boat carrying Thomas on an unsuccessful peace mission returned, why did Captain Page panic and attempt to make a run for it? All he managed to achieve was to run his vessel upon a sandbank where it stuck. Panicked by the irate crowd, the crew further enraged hostility by firing the *General Sherman's* cannons, killing civilians.

It is unclear whether, at this point, Governor Park Gyu-su's patience ran out and he gave orders for the *General Sherman* to be attacked, or whether the crowd spontaneously attacked the stranded vessel and set it alight by using small boats piled with brushwood as makeshift fireships. Certainly, no quarter was shown to crew or officers, who were all killed. One account suggested two survived the initial onslaught, Robert Thomas and a Chinese, though both were shortly afterwards put to death.[4] Another interpretation of these confused events is the one that Ross offers, who after hearing of Thomas' death from Williamson, and not wanting to ruffle feathers on either side, advanced the theory that an innocent navigational error led to the *General Sherman* being stranded, with the local people, for the first few days at any rate, treating the American owner, master and mate, and their Malay (not Chinese) crew kindly. Ross alleges that it was only after orders were issued from the capital that the popular mood changed, and the crowd became aggressive, setting the vessel alight, and then, luring the crew ashore, executed them all.[5]

Later claims, but whether factual or fictitious it is hard to say, include the story that one of the first elders of the Thomas Memorial Church in Pyongyang was the son of the man who put Thomas to death, 'who, having picked up Thomas's own [Chinese] Bible, and being impressed by the Welshman's courage and ardor, read the Scriptures and later asked for baptism.' George Paik (Nak-chun Paek) tells how in 1893, three years after Samuel A. Moffett settled in Pyongyang, he discovered that one of the participants of his catechumen class claimed that thirty-three years earlier he had received a Bible from Thomas very shortly before he was killed.[6]

We may never know the whole truth about the *General Sherman* incident, but not wanting to spoil a good story for the sake of a few facts, North Korean propaganda has made much of the affair. A vast canvas, displayed in the Mankyungdae Museum in Pyongyang, depicts the patriot Kim Ung Woo, Kim Il-Sung's putative great-grandfather, raising a flaming torch and directing the mob in repelling the foreign infiltrators, while in the distance the *General Sherman* is consumed by flames. More credible is the claim that Robert Jermain Thomas may be considered the first Protestant martyr in Korea. In 1932 the commemorative 'Thomas Memorial Church' was built near to the spot where he perished. Now, the church has itself fallen victim to the Pyongyang regime's purge of all vestiges of Christianity, with Pyongyang University of Science and Technology occupying the site, obliterating all signs of the church which formerly stood there.

On returning to Chefoo in 1871, with hopes of fulfilling his vision of somehow reaching Korea, and wishing at the same time to honour Thomas' sacrifice, Williamson proposed getting a missionary to Manchuria and therefore closer to the Korean border than if stationed at Chefoo. Having heard, probably from MacGill, of the prospect of John Ross joining the United Presbyterian Mission, a plan began to develop in Williamson's mind. He wrote therefore to MacGill the letter which swayed the Foreign Mission Board, and became the instrument which not only radically altered John Ross' life, by precipitately exposing the pregnant Mary Ann to mortal danger, but set in motion that chain of events that led to establishing the church in Manchuria, the translation of the New Testament into Korean, and the evangelisation of the Korean peninsula by Koreans recruited and trained by Ross.

It did not take Ross long to reconnoitre. In October 1874 he set out on his first journey to Fenghuang and the Corean Gate to see how it might be possible to contact Korean people. His route lay over two hundred miles of poor roads, negotiated in a small travelling mule cart, covering twenty miles a day, weather permitting. Not that he was in a rush. Unhurried travel, with frequent stops at wayside inns, provided important opportunities for meeting people, holding conversations, engaging in public preaching, and distributing Bibles, gospels and pamphlets. He found the curiosity of many Chinese piqued and ready to talk to a friendly foreigner about religion or anything else.

Chinese friendliness could, however, be very frustrating. A well-mannered people, the Chinese, being anything but confrontational, would prematurely conclude conversations by politely remarking that although they thought that Ross' Christianity was excellent, in reality the principles of righteousness and prosperity were much the same everywhere. Underneath this veneer of respect, Ross suspected that most were religiously sceptical and practically materialistic. Such certainly seemed to be the case in regard to an innkeeper whose house and inn contained many images and altars to Ts'ai Shen, the god of wealth. Asking how often he paid devotion to this god, Ross was told twice a month. That didn't strike him as very often, so he asked the innkeeper why he didn't worship his god more frequently. Back came the cynical reply, 'Frequent or seldom, it is all one; he will not give wealth.'

Fenghuang was an agricultural town with a population of around twenty-thousand with an unenviable reputation for being the most lawless town in China. Having to wait for a few days before the Corean Gate would be opened and cross-border trading allowed, Ross used the time to preach and distribute Scripture portion and tracts. He wondered how the town's reputation for lawlessness might be manifested, but apart from hearing lurid stories of robbers being apprehended or pursued, noting the high stone protective walls around the better houses, and being woken in the night by the firing of the watchmen's guns, he found the place rather quiet, with little sign of what he described as 'ruffianly' behaviour. Indeed, far from finding the place hostile, he was invited by some merchants to establish a mission and open a discussion hall. Ostensibly this was to understand his teaching better; what actually lay behind the request he could not fathom, though he suspected an ulterior motive.

The Corean Gate lay about one hundred *li* beyond Fenghuang (a *li* was about one third of an English mile). After six days in the town, Ross commenced this last stage across 'a magnificent pile of mountains'. These are known today as the Changbai-sanjulgi, or 'Perpetually White Mountains'. He noted that their highest peaks rose over eight thousand feet and were snow-covered, if not 'forever', then at least during the winter months. The region, he heard, was a haven for wildlife, including tigers, wolves, deer, and pheasants 'without number'. A keen observer of nature, Ross included in his reports to Scotland, and in some letters to the *Chinese Recorder and Missionary Journal*, descriptions of Chinese trees, plants, birds and animals, often comparing them with Scottish flora and fauna.

He also learned that this mountainous region was said to be the abode of Taoist hermits or recluses, who living in caves, subsisted as vegetarians, eating only on what they could forage in the harsh environment. Such reports he found incredible, feeling obliged to say in a report published in the *United Presbyterian Missionary Record* that the hermits' diet, 'must be scanty fare indeed, if not more abundant than I could discover, on the high and steep hill which I scaled.'

After his brief visit to the borderlands, Williamson wrote about the Corean Gate, but failed to describe the place and its functioning as thoroughly as Ross. The village was named after a literal gate between Manchuria and Korea which stood at the east end of its long main street. Located in a house, about thirty feet long, set at right angles to the road, Ross saw not just one, but two gates, one Chinese, the other Korean. The very structure of the two gates was itself a witness to the degree with which each nation prized its isolation: the Korean most intensely, the Chinese more laxly. The Korean border gate, on the east side, was made up of solid boards secured with a large, sturdy iron lock. On the western side, the Chinese side, the way was barred by a gate of perpendicular wooden spars that did not appear overly strong.

On fair days these gates were unlocked by their respective keepers, the tax collectors took their place in the area between the gates to assess duty on all the goods imported or exported to either country. Outside the house, the boundary line was continued by a row of elm trees, on either side of which was a no-man's-land. On the Korean side, this neutral ground extended for over twenty-five miles along the Yalu River, which formed the international boundary. The nearest Korean town was about seven miles beyond the river.

On the morning of 10th October, Ross heard that Korean traders had crossed the river and were encamped in the neutral territory waiting for the gate to be opened. Later that afternoon their servants turned up in the town to secure lodging for their masters, and the following day a formal deputation waited upon the Magistrate of Fenghuang to announce their arrival and to request the opening of the gate. The formalities were completed the next day, with both the Chinese and Korean magistrates officiating at the traditional ceremonies marking the opening of the fair. Matters progressed very slowly, and it wasn't until the following week, after the officials had withdrawn, and the traders felt less under scrutiny, and therefore less inhibited, that the market got into full swing. All this time Ross preached and sold Bibles and tracts to the Chinese, and although he was aware of Koreans listening to what he had to say, none were willing to purchase a Bible or receive a tract. As the fair came to an end, and having seen much to pique his interest, Ross departed with the firm intention of returning as soon as possible.

The next opportunity came eighteen months later, in the spring of 1876. Ross and Macintyre had been hindered in setting out earlier by the responsibility of training Chinese workers in Newchwang, Mukden and elsewhere. As a result, they had been taunted by Chinese Catholics that the absence of Protestant missionaries in Korea was due to the fact that they were soft, trammelled with wives and susceptible to the comforts of their homes. Celibate Catholics, they alleged, were much more willing than Protestants to accept personal sacrifice and brave the hardships of pioneer mission. Sensitive to the charge – in Ross' case, maybe severely stung by it – it was decided that Macintyre would remain and concentrate all his efforts around Newchwang, Mukden and the outstations, while Ross would visit Fenghuang and the Gate once more, covering his costs by drawing on funds donated to the United Presbyterian Mission by the eccentric millionaire philanthropist and missions' supporter, Robert Arthington of Leeds.

To Arthington belongs a special place in late-nineteenth and early twentieth century missions. Although he 'never left his native shores in Victorian England, never wrote a book, was never on the board of any missionary society, and can only with some question be regarded as an original missions thinker [he] did more than any other... to facilitate the growth of British Protestant missions.'[7] Motivated by strong premillennial beliefs, Arthington spent his fortune in encouraging pioneer missions, believing that they were most likely to spread the gospel both rapidly and broadly and so hasten the return of Christ. Although the greatest beneficiary of his generosity was the Baptist Missionary Society, Arthington had broad sympathies and funded projects run by other groups and denominations, including the United Presbyterian Church.

MacGill in the January 1877 *Missionary Record* refers to Arthington as a 'friend'.

Drawing on Arthington's generosity, John Ross made the long journey back to the Gate. On arrival, he went down once more to the banks of the River Yalu to distribute tracts, sell gospels and books, and preach. Although received respectfully, he was less than successful in gaining a hearing for his message. Sometimes this was his own fault, as when he once clumsily and unfavourably contrasted Confucianism with Christianity, but more often the reticence of the Koreans erected a barrier to communication. Ross was only marginally more successful in inducing Koreans to take his tracts and books, though in one notable case a Korean merchant took a few tracts and later passed them on to his grown-up son, Paik Hong-jun. Paik was converted and eventually joined Ross' translation team. Only very rarely could Koreans be induced to buy books, despite the fact that several Chinese felt free to do so. A typical response was that of a young man who, eying the books with keen interest, turned suddenly away after an elderly man, with a look of grave suspicion, whispered something in his ear.

It was not that the Koreans were disinterested, indeed far from it; they were very keen to know all about Ross and endlessly quizzed him, but the intensity of their interest was equalled only by their reluctance to divulge knowledge about their land or themselves. Yet, despite themselves they did reveal much to Ross who, patiently, by tactful personal interviews and keen observation, gleaned information about the land, its agriculture and industry, its language and history, and its culture and religion. A trained espionage agent couldn't have done better. Six years afterwards, Ross revealed one of the clever ploys he had adopted:

> One day I took pencil and a piece of paper, wrote out a few of the letters I had learned, and handed the paper to a Corean who had just emphatically denied knowing any language save Chinese, asking him whether he knew what that was. He opened his eyes in amazement, and said, 'Why, those are our letters; how did you come to know them?' Seeing I knew a few, he apparently took for granted that I knew all the letters, and having never before seen a pencil, he asked permission to use it. I handed him pencil and paper. After writing

> some sentences, he threw down the paper, handing me back the pencil. Though I could not decipher the paper, I saw the writing was not Chinese, and therefore kept it carefully till all then present went out of my room and others came in – for they came and went most of the day. To one of the new-comers I presented the paper after some conversation, and asked him whether he could read that? 'It is our own language,' he replied, and read it, when I took down the sounds. In this same way, getting some to write and others to read, I soon became acquainted with the alphabet.[8]

In addition, there were books. On his first visit to the Gate, Ross was pleased to be able to buy from a Chinese merchant 'at an enormous price' some old Korean books in manuscript. These had been dismissed as 'historical novels', but were to him extremely helpful guides to the use of the Korean language.

Desiring to see a little more of Korea than was visible from the Chinese bank, one day Ross asked his landlord, a distiller, to negotiate with one of the many boatmen who were plying for business on the Chinese side to row him up and down the river. Despite his willingness to pay above the odds, none could be induced to help, so convinced were they that his proximity to the border would spark serious trouble. Indeed, in his report of his first visit to the Gate, printed in the *Missionary Record*, Ross intimated that it was his belief that any infringement of the border by a Chinese would speedily result in death, and he had few doubts that should he attempt to do the same, he would be surrounded by hostile Koreans and driven back, if not worse. On this second visit, he further learned that the risk entailed was now greater than formerly. The Koreans had enhanced border security by stationing special officers at intervals of every two miles or so, to ensure that no one crossed the river.

Nevertheless, it was from the river that the first sign of a breakthrough came. A merchant on his way to the fair had his boat capsized by a strong squall of wind, with the loss of all he had. Now destitute, and unprotected from his debtors, he urgently sought an alternative source of income. On hearing that a foreigner wanted a language teacher and was willing to pay handsomely, he threw caution to the winds and offered his services, with the strict proviso that his security must be safeguarded by their meetings being kept secret, held only at a distance from the village, and undertaken at night. Ross was more than happy to comply, and so with these reassurances and two months' wages paid in advance, the merchant agreed to help.

It was decided that they would meet the next day for an early breakfast at an inn some miles to the west and afterwards, to avoid detection, would travel about in Ross' cart. To further hide his identity, the merchant removed his distinctive Korean garb, handing it to Ross who hid it. He was then loaned the clothes of Ross' Chinese servant. As Ross took up his place in his travelling cart, with pencil and paper to hand, his new Korean informant sat on the shaft. It turned out to be a very productive morning. As they jogged slowly along, Ross was able to jot down a complete list, in their proper order and pronunciation, of the Korean letters, as well as a number of basic Korean phrases. This collaboration continued for a few days, but his informant's fear eventually outgrew his need for money, until sometime during Sunday night he disappeared, to make his way back across the border, with two month's wages in his pocket. Ross was hardly surprised, as he recorded later: 'Having seen his terror visibly increase daily, I was not unprepared, though bitterly disappointed, at this destruction of my hopes.'

An intriguing question now arises as to this man's identity. Some have thought that he was Yi Ung-chan, who collaborated with Ross on the translation of the New Testament. But Dr Peter Ahn-Ho Bae thinks not, as Ross' account of his meeting with Yi Ung-chan provides nothing to link him with the merchant, and appears to have taken place not at the Gate but later in Mukden. Ross writes:

> At last success crowned my efforts, a man [Yi Ung-chan] came who was able to remain a few months. Knowing how insecure was the tenure of his office, I employed him without stint. Through him, besides other useful work, I had the Gospel of John translated, and subsequently that of Mark. Having a very fair knowledge of Chinese, he was able to make use of the Chinese versions of the Scriptures, in both the literary and the colloquial styles.[9]

The problem of identity is further exacerbated because of Ross' and Macintyre's regrettable failure to carefully identify their language collaborators.[10]

The real significance of Ross' encounter with the bankrupted merchant, argues Bae, is that it served to spur his determination to secure a language teacher as speedily as possible, knowing full well how stressful this might prove to anyone willing to occupy such a role, and how temporary such assistance might prove.

Just as God had opened for St Paul a wide-open door for effective work in Ephesus, along with many difficulties, so he was now at work opening another door that no one could shut, despite the many challenges entailed. Of all the difficulties, without doubt, the main one was the fear of collaborating with foreigners in violation of the Korean government policy of extreme isolationism. Repeated attempts at intrusion by the western nations had heightened Korean mistrust to the point of paranoia. Some years later Ross wrote of the situation as it had prevailed in the 1870s:

> The laws against intercourse with foreigners had always been stringent; but after the failure – first of the French, and then of the American Squadron, for lack of water – to force their way to the Korean capital, the Regent issued a still more severe law against any communication with Europeans. Hence the difficulty in obtaining information or service.[11]

What was becoming increasingly clear to Ross was that it would be one thing to gain a grasp of Korean culture and language, but altogether another to enter the country itself, to say nothing of preaching the Christian gospel to the people of the land. He was now convinced more than ever that if the Good News was to penetrate Korea it would not be by foreign missionaries, such as himself, but by Koreans.

12

The Trials of Bible Translation and Publishing

Because [the] original tongues are not known to all the people of God, who have right unto and interest in the Scriptures ... therefore they are to be translated into the vulgar language of every nation unto which they come.

The Westminster Confession of Faith, I.8

AN important lesson that Ross learned from his visits to the borderlands was the enthusiasm of Koreans to own and read portions of the Bible, despite official sanctions forbidding possession of western books, and despite their reluctance to speak to him or be seen taking books from him. He therefore returned to Mukden eager to translate the New Testament into Korean and distribute it through the agency of Korean colporteurs. Ross' and Macintyre's decision to invest so much of their time and energy, and so much of other people's money in this project, was not borne out of missionary pragmatism, but came from a deeply held conviction.

In common with other Protestant Christians, Ross and Macintyre regarded the Bible as God's Word written. Holy Scripture was, therefore, no mere adjunct to church life, nor accessory of personal spirituality, but an absolute essential. The reverberating echoes of the Reformation's *sola Scriptura* rang in their ears, reinforced by how at their ordination they had affirmed 'the Scriptures of the Old and New Testaments to be the Word of God, and the only rule of faith and manners.' This foundational doctrine undergirded all they did. It informed their entire missionary strategy and galvanised all their work.

Bible translation for Presbyterians was axiomatic: the principle was clearly embodied in the first chapter of the Westminster Confession of Faith, which not only taught the divine origin of Scripture, and the necessity, authority, sufficiency and clarity of the original Hebrew and Greek manuscripts, but also that they must be translated 'into the vulgar language of every nation unto which they come, that the Word of God dwelling plentifully in all, they may worship him in an acceptable manner; and, through patience and comfort of the Scriptures, may have hope.'

Although, like all Scottish Presbyterian ministers at the time, Ross and Macintyre had promised to adhere to the teaching of the Westminster Confession, the current mood in the United Presbyterian Church was not to be overly rigorous in that regard. Indeed, an Act passed by the Synod of 1879 granted liberty of opinion on some matters. Whatever may be said for or against the Act, it would be wrong to suggest that it had lessened the Confession's evangelistic implications. Indeed, some would argue, it gave them a fresh energy.

In preparation for the hoped-for union of the two denominations, the Free Church of Scotland adopted a similar Declaratory Act in 1892. A conservative Highland element considered this irredeemable, and they seceded the following year to form the Free Presbyterian Church. Their views were not shared by the great majority of Free Church missionaries, who joined the United Free Church at its formation in 1900. Aware of the Act's negative aspects, they welcomed the manner in which it undermined latent hyper-Calvinistic tendencies by an insistence that all ministers and office bearers not only give intellectual assent to the Westminster Confession, but accept it as their duty to extend the 'free offer of salvation to men without distinction', and impress upon their hearers their personal responsibility to respond to the gospel with faith. It was this element, present in both Declaratory Acts, that gave fresh impetus to the missions of both denominations in the last quarter of the nineteenth century. Those who formed the Free

Presbyterian Church in 1893 strongly disagreed and went so far as to assert that the section on the free offer of the gospel 'puts a dagger into all true missionary effort'.[1]

Declaratory Acts apart, Ross' and Macintyre's loyalty to the Westminster Confession made the task of translating the Bible into Korean a necessary aspect of their missionary plan. They were not, of course, the first Protestant missionaries in the Far East to see the importance of translating the Bible into Asian languages. Robert Morrison and William Milne completed their translation of the Chinese Bible in 1819. This was followed three years later by the version published by the Serampore missionaries in India, led by the Armenian scholar, Hovhannes Ghazarian (Joannes Lassar) and Joshua Marshman, working together with an unnamed Chinese collaborator from Guangzhou. In 1847, Karl Gützlaf produced his translation of the Bible, with contributions from Walter Medhurst, Elijah Coleman Bridgman and John Robert Morrison. Gützlaff had also worked on Thai, Khmer, and Lao translations, just as Ghazarian and Marshman in India had produced translations in Hindustani, Bengali and Sanskrit. Others worked assiduously at Bible and book distribution: Alexander Williamson, as well as serving with the United Presbyterian Church and the National Bible Society of Scotland, set up in Scotland the Chinese Book and Tract Society, and opened in Shanghai a publishing house. He personally distributed enormous quantities of Christian literature during his extensive itineraries in China, Mongolia and Manchuria.

To commence translation required finding ways of circumventing the Korean government's prohibition of Koreans associating with foreigners. Ross and Macintyre were able to gather at Mukden a team of language informants, printers, colporteurs and evangelists, facilitating a thorough study of the language, culture and history of Korea. In less than two years, and before the Korean language was standardised, Ross was able to compile the first Korean language primer, *The Corean Primer: Being Lessons in Corean on All Ordinary Subjects, Transliterated on the Principles of the Mandarin Primer,* published in Shanghai in 1877 by the American Presbyterian Mission Press. Prof. James Grayson suggests that the Mandarin Primer of 1876 may well have served Ross as a useful tool in studying the Korean language by his adopting the expedient of asking a bilingual teacher what the equivalent of a Mandarin word in Korean was, and in the Korean script.[2] At any rate, *The Corean Primer* earned its place as the first textbook of the language. After thorough revision and enlargement, a final edition was published in Shanghai by Kelly and Walsh in 1882 under the title, *Korean Speech, with Grammar and Vocabulary.* This was reprinted in Seoul as recently as 1979.[3] Ross' English language history of Korea, *History of Corea, Ancient and Modern, with Description of Manner and Customs, Language and Geography,* was published in 1889.

Ross was not the first to publish in the Korean language. His work was preceded in 1832 by Gützlaff's very brief *Remarks on the Corean Language*; in 1864 Léon de Rosny's *Aperçu de langue coréenne (The Korean Language Overview)* appeared in print; and a decade later Charles Dallet's *La langue coréenne.* Dr Pawel Kida of the Seoul National University makes the point that these early foreign works provided a useful foundation for the grammars that were compiled by Korean authors after 1910.[4]

In contemplating Bible translation into Korean, Ross had to take into consideration that for centuries classical Korean literature had been closely allied with Chinese literature, with the Korean intelligentsia writing in Chinese. There was, however, a Korean script known as *Han'gŏl*, or Great Script, that had come into existence in the mid-fifteenth century. Aware that the elite disdained *Han'gŏl,* Ross was sensitive to the risks of using it: 'As [this] class [of scholars] are all educated in Chinese, read and write only a high-class Chinese style, they contemptuously ignore the "vulgar" tongue, and will neither read nor write in that tongue.'[5] *Han'gŏl's* simplicity attracted Ross. He once commented: 'The Corean alphabet is phonetic, and so beautifully simple that all men, women and children of years of understanding can read it: for being phonetic it is necessary only to learn the alphabet to be able to read any book printed in that alphabet. The importance of the Bible translation into such a language of 12 to 15 million of people cannot be overestimated.'[6]

Moreover, there was a precedent; in the early days of the script, Buddhist scriptures and religious poems had been translated into *Han'gŏl*, thus creating something of a Korean religious vernacular literature.[7] Now, in its turn, the Bible in *Han'gŏl* would contribute to Korean literature, embed the gospel in Korean culture, enhance the reputation of *Han'gŏl* as a medium of sophisticated expression, and contribute to a burgeoning sense of modern Korean national identity.

So it was that at Mukden, Ross and Macintyre, with their Korean colleagues, set themselves to translate the New Testament into Korean. The Greek text that Ross finally settled on for this work was Westcott's and Hort's 1881 *Revised Greek New Testament*, and the main reference resources were what was known as the Delegate's Version of the Chinese Bible, and various English versions. The principles of translation followed were later succinctly set out by Ross:

> These are, first, an absolutely literal translation compatible with the meaning of the passage and the idiom of the Corean language and second, the Greek of the Revised Version is made the standard rather than the English. My main object being an accurate and faithful representation of the sense, in the best attainable idiom. Where that sense is rendered by periphrasis in Chinese I have followed the literal language of the Greek.[8]

A special challenge was how best to translate indigenous religious terminology, not least finding the most felicitous way of translating the name of God. For Ross and the United Presbyterian missionaries, no less than for their Korean associates, this choice was fraught with the difficulties of prior associations. Sebastian and Kirsteen Kim in their *A History of Korean Christianity* point out how another contemporary translator, Yi Su-jeong, 'used *sin*, the Korean version of the generic Chinese name (*shen*) for God, or gods or spirits .... Ross, [however], claimed that he had identified a distinctive and almost universal Korean name for God — *Haneunim*/*Hananim*.'[9]

Modern scholars point out that while there may be some debate as to the historicity of *Haneunim*/*Hananim*, which apart from one important old text may not have been as widespread as Ross thought, and for different reasons was unacceptable to Yi and to Roman Catholics, it was nevertheless an authentic Korean name (not a fabrication by Ross, as his opponents claimed) which at the time enjoyed popular support. It also served the useful purpose of immediately distinguishing Protestant from Catholic literature.

Faced with these and many other challenges, it is not to be wondered at that Ross' early work was less than perfect. In analysing the Ross primer, Dr Sung Il Choi reached the conclusion that aside from some grammatical issues (there was no fixed Korean grammar at the time) Ross used archaic terms, misspelled a number of words (which may have been the fault of the typesetter), and 'in many places' adopted 'over-free translations, totally wrong translations, and direct use of difficult Chinese words.'[10] But for some, the primer's most objectionable flaw was that 'it reflects the local dialect of the northern-western part of Korea,' the area from whence came Ross' language informants. Although this caused no problem with regard to general comprehensibility, it was argued that it unhelpfully fixed the Mukden work in a regional dialect and idiom, rather than that of the capital. This became a ground of negative criticism with American missionaries.[11] But that, however, is perhaps neither here nor there. The question as to whether or not Ross' translation succeeded was, and remains, for Koreans themselves to decide.

In 1879 Ross returned to Scotland for a period of home leave, taking with him manuscripts of the Four Gospels, Acts and Romans. He travelled with the hope of finding sufficient funds to underwrite the publishing costs of an urgently needed work. Others were not so convinced. Even as Ross was knocking on the doors of Bible Societies, Samuel Dyer wrote to the committee of the British and Foreign Bible Society in London suggesting that the costs of funding Ross' project be shared with the National Bible Society of Scotland, arguing that 'It would be a good thing for both Societies to publish, so that the more might be circulated.' But, adding the dampener, that 'Perhaps the door of Corea is too thoroughly shut for much benefit to arise from such a procedure.'[12]

Thankfully the British and Foreign Bible Society editorial committee thought otherwise. They interviewed Ross 'very cordially' and decided to support the printing of a Gospel, intimating their decision in the October issue of their periodical, *The Record*, and again in their annual report.[13] Furthermore, they arranged for specimens of Korean type to be forwarded to Newchwang from Yokohama in Japan, so that the work might begin without delay. The reference to Japan is significant as it opens up another facet in the story of the translation of the Bible into Korean. In the early 1880s, a progressive Korean government officer named Yi Sujŏng visited Japan on government business. He was converted and, at the request of the American Bible Society, rendered Chinese tracts, the Gospels of Matthew and Mark, and The Acts of the Apostles into Korean *Han'gŏl*. Yi's Mark's Gospel was published in Yokohama in 1884 and clandestinely circulated in Korea. To Ross' critical eye, Yi's work was flawed because, instead of translating from the Greek New Testament, he had transliterated the characters of the Chinese Bible into *Han'gŏl*. As Ross saw it, this was neither adequate nor did it make the Gospels and Acts accessible to ordinary Koreans who were not fluent in Chinese. Ross rather scathingly wrote:

> I have read a great deal of a translation being made in Japan. Specimens have been sent me of the Gospels and Acts. It is not a translation ... this 'Version' leaves matters exactly where they were. To a good Chinese scholar they are of little or no value as he could make them for himself, while to ... the nine tenths of the population who know not Chinese nothing can be of any service which is not written in their own language.[14]

Nevertheless, it was Yi's version that was adopted by Underwood and his American Presbyterian colleagues, the first foreign Protestant missionaries to Korea.[15] Choi irenically and aptly comments, 'every bit of [this] effort was a further preparation of the ground for the foundation of the Korean Church.'[16]

Ross' ungenerous critique of Yi's work reminds us of a somewhat dismaying aspect of his character, a tendency to lose patience with those with whom he disagreed. Harsh though it may sound to modern readers, plain speaking was unremarkable at the time, but in Ross' case it cannot be so easily dismissed as it tended to mar his relationships with supporters of his work, such as Robert Arthington, the wealthy recluse of Leeds, and the committee of the National Bible Society of Scotland, which included such deeply sympathetic men as Robert Candlish, Principal Patrick Fairbairn, Robert Haldane, and Henry Moncrieff, as well as Principal John Cairns. What makes it so regrettable is that Ross had known most of these men, at least by repute, from his time as a student at the United

Presbyterian Divinity Hall in Edinburgh. Even more unfortunate were his irascible exchanges with his own denomination's Missions Board. It was of course a challenge for such men to enter fully into the difficulties of the man on the ground, though all were sympathetic. It ought to go without saying, that if not from self-interest, then out of courtesy, it was Ross' Christian duty to maintain good personal relations with these people. But forbearance and patience appear to have been in short supply in Ross' character, at least when he was under pressure. His abruptness created numerous relationship problems which are well documented.[17]

United Presbyterian elder, William J. Slowan, the secretary of the Western (Glasgow) branch of the National Bible Society of Scotland, found Ross exceedingly difficult to deal with, as this note to his counterpart in the British and Foreign Bible Society indicates:

> I might reply in more detail to the charges against myself incidentally made by Mr Ross in his letter to you of 26th March last; but this kind of thing is very distasteful to me, and I am content to leave the minute to speak for me as well as for itself.
>
> We think that we and others have some reason to complain of the way in which Mr Ross has treated us in connection with this matter. Should you accede to his request, we trust that your experience may be of an agreeable character.[18]

Slowan wasn't the only one to suffer Ross' irritability. The eccentric Arthington was another. Ross didn't trouble himself to travel to meet Arthington during his time in Britain, and this wasn't because Arthington was unwelcoming. Indeed, far from it. He had expected Ross to have visited him in fulfilment of a promise he understood to have been made. Ross, instead, wrote bluntly requesting money to fund three thousand copies of Luke's Gospel. Arthington was keen to help, but understandably upon his terms, or at least terms he might negotiate with Ross person to person. Ross, however, brooked no compromise to his plans. It is not hard to detect disappointment in Arthington's note to the British and Foreign Bible Society.

> I not only wish to encourage my dear brother Mr Ross, but to express the intense interest and sympathy which I feel constantly in the Corean work and with him; so that we may make known the glorious

> Gospel to the Coreans, as to every nation and people under the whole heavens over the face of the globe. Let us all do this with the utmost intelligence and diligence, and good speed, promptly and well, until every people on the face of the earth can either read in their own tongue, or hear read or taught intelligibly … the Word of God as it is set forth clearly and invitingly in the New Testament Scriptures …. Mr Ross seems to have proceeded independently of me since leaving China or arriving in this country. I am not aware that I have failed to fulfill any promise to him.[19]

Although this was not addressed directly to Ross, there is no doubt that he was aware of Arthington's sentiments, which he impatiently dismissed as a pietistic evasion of the one thing he needed for his work: namely, money.

In mitigation, it does appear that Arthington was moving painfully slowly in response to Ross' appeals, causing Ross to add, by way of explanation, if not self-justification, that he and Arthington had been in touch for seven years, with Arthington all the time promising to pay the cost of producing the Gospels of Luke and John, but as yet providing nothing. In the event, the main part of the cost of the first edition of the Gospels of St Luke and St John was borne by the National Bible Society of Scotland.

It is impossible to offer an accurate analysis of Ross' frame of mind – we simply do not have sufficient evidence to attempt the task – but it is possible to make an informed estimate of some of the factors which may have lain behind his irascibility. Like many other pioneering missionaries, Ross may have resented overly close scrutiny from people who did not possess firsthand knowledge of his situation, and who appeared to know better than the missionary on the ground. He was disappointed to encounter in the National Bible Society of Scotland and in Arthington, people who claimed to share his vision for Bible translation, but who were, as he judged, bound by inertia, lack of vision, weakness of faith, and aversion to risk. Certainly, in the face of the financial burden he personally carried, both for the work and support for his family, he found having to haggle for funds deeply disagreeable. In a letter to the British and Foreign Bible Society, dated March 1882, he wrote:

> I have had half a dozen men, four Coreans and two Chinese printers, constantly at work for half a year and as yet have had no money save my own salary with which to pay them and the other expenses connected with printing. I still expect that Mr Arthington of Leeds, though I have never seen the gentleman, will implement his repeated promise to provide the expense incurred for two gospels. But I could have wished that he had saved me the annoyance of having to work meantime on my own salary and when it fails on borrowed money. From such annoyance I hope to escape in future by your generous help; it is partly on this account that I now ask you to kindly send some money in advance, for the six men must be regularly paid, and paper etc. cannot be had without ready money. [20]

Could these people not see that the almost intolerable strain under which he worked might be eased, if not eradicated, by printing everything he had translated, and in the large numbers needed for the day when Korea would open its doors to the outside world? Were they all, like Dyer, failing to share his optimism that that day would soon dawn? Yet, we might add, how could they share his vision? Unlike him, they had not witnessed at firsthand the enthusiastic faith of the Koreans, nor the alacrity with which they had seized upon any book or pamphlet that might nourish that faith. They had not sensed what Ross had sensed, the thrilling irresistible divine momentum which was driving this work forward at a speed with which he and his Mukden colleagues could scarcely keep up. Nor were his backers able to recognise that below the level of human consciousness, beyond the ken of committees and officials in an orderly and spiritually prosperous Britain, lay a reality which all might acknowledge in theory, but which few had actually encountered, as he had done: the great relentless spiritual struggle as the Enemy sought, in his venomous subtlety, to frustrate all who had the temerity to encroach upon his domain of darkness.

It is as well perhaps to suspend our analysis of Ross' flaws of character at that point, for it would appear that at an interpersonal level he did little to enlighten those whom he judged to be fickle supporters. Thankfully, the British and Foreign Bible Society was persuaded of the soundness of publishing a fresh edition of five thousand copies of St John bound up with Ephesians, on the grounds, as Ross put it, that 'an Epistle would explain the subject of the Gospel, [and] the Gospel would illustrate the basis of the Epistle.'[21]

Finally, in 1887, much to everyone's great relief, the stress and strain of ten years of sacrificial effort and a heavy investment of nervous energy, along with the diligence and patience of all in the team, and the indispensable commitment and prayers of the home supporters and others, was rewarded by the publication of the full New Testament. But that is to run ahead of ourselves. First, we must backtrack to Ross' return to Mukden after his 1879 furlough in Britain.

With the National Bible Society of Scotland having agreed to provide part funding for the printing of the Gospels of St Luke and St John, and with the rest being contributed by private individuals, Ross now had to determine the best way to distribute the thousands of copies shortly to be in his hands. At the time, much was made of his far-sighted belief that Korea would shortly open its borders. His optimism was exonerated when in 1882 the Korean government capitulated to pressure from the United States of America, signed a treaty, and opened up the country to outside influence. Despite the dawning of a more liberal day, Korea would, however, remain closed for another two years as far as a missionary presence in the country was concerned, and the open circulation of the Bible would not until then be allowed. In the meantime, Ross had two problems. The first was financial: he needed money to arrange distribution of his Gospels. The second was logistical: how best could he establish a network through which he might spread them across Korea, rather than concentrating them all in the north? He must have had something akin to Jewish *chutzpah*, because, to resolve the first, he boldly wrote again to Arthington soliciting funds:

> I should much like if you send on £50 to cover cost of John's Gospel. If you so desire it, £10 or £12 more might be sent to engage a member as colporteur and within the year 6,000 copies of the Gospel would be circulating and preaching in as many centres throughout the length of the land from our shores to those of Japan. From what the Coreans tell me, I believe that though having to distribute in secret, the sales would cover travelling expenses.[22]

Arthington obliged immediately and with a degree of eccentricity sending off £50 not for John's Gospel, but to translate Acts, and print and bind three thousand copies together with Luke's Gospel. It would seem he was not going to be told by Ross how to spend his own money, nor did he respond to the appeal for funding for an extra colporteur.

Ross' observation, that the distribution of the Bible might have to be done in secret, explains why his three-pronged strategy was nothing if not ambitious. First, he would get Gospels into the hands of the many Koreans resident in the northern valleys of Manchuria, as well as those who might visit the country in the course of business, such as the members of the annual embassy to the Chinese court in Beijing. Secondly, by using Manchuria as a base, he would organise a smuggling operation to get books across the Yalu River border. Thirdly, part of his stock he would have sent to Japan, from where he would export them into Korea through the ports Korea had opened up by the Treaty of Amity of 1876. These would be clandestinely distributed in the southern part of the country.

In pursuit of the third prong of his strategy, Ross arranged for the National Bible Society of Scotland to send one thousand copies each of St John's and St Luke's Gospels to J. A. Thomson, a United Presbyterian Church colleague, who was the National Bible Society of Scotland's agent at Yokohama.[23] Thomson in turn recruited as a courier a Japanese Christian called Nagasaka, who had been previously employed by the Bible Society in Tokyo. Rev. Hugh Waddell of the Presbyterian Church in Ireland, then serving in Japan with the United Presbyterian Church, reported that Nagasaka and his books arrived in Korea in June 1883 on board a Japanese man-of-war, adding, 'Truly never was ship of war better employed; and let us hope that this incident may be the omen of a peaceful future for these sister kingdoms.' In view of Japan's history of interference in Korea and her looming menace, Koreans might have seen it differently, considering Nagasaka's good intentions compromised by association with their enemy.

That same year, recognising the good sense of Ross' scheme, the National Bible Society of Scotland ordered, for distribution in

Korea, another thousand copies of all available portions of Scripture from the Mukden press. The following year, when clandestine operations were unnecessary, Thomson openly visited Korea with his wife, making Mrs Thomson the first European woman to enter the country. Their purpose was to establish another National Bible Society of Scotland agent, Sugano, and his wife Miura, to assist Nagasaka in distributing Bibles. In 1885 Sugano distributed over a thousand copies of St Luke and St John, and one thousand two hundred and fifty copies the following year. Between 1883 and 1886 around fifteen thousand seven hundred copies of the Gospels in the Ross translation had been circulated.[24] When supplies of the Ross version ran out, National Bible Society of Scotland agents distributed instead the Yi Su-jong version, with which Ross had found fault.

In Korea, the newly arrived American missionaries were, as we have noted, dissatisfied with *Yesu syŏnggyo chŏnsŏ*, the Ross version of the New Testament, and in 1887 set up their own translation committee to prepare a new version. Hearing of this, Ross, ever ready to improve his version, wrote to the Americans, inviting them to send to him a list of the defects as they saw them. There was no reply.[25] The American version only very gradually diminished the status of the Ross version which exerted its greatest influence during the two decades, 1890 to 1910, the most formative in the life of the Korean Church. In 1964, Bishop Richard Rutt, the Anglican Korea scholar, Warden of Bede House at Seoul University, and Assistant General Secretary of the Korean Bible Society, voiced his opinion that as far as intelligibility was concerned, 'the best piece of translation work so far done in Korean was Ross.'[26]

It was not only in the area of linguistics and Bible translation that American missionaries asserted a different approach; the same was true of worship. The first Korean Christians had become accustomed to singing Chinese hymns with Korean pronunciation to indigenous tunes, but by the 1890s missionaries of both American Methodist and Presbyterian missions took a retrograde step by imposing translated English hymns in western four-part harmony.[27]

The second aspect of Ross' distribution strategy was a smuggling operation, using Korean colporteurs and evangelists to spread the

Scriptures throughout northern Korea. One such evangelist was Yi Ung-chan, Ross' first Korean language teacher. Another was Paik Hong-jun, baptised by Macintyre in 1879, whose work in Uiju laid the foundations of a congregation that may be considered one of the very first Protestant churches established in Korea, of which more anon. In 1883, Ross sent a colporteur to Pyongyang with a stock of seven hundred Gospels of St John and about two hundred and fifty of St Luke. Between them the colporteurs and evangelists distributed all that had been given to them.

Their work was not without significant risk. The law prohibiting the propagation of Christianity was still in force, and some of the colporteurs, with other Korean Christians, ran foul of it. Paik, returning to Mukden to restock, brought Ross the troubling news of Korean Christians being caught and imprisoned for a month. Paik's books had been confiscated and burned. As late as 1880 Macintyre parcelled up for Paik some Chinese Scriptures and some Christian and general scientific books. These were intercepted by Korean Customs officials, who opened them and on discovering Paik's name had him arrested and imprisoned. He was not released for three months.

All involved in this hazardous undertaking – Ross and Macintyre, their backers and supporters in Britain, the colporteurs and evangelists, including those who had been imprisoned – were united in agreement that all the risks run, and all the suffering entailed, had been more than worthwhile. Under God's blessing, their efforts had brought about marvellous results: the Bible had been distributed, the Gospel preached, and the Church established. The American missionary, Horace Underwood, may have had reservations about Ross' version, but he was unstinting in recognising its huge influence. He wrote: 'Applications for baptism are coming to Seoul to-day by the hundreds from all parts of the land where copies of the gospel have been distributed.'

But what, we may ask, of the first part of Ross' three-pronged strategy, the use of his translations for the evangelisation of the Korean valleys in the northern part of Manchuria? As far as this account is concerned, it is that attempt that is so important, as it was the one in which Ross himself was most directly active. To that story we now turn.

13

The Korean Valleys

The valley of Achor as a door of hope.
HOSEA 2:15

TO a discouraged Israel, the prophet Hosea suggested that the valley of Achor, a place redolent with the struggles and failures of the past, would become a motif of hope, a door opening to a brighter future. In the *Commentary Critical and Explanatory on the Whole Bible* (JFB), by Robert Jamieson, Andrew Fausset and David Brown, Fausset, an older contemporary of John Ross, interprets Hosea 2.15 as follows: 'the very trouble of Israel's wilderness state will be the "door of hope" opening to better days.' Whether or not Ross had purchased a copy of the newly published JFB in 1871 and had taken it to China is unclear, but it is likely that he had, and possible he had read these very words. At any rate, Ross was to experience Jamieson's meaning in connection with his attempts to contact Koreans and win them for Christ. A door of hope was opening on Korea.

To test the accuracy, effectiveness and acceptability of their translation of Luke's Gospel, before its widespread distribution, Ross and Macintyre printed a number of copies to be distributed with a simple tract 'briefly and intelligently setting forth Christian doctrine'. Should the translation find acceptance, more would be printed. But before that could happen it was necessary to find a Korean who could be trained to set the type. Koreans in Mukden were, at that time, a rare sight, but even rarer was one who might be persuaded to help. Providentially, the right person came their way. As it so happened, the local Chinese people had a high regard for Korean medicine, making it relatively easy for a smooth-tongued salesman to make a small fortune, but if you happened to be tongue-tied and clumsy, wealth would elude you. So it was that would-be medicine seller Kim Ch'ongsong, impoverished and desperate, came one day as a beggar to the mission house. Keen to abandon the medicine trade and save sufficient money to one day return to Korea, Kim was ready to take on any task.

Ross offered Kim the opportunity to prove himself as a compositor, but it was soon apparent that had he had a choice in the matter Ross would certainly not have chosen Kim. Ross' assessment is unflattering: 'His eye was sleepy, his fingers clumsy, his gait slow, his thoughts of the most sluggish. To understand any process, he required four times as much explanation as any ordinary man.'[1] Kim was only just able to keep himself ahead of the printers who were running off at full speed three thousand copies of the page he had just set. In his favour, Kim was entirely trustworthy, satisfactorily, if clumsily, carrying out each task he was set. Moreover, he had curiosity. In setting the Korean type he necessarily had to read every word on every page, noting every detail of sentence construction and spacing. The words and sentences and pages carried ideas, ideas which were new to Kim, and not only fascinating and challenging, but, he discovered, very relevant to him personally. Turning to the Christian Chinese printers, he asked them in his broken Mandarin the meaning of these things. They instructed him so well that by the time the Gospel of Luke was typeset he felt ready to ask for baptism. Ross, of course, did not take such applications routinely, invariably submitting candidates to close scrutiny, but to his great delight, he discovered in Kim a deep knowledge and a sound experience of Christian faith, and unhesitatingly agreed to baptise him.

A further important development took place when the unofficial Korean intelligence service communicated news of the translation to official circles in Pyongyang. Whilst no sanction was set against it, no official acknowledgement recognised its existence; consequently, some younger lower-placed officials, accompanying the annual embassy bringing tribute from the Korean King to the

Chinese Emperor, were not discouraged from calling in at the mission printing shop when passing through Mukden. One of these young men was the temperamental opposite of Kim. Ross described him – though he unfortunately fails to give us his name – as 'nimble-fingered, quick-eyed, and smart in speech, in thought, and action.' He was engaged, replacing Kim Ch'ongsong as the Korean compositor.

For Kim, Ross had another task in mind, one to which he believed his experience, temperament and Christian character better suited him. He was to be sent with three hundred copies of the Gospel of Luke, and many tracts, the four hundred miles and two weeks' journey to his native place in the Korean valleys of Kando, close to the Korean border. For six months, nothing was heard from Kim until one day he reappeared in Mukden, claiming to have sold all the books, that they were being read avidly by many people, and as a consequence some of the villagers wished to be baptised.

Ross, however, suspected that Kim was telling him only what he wanted to hear but, without travelling four hundred miles, was unable to prove it. Ross bluntly confessed, 'I paid no attention to it.' Nevertheless, Kim was sent off once again to visit some of the other Korean valleys, with a fresh supply of Gospels, books and tracts. Once more, six months later, he returned with essentially the same story: all the books had been sold, their purchasers were devouring the contents, and more people had been converted. Now, what was Ross to believe?

In the meantime, significant changes were taking place in high official Korean circles, opening the country to foreign influence. In 1876 an unequal treaty had been signed with Japan, and in 1882 another with the USA. With America getting its toe in Korea's door, Britain and other western powers speedily negotiated their own treaties, ending Korea's seclusion from the rest of the world. This fulfilment of what they had long anticipated brought great joy to Ross and his team at Mukden. A door of hope had been opened for the Good News of Jesus Christ, allowing Korean colporteurs and evangelists some freedom to evangelise in their own country.

The changes brought about by the Progressive Movement, and the undermining of Chosŏn traditionalism, were not accomplished without reaction, violence and bloodshed. In the ensuing struggle, many political progressives had been killed, some were imprisoned, and others had fled across the border to become refugees in the Korean communities in the Kando valleys. Some even reached Mukden where they found the United Presbyterian mission and saw the Korean books that Ross and Macintyre were printing. This aroused their curiosity, leading some to remark that they had come across the very same books whilst travelling through the Korean valleys.

Not only had they seen books, but they had met those who were now praying to the God of Heaven. By such simple and uncontrived comments, from men who had no idea of the significance of what they were saying, Ross was deeply humbled, greatly regretting his earlier dismissal of Kim Ch'ongsong's reports. Forced now to believe Kim, Ross saw that these fresh reports were far too significant to be any longer neglected. He set his mind on visiting the Kando valleys to see for himself what Kim had claimed God had been doing. This time Rev. James Webster agreed to accompany him 'with his characteristic courage and enthusiasm'.[2]

By this time, all the Korean refugees at Mukden had become Christians. The oldest was a *yangban*, holding the highest Korean literary degree; he was respected as a man of character, learning and dignity. It appears that during his flight from Korea, he had met a colporteur in one of the valleys, in all probability Kim Ch'ongsong, from whom he had bought some Christian books. Coming to Mukden with an open and enquiring mind to hear more fully the way of salvation, he was converted and baptised, the first of the Korean refugees to be received into the Church. Being the esteemed person that he was, he was invited by Ross to act as their intermediary with the residents of the Kando valleys, joining Webster and himself in what would prove a most arduous but remarkable journey.

It was now the summer of 1884. The heavy autumn rains would soon come and, until the winter freeze, the roads would be a sea of impassable mud. Ross, Webster and their Korean friend set out in the middle of November. They managed to accomplish the first half of the journey with Chinese carts, but when conditions became too difficult for wheeled vehicles, they transferred their baggage and scant provisions on to pack mules, themselves riding small Manchurian ponies. An abominable road ran gently uphill until it reached a height of some two thousand feet above sea level, where an inn provided a resting place for the night. Beyond, deep snow covered the road, through which a narrow pathway had been beaten by the feet of a few daring travellers. Ross recalled in an article in *The Missionary Review of the World* how the next stage demanded all the endurance they possessed.

> About 3 A.M. next morning, in brilliant moonlight, we set out to scale the two passes which lay between us and the Koreans. From the west fort of the one pass to the eastern base of the second was a distance of thirty miles. Once we tried to ride; but soon had to dismount, and made no second attempt, as the path was so steep, narrow and rough. With a halt on the top of the first pass, we had to walk the whole distance, and thoroughly worn out we at last came in sight of a house, which to our delight proved to be a Chinese inn. Entering the gateway, and throwing our horses' reins to the nearest attendant, we moved into the inn, threw ourselves on the [heated] brick bed, resolved to rest there till next day before searching out our Korean friends.

But their rest was suddenly disturbed:

> In marched a body of about a dozen Koreans, gentlemanly in appearance, garments, manner and speech. They came in to welcome us. This they did with a smile lighting up their faces, as though they had been welcoming long lost and very dear friends. Being hospitable, it would have been a disgrace to them had we remained in the inn, so, perforce, we had to go to be their guests. We were conducted into the home of the principal farmer, in whose guest-room we found a crowd of men filling the warm, close room.[3]

The missionaries learned that there were those who wished to be baptised, and the next day requested their Korean intermediary to ascertain the genuineness of these people's Christian profession. He returned late at night with an encouraging report. The following morning thirty well-dressed farmers and heads of families came to meet the missionaries. Ross continues the story:

> Their women and children were, they said, believers; but they thought the younger people would not be received, and their women, for social

> reasons, could not present themselves where the men were met. As this was the only opportunity for investigation, the examination through which the men had to go was pretty thorough. Some were baptized, and some postponed for further Christian instruction.[4]

Refreshed with the renewing energy that comes to missionaries from the encouragement of knowing that the Spirit God is at work in human hearts, Ross and Webster, with their Korean colleague, set off that afternoon to meet another group in a further valley, notwithstanding the taxing journey of the day before and an already demanding morning's work interviewing and baptising new converts. There, they had a very similar experience, and administered more baptisms. The next day they traversed a yet higher mountain range, which Ross remembered as 'picturesque', to enter another extensive valley. Here nearly one hundred men, from sixteen to seventy-two years of age, presented themselves for baptism. Altogether, in three days, in three valleys, eighty-five men were baptized, and many more asked to further prepare their minds and hearts for baptism at a later date. But that was not all. Ross and Webster now heard that in all of the next twenty-eight valleys were even more who desired to profess faith in Christ, be baptised and received into the Christian Church. To some people such Gospel progress might have sounded incredible, fantastical, exaggerated, beyond belief, but Ross, now thoroughly cured of his earlier scepticism, drily remarked that from what they had already seen they 'were now prepared to believe almost anything'.

Regrettably, however, they could go no further as they had been warned that a severe snowstorm was expected which would block the passes for three months or more. If they wished to return to Mukden before winter was over, they must hasten away immediately. The Koreans were saddened to let them go, but there was little reluctance on the part of the missionaries, confident as they were that the Holy Spirit would do his own work and that those who had been baptised would, over the coming winter months, help the applicants to appreciate more fully Christian instruction and the commitment of life necessary to become members of the community of the God of Heaven.

Early next summer, 1885, Ross and Webster returned to the valleys, eager to meet the believers and to examine and baptise the waiting candidates and others who might be ready to profess their faith. It soon became evident that serious and detrimental changes had taken place, threatening the physical and material wellbeing of the Korean Christians, if not their spiritual health. Although they received a very warm welcome on arrival and the offer of guides to accompany them wherever they wished to travel, they also heard stories of persecution instigated by the Chinese landlords.

Traditional rural Korean society was a threefold hierarchy. At the apex was the *yangban* class of wealthy landed aristocrats, educated, economically privileged and politically influential. Beneath the *yangban* was the *yangin*, small landowning or tenant peasant farmers. Below them, were the *ch'ŏnmin*, landless indentured servants and others whose occupations held no social cachet, such as butchers, shoemakers, metalworkers and mendicant monks.[5] In the Korean valleys of Manchuria the *yangban* had been displaced by Chinese landlords, to whom they were subservient and for whom they now worked. As the missionaries had, wisely or unwisely, confined all their efforts to the Koreans, the Chinese landlords, fearing that Christianity was a plot designed to oust them in favour of the Korean *yangban*, worried that the social order might be disrupted, and they be deprived of their traditional workforce. They had therefore resorted to violence, calling in the services of local thugs to intimidate, though not to kill, the Korean Christians. The missionaries heard harrowing tales of cruel beatings, slashings with swords and many broken bones, and not wanting to add further to their suffering considered immediate retreat to Mukden.

Despite strong requests for the missionaries to remain for six months longer, Ross considered it unfair to further complicate the lives of the Christians by pressing deeper into the valleys, or by prolonging their visit when there were other pressing responsibilities awaiting them in Mukden. Explaining their decision as clearly as they could, and taking every opportunity to remove suspicion from the Koreans, they determined to return to Mukden. Even so, the Koreans would not let them depart immediately. Persecution or no persecution, there were those who would not allow anything to stand in the way of their baptism and membership of the church of Christ. Ross never did return to the valleys, but he continued to support the work of Kim Ch'ongsong, and also enlisted a Mr Atkinson of the British and Foreign Bible Society, and 'another' worker – Ross was never good at remembering names – whose combined activity facilitated further progress. Ross was now confident that on both sides of the border were thousands of Koreans who daily read Scripture, and prayed to God.[6]

14

The First Korean Churches

In Korea and part of Manchuria the evangelistic spirit is so strong that … the entire Church is a missionary organisation.

Report on Spiritual Fruitfulness, Edinburgh 1910.

SO far, we have met Korean Christians either as individuals or as those belonging to informal indigenous Christian communities in the Kando valleys of Manchuria, such as Ross' language informant Yi Ung-chan, baptised by Macintyre in 1879, and the evangelist and colporteur, Kim Ch'ongsong. To them may also be added the name of Paik Hong-jun, who came to Macintyre for baptism after reading his father's Chinese New Testament and a slender volume of basic Christian teaching in Korean called *Peep of Day* by Favell Lee Mortimer, published in English in 1883.[1] This idiosyncratic volume was originally intended for small children, but its general theological accuracy and simple clarity of expression made it suitable for translation and circulation among those for whom the Christian message was new. Paik's father received a copy from Ross on his first visit to the Corean Gate in 1874. The same copy led to the conversion of Paik's friend.

Then there was Kim Jin-gi of who we know little, and Yi Ung-chan whom Ross once referred to as 'my chief assistant', but did not mention again.[2] There were others too, their names unrecorded by the missionaries, omitted from mission records, or lost in the upheavals that convulsed Korea during the twentieth century. If before Kim Ch'ongsong's first visit to the Kando valleys Korean Christians could be numbered in the hundreds, by 1890 there were thousands of praying believers.

Although informing the supporters of the mission in a general way through *The Missionary Record of the United Presbyterian Church,* the missionaries themselves were very reticent to count heads or provide statistics merely to satisfy an appetite for success stories. Though they rejoiced over every new Christian, they did not feel that their work was fully rewarded, nor their prayers answered simply by individuals coming to faith in Christ, no matter how many of them there may have been. From the outset their goal had been the formation of Christian communities, properly constituted congregations, on sound principles of church government and sustainable in the local context. For Ross the real answer to China's spiritual needs, and Korea's too, was indigenous churches motivated and empowered by the Holy Spirit, able to engage in spontaneous evangelism, and, essentially, independent of foreign missionaries and overseas supporters.

As we have noted, from the time of the conversion of Wang Ching-ming, Ross made it his aim to invest time and energy in equipping indigenous evangelists and local church workers. Although willing to provide temporary subsistence allowances for such men, if necessary, out of his own pocket, his ultimate goal was to establish churches that were financially self-sustaining, self-propagating and self-governing.

How did this go down with the converts themselves? Did they misinterpret Ross' good intentions as mean-spiritedness, or worse, an expression of racial prejudice? In the face of claims that many eastern people became Christians in order to benefit materially from inducements offered by misguided missionaries – the old 'rice Christian' canard – it may be thought that approaches such as Ross' might have been met with resistance, if not outright opposition from local Christians. In fact, the opposite appears to have been the case. Both Old Wang and Blind Chang epitomise the Chinese Christians' spirit of independence. Not only were they a people proud of an ancient identity, culture and civilization, but they were also newly confident of the Holy Spirit's power and provision. Old Wang had spoken for most when he sternly repudiated all allegations that he was dependent upon the missionaries by trenchantly asserting: 'Let the foreigner depart, we have the Bible, and we know the truth, and we will teach and repeat it even if there are no foreigners in the land.' Precisely!

As John Nevius and John Ross both thought out coherent schemes built upon Venn's Three Selfs doctrine, it has been wondered whether Ross' scheme was derived from Nevius' method. On the face of it that might seem plausible. John Nevius was senior in age and mission experience: he and his wife Helen having lived in Chefoo for ten years before John and Mary Ann Ross had arrived in 1872. It is also unlikely that Ross was altogether ignorant of Nevius' thoughts. Although, by the time Ross was in Chefoo, they were not sufficiently developed to have been published, their general principles were probably well enough known, discussed and debated by the missionary community. Ross and Nevius may have been personally acquainted, though there seems to be no record of them meeting, let alone discussing mission strategy.

Nevius' scheme matured some considerable time after his move to Chefoo, evolving through his experience of running summer training sessions for groups of Chinese Christian leaders from Shantung Province. It would not be until 1886 that his *Manual for Inquirers* would evolve into his *Methods of Missionary Work.*[3] The general approach of the United Presbyterian missionaries derived not from the theories of Nevius, but from the example of William Chalmers Burns, undergirded by their denominational voluntary principles. These ideas Ross rigorously thought through, adapted and developed, so that by the early 1880s his principles were widely adopted by his colleagues. They were also implemented by Ross' Korean evangelists who had crossed the Yalu River into Korea, thus fostering a spirit of independence in the very first Korean churches. After almost two decades of locally sustainable church planting and development, Ross published the history and theory of his approach in his 1903 book, *Mission Methods in Manchuria*. By contrast, the Nevius method was not implemented in Korea until after 1890, subsequent to his having been invited by the American missionaries to explain his ideas. From then on, Nevius' version of the Three-

Selfs principle became the cornerstone of American missionary strategy, shaping the church that resulted from their efforts. There appears to be no evidence that Ross and Nevius were dependent upon each other. Although their strategies were broadly similar, they developed independently of each other in response to broadly comparable challenges. Moreover, neither scheme was truly original, for both leaned heavily on the ideas of Venn and Anderson.

The core principle at the heart of both strategies is faith in and dependency upon the Holy Spirit, specifically in relation to the lives of new converts and young churches. Both the missionary and the new converts must learn to be reliant upon the Holy Spirit, rather than upon each other. Despite the temptation to manipulate, mould, shape and patronise, the missionary must remember that the Holy Spirit is the instigator of both new life and Christian maturity, and cease from unnecessary interference in the lives of young Christians. Likewise, new Christians must learn to trust the Holy Spirit residing in themselves and refuse to lean upon transient foreign help.

One of the strongest and most articulate proponents of this new and challenging way of thinking was neither Ross nor Nevius, but their younger contemporary, the High Anglican missionary strategist and thinker, Roland Allen. In 1895 Allen went to Beijing as part of the north China mission of the Society for the Propagation of the Gospel. In 1900 he became chaplain to the British legation trapped in Beijing by the Boxer uprising, where his experiences provided material for a series of three articles for *Cornhill Magazine* in late 1900 and 1901, when he was on furlough. Allen recognised the need for social change in China, was blunt about the misrule of the Qing court, deplored the unprincipled scramble of competing foreign powers for concessions, and was utterly appalled at the brutality of the international force in suppressing the Boxers, which, he believed, would be a major hindrance to the acceptance of 'foreign' Christianity by the Chinese. After furlough, Allen and his new wife, Mary Tarleton, returned only briefly to China before ill health led to his resignation from active missionary service. In 1904 he became parish priest at Chalfont St Giles in Buckinghamshire, but resigned three years later. For most of his life he held office neither in a mission society, the Church, nor in the academic world. He wrote and published his first book, the highly influential *Missionary Methods: St Paul's or Ours?* in 1912, and *The Spontaneous Expansion of the Church and the Causes which Hinder It* in 1949. Both have remained in print, more or less since they were first published. Looking back on Allen's contribution, Lamin Sanneh, Professor of World Christianity at Yale University, described it as 'resonant with contemporary meaning' and 'vindicated by the current post-Western Christian resurgence'.[4]

During his life Allen's work rarely found approval, being frequently rejected as irritatingly eccentric and impractical. He had no illusions about this. When his grandson, Hubert Allen, once asked to read his books Allen replied: 'Oh, yes, you can read them by all means – but you won't understand them; I don't think anyone is going to understand them until I have been dead ten years.'[5] That typically self-deprecating comment was, however, very wide of the mark. John Ross and his colleagues were very well aware of Allen's thought and work, and much appreciated it. James Inglis in 1916, the year after Ross' death, made this comment in his tribute to Ross:

> To a large extent Dr Ross followed the methods advocated by Roland Allen as being those of St Paul – he had an unbounded faith in the capacity of the Chinese race, and he believed in devolving a large measure of responsibility on those whom he baptized, so that the evangelisation of China might be speedily accomplished by the people of that land.[6]

Inglis' statement ought not, however, be read to imply that Ross depended upon Allen, but rather his work followed the same methods that Allen articulated. In this case Ross' practice came ahead of Allen's theory, but both were consciously dependent upon the principles of St. Paul and therefore it is unsurprising that their thinking tallied. It would be interesting to know to what extent Allen had absorbed ideas from Ross' thought and practice.

In a manner which would have gained the approbation of Ross and his United Presbyterian colleagues in Mukden, Allen recognised that of the very many hindrances to the spread of the gospel, the worst was the foreign garb it was dressed up in when presented by westerners. It was not enough for missionaries to wear Chinese dress if the language they used to preach the gospel, even if it was ostensibly Chinese, was redolent of an alien culture. Ross' translation work brought him to recognise, what Allen later learned, that every reference to God, redemption, love, sin, grace, faith, revelation, or any other biblical concept, invariably communicated to the hearer not what the preacher intended, but what the hearer already associated with the words he heard. If the missionary failed to be aware of this communication gap, he would make no effort to counter it and would blunder badly. Such miscommunication could have dire consequences. Allen once warned, 'If the church bears the mark "made in the West" ... many will turn away from her who would not turn away from Christ.' As an antidote, he advocated handing over full responsibility to indigenous Christians, in the shortest possible time. Before he could possibly have read Allen, Ross already agreed.

Allen articulated something else that Ross understood very well which is that a reluctance to establish locally sustainable self-governing churches might be motivated by a badly misguided, even if sincere, attempt to preserve orthodoxy. Such motives he held to be quite wrong. Orthodoxy could not be maintained by handing over to a local church the mission's funds, property and facilities with such a string of conditions attached that it had no room to be itself. Such paternalism and manipulation doomed the work to failure. Allen argued that 'Orthodoxy based on ignorant acceptance of authority or upon fearful obedience to rules is not orthodoxy .... It is a house built on sand.' In another place he asked rhetorically, 'What is to ensure orthodoxy?' And then answered convincingly, and predictably, 'Nothing: no power can ensure orthodoxy but the power of the Holy Spirit.'[7]

Of course, such policies were fraught with risks, but then, as Ross and his colleagues well understood, all missionary endeavour entails risk, but trusting the Holy Spirit in the new converts provided significant risk mitigation, transforming what would otherwise be a gamble into an act of faith. Both in Manchuria and in Korea, Ross and his colleagues took many calculated risks, but they were hedged about by prayer and undergirded by an assured confidence in the loving nurture and jealous care of the all-powerful Christ. They bore fruit. The American Presbyterian missionaries in Korea were much more risk averse, indeed excessively cautious over identifying with local culture, and timid about handing over the churches to Korean leadership. It is no exaggeration to say that it took a most remarkable divine intervention to bring about the latter. But that is to anticipate a latter episode.

If Ross' principles were adopted in Manchuria, they were applied even more rigorously in connection with the evangelisation of Korea. There Ross could not and did not go, but Korean Christians could, and, by trusting in the Holy Spirit, did all that needed to be done. Ross determined that he would evangelise Korea without western missionaries. The first Protestant Korean Christians to be baptised were those in Manchuria, the earliest being the Korean refugees gathering in John Macintyre's home in Mukden. It was this group that became influential in planting a church at Uiju, just across the Korean border, hence the claim that Uiju might be considered the first congregation established in Korea.[8] But this claim has not gone unchallenged.

Ought not the groups in the Kando valleys be considered as the first Korean churches? Certainly, it is inconceivable that Kim Ch'ongsong on visiting the valleys in 1883 and 1884 would have failed to have encouraged corporate worship, even if it only consisted of Bible reading and prayer. Likewise, it is improbable that Ross offered no advice concerning communal Christian life to those baptised in 1884 and 1885, despite spending so short a time among them.

Another contender for the honour of being the first Korean church is a congregation established in Seoul in 1887. Indeed, it appears that Ross himself thought so. That year, thirteen years after his first visit to the Gate, Ross crossed the border for the first time to meet the American Presbyterian missionary, Horace Grant Underwood. Ross' account of this journey, written for *The Missionary Review of the World,* carries the subtitle, 'The First Korean Congregation,' though it is proper to point out that that was not Ross' title. His title was 'The Christian Dawn in Korea'. This is part of what he wrote:

> I went to the capital by sea, which made the journey both possible and easy, arriving on an evening which was to me of peculiar interest. My host, the Rev. Mr Underwood, informed me that he was to go

> [to] his little chapel that night to organize his small company into a Presbyterian Church. Gladly accepting his kind invitation, I accompanied him and his medical colleague, when the darkness had fairly enmantled the city. Crossing the wide main streets, which, like all those eastern city streets, are unlit, we were guided by a Korean, with a small lantern, among narrow lanes till at last we were ushered into a small, open courtyard, whose gate was opened to our knock. A gentle tapping at a paper window secured our entry into a room, where we found a company of fourteen well dressed, intelligent-looking men. One of these was baptized that night, but the principal business was the election by the others of two men to be their elders. Two were unanimously elected, and the next Sabbath ordained.[9]

Ross had been aware of the existence of a group in Seoul for some time. The person responsible for planting this church had been Seo Sang-yun, whom Ross knew from Mukden, and whom he highly regarded as one of the ablest of the younger men. Ross said that he 'seemed ... to possess greater force of character, and a more fearless disposition than the others, while he was also a fair scholar.' Indeed, it was Ross who ensured that Seo Sang-yun received special training, to become an agent of the British and Foreign Bible Society. The night that Ross visited the Seoul congregation, Underwood was setting apart two men as elders in the congregation; both cousins of Seo Sang-yun. Ross himself, however, made no claim in the *Missionary Review* article that this was the first church to be established in Korea. The claim, as well as the title, appears to have been the editor's choice. He was, of course, mistaken, but the mistake grew legs and was repeated by Mrs M'Laren in her official United Presbyterian history, *The Story of our Manchurian Mission,* published in 1896. So, if not the Seoul congregation, then which was the first Protestant church to be constituted in the land of Korea? The answer is that historians appear somewhat uncertain and inclined to suggest two possibilities, either of which has a claim, though perhaps one is better attested than the other.

Some allow that the first church was at Uiju, just across the Yalu River close to the Manchurian border. It was here, according to Sebastian and Kirsten Kim, in their *A History of Korean Christianity,* that at least as early as 1879 Paek Hongjun commenced cross-border journeys to smuggle Christian literature and engage in evangelistic activity. By 1885, Paek Hongjun, with the help of a colleague, had gathered together eighteen people who regularly attended his gatherings.[10] As Bae points out, the majority of the Koreans in Ross' team at Mukden, including Paek and his friends, had come from Uiju, and now were returning to smuggle in Gospels and engage in witness among their family and friends, activities which carried their own joys, but also their dangers. So, was Uiju the first Protestant church in Korea?

Both the Kims, as well as Bae and Choi in their doctoral research, raise doubts against the claim. Bae and Choi refer to something Underwood said as justification for their doubts. Underwood spoke of visiting Uiju in 1887 and tells of finding 'A most promising work … [where] at one time there were gathered at this city from the surrounding villages and counties men to the number of over one hundred who asked to be received into full membership.'[11]

Bae and Choi draw our attention to the qualifying comments, 'at one time' and 'who asked.' What this appears to suggest is that not only were such numbers a thing of the past, but those who had asked for membership may not have received it. When Underwood returned to Uiju two years later, he, according to Choi, 'baptized thirty-three,' but made no claim that a congregation had been constituted, either by Korean agency or by a missionary.[12]

Against all that, it might be argued that it is unseemly to quibble over whether Uiju was the first constituted church or merely a prayer meeting from which a constituted congregation later organically emerged. But the problem is that there is another claim to be considered, that of the famous congregation at Sorae, a coastal village in Hwanghae province, approximately eighty miles west of Pyongyang. Here, a congregation was established by Seo Sang-yun and his brother Seo Kyeong-jo. The elder brother we have already met in connection with the Seoul congregation established in 1878. On a visit to Manchuria, Seo Sang-yun had fallen dangerously ill with enteric fever at Newchwang. He was admitted to the mission hospital, and afterwards cared for by John and Catherine Macintyre until he had fully recovered. More significantly, he was converted, and later baptised by Ross who was deeply struck by his 'indefatigable evangelising zeal and courage'.

In 1883 Ross appointed Seo Sang-yun an evangelist and colporteur. At some considerable risk, that same year he visited Sorae and gathered a congregation. The following year his brother, Seo Kyeong-jo, settled in Sorae, becoming the unbaptised and unordained pastor of this informal congregation. This arrangement, driven by exigences of the circumstances, has to be considered informal, and maybe also irregular, though certainly not invalid, because it appears that Seo Kyeong-jo was unbaptised and unordained, though through no fault of his own. The truth is that none of the believers were able to obtain baptism until 1887. Ross had been unable to visit them in 1883 and 1884, and Underwood declined to go in 1886.

It was not until January 1887, when Seo Sang-yun escorted four of the Sorae believers, including his brother, to Underwood at Seoul that the irregularity could be rectified. Underwood immediately recognised Ross' influence and just before the baptisms wrote, 'We are to have several baptisms on next Sunday and the men who have applied seem to be thoroughly in earnest. They are some of the offshoots, as it were, from some of Ross' work in the North.'[13] Years later, Underwood vividly recalled how this encouraging event bore a hallmark characteristic of Ross' work: financial independence.

> Not long after, he [Seo Sang-yun] returned with a delegation of four, who asked for baptism. They were rigidly examined in the presence of and by Dr Allen, Dr Heron and myself. They were seen on several occasions by us all during a stay of several days in Seoul. At the end all felt and said that we had no right to refuse baptism, and they were baptized. Of course they paid all the expenses of coming up, going back, and their hotel charges in the city. They all again urged me to go down to their village, but the way did not seem open.[14]

The first church building erected at Sorae was funded entirely at the cost of local Christians. Not only were they self-supporting, but through their evangelistic zeal could also claim to be self-propagating. Within a short time, their church was attended by the residents of fifty of the fifty-eight houses in the village.[15]

Scholars may want to debate the primacy in time of individual congregations, but there appears to be a strong consensus, following the research of Dr L. G. Paik, that asserts Sorae's claim to be considered 'the cradle of Protestant Christianity in Korea'.[16] But was Sorae anything other than numerically the first church? It may indeed be said that it was. Sorae was not only an exemplary self-sustaining congregation (even the candidates for baptism preserved the integrity of their independence by paying for their own travel and hotel expenses), it was also a self-propagating church from which many Korean Christian leaders were to come. Both Uiju and Sorae were prime examples of the effectiveness of the work of indigenous evangelists, often young in the faith, some highly gifted, others maybe of more modest attainments, who justified Ross' general missionary strategy that evangelism could be carried out effectively and churches planted without a single foreign missionary setting foot in the country.

When in 1890 the American missionaries adopted Nevius' plan, there were already in existence locally sustainable churches founded on Ross' approach. And by 1910 a report to the Edinburgh Missionary Conference could claim that the 'Church in Korea ... furnishes at present the brightest and gladdest example of a Church filled with evangelistic fire. In some cases it is made a condition of Church membership that the applicant should have endeavoured to win others to Christ.'[17]

15

Death and Resurrection

Verily, verily, I say unto you, except a grain of
wheat fall into the earth and die,
it abideth by itself alone; but if it die, it
beareth much fruit.

JOHN 12.24 (RV)

THE decade spanning 1894 to 1905 was dangerous, disruptive and cruel. Twice Manchuria was convulsed by war and once ravaged by a fierce civil uprising. Unspeakably difficult years they may have been, but it ought not be thought that these savage upheavals were entirely unproductive of good. Rather they are a most remarkable example of God working all things together for the good of his people. Both during and after these traumas Christians grew in faith, church membership increased, and new congregations were established. Though temporarily set back by a loss of personnel and property, the Manchurian Church passed through this crucible refined for further usefulness. As Iza Christie summarised it, 'Each successive trial became a stepping-stone towards greater service and wider influence.'[1]

On 1st August 1894, Japan declared war on China, provoking hostilities in order to lay claim to Korea, over which Qing China claimed suzerainty rights, and in recognition of which Korea paid tribute to the Imperial government in Beijing. As tensions between reforming and conservative elements threatened the internal peace of the nation, the Korean government, as a dependent state, requested Chinese military help to quell insurrection. In response, China moved quickly, sending several thousand of its troops across the border. Claiming this violated its treaty rights, Japan despatched a large task force to seize strategic points, eventually driving Chinese forces northwards from the peninsular. It was an unequal conflict. Japan's army was fully modernised and properly trained. The Chinese army was unprepared and ill-equipped, having changed little from medieval times.

Among the Chinese forces marching south to the border in early August were Manchu irregulars, with a deserved reputation for brutality and ill-discipline. Knowing little of the wider world, they considered their sole military objective to be the eradication of all 'foreign dwarves' who had insulted their emperor. A detachment of such men arrived at Liaoyang. On learning that there were foreigners in the town, including the United Presbyterian missionaries Rev. James Wylie, Dr David Gray, Rev. and Mrs George Douglas, Rev. Alexander Westwater, and Miss Sinclair, one of the officers ordered them all to be killed. After wrecking their chapel, an unsuccessful attempt was made to force entry to the mission compound. Besieged within their own walls and out of contact with the outside world, the missionaries agreed to allow Wylie and Liu, a silversmith and earnest Chinese Christian, to attempt to break through to the Yamen, to get help from the chief magistrate. It was a forlorn hope. Found on the street by the irregulars, Wylie was brutally attacked. With his jaw smashed and his teeth knocked out, he was left for dead. Worried by Wylie's prolonged absence, Dr David Gray went to look for him. Meeting up with a regular army officer and some disciplined soldiers, he asked them to help him find the missing men. They were soon located, but Wylie was unconscious and beyond help. Liu, though injured, had bravely continued to shield Wylie from further assault, and remained with him until help arrived.[2]

Word was sent to Dr Christie at Mukden, who immediately set out for Liaoyang. Normally, he would have travelled by horseback, but a painful injury to his foot meant that he had to use an official sedan chair. This probably saved his life. An official chair was customarily respected, and its closed curtains hid Christie from the sight of the irregulars posted beside the road. All went well until they came to a ferry across the river, where Christie had to alight. He was immediately spotted by a keen-eyed soldier on the bank, who opened fire. An officer ordered the firing to cease just as the ferry boat reached the far bank, and Christie's sedan chair bearers sped off in the direction of Liaoyang and the traumatised missionaries there. Following the burial of Wylie, the members of the Liaoyang congregation sent a moving letter to his parents, grateful that he had, at great personal inconvenience, come to preach the gospel to them, whatever the time, the weather or the distance. Their letter, bearing eloquent testimony to the impression that he had made upon them, included the words:

> Your honourable son came across the great seas to arouse the people .... In the service of his invisible Lord, his deep earnestness was remarkable. In his love of visible man, his actions are well worthy of imitation. When he saw the hungry, he fed him; he gave drink to the thirsty; he provided lodging for the wanderer; he clothed the naked; he cared for the sick; he visited the prisoner .... His goodness is worthy of being ever recorded, and is fitted to be a noble example. Our pastor is gone, but his life lives in brightness before the eyes and in the ears of men.[3]

When the victorious Japanese army drove back Chinese forces and crossed the Manchuria border, panic erupted. In Mukden, two-hundred miles or so further north, the population was highly susceptible to rumours. Hospital patients discharged themselves and fled to their homes. Officials abandoned their posts. General confusion prevailed. The missionaries evacuated the women and children, and even some of the men, to Newchwang. Later, when road travel became unsafe, the remaining male missionaries departed by river boat to join the others. Then, on the morning of 6th March 1895, Newchwang itself fell to the Japanese. As spring advanced, the occupiers settled down to administer the region. It appeared both to the missionaries and the Chinese population alike that the Japanese were there to stay. But, with an eye to its own imperial ambitions, Russia, backed by France and Germany, insisted that the terms concluding peace would require Japan to leave Manchuria and recognise Korea's independence.

Within weeks of the ceasefire, in April 1895, the Mukden missionaries returned to their homes and work, but although the dispensary and hospital reopened immediately, it was months before normal life could be resumed. One day, as a portent of what was to come, posters appeared on the walls of the town proclaiming that the Emperor had ordered the deaths of all foreigners and all Chinese Christians. The date set was 28th September. It soon transpired, however, that the posters were fraudulent and had been pasted up on the orders of a disaffected officer of the kind of levies which had murdered James Wylie. The date passed without incident.

John Ross was now in his early fifties, with over twenty years of arduous service behind him, and now the stresses and strains of wartime were beginning to take a toll on his health. He badly needed a protracted period of rest. His last furlough, five years earlier, had been anything but restful, as most of his time had been taken up with canvassing support for his translation of the New Testament into Korean and organising the publication of two books, his *History of Corea: Ancient and Modern*, and *The Manchus; or, the Reigning Dynasty of China: Their Rise and Progress*. But it wasn't until late November that he and Isabella and their children could reach Shanghai to embark for Scotland.

A few months earlier, the Senatus of the University of Glasgow had conferred upon Ross the honorary degree of Doctor of Divinity in recognition of his work in China, having noted the importance of his two historical books, his Korean translation of the New Testament, and his founding of the Dongguan Church in Mukden. It was not, however, until he reached Shanghai that he found time to write to the clerk of the Senatus:

> Sir,
>
> The serious disturbances which have for long unsettled our people and work in Manchuria must be my apology for failing to write you long ago. For though Dr [George] Robson, Inverness, will have written you on my behalf long ago, it was my duty to acknowledge to you directly my sense of the honour conferring upon me the degree of D.D. Upon me the sense of obligation lies all the more heavily inasmuch as my life has been spent so far away from the supervision of the Senatus.

> My brethren in Manchuria, several of them alumni of Glasgow university, expressed themselves as grateful to the Senatus; inasmuch as the honour bestowed reflects upon the whole of our mission staff and work here.
>
> Will you therefore kindly express my sincere, though tardy, thanks to the Senatus.[4]

Academic matters, though certainly not his own honour, had occupied much of Ross' time and thought during the previous months. Early in 1894 the missionaries of the United Presbyterian Church and the Presbyterian Church of Ireland had agreed to establish a joint four-year Scheme of Training for Native Agents; although this had to be deferred until more settled times, it was not forgotten and would be implemented in 1898.

Military defeat at the hands of the smaller nation of Japan had acted upon China as a catalyst for change. Both John Ross and Iza Christie noted how many Chinese, including the reform-minded Governor-General of Mukden, attributed the Japanese victory to that country's embrace of modern technology. This deepened their own growing misgivings about China's old-fashioned ways, conservative politics and reactionary leaders. Iza Christie had noted public opinion favouring change even before the war, after which it greatly accelerated. As earlier in Korea, so now in China, the national trauma created a new openness to Christianity as a vehicle of change. Popular regard for the missionaries rose. Not only had they cared compassionately for wounded and ill soldiers retreating from Korea, but they were also seen as in the vanguard of much needed modernisation. Mrs M'Laren recorded one soldier's expression of gratitude. 'Pastors,' he had said, 'we are returning to our camps, and we will tell our officers, from the general downwards, what the foreigners have done for us; and when we return to our homes, we will make it known to our fathers and mothers, our wives and children, and they will hand it down to their children's children, and you will not be forgotten for ten generations.'[5] Flamboyant as his language may have been, it was sincere and betokened a real change of attitude.

Throughout Manchuria the preaching halls became crowded with hearers, the schools inundated by new children, and the missionaries overwhelmed with applications for baptism and admission to the church. But, following their characteristic caution, instead of throwing the doors wide open, the missionaries, if anything, tightened the criteria for a credible profession of faith. None were included, even in the list of catechumens, without evidence of sincerity and a change of life. None were baptised until a nine months probationary period had been completed. Yet notwithstanding this circumspection, Rev. Thomas Crosby Fulton of the Irish Presbyterian Church could report that, as a result of a single journey in 1897, he baptised two hundred and ninety-nine persons, adding that not one of them was the result of what he called 'the present rush', and adding that they been all on probation for some time. A little later, on a single round of his immense area and only able to call at each station once, he admitted four hundred and eight-one people to church membership.[6]

In reality the missionaries were caught up in a mass movement of Holy Spirit-induced church growth, which had its own divinely generated and humanly uncontrollable momentum. With literally thousands attracted to Christian faith, the words of Christ, which so often had been little more than a cliché, were now seen as literal truth: 'The harvest is plentiful, but the labourers are few.' Iza Christie prayed that both the Chinese evangelists and missionaries might be multiplied tenfold. Her hopes in regard of more missionaries were not fulfilled. In 1896, only twelve men and women came from Scotland, a few came from the Irish church, and the Danish Lutherans commenced their own nearby mission. Immediately after the war, the membership of the Manchurian church was estimated at under six thousand, but by the end of 1899 it was closer to twenty thousand. Moreover, Iza Christie testified that 'many of those who came in on this flood-tide of enthusiasm proved themselves afterwards most staunch followers of Christ.'[7]

Ross identified a further benefit conferred on the Chinese church by the Japanese war: the welcome exercise of a spirit of dependence upon God. This was exactly what he had sought to inculcate. For him, it was no sin to leave his converts in troubled times, though it would have been wrong had he neglected to teach them how to get on without him. 'We compel them,' he once wrote, 'to learn self-reliance – as far as human wisdom is concerned.'[8]

The necessity for change was recognised even within the palace at Beijing, though not by all. The young Guangxu Emperor, who had come to the throne in 1875, ruled under the sufferance of the Empress Dowager Cixi, who was *de facto* supreme ruler of China. In 1898, the restive Emperor seized an opportunity for effecting radical and far-reaching cultural, political, and educational change, by ushering in what has become known as the Hundred Days Reform. His modernising plans failed, however, when supporters of the Empress Dowager instigated a coup d'état. Cixi took over as regent, confining her nephew to the Summer Palace until his suspicious death in 1908. Six of the leading reformers were publicly executed. The Dowager Empress would only tolerate reforms that enabled her to consolidate her power over the Empire.

A further destabilising factor, playing into the hands of the conservative faction, had been a clamour by the western powers to establish their own spheres of influence in China. After the Japanese withdrawal in 1898, Britain leased the territory of Weihaiwei on China's north-east coast. Then, in Shantung province, the violent death of two German Catholic priests gave a pretext for the German appropriation of Kiaochow. Expansionist Russia gained a concession to run a branch of the Trans-Siberian Railway down the Liao-tung peninsula from Harbin, southwards through Mukden, Liaoyang and Newchwang to Port Arthur, in the hope of securing a warm water port as a base for its Pacific fleet, which was ice-bound in Vladivostok for much of the year. Yet other European powers put in their bids, causing in China a deep resentment and an increasing sense of injustice. The call for violent anti-foreign reaction steadily grew.

16

The Blood of Christians is Seed

We multiply when you reap us. The
blood of Christians is seed.

TERTULLIAN OF CARTHAGE

AMONG the traditionalist groups supporting the Qing dynasty was a Shantung occult martial arts secret society which combined belief in the spirit possession of their followers with martial arts 'boxing', as well as Tai Chi calisthenic rituals and deep-breathing exercises. All these elements, they believed, combined to make them invulnerable to injury from bullets or thrusts from edged-weapons. In 1898 the movement gained quasi-official approval. To reflect its new status, a new name was used; it was now known as the Yihequan. The most common contemporary English translation was 'Righteous Harmony Fists', or simply 'The Boxers'.

Most expatriates, missionaries included, saw the Boxer movement as militantly anti-Christian, but Ross disagreed. What lent credence to this view was the fact that the only foreigners most Chinese met were missionaries, whether Protestant or Catholic, and it was indisputable that some missionaries had allowed their zeal to outrun their prudence and had shown disrespect towards Chinese values and culture; yet, Ross acknowledged, on nothing like the scale as expatriates in the ports. The Roman Catholics had earned opprobrium by persistent disrespect of officials, defiance of the law, and by their leaders going about pompously with a retinue of armed men as if they were high officials.[1] A misunderstanding had also arisen over the meaning of the term 'convert'. In popular Chinese thinking a convert was someone who sided with foreigners 'bent on subverting Chinese rule and on changing Chinese customs'.[2]

If Ross saw the Boxers as anti-foreign rather anti-Christian, modern scholarship goes further, acknowledging that the motives behind the phenomena were highly complex, having their roots in traditional ideas of harmony and equilibrium, including aspects of environmental protection and cultural balance sometimes overlooked by older writers. In the eyes of the more conservative Chinese, the presence of foreigners in the land, the wars instigated by the machinations of foreign governments, the introduction of the Christian religion, and the adoption of western innovations such as railways and telegraph lines, had so upset the dynamic balance of Chinese cosmology (*feng shui*) that disaster seemed inevitable. This dissonance, it was argued, caused the destructive flooding of the Yellow and Yangtze rivers in four consecutive years from 1896, as well as the drought of early 1900, with resultant crop failures and widespread famine. Such imbalances, if left uncorrected, offered a gloomy prospect to traditional Chinese sensibilities, provoking deep anxiety.

Exacerbated by the thought that the greed-driven goal of the Western nations was to occupy China and deprive it of its wealth, Chinese insecurity was channelled into violent solutions that sought the complete eradication of western infrastructure, such as railways, telegraphs, hospitals, schools, church spires and the like, as well as the extirpation of all foreigners and their Chinese associates.[3] This was explicit in the Boxer's own propaganda. The missionaries at Mukden saw posters being pasted up inciting the population to get rid of foreigners on the grounds that 'Until this is done the heavens will withhold the much-needed rain; peace and prosperity will not return to the country.'[4]

Another popular slogan of late 1898 was 'Protect the Qing [dynasty], exterminate the foreign.' This slogan was articulated in posters pasted on walls, repeated in pamphlets, and passed on through village gossip. With a mobile population, such ideas spread with great rapidity along China's main transport arteries, bringing consternation to the missionary community, even in faraway Manchuria. Fears were exacerbated by stories of the destruction of railways, the burning and looting of foreign owned buildings, and, more ominously, the murder of Chinese Christians and two British missionaries. Then in June 1900, the Boxers rose and penned up foreigners in the Legation Quarter in Beijing. A large number of American and British missionary families were besieged in the British legation, and remained so until 14th August, when relieved by an international force under General Sir Alfred Gaselee.

Elsewhere in the country there was a mass slaughter of Christians. Estimates vary, but maybe as many as thirty-two thousand Chinese Christians were martyred, as well as two-hundred and thirty-nine foreign missionaries. The China Inland Mission lost fifty-eight adult missionaries and twenty-one children. The Christian and Missionary Alliance lost twenty-one missionaries, twelve children and three Chinese Christian assistants. In Manchuria the losses were lower: three hundred Chinese Protestants were killed, and no missionaries.

The Boxers arrived in Mukden on 10th June. Determined not to display anxiety, the missionaries kept calm and carried on with their plans for a relaxed picnic beside the river. But, as Iza Christie recorded, 'This was the last hour of unsullied quiet, for events moved quickly.' The attitude of the Governor-General, who was usually very friendly and supportive, abruptly changed. He permitted the Boxers to recruit openly and drill publicly. The intimidating slogan, 'Protect the Qing, exterminate the foreign,' was plastered all over the town. Perhaps, naively, the missionaries believed that popular opinion was still on their side, but fear of the occult powers of the Boxers appeared to have paralysed any local resistance. Another more ominous placard appeared on the walls calling on the populace to rise and burn every foreign building and drive out every foreigner. Dr Christie, inclined to play down the seriousness of the situation, became greatly alarmed to receive on 21st June a clandestine message from an envoy of the Governor-General disclosing that his change of attitude was due to the arrival of orders from Beijing, commanding the two local units of the Imperial Army in Mukden to drill in the red Boxer uniforms. The message warned Christie that it was no longer safe for the missionaries to remain.[5]

On 23rd June, the remaining women and children with Revs H. W. Pullar and J. Miller Graham, with Dr Christie escorting them, made their way to a station on the Chinese Eastern branch of the Trans-Siberian railway, about ten miles distant. Here Christie bid an anxious goodbye to his family and colleagues and hastily returned to the hospital, pausing only to warn the Russian stationmaster of the imminent danger. The stationmaster retorted that he could not desert his post. Christie subsequently heard that a few days later the station was attacked, and the stationmaster cruelly tortured before being murdered.

By Sunday 24th, the day proclaimed for the rising, only three missionaries remained in Mukden: Christie, his new medical colleague Dr W. A. Young, and Rev. T. C. Fulton of the Presbyterian Church in Ireland. Determined to stick it out with the Christian community to the bitter end, should it come to that, but also ready to beat a hasty retreat if prudence required, they prepared their horses for an emergency departure, before walking to church as usual. At the church they were met by around four-hundred Christians. The service commenced. A reading for the day included Romans 8.31: 'What then shall we say to these things? If God is for us, who can be against us?' This was taken as a providential signal to fortify fearful hearts. The service continued with extraordinary earnestness as prayers were offered for strength, guidance and protection. When it concluded, the congregation quietly dispersed, not to meet again for many months, and then only as a broken fragment of what had been.

Although large and ominous crowds gathered outside the church, there was no interference, and some Christians began to think that the danger might pass, and life return to normal. But later that day came news of the siege of the legations in Beijing. Pastor Liu, some of the elders, hospital assistants and others sent word asking the missionaries to meet them that evening. When they did, they were urged to leave speedily. The Chinese leaders were perplexed when the missionaries seemed inclined to reject their counsel and stay. One by one the Christians unitedly counselled against such an unwise decision; finally one of the hospital workers confronted the missionaries with the probable consequences of staying. 'If you remain,' said he, 'we will stand by you, and we'll all die together. If you go, your lives will be saved, and we can look after our families and ourselves.' There was no dispute. Early the next morning the missionaries, in disguise, made good their escape on Chinese carts. It was none too soon.

Sometime earlier there had been strong disagreement among the missionaries about what to do in the face of such an eventuality, so strong that it seems to have strained personal relationships. The doctors at Mukden – Christie and Young – were all for remaining whatever the personal risk, if necessary dying beside the Mukden Christians. Ross disagreed. A section in his book *Mission Methods in Manchuria,* published in 1903, but written much closer to the events, casts light on the issue. In discussing, in the abstract, asceticism in missionary service, including the question of self-sacrifice, Ross, citing the example of the Boxer uprising, warns of the dangers of holding fixed theoretical opinions and argues that the right decision can only be made in the light of circumstances. If, by remaining at his post and sacrificing his own life, the missionary might save the lives of others or alleviate their suffering, he hoped that most would not hesitate to do so. But he thought it was 'criminal rashness' to make oneself a martyr, adding: 'The man who in the service of his Master is not ready to encounter hardship, privation, danger, and sword, is not worthy of him. [But] the man who runs to meet avoidable danger ... is guilty of the sin of presumption.'[6]

Whichever way we read Ross' argument, it is hard to avoid the conclusion that it is in some degree a justification and exculpation of his own prompt withdrawal from Mukden, which to others, especially Christie and Young, may have seemed like running away, when they remained until the last moment. In mitigation it is worth noting that Ross was ten years older than Christie and almost thirty years older than Young. It may or may not be the case that this difference of opinion resulted in permanently strained relations, but it is a fact that in their three books, covering their long service with Ross in Manchuria, Dugald and Iza Christie only mention their neighbour and colleague a handful of times, and then with scant appreciation; though in 1934, in old age, Iza Christie contributed a warm appreciation of Ross in an article she contributed to a series on missionary pioneers for the Church of Scotland's periodical,

Life and Work.[7] Ross was equally sparing in his references to them, mentioning Dr Christie but twice in his *Missionary Methods*.

With the withdrawal of Christie and Young, all the Mukden missionaries had pulled back to Newchwang on the coast, one hundred and twenty miles to the south-west, where, over the following weeks, they received news of the destruction of their homes, the Dongguan church, the hospital, the Bible Society premises, and six preaching-chapels; but most distressing of all, they heard of the suffering of Chinese Christians. They learned that marauding bands of Boxers had found few Christians in the city. Like the others, Pastor Liu and his family had escaped by the skin of their teeth, though an evangelist had been caught in the street and cut down. Christians were given no quarter in this orgy of savagery: when caught they were butchered. Later, after passions had somewhat subsided, they were offered a chance of life if they would burn incense in a temple as a sign that they had renounced Christianity. Failing that, they were killed. Many, including women, school children, and even un-baptised catechumens, chose death. On the door of one preaching chapel hung eighteen Christian heads, a grisly testimony to undying faith. The majority of Christians who fell into the hands of the Boxers were decapitated, but death did not always come so swiftly or easily. Others were wrapped in cottonwool soaked with oil and burned alive. At least one was given the 'fiery crown', a thick ring of oily cottonwool placed around his head and set alight. Some suffered *lingchi*, a slow death by a thousand cuts, being given a fresh chance to recant after each slice.

Ross was able to verify one such horrid execution and its consequences. Li Ru Tang was captured but refused to deny Christ even though his eyebrows were cut off, then his ears and lips. When despite these appalling tortures, he still adamantly refused to abandon the faith, his heart was cut out and publicly displayed in a theatre as a warning to others. A fourteen-year-old girl was caught hiding in a field of millet; her Bible, from which she had refused to be parted, was the only incriminating evidence against her; but, when questioned, she unhesitatingly affirmed that she was a Christian. When asked if she was not afraid, she answered frankly:

'Afraid or not afraid, it is all one.' Ross heard that 'with a smile she met the sword that cut her down'.[8]

What is most moving about Ross' accounts of the deaths of Chinese Christians is the fact that most of them were people he knew intimately. In addition to Li Ru Tang, Ross could tell of a person called Wang, an old man named Swun, two deacons, Yieh and Chang, and most movingly Mrs Hsia, who was fervently singing the hymn *At the Gate of Heaven*, when they cut off her head with a single blow. And so on.

Others had most remarkable, indeed, miraculous escapes. A hospital dispenser, recognised by some soldiers, thought death was imminent, but a soldier told how after an accidental explosion he had been taken to the hospital and his life had been saved. The officer, moved by this account, freed the dispenser and invited him to accompany them for a number of days until safely away from the area. A student on his knees preparing himself for the blow of the sword that would end his earthly life was taunted by his executioner that, unlike the Christians, he was invulnerable to attack. To prove it, he frenziedly stabbed himself with his bayonet and fell seriously injured. The student shouted out that he could heal him. A swift bargain was struck that, if he did so, he and his father, but not his brother, could go free. The brother was immediately executed. The Boxer recovered, the bargain was honoured, and the student and his father walked free. In the Christian village of Hsia-fangshen two men were sentenced to be beheaded and left for dead. But despite severe lacerations to their necks, Ross reported that 'like Paul in similar circumstances, they both recovered.'

The resolve of some, however, failed under the intimations of their enemies, and they chose life by renouncing their faith. As evidence, a kitchen-god might be hung up, whilst others took to smoking opium or gambling to create the impression they were no longer Christians. There were those who, in a remarkable echo of the persecution by the Roman emperor Trajan in 250 A.D., burned incense to false gods set up by their persecutors. Whilst others, just like the North African Christians, bought and displayed recantation documents certifying that they had 'rejected the false and returned to the true'.

Among those unable to escape was Blind Chang, who at that time was visiting the beautifully named Valley of Victory. And such it was to prove. As the missionary closest to Chang, Dr Christie recorded the moving story:

> Chang was again in the Valley of Victory when the Boxer storm broke. It is a mountainous region where the concealment of individuals is not difficult, and he being a marked man was hidden away in the recesses of the hills, the faithful people sending him food. The band of Boxers, exasperated at losing their most conspicuous prey, threatened not only to kill the Christians, but to lay waste the whole valley with fire and sword. At last someone told Chang, and at once he came forth from his hiding-place and let himself be taken prisoner. He was brought to a neighbouring town whose headmen were allied with the Boxers, and in a temple was ordered to worship the idols or die.
>
> 'I can only worship the one living and true God.'
>
> 'But we will kill you.'
>
> 'That is of no importance, I shall rise again.'
>
> 'Will you not repent of your wickedness in following the foreigner?'
>
> 'I can only worship the one living and true God.'
>
> 'I have repented of all my sins.'
>
> 'Then you will believe in Buddha?'
>
> 'No, I believe in my Lord Jesus Christ,' and he began to preach to them.
>
> Afraid to kill him themselves, his captors sent some distance for some Boxers, and for three days Chang lay in prison. Then he was bound and taken through the town in an open cart, the Christians following behind, and marvelling at his fortitude as he joyfully sang the old hymn learned in the Mukden hospital, 'Jesus loves me, this I know.' Outside the town, in front of the temple, he was made to kneel down. 'Heavenly Father, receive my spirit,' he prayed. But still the sword tarried. A second and a third time he prayed, saying the same words. Then 'they gnashed on him with their teeth, and cried out with a loud voice, and ran upon him with one accord,' attacking him from behind with their swords, and cutting him to pieces.
>
> When the deed was done, the superstitious fears of the murderers began to work. He was a blind man, and therefore specially under the protection of spirits and demons. And what did he mean by 'rising again'? To prevent such a possibility they burned his body, and scattered the ashes on the mountain streams. Still their fears were

> not laid. He was a good man, so much so that he might become a god. His ghost was said to be haunting the place, and the Boxers departed precipitately, leaving the Christians of that district unharmed.
>
> Some years later the Government erected a monument to Chang's memory in the county town of that district, but none marks the resting-place of his ashes, for they are scattered afar, fit emblem of the Gospel he loved to preach. Indeed, he and the other martyrs have already 'risen again,' in the many churches and little Christian gatherings which have sprung up all over Manchuria since that terrible Boxer summer.[9]

After narrowly escaping from Mukden, Pastor Liu hid out in the fields with his family. Discovering there was a price on his head, he left his family in the care of trusted non-Christian friends and went on the run. Li struggled greatly to get food or even water. An imaginary fear that Christians might retaliate by poisoning the wells had led villagers to lock them at night. After more than once being recognised, Liu disguised himself as an itinerant Buddhist monk, but he was unconvincing, and people suspected him. Eventually he found work, and months later returned safely to Mukden, traumatised after witnessing the murder of a Christian women and being helpless to save her.

In August, after forty-one days of Boxer terror, the reform-minded Governor-General at Mukden heard by wire from Beijing that Boxer and Qing government forces were daily suffering defeats at the hand of the foreign coalition army as it swept towards the capital to liberate the legations. Now, with the Boxer's local ally, the Lieutenant-Governor, absent, the Governor-General seized the opportunity to bring the matter to a conclusion. He issued a proclamation denouncing the Boxers, then ordered his troops to kill every Boxer they could find. Many died, others fled, the remainder disappeared into the local population.

In the aftermath of the uprising, the church was perplexed with the old question of how to deal with those whose courage had failed and had denied the Faith. A missionary conference was set for 27th November 1900 in Newchwang to determine what guidance should be offered to the church, and what disciplinary measures, if any, ought to be taken against those who had denied the Faith. Once more, the missionaries failed to achieve unanimity. Dismissing the lapsed as

'Christians of a day', to whom 'it seemed a light thing to tell a lie', Dr Christie took the harder line, denouncing all who had bought their safety by defection.[10] James Miller Graham was more lenient, especially in regard to those who had made use of recantation documents:

> … it is only fair to state that most of them do not seem to have realised at the time the seriousness of their action. They regarded it merely as a temporary expedient for the saving of life, or as a means of escape from torture, but not as in any sense, implying a final abandonment of Christianity. As they themselves naively confess: 'By the grace of God we were permitted to tell a lie.' This, of course, reflects upon the imperfect development of many of the members, whose Christian faith, be it remembered, is but of yesterday.[11]

With such strong differences of opinion matters could not be resolved; it was not until six months later, in May 1901, when passions had subsidised, that a motion could be brought forward. It was proposed: 'That any Christian who during the recent persecution by word or act deliberately led another person to believe that he was not a Christian had denied his Lord.' This form of words satisfied a majority of seven, some abstained, but three opposed the motion. For Ross, Webster and Fulton, the statement was going too far. Not only did they vote against the proposal, but they also required their dissent to be recorded in the minutes. Regrettably, we do not know the precise grounds of their opposition as they did not require their dissent to be recorded with reasons, a provision available in Presbyterian church courts. We can, therefore, only conjecture that they found it distasteful to be acting as the conscience of the Manchurian Church, when its wounds were, in some cases, quite literally still raw, especially when they and their families had been able to get away to safety. Firm though Ross, Webster and Fulton could be in disciplinary matters, Ross especially, they nevertheless appear to have found it impossibly difficult to attempt to deal with such matters dispassionately, when memories of suffering friends loomed before them, and they were able vividly to recall the hideous pressures the Boxers put on the Christians to renounce the Faith.

The conference was none too confident in its conjoint mind, and so it passed a supplementary motion: 'That as a general rule only those should be regarded as having recanted who have publicly denied their faith.'[12] This was approved by ten, and two dissented. The two resolutions reflect the dilemma: how could the missionaries legislate for those who had failed the test of loyalty when faced with great cruelty, when they had come through persecution virtually unscathed?

Before we hasten to take sides, we do well to remind ourselves that the early church had also had some hard thinking to do about the same matter. The fierce third-century persecutions instigated by the Roman emperors Decius and Valerian had been designed to induce apostasy and reversion to paganism. They too had offered almost identical expedients for Christians to save their lives: burning incense to a god or purchasing a certificate of recantation. Just as the missionaries in Manchuria were of two minds, so too had been the leaders of the North African church. Some sided with the brave but maverick Tertullian of Carthage, who refused to receive back the lapsed. Others sided with Cyprian, Bishop of Carthage, who could not bring himself to see the lapsed as irredeemable, but called on them to face their weakness, confess their sins, demonstrate a spirit of true penitence, and in time be restored to fellowship and the sacraments. And, we ask, was that not the way of Christ himself, who was not only reconciled to those who had deserted and doubted him, but made a special point of asking for the shamefaced Peter who had so vehemently denied him?

It was, of course, Tertullian who famously said of the martyrs that their blood was the seed by which the Church multiplied, and so it proved in the days of the Boxers. In God's economy which determines every vicissitude for the good of his people, suffering, though painful, is productive. The bitter is sweet. The medicine is food. Under this redemptive regime, a sanctifying spiritual influence was felt, and the Manchurian Church matured.

One evidence of the work of the Spirit was a disinclination, both on the part of the Chinese Christians and the missionaries, to seek retribution. Nor is there any record of Manchurian Christians taking vengeful action. The Scottish and Irish missionaries were of the same mind as most Protestant missions, that reparation would send entirely the wrong signal and would not be sought nor accepted from the Chinese government, whether for damage to buildings or for loss of life. Ross and Fulton were appointed by the British government to negotiate reparation with high authority in north-east China, but they made only token demands. This may have disappointed British interests, and maybe some of their colleagues, but their graciousness endeared them and their cause to their Chinese interlocutors. When the Governor-General of Mukden insisted that some compensation be made for the losses the Christians had sustained, it was accepted only with the proviso that it was recognised that the recipients had chosen to abstain from any kind of litigation against those from whom they had suffered. As was pointed out at the time, this was something highly remarkable for a naturally litigious people. Generous monetary assistance to rebuild the shattered work came from supporters in Scotland and Ireland who had been greatly moved by accounts of the persecution.

Refusing reparation, the missionaries asked for a public proclamation legitimising their ministry, and perhaps, a tangible memorial to the martyrs. The Court of the Emperor issued an edict affirming the right of missionaries of the 'Jesus Religion' to build churches and preach in China, made it illegal, on pain of 'severe punishment without mercy,' to libel or harass Christians, and ordered the immediate return of all expropriated buildings. At least one copy of this proclamation has survived and is now in the Church of Scotland's collection of missionary records.

Rev. A. E. Glover, a missionary with the China Inland Mission in Shan-si Province, further west than Manchuria, who, with his colleagues, had suffered far more than had any of the United Presbyterian or Irish missionaries, vividly described his flight from the rebels, during which he lost his wife, as *One Thousand Miles of Miracles.* In retrospect he was able to say:

> I thank God, too, for the lessons he taught me through the spirit of brotherly love that prevailed in our midst .... No man sought his own, but each his neighbour's good [in] self-denial ... ministering to all ... in the very spirit of Christ's sacrifice. ... and how faithfully, zealously and self-forgetfully, [with] tender-heartedness, the outcome of meek submission to the known will of God, which was recognised at all time to be 'good, perfect and acceptable,' breathed through

> all our relations with one another, infusing into them a certain cheerfulness that killed irritability in the germ … for his right hand had holden us up, and his gentleness had made us great. To him be glory for ever. Amen.[13]

Ross, characteristically, said little of his family's relatively light privations, preferring to speak of the positive effect of the trials on the inner spiritual life of the Manchurian Christians:

> The conduct of Protestant Christians in Manchuria during and subsequent to the Boxer troubles has gained them a reputation, such as almost nothing else could secure, for the possession of a truly religious spirit, exhibited in the manner in which they bore persecution. Not one of them has been known to fire a shot or to strike a man. Nor, after deliverance came … did they seize the opportunity of wreaking vengeance on their persecutors.[14]

J. Miller Graham similarly summarised the spiritual gains brought by the persecution:

> Among the three hundred who were slain, there were many undoubted martyrs, men and women who had every opportunity given them to deny their Lord, but who steadfastly refused. Their heroic and noble witness has raised the native Church to a higher spiritual level …. It has done for Christianity what years of preaching could not have accomplished … the Church has emerged from its baptism of fire with a much-needed touch of other-worldliness upon it. To be a Christian is a matter of profounder import than hitherto realised. Faith has been vivified, and the personal relation of each believer to the Saviour more sharply defined. A deeper appreciation of the means of grace, and a new-born hunger for spiritual instruction now marks the assemblies of believers. In a word, the Church has perceptibly risen to higher spiritual levels. It may be temporarily reduced in numbers, but it has indisputably become purer in spirit.[15]

Subsequent history has shown that Graham was correct. After the Boxer persecution, there was no steep increase in the membership of the church as there had been after the first Sino-Japanese war. Even their enemies had been moved by the courage of the martyrs and awed by the fortitude of the Christians, and many would yet become followers of the Jesus Religion. For the survivors, however, their experience of living on the very brink of heaven itself had created an inward and hidden change, a great deepening of their spiritual life, a true reviving of Christian grace, giving what Graham called 'a touch of other-worldliness'. Many of these people would go on to lead the Manchurian church in coming years. Moreover, their experience had reinforced the importance of being independent of transient missionaries and those outside their immediate circle, thus putting into practice principles of church survival based on what they had learned from Ross and others.[16]

Meanwhile, over five thousand miles away in Scotland, many, though not all, saw another reason for optimism. In 1900, after protracted negotiations, not a few compromises, and a significant secession, the Free Church of Scotland joined with the United Presbyterian Church to form Scotland's largest denomination, the United Free Church of Scotland. This brought a breath of fresh air to the missionaries of both churches who, being less interested in maintaining denominational traditions and distinctives than in evangelising the world, unanimously joined the new church. The cost of union was highest to the Free Church, who in 1892 had suffered a secession by a substantial conservative, mainly Highland, minority affronted by the passing of a Declaratory Act accommodating both the voluntary United Presbyterians and those who felt unable to subscribe to the Westminster Confession of Faith on the old terms.

Back in China, some missionaries, including the young Roland Allen, felt less than optimistic about the future of Christianity in China. As an Anglican chaplain to the British legation in Beijing, Allen had had a grandstand view of the siege of Beijing and its brutal relief by the international force, whose severe actions have been described as 'illegal, immoral, and heinous.'[17] Throughout the siege and during its relief, he had kept a diary, which he later published as *The Siege of the Peking Legations*. Towards the end of his account, as he sailed down the Yongding river to safety, he angrily recalled the atrocities committed by the relief force and observed all around the devastation of war: Chinese villages in flames and dead bodies floating in the river or stranded upon its banks. It sent a chill up his spine:

> We shuddered to think of the deeds committed by Christian troops and of the effect which they must have upon the Chinese, and of the undying hatred which was being planted with ever-deeper and stronger roots in their minds.[18]

United Presbyterian and Irish Presbyterian missionary accounts of the uprising in Manchuria naturally focused on the towns and cities where they lived – Mukden, Liaoyang and Newchwang, etc. – as well as events of which they had received eyewitness accounts. They recorded little beyond. Which leaves us wondering what may have happened when the Boxers reached the Korean Christians in the northern Kando valleys. There too the litany of terror appears to have been the same, with violence and destruction raining down upon Christians fleeing for their lives, leaving behind their burning homes and churches. Dr Choi believes, however, that most of the Korean Christians in Manchuria escaped across the border to Korea or into Russian territory. He quotes a letter of Ross, dated 21st September 1901, in which he states: 'To-day I was glad to see … the colporteur, who originated the work in the Korean valleys. He and the evangelist Li Tai-gao, the ex-mandarin, escaped across to Korea.'[19] As James Webster observed, these refugees took with them the gospel, bringing Christ's love and hope wherever they went.

17

The Maturing of the Manchurian Church

It is hardly an exaggeration to say that
every Manchurian Christian is a missionary.
ALFRED COSTAIN[1]

Truth is not selfishly private.
EPISTLE FROM THE MANCHURIAN CHURCH.[2]

IN *Hamlet*, Shakespeare, pondering the problems of life, concluded that they rarely come singly: 'When sorrows come, they come not single spies, but in battalions.' Certainly, they did in Manchuria. To the battalions of the first Sino-Japanese War of August 1894 to April 1895 was added the Boxer forces of 1900, and then in February 1904 the Russo-Japanese hordes. Three times in a decade the second horseman of the Apocalypse rode his blood red steed across the land, taking peace from the earth and inflicting the ravages of military confrontation.

The latest conflict, in which so many Chinese suffered and died, was not the result of any quarrel of theirs. It was fought out by foreign powers on Chinese soil. Following Japan's victory in 1895, the interventions of Russia, Germany and France to force Japan to concede the territory it had conquered, opened the way for Moscow to occupy large parts of Manchuria. In 1897 Russia seized the warm water port of Port Arthur for its Pacific squadron and continued its 'conquest by railway', the extension of the Trans-Siberian Railway through the Liaodong Peninsula, with plans to penetrate deep into Korea. Although the Chinese nominally governed Manchuria, Russia was the real power, having intruded into the country a force of some one hundred and seventy-seven thousand troops, ostensibly to protect their railway network, but in reality as an army of occupation. Everywhere Russia's presence was evident. In Mukden the old pro-reform Governor-General had returned, but behind him was a Russian government official. In commercial life too Chinese institutions had been overtaken by Russian banks and trading companies. Russian soldiers, hated by the Chinese for their boorish and brutal behaviour, roamed the streets, threatening the security of Chinese homes and the safety of Chinese women. Ross reported that in Mukden, 'Under the Russians the utmost anarchy still prevails, and business is extinct in the city.' As a result, many were suffering, not least the Christians.[3]

After the First Sino-Japanese war, an international agreement required all Russian forces to be withdrawn from China by 1905. Yet by 1903 Moscow showed no signs of compliance; rather, with Japan again threatening the Korean peninsula, Moscow strengthened its position in Manchuria and was intent on military confrontation. It was against this unsettling background that the Mukden missionaries returned to rebuild their shattered work. Despite investment from the home churches, practical problems in securing skilled tradesmen meant that reconstruction of church buildings and hospitals had not begun, though work was underway on some of the houses as well as the women's hospital. In the meantime, Dr Christie rented a building for a dispensary which might also accommodate a few inpatients. Many of his old assistants flocked back to serve under him once more.

The missionaries felt they were living on top of a gunpowder keg waiting for a careless spark to send everything sky-high. On 8th February 1904, that spark was provided by Japan declaring war on Russia, having three hours earlier launched a sneak attack on the Russian fleet at Port Arthur, crippling two battleships and a heavy cruiser. Mukden was placed under martial law. Acting on British consular advice, the missionary families once again evacuated, this time to Pei-Tai-Ho, a pleasant seaside resort, four hundred and thirty miles southwest around the Liaotung Gulf.

From April to December, Japan bottled up the Russian fleet in Port Arthur. In August, with a major land battle at Liaoyang seeming imminent, Christie and Ross determined to return to Mukden. Their journey, although difficult, was eventually successful and they arrived safely, just before battle commenced on 24th August. The Russian failure to gain the offensive led them on 3rd September to retreat northwards towards Mukden, there to await reinforcements arriving by railway. A week later, tens of thousands of dejected Russians and droves of displaced Chinese descended on the city. The Governor-General set up a local relief committee, under the direction of two Chinese officials, together with Dr Christie and James Inglis, who were also official agents of the Red Cross, as was James Webster at Newchwang. Reuter's correspondent covering the war was the twenty-two-year-old Lord Brooke who, in his *An Eye Witness in Manchuria*, commended in the highest possible terms the missionaries' diligence in caring for suffering refugees:

> The Chinese Relief Committee worked hand in hand with the British missionaries, who proved the truest helpers of the refugees, as they could care for the sick and wounded as well as for the destitute. Dr Christie, Dr Ross, Dr Young, Mr Inglis, Mr Pullar, and Mr Fulton, all members of the Scotch or Irish Protestant missions in the city, were untiring in their care of these poor people, giving them food and lodging, clothes and money to the utmost extent of their ability. Besides this, Dr Christie and Dr Young, assisted by Chinese medical students they had themselves trained, relieved hundreds of the Chinese wounded in their magnificent hospital.[4]

Throughout the winter months the medical work was sustained, though it was exhausting and harrowing. The sufferings of the civilian population were terrible; neither of the armies had any care whatsoever for their safety. Christie documented Russian atrocities, including systematic destruction of Chinese homes and the summary execution and torture of non-combatants. In February 1905, it was deemed safe for Iza Christie and the children to return to Mukden. The decision was ill-advised as they arrived just before the battle of Mukden commenced on 20th February. Once again, Japan gained the upper hand and drove the Russian forces into retreat. On 7th March, the missionaries saw a seemingly unending line of disconsolate Russians limping northwards out of the city. On 9th March a severe dust-storm hindered the withdrawal, but after a brief artillery barrage at dawn on the 10th, the guns suddenly fell silent. The city had fallen, and the Japanese entered unopposed. Dr Christie and his staff hardly had time to notice the Russian ebb and the Japanese flow, as they found themselves treating patients from both armies, as well as indigenous Chinese, all of whom sought shelter under the neutral sign of the Red Cross.

With the arrival of peace after a decade of appalling devastation, death and destruction, the missionary community and the church took stock, sought to evaluate its present strength, and began making tentative plans for future advance. Surprisingly, the overall picture was not discouraging. Evaluating the growth of the missionary force, in the period between the death of William Burns in 1867 and 1905, J. W. Inglis counted fifteen men and twenty women with the Irish Mission, and fifteen men and twenty-two women with the United Free Church of Scotland. The total of seventy-two missionaries might seem impressive, but they seemed few when compared to an estimated twenty million Manchurians.[5] Nevertheless, he reckoned that the total baptised membership of the congregations within the Presbytery of Manchuria now stood at a heartening eleven thousand, five hundred and eight-four, with a further three and a half thousand catechumens under instruction.[6] Ross calculated differently and thought the number was more than twenty-seven thousand on the rolls of the Church, either as baptized members, or as accepted applicants for baptism.'[7] Iza Christie offered a mediating figure of almost twenty thousand.[8]

Whatever the true number was, both Ross and Inglis agreed that it was due to the evangelism carried on by the Chinese themselves, both as official agents and as spontaneous witnesses to the gospel. Ross beautifully visualised the process:

> Under the shadow of a great elm or willow on a summer evening, or seated on the hot *kang* [communal bed in an inn] on the long winter

> nights, the neighbour who knew has instructed his fellow-villager who was ignorant. Among the endless stream of foot-travellers toiling north or south on the main road, the rare Christian among them introduced the doctrines of grace into the conversation with which travellers always beguile the tedium of their long journey .... On one occasion I came in contact, at a village in the eastern hills, with a quiet and apparently respectable Roman Catholic, who had been there fifteen years, and who declared that no one there knew him to be a convert. Of our own people I have never known one who would be as many days in a place without letting some people know of his Christianity. Hence it is that Christianity has so marvellously and so rapidly spread over so great an extent of country.[9]

Ross was disinclined to draw too close a connection between the growth of the Church and the efforts of missionaries. Indeed, missionaries had often discovered how Chinese Christians had gone ahead of them, so that when examining people for baptism they discovered that many had first heard the gospel from ordinary Chinese Christians who had witnessed to them in the course of their everyday occupations. It was much better to describe growth in simple organic New Testament terms as the spontaneous expansion of the church through the witness of ordinary Christians. That was generally the way in which the work went on: a father taught his children, an employer his men, a labourer his fellow-workmen. This was the way in which the power of the Spirit was manifest. This was the way by which the glory of God was revealed. With this John Ross was content.

Much better than disputing statistics, is to join in the joy of the missionaries, when in their gatherings, they sang the words of the Scottish Metrical version of Psalm 126:

> Who sow in tears, a reaping time
> of joy enjoy they shall.
>
> That man who, bearing precious seed,
> in going forth doth mourn,
> He doubtless, bringing back his sheaves,
> rejoicing shall return.

As the number of baptised members grew, three things became evident. The first was the necessity of organising a united indigenous church on a contextualised Presbyterian basis. Second was the challenge of evangelising Chinese women and training them to reach their sisters. The third was to establish a proper theological course to train an indigenous ministry.

From 1872 onwards, there had always been the possibility of two churches emerging in Manchuria, one started by the Irish missionaries, the other loyal to the United Presbyterians. As each would have been little more than a clone of the other, it was fortunate that both churches agreed that, while historical differences and divisions might be tolerated at home, they ought never to be exported to China. According to Webster, Ross proposed a somewhat utopian solution: the cooperation of the two missions in producing a single church. Even more surprisingly, the General Assembly of the Irish Church and the United Presbyterian Synod agreed. Each mission would have its own home support base, but in China there would be a joint missionary conference and one Manchurian Presbyterian Church. The union became a reality in May 1891 at a conference in Mukden when an interim Presbytery of Manchuria was established. Ross describes what happened:

> The first meeting was composed of the foreign missionaries only, and was conducted in English. One of the first resolutions, however, was that the presbytery should be the Church Court of the [Chinese] Church, which would be called the Presbyterian Church of Manchuria; and that all its business should be transacted in the Chinese language. It was resolved that meantime every foreign missionary be a member of this presbytery, till the Chinese should have become familiar with the transaction of business. As [Chinese] elders were not numerous, and as it was desirable they should all become as speedily as possible acquainted with the forms of business, every elder was made a member of presbytery. Now the elders outnumber the foreigners; but the reasons are still in force which made them all members in the beginning. They have taken an increasing interest and share in the proceedings, so that they have the largest share of the speaking, and virtually all the voting.[10]

The following year the first proper meeting of the presbytery was convened, with Chinese elders outnumbering foreign missionaries. As the proceedings of the previous year had been in English, they were not considered to be binding until they had been thoroughly discussed in Chinese, amended as necessary, voted on by the presbytery, and finally minuted in Chinese. This indigenisation stemmed directly from Ross' *de facto* leadership of the missionary community. He abhorred the patronising tendencies too common among foreign missionaries that led them to dominate the local church. Rather, he insisted that the Chinese church, guided by Scripture and the Holy Spirit, should make decisions for itself. Ross' *Mission Methods* provides us with a clear insight into the rationale behind the procedures adopted by the interim presbytery:

> National differences will have their own influence on the future development of the Church, though in everything affecting the moral character and conduct their mind will become more and more assimilated to ours the more thoroughly [we both] become leavened by the spirit of the teachings of Jesus. They have meantime their own ideals, and to some things they and we attach varying degrees of importance. Hence a possible difficulty in presbytery. The safest way, however, is to let the Chinese decide their own affairs from their own sense of right; while we carefully instruct them … till they perceive the [Scriptural] duty. They should never be compelled to act in a certain way merely because it is the will of the foreigner. Coercion is unwise. True religion is ever voluntary and hearty. Whatever is opposed to this makes religion a bondage and a burden. Obedience to a purely arbitrary rule, whose living principle does not evoke a corresponding response in an enlightened conscience, is of no moral value. Nay, is it not true that 'whatever is not of faith is sin'? Faith, to be worthy of the name, must be intelligent. It is worthy of the name only when the man is 'fully convinced in his own mind.' The divorce of reason from religion is suicidal. Hence the necessity for endless instruction—the great duty of the missionary.[11]

The presbytery also decided to draft a creedal statement for the church, and fix terms of admission and rules of conduct for its members. Additional procedures would be prepared for the proper functioning of local elders in their congregations and also as members of the presbytery. There would be arrangements for the election and installation of deacons, elders, and pastors, as well as a directory of worship with forms of services, including those for life events such as marriage and burial. Great care was taken to make all these both authentically Chinese and thoroughly biblical, carefully 'eliminating … whatever savoured of idolatry,' whilst retaining non-idolatrous Chinese customs. These documents took almost ten years to complete.

It must have been with great satisfaction and gratitude to God that Ross and his missionary colleagues saw legislation enacted by their Chinese colleagues, entrenching in the constitution of the church the key principles they had themselves followed. Most importantly, these were the ultimate authority of Holy Scripture as the only rule of faith and conduct, the desire to adopt a credal statement, and their loyalty to Ross' conviction that an authentic indigenous church should be, as far as possible, self-supporting, self-propagating and self-governing.

The presbytery initially consisted of the ministers and elders of the Newchwang and Dongguan (Mukden) churches, which also included the many preaching stations and groups connected with the Dongguan congregation, in an area with a radius of over twenty miles, while to travel through all the groups connected with the Newchwang church took up to five days. Later, other congregational districts were formed and incorporated into the presbytery, including one for the Kando valleys. Eventually the presbytery was made up of representatives from fourteen such districts.

So much for the presbytery, a domain of men, but that left to be addressed a challenge that had been present from the very beginning. A significant weakness in the church had been the low number of women members and catechumens. Chinese women required specialised sympathetic and contextualised training and support if they were to win other Chinese women. For obvious cultural reasons it was impossible for male missionaries to provide this training, and not at all easy for foreign women. The challenge could only adequately be met by well-trained Chinese Bible-women.

The first attempt to address the issue was the arrival of Miss Barbara Pritty, who came to Mukden with John and Isabella Ross when they returned from furlough in 1881. Miss Pritty had been recruited by the United Presbyterian Church Zenana Mission founded the same year. The word *zenana* was borrowed from Hindi and meant the segregated women of a Muslim *harem*, or its equivalent in other cultures. Zenana missions, then, were missions for women by women, organised and financed by women's committees at home. Miss Pritty was the first of the United Presbyterian zenana missionaries.

Showing considerable initiative, she opened a small boarding school for around fifteen girls to provide basic instruction in Christian doctrine and Bible knowledge. The school continued under her direction until 1886, when she married Rev. Thomas Fulton of the Irish Presbyterians, leaving Isabella Ross and Eliza Webster temporarily in charge until a Miss Struthers and a Miss Wilson arrived from Scotland towards the end of 1890. Miss Wilson's health broke down almost immediately, and the following year Miss Struthers married Rev. George Douglas.[12] In Mukden, the Zenana Mission was doing sterling work in providing missionary wives, but it was much less effective in securing Chinese female evangelists.

In Liaoyang, fifty miles south of Mukden, after the death of Rev. Alexander Westwater in 1886, his widow stayed on to run a girl's elementary school, to preach at services for women open to the gospel, and to start a small training home for Bible-women. Through the work of four of her trainees, well-attended Sunday services for women were commenced. These in turn fed into a weekly inquirers class. Within a very short time fourteen women sought baptism. One described her conversion in these striking terms:

> We used to feel as if we were walking in the dark; we knew that we must die some day, but we did not know where we were going. Now we are walking in the light, and know that when we die we are going to the heavenly home which Jesus has prepared for us, and we have nothing to fear.[13]

Such testimonies confirmed how important it was for Manchurian Christian women to be trained as evangelists and Bible teachers to their countrywomen. It was even more true of women than it was of men, that Chinese agency became the method which God most blessed.[14] Many Bible-women came from very humble backgrounds, but that did not mean that their spiritual or intellectual abilities were limited, as the moving story of Mrs Liu demonstrates.

In the early 1890s, largely due to the hard work of a Chinese evangelist called Chao, a new church had been established in Shuang-cheng-pu, north of Mukden. The congregation soon had more than twenty-five baptised members, among them a Mr and Mrs Liu. Liu had been slow to respond to the gospel, but not so his wife. Unable to read until she came in contact with the Bible, she quickly learned, readily understood and wholeheartedly accepted what she read. She sought and received baptism. Mrs Liu was a woman of considerable intellectual ability and deep spirituality, and the Rev Daniel T. Robertson was greatly moved when he came to baptise her:

> She stood so modestly, … and yet I felt like Samuel anointing David, for I knew a genuine religious earnestness stood before me, humble, contrite, and pure, and I saw one of our future Bible-women in the north, – a Manchu woman, strong, clever, and earnest.[15]

In 1901, after the Boxer terror, Miss Mary Davidson arrived to re-establish the training of Bible-women at Mukden. In March 1902, she wrote home about plans she had to hire a room and open a girls' school; but on further reflection, she changed tack, and in May notified the *Women's Missionary Magazine of the United Free Church* that, in the aftermath of the uprising, her priorities had changed:

> … it will be impossible for foreign women to take up their former method of work of itinerating in the towns and villages, and more dependence than ever will be placed in the Bible-women. More and more of our time and strength will thus be devoted to the work of fitting them for this important work.

Mary Davidson continued her work until, by 1913, many of her students had become colporteurs and evangelists in their own right, each doing work that no foreign missionary could ever have done.

At the end of the Sino-Japanese war, while Dr Christie and his medical colleagues busied themselves reinstating the Mukden hospital and its medical services, John Ross found himself engaging in what was to become the main activity of the last period of his active missionary service – the establishment, delivery and administration of theological training for the Manchurian church. This was no sudden notion, but the logical outcome of a process.

In *Mission Methods*, Ross describes the evolution of theological training in Manchuria. In the early days, the missionary was able to spend considerable time with each new Christian, giving daily instruction and encouraging their spiritual, intellectual and moral growth. The criteria for determining who was best suited to be an evangelist was both practical and simple. An evangelist was chosen for his 'earnest and influential piety'. To put it another way, a man was trained to be an evangelist who had already proven himself adept at winning others for Christ.

Just before the outbreak of the Sino-Japanese war in 1894 it was evident that this informal arrangement was breaking down under the sheer weight of numbers. It needed to be replaced by a properly thought-out theological training scheme. The pressure increased markedly after the war when scores, even hundreds, of men sought training. Under Ross' new measures, student evangelists were placed with established senior evangelists, men in charge of a preaching chapel. Their mornings were dedicated to studying a set course of reading, their afternoons and evenings to gaining experience of evangelistic preaching, assisting with corporate worship for the believers, and instructing baptismal candidates. Each spring, usually in April, the students were brought into Mukden, where they lived in community for a month attending a course of lectures arranged by Ross, who was helped by Webster, Wylie and Inglis.

The curriculum consisted of four subjects each year; each was related to biblical and theological disciplines, with the exception of a short course on aspects of Confucianism, included at Ross' behest. For example, in one year Ross taught First Corinthians, T. C. Fulton taught Joshua and Judges, and James Inglis taught the Shorter Catechism.

Though some may have looked askance at classes on Confucianism, Ross' reasoning was sound. Not only did he know how ignorance of or clumsy attacks against Confucianism were detrimental to the credibility of Christians, Ross also saw how an appreciation of the *Analects,* when compared with Scripture, exposed how unfitted they were to lift people out of sin, deliver them from the burden of guilt and reconcile them to God. This class excited great interest among the students, resulting in 'keen discussions which took place in the evenings, when the members were by themselves, indicating the thoughtful interest that was awakened.'[16]

At one level this proved that the 'Manchurian convert has not been asked to shed his patriotism, nor his child expected to grow up ignorant of his national literature.' At a higher level, traditional wisdom was shown to be impotent in changing a person's heart or providing the comfort of pardon and the assurance of acceptance by God.[17] It was perhaps never better said than it was in a remarkable communication from the embryonic Manchurian Presbyterian Church to the United Presbyterian Synod meeting in Edinburgh in 1888:

> Truth is not selfishly private. Through the close investigation of ancient times, we find that the proclamation of the doctrine of heaven was not unknown in Flowery China. We acknowledge the value of the Six Classics and the Four Books; but how could Confucius and Mencius repair the ruins of man's heart? Happily Heaven has not forsaken the Flowery Nation, though the Lord of Salvation was born in Judea, at length the doctrine, able to make all under heaven one family, has entered the Central Flowery Land.[18]

Students showing an aptitude for ministry could be fast-tracked into a senior pre-ordination course. Someone who was struggling academically, and might be judged unsuitable for ordained ministry, might yet become a senior evangelist, provided he could demonstrate good preaching ability, tact in his relations with others, and responsibility and faithfulness in the conduct of his work. He might eventually be given sole responsibility of running a distant station. But if he lacked what Ross called 'the moral backbone needful to face the duties and temptations of a remote station', he would likely be located near a missionary and under his close supervision.

Such was the scheme as it ran for the first five years or so, but Ross was dissatisfied; he longed to establish a proper, centralised theological institution in Mukden: a Theological Hall. Hindered by the outbreak of the Russo-Japanese war, this was eventually organised with Ross and T. C. Fulton as the first full-time teachers. As had been the case with the old scheme, the Mukden college course for students for ordination was part-time, spanning only the winter months of October to April, when movement was more restricted and itinerant work not easily undertaken. With Ross keen to include as many church workers as possible in formal training, the college also provided courses for junior evangelists and classes for Bible-women.

No scheme of theological training ought to be assessed by the quality of its buildings, the excellence of its facilities or even by the calibre of its teachers. Ultimately its only test is the quality of the ministers it produces. Certainly, many students were extremely diligent. Ross remarked that although the Chinese usually retire early to bed, it was often midnight before students went to sleep. Conscientious application of traditional learning methods resulted in students becoming extremely proficient at learning the lectures by rote. Some could memorise a number of lectures in their entirety. One, who sat thirteen papers, each with a possible score of one-hundred marks, was able to earn an average of ninety-eight percent. Half the students exceeded ninety, and even the lowest was awarded seventy-one and a half. But Ross understood the dangers of such learning, and throughout his time as Principal longed for his students to be both 'spiritually fired and intellectually illumined'.[19] As he put it in reports in the *Missionary Record,* the aim of the Theological Hall was turn out people who were 'the cream of the theological training of many years', men of 'scriptural enlightenment and sound judgement, as well as sterling piety.'

The very first student to pass successfully through the college course set the bar very high for his successors. As a young Christian, he had suffered much for his faith, but was glad of it. His name was Liu Chuen-yao, a onetime pupil of Blind Chang. He became a highly regarded senior evangelist, one of the first deacons in the Mukden Dongguan church, and later it was his name which was on the call from the church when it was seeking its first Chinese pastor, and it was Liu who was called to be the first moderator of the Presbytery of the Manchurian Presbyterian Church. This latter appointment delighted Ross and led him to remark that Liu had now been 'placed officially on an equality with the foreign missionary'.[20] Then, following that heady time, Liu experienced the ferocious Boxer persecution and was driven into hiding, from which, as we have seen, he did not emerge unscathed. Yet, having passed through the fires, he once more took his place as the much loved and highly esteemed minister of Dongguan.

In those busy days, when he was establishing the theological college, there were heavy demands on Ross' time, as many sought his help. J. Miller Graham, then secretary of the Manchuria Missionaries' Conference, sought to relieve the pressure by informing the committee in Scotland, and his missionary colleagues too, that:

> Ross's time being thus almost wholly occupied with teaching, they [other missionaries] cannot reckon on him for the ordinary work of the station as hitherto; it is of the most urgent importance that the scheme for the training of native pastors be entered upon at once, and with enthusiasm, if they are to gather up the rich spiritual harvesting of the past three years.[21]

Although Graham was without doubt correct that Ross' time was 'almost wholly occupied with teaching' and he could spare precious little for other things, there was an exception: his hobby of botany. In an early report published in the *United Presbyterian Missionary Record*, Ross couldn't restrain himself from remarking on the rich wild flora everywhere around him: 'a thick undergrowth of flowering bushes, with wild grape and other creeping plants, all are nature's planting.' He noticed too the cultivated fruit trees – apricot, peach, pear, cherry – that had been planted on the slope of the hill up which he was walking. Looking out from the height, his keen eye took in the plain dotted with orchards and covered with millet, wheat and barley. All this fruitfulness he saw as a living parable: 'The day will come when the district will be as fruitful spiritually .... The great Husbandman will yet apply the chemistry of his truth to destroy or counteract the unproductiveness, and the natural excellency of the soil will appear in bringing forth fruit many fold .... The process is commenced; God speed it!'[22]

On another occasion, he enthusiastically, though incidentally, shared some of his discoveries with readers of the *Chinese Recorder and Missionary Journal* in 1875.[23] Among the proliferation of wildflowers Ross saw in China were many that he could not identify from his copies of Cardale Babington's *Manual of British Botany* (1843) and John Loudon's *Encyclopaedia of Plants* (1866).

On his journeys around Manchuria, he kept his eyes open for such interesting plants, sending specimens, carefully labelled, to the professionals at Kew Gardens for identification and classification. One collection was the first of its kind ever seen in Europe. Ross' botany was taken seriously, and his collections written up in *The Linnean Society Journal* by J. G. Barker and S. Le Marchant Moore, under the title 'A Contribution to the Flora of Northern China.'[24]

As well as collecting for Kew, Ross also was in touch with Emil Bretschneider, a botanist and sinologist of Baltic German ethnicity, who from 1866 to 1883 was physician to the Russian legation to Pekin. In 1898, Bretschneider published *The History of European Botanical Discoveries in China* in which a number of Ross' specimens are listed. Bretschneider also records that two of Ross' collections, one sent to The Linnaean Society and the other to himself, included a number of 'novelties'. In other words, these were plants hitherto unknown to western science, five of which were named in honour of the discoverer: *Anemone rossii, Viola rossii, Saxifraga rossii* (renamed in 1935 as *Mukdenia rossii*), *Iris rossi* and *Tovaria rossi*.[25]

Productive hunting grounds for Ross included ancient cemeteries close to Mukden where early Manchu Emperors had been laid to rest, as well as at Fenghuang where in 1875 he gathered specimens for the professionals both at the Corean Gate itself and from the banks of the Yalu river. In his ability to see beyond books and work, Ross shows a refreshing and life-affirming appreciation not only of the work of grace in the lives of those he came to win for Christ, but by carefully considering the lilies of the field, he celebrated the rich fabric of his Father's world. A few paragraphs from the *Chinese Recorder and Missionary Journal* are worth recording:

> Some hills were well covered with oak and hazel saplings, used to feed the silkworms; the greater number were bare as they could be, their wood long ago cut down for fuel. The willow and elm trees of the plain were also found in the glens. One variety of poplar, very handsome with white bark resembling birch, reminded one of the aspen with its tremulous leaves; another variety was like the home poplar. The ash occurs, and the birch, though infrequent. Several varieties of thorn were common; the haws of the dog-rose abounded over thirty or forty

> miles. One graceful tree called *sai* had small elm-like leaves. The inner bark of another, the *dwan* tree, was used by some of the natives in long narrow strips for a waterproof coat; chestnut and walnut trees abound, but not by the road side. The fir is not common; mistletoe of two varieties, one with yellow the other with scarlet berries, is plentiful. There were also some berry-bearing shrubs, which I did not recognise.
>
> The only flowers surviving were compositæ, various shades of blue, pink, yellow and white, outer row only ligulate, but very large. A lovely gentian grew everywhere, sometimes attaining a foot in height. One very large blue flower, the petals of which were just withering, is well known to the Chinese herbalist. Another flower was precisely like the blue bell of Scotland, but had a very different leaf.
>
> On some large old firs battling for life on the top of a high and steep hill which I scaled, I saw a woodpecker the size of a thrush, its variegated green plumage reminding one of a cockatoo. The natives call him the 'mountain magpie,' on account of his cry. Another woodpecker of similar size, with a rich scarlet throat, is also said to be seen only on the higher mountains.[26]

The new missionary of 1872, coming to China with eyes wide open to all that was new, had by the beginning of the twentieth century become a shrewd observer of the complexities of China whether geographical, political, religious, cultural, anthropological, linguist or, indeed, botanical. Now in his early sixties, Ross was a respected missionary statesman who still did not spare himself. Although in declining health, he remained active in teaching at the Theological Hall, instructing the Chinese evangelists and Bible-women, supporting the newly established Arts College, and yet always found time to stop and stare wonderingly at the flowers at his feet.

18

Revival in Korea

Terrible agony on account of sin and great joy
and peace resulting from confession of it.
REV. GRAHAM LEE, PYONGYANG.

THE Korean church expanded spontaneously and very remarkably in the two decades following the distribution of Ross' Korean New Testament in the Kando valleys of Manchuria and in Korea itself. The part of the church planted by Ross' Korean colporteurs and evangelists came under the care of North American Presbyterian missionaries in 1892, and by the early twentieth century it was a flourishing and mature church. The first American Northern Presbyterian missionary to Korea was Horace Grant Underwood, who arrived at Inch'ŏn, twenty miles southwest of Seoul, on Easter morning 1885. With Underwood came Northern Methodist Episcopal missionary Henry Gerhard Appenzeller. Unlike the strained relations that existed between the Irish Presbyterians and Scottish United Presbyterians in Manchuria a decade or so earlier, the relation of American Methodist and Presbyterian was very cordial; and, despite a number of long-established doctrinal differences, the missionaries of both traditions cooperated closely with each other, sometimes socialised together, and found themselves caught up in the revival of 1907.

As much of the following narrative focuses largely upon the Presbyterian missionaries, it is worthwhile sketching in an outline of their Methodist friends. From the very beginning, a marked feature of the Methodist approach was sensitivity to the Korean government's prohibition of Christian evangelisation, coupled with a keen awareness of the violent persecution of Korean Christians two decades earlier, in which it is said as many as two thousand Catholics had perished.[1] As there were no restrictions on evangelising Japanese people in Korea, Henry Appenzeller commenced his work among them, whilst also gaining royal approval for a school for young men which he established in 1887. The Methodists would become leaders in the provision of Christian-based modern Korean education.

When the ban on Christian public worship was lifted in 1887, Appenzeller founded the Bethel Chapel, later to be known as Chong Dong First Methodist Church, of which he was lifelong pastor, though he depended greatly upon Korean leadership. The same year he baptised a Korean convert, Park Jung-sang, who, it appears, first heard the gospel in Japan. By 1894, Appenzeller had opened a bookshop, was editing two English-language journals aimed at making Korea better known in the West, had established a publishing house, the Trilingual Press, which produced the first Korean-language newspaper, and had also established a theological school. He died, aged only forty-four, in 1902, in a shipping disaster.[2]

Much as the United Presbyterians had done in Manchuria, the Methodists in Korea undertook work among Korean women through the agency of trained Bible women. By 1898, Mary F. Scranton, the mother of Appenzeller's colleague Dr William B. Scranton, and the first Methodist female missionary, was employing eight Korean Bible women in Seoul, and had established a women's training school.[3] A decade earlier, in mid-1886, she had set up a school for girls which, in the following year, gained official recognition by the government conferring upon it the name of *Ewha Haktang* (Pear Blossom School).[4]

Although Appenzeller's work was focused largely on the region around Seoul, he set out in 1888 on an exploratory journey to Pyongyang with the Presbyterian Horace Underwood. He and Underwood discovered, what other missionaries who explored the country also found, that the way had often been opened up before them by Koreans directly or indirectly influenced by Ross.[5] As the number of converts grew, the missionaries noted a significant change. Instead of having to go out to make converts, so attractive had the Christian message become through the advocacy of Korean Christians, that people came to the missionaries seeking Christ for themselves and asking for instruction.

A second wave of Methodist work, led by Clarence F. Reid of the Southern Methodist Mission, commenced in 1896. This too saw significant success establishing, within a decade, churches at Seoul, Kaesŏng and Wonsan. In the period between 1896 and 1905 the Methodists saw very significant growth, described by one historian as 'beyond missionary control'.[6] One missionary reported there were 'groups of believers springing up all over the territory, even in places that have not been visited by a missionary but only native helpers.'[7] Edward Poitras summarised the salient features of Korean Methodism as 'evangelical spirit, fidelity to the Bible, concern for social justice and Korean independence.'[8]

Attention is sometimes drawn to the greater numerical growth that the Presbyterians saw, and the popular explanation is offered that this was largely attributable to the implementation of the so-called Nevius Method, a range of strategies formulated by John Livingstone Nevius, but very similar to those developed earlier by John Ross. That may, however, overstate the case, as reasons for church growth are rarely attributable to any single issue. Indeed, where Methodists and Presbyterians worked side-by-side they often adopted different methods but nevertheless saw similar growth.[9] Both missions benefitted from the foundational work undertaken by Korean evangelists trained by John Ross.

Whatever the similarities of their strategies for church planting and nurture, Ross and Nevius diverged significantly in the degree to which they were comfortable to conform their personal life to the prevailing culture. Moving to Chefoo in 1871, Nevius had not 'gone native', as his fellow expats might have disdainfully described it. Ross and his Scottish colleagues, however, followed the practice of William Chalmers Burns and his protege James Hudson Taylor, generally wearing Chinese dress, enjoying Chinese food, constructing their buildings according to Chinese architectural style, and carefully conforming to Chinese social etiquette. The American Presbyterian pioneers were different, despite knowing how much their foreign ways amused the Koreans. William N. Blair tells how, when they were first seen in the streets of Pyongyang, the Koreans thought them 'crazy', with their great height, white hair, large beak-like noses, and startlingly narrow trousers.[10] What had been more or less an unthinking retention of American dress and ways, changed to a formal policy when cultural compliance was actively discouraged following the suicide of William J. Mckenzie in June 1895. Mckenzie's death was bizarrely attributed to his habit of wearing a small Korean hat, which, it was said, did not adequately shield his head from sunstroke, exacerbating his mental insanity. But more of McKenzie in due course.

Despite superficial differences, the missionaries of both denominations were evangelicals, agreeing that there is salvation in no other name than the name of Jesus, and working sacrificially and diligently to establish churches based on what they understood to be biblical principles. In Korea, as in Manchuria, the result was a church that was zealous in witnessing, delighting in prayer and Bible study, generous in giving to support the work, and with members eager to play their part in the church's spiritual oversight. One difference, however, was that by 1890 the Manchurian Presbyterian Church was under Chinese control, but the Korean Presbyterian church, though strong, was only semi-independent. Encouraged by the church's general state, the calibre of its pastors and elders, and a promising group of ordinands due to graduate from the theological seminary in 1907, the American Presbyterians chose that year as the time when they would relinquish control in favour of Korean leaders.

The closer the date came, however, the more uneasy the missionaries became. It was hard to let go. The patronising instinct, built on a sense of western superiority, was strong. Questions were raised. Was the Korean church *really* mature and wise enough to cope? Would they, the missionaries, *really* be acting prudently to entrust power into 'untried hands'? Isn't there something insidious and insatiable in that word '*really*'? A few were optimistic, but the naysayers predicted disaster. All were cautious. Nevertheless commitments had been made and it would be bad faith to change the date.

After the 1904–05 war, and the victorious Japanese had enveloped Korea within its empire, and the world powers had acquiesced, the Koreans had, at first, unresistingly, accepted their fate. Then suddenly there was a reaction. What years of Chosŏn ultra-traditionalist rule had failed to do, the Japanese occupation achieved in a moment: patriotism was born.[11] A resistance movement was set up, groups conspired to strike against the Japanese, and a sporadic guerrilla war broke out. Slogans for Korean independence were everywhere seen and heard.

For Korean Christians, a crucial question was where the church ought to stand in relation to this patriotic nationalist movement. As the largest and most influential western-aligned body in the country, many expected the church to openly side with anti-Japanese feeling, providing political as well as spiritual leadership in the struggle for independence. But the American missionaries, especially the Presbyterians, for whom the separation of church and state was axiomatic, encouraged the church to stay out of the conflict. As Blair put it, it 'took high courage, coupled with wisdom and great love to lead the church aright, to stand up before men burning with indignation at their nation's loss and preach a doctrine of love and forbearance, and forgiveness even of enemies.'[12] Maybe not all would have agreed with this policy.

Some of the more pietistic missionaries counselled Christian activists to abandon their political aspirations in the hope of heavenly benefits, bizarrely suggesting that the verbal similarity in English between Chosŏn and 'chosen' indicated that, just as he had led ancient Israel, so God would lead his elect Korean people, in his own time and way, to their predestined destiny. Such arguments may have been used because their proponents felt that resistance might be futile, and costly in human lives and suffering. Whatever the rationale, most missionaries and many Korean Christian leaders sought to turn attention away from politics to spiritual concerns. Developments and influences such as these helped set the stage for the Korean revival of 1907 which, no more than any other revival, cannot be separated from its specific historical and national context, and the many non-spiritual factors which impinged upon it. In part, the revival can be seen as God's response to the crisis of hopelessness through which Christians in Korea were then passing, his way of preparing them for the coming traumatic events later in the century, and maintaining them in a state of spiritual usefulness.[13]

The first glimmers of revival, it is said, were seen in 1903, three years before the political ferment of 1906 engulfed the nation. In Wonsan, a city situated on Korea's Japan Sea coast, about a hundred and thirty miles east of Pyongyang, in August 1903, two missionary ladies commenced a prayer meeting. They were an American, Mary Culler White of the Southern Methodist Mission, on vacation from her missionary work in China, and a Canadian, Louise Hoard McCully, of the Canadian Presbyterian Mission. McCully, from Truro in Nova Scotia, had gone to China in 1887 and although a Presbyterian was, like White and some of their missionary colleagues, inclined towards the teachings of the Higher Life Movement. Adopting the jargon of that movement, the two women said that they prayed for 'the Holy Spirit to indwell abundantly not only in them but also in all other missionaries working with them.'[14]

Those missionaries, including Dr Robert Alexander Hardie, plus some Korean Christians, started to attend the prayer meetings. Hardie, a medical doctor and an evangelist, had been working as an independent missionary in Korea for thirteen years, having taken up missionary service following a pledge of support by Toronto University Medical Students Young Men's Christian Association. Located at first in Seoul, he then moved in 1891 to Pusan, where he was joined by his wife and children. When he fell ill that year, the family moved briefly to Nagasaki in Japan, returning to Pusan in 1892. Faced with considerable financial hardship, and some unkindness from fellow missionaries, the discouraged Hardies moved to Wonsan.[15] Hardie now associated with the American Methodist Episcopal Church, the same denomination as Mary Culler White. Less than a year later Hardie again took up work in Seoul, where in 1900 he was ordained as a deacon by the Methodists, ceasing medical work to concentrate solely on evangelism. In 1902, the Hardies returned to Wonsan, which remained their base until

1909, when Robert went to teach at the Pierson Memorial Union Bible Institute and Union Methodist Seminary in Seoul.

In August 1903, Hardie found himself at the centre of an event that has been regarded by some as the dawn of the revival of 1907. He was present at one of Mary White's and Louise McCully's prayer meetings, feeling deeply discouraged and in a very low mood. Thinking his ministry fruitless, he publicly confessed what he considered his failures. Both at the time and subsequently, Hardie's confession has generally been taken at face value, and unquestionably attributed to the Holy Spirit's ministry of conviction of sin. But, before jumping to such conclusions, it is as well to ask if there was evidence of any predisposing factors that led him to say what he said and do what he did that day.

The answer is that there were indeed factors that contributed to Hardie's low mood. First, there was the emotionally destabilising effect of having moved home seven times in little more than ten years. This had denied his family the opportunity to settle, and robbed himself of a proper pattern of ministry. Then there was the cumulative effect of years of inadequate financial provision and poor moral support, and on top of that the family's health was not good. They all suffered from malaria. His wife Abigail had bouts of louse or tick-borne relapsing fever, which sometimes put her life in jeopardy. Then, after losing a child, a daughter called Marie who survived just one day after her birth on 9th August 1893, Abigail's mental health gave way. Two years later, Hardie himself was close to a nervous breakdown. In 1896, a friend and missionary colleague, Malcolm C. Fenwick, reported on the dire condition of the Hardies' circumstances to the philosopher/psychologist, Professor James Gibson Hume, then head of the Philosophy Department at the University of Toronto, and presumably one of Hardie's Toronto supporters. Fenwick wrote:

> Spiritually, I found [Hardie] growing indeed, but physically his health, I am afraid, has received a terrible blow. What with living in schoolhouses, native rooms, and dispensary, he has contracted malaria .... Bessie is but a shadow and still having very hard night sweats. Eva is malarial, and Mrs Hardie not only malarial, but badly afflicted with nervous prostration. The babe [Gertrude Abigail, born on November 27, 1894] is the only strong member of the family.[16]

In addition, Hardie's giving up medicine to concentrate on evangelism meant that he had turned his back on the reason that had brought him to Korea in the first place. His motive in gaining a medical degree had been to use his skills as a doctor to open up opportunities for witness and evangelism. He once wrote, 'few men had more opportunities and influence for good than Christian physicians, I decided that night that I should study medicine.'[17]

To these predisposing factors must also be added the reawakening of painful recollections of the death of his Canadian colleague, Rev. William J. Mckenzie, in June 1895. It is inconceivable that distressing memories were not stirred when he found himself in close contact with Louise McCully at the very time when her sister Elizabeth, back in Canada, was busy writing Mckenzie's biography, *A Corn of Wheat*, published in Toronto the following year, 1904. Not only so, but there was also an added sharp edge to these recollections for Hardie. His Canadian colleagues conspired to suppress that Mckenzie's death was suicide. Hardie alone had broken the conspiracy of silence by reporting in the October 1895 issue of the *Canadian College Missionary Magazine* that Mckenzie had in fact shot himself.[18]

Profoundly shocked by Mckenzie's death, and aware of the fragility of his own health, Hardie warned his missionary associates, including Horace Underwood and other Presbyterians, not to fail to learn the lessons it taught. These he believed were threefold: first, no missionary ought to be isolated as Mckenzie had been; secondly, no missionary should 'conform to the native mode of dress, food, etc.' as Mckenzie had done; and thirdly, all missionaries would be better off without firearms of any kind. As there was already a disinclination to follow Mckenzie or their missionary contemporaries in China in adopting an Oriental lifestyle, Hardie's advice was taken. The majority of missionaries in Korea retained a westernised way of life.[19]

As if that was not all, Hardie, like many others associated with the revivals of the early twentieth century, was under the influence of the naïve, theologically untenable, and pastorally disastrous Higher Life teaching. This very fashionable but seriously aberrant theology was rooted in the thought of John Wesley and developed by Charles G. Finney and Asa Mahan as Oberlin Perfectionism. From 1875, the doctrine was promoted through the very influential

Keswick Convention, held annually in England's Lake District. Perfectionism's flaws were meticulously exposed and devastatingly repudiated by Benjamin Breckinridge Warfield, Principal of Princeton Theological Seminary from 1886 to 1902.[20]

With great clarity, Warfield demonstrated that all perfectionist notions ultimately emanate from a fundamentally deficient view of the redemptive work of Christ. The historic confessions of the church teach that sanctification, though a work of God's grace, entails the lifelong commitment and cooperation of the believer in overcoming sin. In the words of the Shorter Catechism: 'Sanctification is the work of God's free grace, whereby we are renewed in the whole man after the image of God, and are enabled more and more to die unto sin, and live unto righteousness.' Likewise, the Westminster Confession insisted that sanctification was 'imperfect in this life' and called the believer to engage in 'a continual and irreconcilable war' with sin wherever encountered. More graphically, the Anglican baptism formula calls on the Christian 'manfully to fight under his banner, against sin, the world, and the devil and to continue Christ's faithful soldier and servant unto … life's end.'

Higher Life, as taught at Keswick, rejected all ideas of active struggle. Sanctification was achieved passively by faith, through a second work of grace, which was referred to as the baptism of the Holy Spirit, or simply, the Second Blessing. This experience, it was said, enabled the believer to 'yield' or 'surrender' himself to God. Keswick claimed too much for sanctification, assuring believers of the possibility of its entire fulfilment in this life. This outcome was referred to as 'complete victory'. Not only was this teaching contrary to Scripture and the confessions, but it was and remains pastorally calamitous, leading some to experience immense frustration, disillusionment, depression and ultimately emotional instability.[21] Instead of living life in glorious tranquillity lifted up to a higher spiritual plane, as promised in the convention tent, Christians with their feet back on the ground found their progress in grace after the Second Blessing no easier than it had been before.

Adding this teaching to all his other personal problems, it is not difficult to understand why Hardie felt anxious, despondent and stressed, especially in the highly charged atmosphere of the prayer meetings, where the explicit longings of one for higher spiritual attainment could so easily be taken by another as implicit criticism of their own spiritual standing. In such an atmosphere, it is unsurprising that Hardie felt emotionally overwhelmed and induced publicly to confess as sin his incompetence as a missionary and the fruitlessness of his work, concluding that he had never been 'filled with the Holy Spirit'. The specific faults Hardie admitted included pride, hardness of heart, lack of faith, and, tellingly, his 'superiority as a white man'. How much of his confession that day was due to his mental condition, how much was the work of the enemy acting as the Accuser, and how much might have been attributable to the conviction of the Holy Spirit, and how each might have interacted with the others, is now impossible to say. Wisdom, however, requires that at the very least Robert Hardie's experience ought never to have been set up as normative, a spiritual example to be emulated. Rather it ought to have been recognised for what it was, a complex of signs and symptoms indicating a deeply floundering Christian in great need of wise pastoral support, sound instruction and friendly guidance.

Hardie, however, believed not only that he was prompted by the Holy Spirit to confess, but that the very act of confession was the immediate consequence and evidence of his being baptised by the Spirit. 'The first duty the Holy Spirit required when he came upon me was acknowledgement to those before whom the greater part of my missionary life had been spent, of my past failure, and of the cause of that failure. That was deeply painful and humiliating.' But as we Christians are notoriously inept at self-diagnosing our spiritual health and effectiveness, it might have been more prudent for his colleagues to have paused for reflection rather than to take his pious, though doubtless sincere, confession at face value and promote his experience as a standard for others to follow. Had they done so, some of the more unhelpful and distracting phenomena that accompanied the revival of 1907 might have been avoided.

The following Sunday, however, Hardie again made open confession in a service of public worship at the First Church of Wonsan, though he was less explicit than he had been in the prayer meeting, and failed completely to mention his tendency towards racism. In fact, as Dr Chil-Sung Kim relates, Hardie never seemed truly to repent of 'his superiority as a white man'. This is precisely what got him into trouble ten years later and led to his resignation from the presidency of Union Methodist Seminary. Hardie was not unique in being guilty of white superiority; it was endemic in many, if not most, missionary communities. Sometimes explicit, it more often betrayed its presence in culturally insensitive comments, acts and attitudes, such as the doubtless unintentional but nonetheless demeaning title that Lillias Underwood gave to her memoirs of life in Korea: *Fifteen Years Among the Top-Knots.*[22]

That Hardie's confessions, both to his peers and in public, had been impressive and moving is undeniable, perhaps especially so for Koreans, for whom self-abasement and loss of face is catastrophic. Hardie's example, therefore, had made it easier for Koreans to stand up in public to make startling confessions of what lay in the depths of their hearts. But at the time, Hardie's confessions did not have the aura of sanctity that gathered around them in later revivalist hagiography. Indeed, when reviewing the year 1903 for her American supporters, Mary Culler White made only the vaguest of allusions to the prayer meeting and didn't mention Hardie at all.

> I cannot fail to mention my delightful vacation in Korea, where I was privileged to look into the faces of those I had worked with and loved in America, to talk with them of the things of God, to form new friendships to my lasting good, to be uplifted by a meeting in which God came very close to us, to see the glorious opportunity of the Church in this empire, and to drink in health from multitudinous mountains and a shining sea. Thank God for it all![23]

Placing a meeting 'in which God came very close' on a par with 'multitudinous mountains and a shining sea' seems to indicate that Culler was far from claiming that what had taken place during one of her prayer meetings was anything like revival. The story, however, grew wings and flew. In his *When the Spirit's Fire Swept Korea,* Canadian Presbyterian, Rev. Jonathan Goforth, who we will meet again in Manchuria, wrote a second-hand account of the meeting, playing up its emotional impact.[24] Another hearsay account came from the pen of Dr Lillias Underwood of the Presbyterian mission who, couching her words in the idioms of the Higher Life Movement, wrote: 'Dr Hardie and other missionaries of Won San received a baptism of the Holy Spirit with power .... This experience was extended to the native Christians as well.'[25] Clearly, the Methodist Hardie was not the only one enmeshed in the Higher Life theory; even Presbyterians who subscribed to the Westminster Confession of Faith seasoned their Calvinism with a generous dash of Keswick.[26]

Lillias Underwood reported other stimuli reaching Korea at this time. 'To the other mission stations and communities of native Christians the news of this came, as well as thrilling accounts of what God was doing in Wales, in India and in other parts of the world, and a great longing filled all souls.'[27] Dr Underwood's reference is to the 1904 revival under Evan Roberts in Wales and the Khasi Hills revival in Northern India in 1905.

The Welsh revival has been chronicled in great detail, so suffice it to say that although there was undoubtedly some genuine blessing, it is also true to say that it was heavily adulterated by Finneyism, Higher Life teaching, emotionalism and decisionism. Evan Roberts' approach to ministry was exaggeratedly pietistic but also casual; after a prelude of an hour or more of singing and prayers, he delivered a message, often without preparation, spontaneously taking as his text a Bible verse stencilled on the wall above the pulpit, or sometimes even the church clock as his theme and inspiration. He typically told his audience that if they wished to be filled with the Spirit they must 'make the past right' by thorough and detailed confession; they must purify their lives by abstaining from anything doubtful; they must also fully submit to the Holy Spirit; and then and there in the meeting publicly stand up and confess Christ. Such a lack of intellectual investment resulted in Christians unable to resist the encroachments of theological liberalism and the secularising spirit of the twentieth century, even then sweeping across Europe. Many of Roberts' more thoughtful Welsh contemporaries recognised his weaknesses, but claimed they were too fearful of quenching the Spirit to publicly criticise them, though they had no desire to replicate his methods themselves. Even in Wales, the Welsh revival was not always seen as a pattern to be followed, let alone exported to other countries and cultures.

The revival in the Khasi Hills in north-east India, now Bangladesh, had a Welsh connection as the local missionaries belonged to the Calvinistic Methodist Mission. In 1902 two lady missionaries visiting Calcutta went to hear R. A. Torrey preach. Torrey was an associate of D. L. Moody, a believer in the Higher Life teaching, a supporter of Keswick, and an advocate of the Second Blessing. The missionaries returned home encouraged to pray for revival and pass on the stories they had heard.[28] This resulted in prayer meetings for revival in which emotions rose high and prayers were sometimes simultaneously offered by a number of people. That year the Indian delegates to their local General Assembly, having heard of what was happening in Wales, returned to their villages renewed in zeal to serve God more faithfully. Soon reports came in of revival spreading from church to church. It was estimated that in 1905 there were around eight thousand conversions in the Khasi Hills.

If revival in Korea was to tarry for a while, revivalism was not prepared to wait. The following autumn, Fredrik Franson, a protege of D. L. Moody and founder of the Scandinavian Alliance Mission, visited Wonsan and encouraged Robert Hardie to accompany him on a tour of the country, holding meetings, repeating his testimony and exercising an appreciated Bible ministry, frequently based on the Wonsan prayer meeting passage, the fourteenth chapter of St. John. When Franson departed to complete his international tour of missionary work, Hardie continued to itinerate for another three years, often in company with Jeon Gye-eun and Jeong Chun-su, two Korean Christians from Wonsan. The emotionally charged meetings included prayers for the baptism of the Spirit and fire, and sometimes a number of people prayed simultaneously.

In August 1906, Hardie came to the American Presbyterians in Pyongyang who were, at that time, agonising over whether to hand control of the church to Korean leadership. So reluctant were they that they decided they could only keep their promise if satisfied afresh, in some remarkable way, that it was indeed God's will. To discern that, they set apart a week for prayer and Bible study, inviting Hardie to lead their meetings.

Blair says nothing about Hardie confessing his sins in public or the events at Wonsan. He gives no hint that behind their speaker lay the hinterland of influences of which we have learned. Influences from which, it appears, not even confessional Presbyterians were immune. Blair does say how graciously God used Hardie's exposition of the First Epistle of John, which the missionaries had themselves selected for study, and how fruitful that passage of Scripture proved, becoming, as Blair put it, their textbook throughout the revival:

> How often God's Word seems written for special occasions! We were seeking help in time of need. The Apostle John assured us that everything depended upon fellowship with God, and that divine fellowship was conditioned upon love and righteousness. He who searches the deep things of the heart took the Epistle and made it a living, personal message.[29]

From Blair's account of events at Pyongyang in 1906–07 we see that the most solid foundations of the revival were not the exigencies of the national crisis, even less the emphases of the revivalists, but faithful Bible study and earnest prayer. One result of their intensive reflection on First John, and the prayers which flowed from it, was the humbling of the missionaries. They were given a keen awareness of their own fallibility and knew they could not lightly pass over their failures. They now saw more clearly than formerly that the way ahead would be sacrificial, requiring, as Blair put it, broken hearts and bitter tears. But it would also mean the comfort of the Holy Spirit. They might be inadequate, but God was all-powerful. The week spent with Hardie kindled hope that an outpouring of the Spirit might equip them and the Korean church to tread confidently the challenging road opening up before them. Going out from the meetings, the missionaries had little idea of how challenging their future path would be, but chastened and expectant, they agreed to pray for a great blessing upon their Korean brothers, especially those who would attend the winter Bible-study classes.

These classes had begun in 1890, sixteen years earlier, when Horace Underwood brought seven men together for Bible-study and training. The experiment was so successful that the following year the missionaries agreed to make annual Bible-study classes mandatory in every substation, chapel and private home at which meetings were held. Each missionary was to work out a course of instruction tailored to his own situation, but based upon a common syllabus. The courses were for all members and catechumens, young and old, literate and illiterate, women and men, though in compliance with Korean etiquette the women were usually taught apart from the men, and the young were segregated from their elders. Occasionally the missionary was the main teacher, sometimes sharing the responsibility with Korean teachers, but most often the Koreans took the major part.

Classes typically included prayer, discussion and fellowship, followed by half-an-hour of singing before leaving the building to engage in direct evangelism in the community around. In the evenings there was a united service. The hub on which everything was centred was the daily three hours of Bible-study. Strictly speaking it was New Testament study, as the Korean Old Testament would not be completed until 1911. At first it was John Ross' New Testament that everyone used, but the Americans so disliked its colloquial Korean that they insisted upon revision and eventually, in 1900, replaced it with a translation of their own, much to the disappointment of the British and Foreign Bible Society which held Ross' version to be more intelligible to the majority of the people. What may have appeared best to the missionaries may not have greatly appealed to the Koreans. Among the New Testaments in use at the Bible-study classes of 1906 and 1907 were well-thumbed and much-loved copies of the Ross version.

Attendance at these Bible conferences was such as to incite the envy of modern ministers in Britain or the USA. In 1904, in the area covered by the American Presbyterian mission, fully sixty percent of all members and catechumens attended. The Pyongyang general class for men brought in eight-hundred to a thousand men, walking from their homes from a radius of up to one hundred miles. Local people had to be excluded because of a lack of space to accommodate them. By 1909 there were eight hundred such classes held across the country, with an aggregate attendance of fifty thousand, twice the number of communicant members. It requires little imagination to appreciate the beneficial effect of such extensive and intensive Bible-study, even without taking into consideration the extraordinary blessing of a revival.

In September 1906, barely a month after Robert Hardie's visit, Dr Howard Agnew Johnston arrived in Pyongyang.[30] From 1899 to 1905, Johnston had been the minister of Madison Avenue Presbyterian Church of New York City, but had resigned his charge in order to visit the Presbyterian Church's Asian missionaries. It was in that capacity that he came to Pyongyang bringing with him first-hand anecdotes of his visit to Wales in 1904, where he had met Evan Roberts. Johnston also told of his time in the Khasi Hills in 1905. His ministry in Pyongyang brought refreshment and welcome calm at a fraught time. Writing the foreword to the 1910 edition of James Webster's, *The Revival in Manchuria*, Walter B. Sloan, who had himself taken the Higher Life message to China in the summer of 1906, quotes with warm approbation the comments of a lady missionary who had heard Johnstone speak just a short time before his arrival in Pyongyang:

> Certainly, there is nothing extraordinary in *what* he says, and nothing fanatical or extravagant in his methods. His manner is quiet, manly, straightforward, and there was an entire absence of egotism in his addresses from first to last. ... We must give up trying to explain the work of such men on purely material grounds; an analysis of the success following Dr Johnston's simple talks on such grounds would utterly break down.[31]

William Blair concurred. Johnstone's visit had increased the desire present in many hearts for an outpouring of grace in Korea. As winter came on, Pastor Kil Sŏnju of the Central Presbyterian Church in Pyongyang daily gathered his congregation for early morning services, leading them in intercession for their troubled nation and praying that God would send revival during the two weeks of the January Bible-classes. Christmas came. For the missionaries this was usually a time of happy festivity and relaxation in preparation for the demands of the coming Bible-classes, but that year there was little appetite for such things; instead prayer meetings were held each evening until the Bible-classes commenced in early January, when they were rescheduled for noon. Hope intensified that a time of refreshing was drawing near.

On 2nd January the Bible-classes began. They were attended by more than fifteen hundred men, with hungry hearts and minds, keen to know more of God's Word. The evening meetings in the Central Church commenced on 6th January. Nothing unusual happened. But, as Blair sagely commented, 'We were not looking for anything unusual.' On the Saturday night he preached. Choosing to speak from 1 Corinthians 12:27, Blair illustrated the words, 'Now you are the body of Christ and individually members of it,' by reference to how, on a hunting expedition, he had shot off the end of one of his fingers, and how much pain that little wound had inflicted upon his head and his entire body. Even so, he said, hatred in a Christian's heart wounds not only those who are members of the Body of Christ, but brings pain to Christ himself, the head. After the sermon some thanked him for what he had said, commented that it had helped them to better understand the effect of their failures upon the church, and confessed their lack of love towards others, especially the Japanese.

Grateful that prayer was being answered, Blair went home. The following Sunday, however, brought an anticlimax. Though the church was crowded, the prayers, he thought, were stilted and the atmosphere leaden. It seemed as if a blockage was holding back God's blessing. At noon on Monday the missionaries met to pray, determined, like Jacob, not to let God go until he had blessed them. Entering the church that evening they were conscious of a very different atmosphere, the whole place seemed filled with God's presence.

Graham Lee's account, *How the Spirit Came to Pyeng Yang,* published in the *Chinese Recorder* for March 1907, relates how he preached a short address, after which a few people engaged in audible prayer; then there were some spontaneous testimonies and, finally, a song was sung. The congregation was dismissed, but told they could remain if they wished. About two-thirds departed. Then Lee invited those who remained to make public confession of sin. 'Immediately the Spirit of God seemed to descend on that audience. Man after man would rise, confess his sins, break down and weep, and then throw himself to the floor and beat the floor with his fists in a perfect agony of conviction.'[32] Confession was accompanied with a chorus of brokenhearted weeping as a wave of emotion engulfed both missionaries and Koreans. In an agony of almost hopeless guilt, unsure if they could ever be forgiven, many cried out to God for pardon.

At one point, confession was broken by prayer. It was this that so impressed William Blair. So many started to pray that Lee, who was leading the meeting, told them not to wait until one had finished before another started, but all who wanted should pray simultaneously. For conservative Presbyterians this might have suggested chaos and cacophony, but, said Blair, it was anything but chaotic. Rather, it sounded to him 'like the falling of many waters, an ocean of prayer beating against God's throne.' Individual prayers were combined into a symphony of contrition and petition, as all with one voice called out to the Father. Blair likened this marvellous surging sound to that of the wind heard at Pentecost in the upper room. His analogy, however, seems to have been misinterpreted by the 1907 Pyongyang Synod to mean that 'there was the presence of a strong wind'.[33] All too easily, especially in the context of revival, fact is distorted, and myths are born.

It was notable that the conviction of sin that fell upon those who confessed was not some imprecise nagging, a vague sense of failure, such as that inflicted by the Accuser of God's people, seeking to depress and discourage. Rather, it was precise, focused, almost surgical, bringing home how in very specific ways people had grieved a holy God, breached fellowship with their fellow believers, and had hated others, especially, though not only, the Japanese occupiers, instead of loving them as they ought. Now, they hated themselves for harbouring such ill-feeling and, initially at any rate, all but despaired of pardon. One man who had worked closely, and in seeming harmony, with William Blair in the Men's Association, confessed to having hated him for some petty grievance, and not only Blair, but others too. He sought and received immediate reconciliation. Another was broken by his adultery and the detestation he harboured in his heart towards his wife. The atmosphere was incredibly intense, very highly emotionally charged. Tears flowed as men were made acutely aware of God's holiness, their sinfulness, and a desperate need of pardon. It continued in this manner until two o'clock in the morning, when physically exhausted, yet spiritually elated, the congregation returned to their homes.

As day after day the movement went on, the carefully scheduled Bible-classes were thoroughly disrupted. On the second Monday and Tuesday, the overwhelming desire to be done with sin as far as possible, to receive God's pardon, and know reconciliation with wronged fellow Christians, spread to the women. Even children at the schools were spontaneously caught up in this movement of the Spirit without, it appears, any attempt on the part of the missionary teachers to influence them. Then the meetings concluded. In reading the accounts, one shares the sense of relief that must have passed through the Christian community now that the stressful emotions of the week had subsided, the pardon sought had been granted, and that the joy of forgiveness and peace refreshed exhausted souls. At the end of his account, obviously compiled very soon after the events it describes, Graham Lee wrote:

> The meetings have closed and the people are rejoicing with a great joy, but out in the country districts the work goes on. Mr Blair and I have just returned from a country class, and at that class the manifestations were exactly the same, terrible agony on account of sin and great joy and peace resulting from confession of it.
>
> And thus has begun in our city a work of grace, for which we give to God our most grateful thanks, praying that what we have seen, may simply be the earnest of the greater blessings that God has yet in store for us and not for us only but for this whole land. To God be all the praise, to whose name be glory for ever and for ever.[34]

Lee's and Blair's accounts are restricted to what happened in the Presbyterian church, but the Methodist students at Pyongyang's Union Theological College were also affected. The revival spread throughout the Methodist congregations in the city, even in those where at first there had been antagonism. As the Methodist students and those attending the Presbyterian Bible-class returned to their villages, some as far as one hundred miles distant, they took with them the spirit of the revival, which now spread across the country, in wave upon wave, sometimes spontaneously, sometimes instigated by the holding of meetings, sometimes from family to family, or from individual to individual. For almost six months the revival maintained its momentum.

The immediate effect was literally cathartic: cleansing. The flood of confession was not spontaneous, but had been instigated, as Lee points out, by the missionaries, influenced by Robert Hardie. Indeed, there was at first a difference of opinion over the legitimacy of public confession. Blair appears to have had reservations, though finally going along with the majority who felt it ought to be encouraged.[35] As a result, said Lillias Underwood, the missionaries saw 'sinners converted, those who had done wrong making confession and restitution of money and goods, the churches crowded to overflowing with inquirers and new believers, the coffers of the Lord's treasury filled, and men of different denominations lovingly joining hands, putting away old jealousies, forwarding the Lord's kingdom shoulder to shoulder.'[36]

It has been said that the movement resulted in a kind of rebirth of the Korean church, coming as it did at the end of the first phase of missionary-led ministry and immediately before the assumption of full responsibility by the Korean leaders. It also renewed confidence in the power of Scripture, instilled a fresh reliance on God's readiness to answer prayer, emphasised the importance of unity among believers, and the need to love all men, even one's enemies. All of which equipped the church for witness and mission in the coming often traumatic decades. It also served as a vivid and unforgettable reminder of the power and presence of the Holy Spirit in the church at all times, not only during revival, but also when his presence was less conspicuous. For those personally touched by the revival it produced a blessing which readied them for the coming days of suffering and grief, when instead of responding with hatred, the persecuted would show love to their tormentors. Others noted how the revival helped to fuse together the missionary emphasis of the salvation of the individual with the Korean hope of national deliverance, by placing the church and its message at the very heart of national life. From then on, evangelical Protestantism broke away from a Western otherworldly pietist worldview, to make a more holistic intellectual, social and spiritual contribution to Korean nationhood.[37]

Despite unsubstantiated claims that the revival 'brought fifty thousand Koreans to Christ', the evidence suggests that it did not produce significant numerical growth of the church, though there was some, such as seven hundred and fifty-six new communicants added to the Pyongyang Presbyterian church.[38] Nor did it contribute, as was hoped, lasting results to the 'Million Souls for Christ' evangelistic campaigns of 1910–11. Little came of that venture, despite the fact that Christians gave sacrificially of their time and money, distributed millions of tracts, and prayed earnestly for the campaign's leaders, who, utilising revivalist methods, gathered large numbers into meetings across the country. Maybe it ought never to have been attempted, not only because it harnessed dubious methodology, but because it was perhaps culturally inappropriate. In his personal annual report to the Board of Foreign Missions, the Rev. James Adams, a Presbyterian missionary of sixteen years of experience at Taegu, concluded with this analysis:

> Every preparation was made along the most approved lines of the Western world revival meetings, and during and subsequent to the meetings no pains were spared. Every night the building was practically filled with an audience of approximately one thousand, the majority of whom were non-Christians. There was an aggregate of between four and five hundred who professed conversion, came forward and gave their names and addresses and were assigned to the charge of some old Christians. Yet after the meetings were over, we were unable to get hold of more than forty or fifty and only a portion of those now remain. It seems manifest to me that the method indigenous to the Korean Christian, that of constant, individual personal work is vastly superior to our Western method of public evangelistic meetings, and the product of it is much more permanent.[39]

It is not hard to imagine John Nevius and John Ross quietly reading these words, sagely nodding, whilst muttering modestly under their breath, 'We told you so!' The reality is that the first stage of explosive growth of the Korean church had already taken place in the years preceding the revival. Lillias Underwood, who was close enough to the heart of things to have known, claimed that in the year 1905/6 adult baptisms trebled and the overall number of communicants doubled. In 1905 there had been four hundred and fifty-seven catechumens being prepared for baptism, but in 1906 one thousand six hundred and ninety-four were admitted by that sacrament into church membership, with another one thousand seven hundred and twelve waiting to join preparation classes. This helps to clarify important distinctions which need to be drawn between revivals and revivalism, sustainable church growth and mere evangelistic campaigns. They are not at all the same thing, neither are they dependent upon each other, nor even necessarily related.[40]

What the Korean revival did do was to inject a fresh stimulus of spiritual life and power into Korean Christians as individuals and into the church corporately, in preparation for the persecution that would break over the church a mere three years later with the annexation of country by Japan.[41]

News of the revival spread as rapidly as did the movement itself, inevitably bringing the curious to see what had taken place, and, if possible, to enter into a vicarious experience. With close links between the church in Manchuria and Korea, the news speedily crossed the Yalu River, reaching the 1907 meeting of the Manchurian Presbytery, which promptly suspended business and turned to prayer, seeking a similar blessing on Manchuria. Two evangelists from Liaoyang, one Mr Chang, a licentiate for the ministry awaiting ordination, the other, Mr Liu, a deacon, were dispatched to find out more and report back. A visitor from Korea to Manchuria, bringing news of the revival, was a Canadian Presbyterian missionary who possessed a most appropriate name for one called to be a missionary, Rev. Jonathan Goforth. John Ross, however, was in Scotland on furlough.

19

The Manchurian Revival: Characters and Crosscurrents

Nothing so proves our guilt as the sense of condemnation which refuses to admit the possibility of mercy and nothing so proves our blindness to the love of God as our blank unbelief of his real, complete and final forgiveness.

WILLIAM STILL

THE practice of holding special meetings for Bible-study and prayer was not unique to the Presbyterians in Korea. It had become customary in Manchuria to have similar events conducted by an invited speaker over the sixteen days of the Chinese New Year celebration, which in 1908 fell on 2nd February. That year the main speaker was the Canadian missionary to Honan, Rev. Jonathan Goforth, who had visited Liaoyang and Mukden the previous year on his return from Korea to share news of the revival. This had piqued the interest of the missionaries, hence the invitation to return. Just as the meetings were about to commence Mr Chang and Mr Liu, the two Chinese workers who had been sent by the Manchurian church to Korea to investigate the revival, returned on fire with enthusiasm to tell of their experiences. They brought with them a letter from the Korean church assuring the Manchurian church of its prayers: 'Remember that our people are praying for you, and that their prayers are mighty and do prevail.'[1]

Among the many details Chang and Liu recounted was the phenomenon of public confession, so pronounced a feature of the

Korean movement. It is perhaps hard for Westerners to appreciate the horror with which Christians from a Confucian background would have looked upon such a thing. T. C. Fulton, an Irish missionary, did understand, and made the strikingly important point that what convinced the missionaries that such an open display of personal failure was generally an authentic work of the Holy Spirit was the Chinese abhorrence of losing face. As Fulton put it: 'no power of man, not even the utmost terrors of criminal law, would have forced such secrets from their lips.' Only an extraordinary influence could induce Chinese people publicly to confess their innermost private faults, indeed nothing other than the power of God. That is not to say however, that public confession was always spontaneous. It was not, for it was actively promoted by example. This had been so in the case of Robert Hardie at Wonsan. He had been stimulated by reports of similar phenomena in the revivals in India. His subsequent retelling of his own story triggered this distinctive aspect of the Korean and Manchurian revivals.

If public confession was naturally repellent to the Chinese, it was an aversion shared by many Scottish and Irish Presbyterians. Their change of mind on the subject, as the revival progressed, was also significant, corroborating that of the Chinese Christians. In Korea, William Blair had said that he had held his own private views of the 'desirability or undesirability of public confession of sin'. But he changed his mind when he was convinced that the confessions were prompted by the Holy Spirit. Fulton, a reserved Ulster Presbyterian, likewise admitted to 'a horror of the emotional in religion'. His revulsion too was tempered by a belief that 'the mighty Spirit of God was working in the hearts of men'. Likewise, James Webster wrote: 'Over and over again, hard-headed Scotchmen, not much given to emotionalism at any time, and with a strong temperamental prejudice against religious hysteria in all its forms, were heard to say one to the other, with a sort of awe in their voice, "This is the work of God."' Even those inclined towards theological liberalism, such as Andrew Weir and Frederick W. S. O'Neil, were compelled to admit that 'emotion, thought and action are equally channels of the Spirit's power,' and that 'the Revival of 1908 [was an] outpouring of the Spirit.'[2]

John Ross was absent from Manchuria at the time, being in Scotland on furlough, but he was fully informed of developments by correspondence from Webster, and he saw no reason to doubt that what was happening was of God. Indeed, he thought that the Manchurian church had been well prepared for revival, both by the ministry it had received and the suffering it had endured. Ross' support did not, however, lead him to suspend his critical faculties. In his preface to the first edition of *The Marvellous Story of the Revival in Manchuria*, transcribed from Webster's letters and published in Edinburgh in 1908, he took pains to counter Jonathan Goforth's pessimistic view of the spiritual state of the Manchurian church before he arrived on the scene. Every word of Ross' well-crafted critique is carefully aimed to hit its target:

> There are two outstanding factors which have contributed to make the Manchurian Church a soil fairly well prepared for this new and deeper Christian experience. One is the Christian doctrines they believed, and the second is the sufferings which they have endured.
>
> The Church has always held a clear belief in the Immanence [omnipresence] of God, not the immanence of hardness in stone, but the immanence of fire in coal—a transforming power. They knew that they required to pray, not that God might come to them, or his Holy Spirit work in them, but that he would open their eyes to the fact that he is with them as the chariots of fire with Gehazi [Elijah's servant, see 2 Kings 5:20-27] though he realised it not....
>
> They knew they did not need to pray to God for mercy as though he were like a heathen God unwilling to grant it, for they knew that 'God was beseeching them to be reconciled to him.'
>
> During the times of persecution, when they were surrounded by the blackness of darkness, they felt as though the hand of God held theirs, and their remarkable spiritual experience, which prevented the fear natural to their circumstances, has made an indelible impression on the character of the Christian people.
>
> The people were therefore thus in a mental and spiritual condition to welcome the more thorough and complete Revival of life which is so graphically set forth in the following pages. The story is incomplete, but enough is herein detailed ... to cause the home Church to sing aloud for joy, and to look for experiences equally influential for good.[3]

Ross repudiated Goforth's curious notion that God had departed from his people in Manchuria and that the remedy was public confession of sin. In doing so, Ross made use of the technical theological word 'immanence' to explain how mightily God's presence, promised to his people at all times, had been revealed in the recent history of the Manchurian church, not least during the Boxer uprising of 1900 when God had drawn close to his people as their consolation and strength, and now once again in the revival of 1908, as a fresh impulse of spiritual life. Ross warned his readers, both missionary colleagues and the general public, not to misconstrue public confession as evidence that because of their sins God had absented himself; on the contrary, it ought to be construed as evidence of his loving presence. Graciously but firmly, Ross struck at the very core of Goforth's message: that God's presence could only be restored to his people upon condition of contrition and repentance. Rather, it was, said Ross, God's unfailing presence which had led his people to repentance and called them onward into a fuller appreciation of their status as his loved children.

Ross' scrupulous analysis of Goforth and his ministry ought not in any way to be construed as resistance to the work of the Spirit. Nor was Ross alone in his caution. Robert Boyd in his *Waymakers in Manchuria* also stated his concern that 'some of the outward manifestations of the of the revival were exaggerated, uncontrolled, and below the highest spiritual level.'[4] Andrew Weir likewise pointed out the danger of inflating the value of the emotional side of the revival. He wrote:

> We need to emphasise the fact that emotion, thought and action are equally channels of the Spirit's power, and should be kept in due balance, otherwise there is a risk of regarding high-strung emotion as the main channel of the Holy Spirit's action, with a consequent craving for excitement, an insistence on one type of experience and growth, and great censoriousness.[5]

There was nothing at all novel in such cautionary statements. It had long been held that all genuine revivals were a mixture of the true work of the Spirit, overwrought but sincere human reaction, downright error, and lapses of understanding and practice.

Jonathan Edwards, opposed to the coldly cerebral influence of the Enlightenment, argued passionately for the place of emotion and feeling in religion, but that did not lead him to abandon restraint. Analysing the mid-eighteenth-century Great Awakening, in which he had played so great a part, he gave a qualified assessment, concluding not that the Great Awakening was 'undoubtedly from the Spirit of God', but that it was 'undoubtedly, *in general*, from the Spirit of God.' Consequently, Edwards felt compelled first to preach and then to publish *The Distinguishing Marks of a Work of the Spirit of God,* in which he insists that not everything in a revival is equally beneficial.

For those with eyes to see it, such caveats had been written into the background history of the Manchurian mission and church. Almost seventy years earlier, in 1839, during Robert M'Cheyne's absence in Palestine, the twenty-four-year-old William Chalmers Burns had been appointed locum minister at M'Cheyne's church, St Peter's, in Dundee and found himself caught up in a revival. Burns, somewhat out of his depth, attempted to add to his own *gravitas* by contriving – as indeed would Goforth – a sternness in his preaching, whilst encouraging the more sensational manifestations relished by the newspapers and his young contemporaries. This brought an immediate and sharp criticism from his discerning mother that it robbed his public prayers and his preaching of their customary sweetness.[6]

Dr John MacDonald of Ferintosh in Easter Ross came to the assistance of the struggling Burns, and under his ministry the more histrionic aspects of the revival immediately fell away. Later, MacDonald could not recall hearing any audible expression of emotion during his preaching, although he had noticed those who silently shed tears or sobbed in contrition. In his understated Highland way, he saw these responses as evidence of 'a general impression from above'.[7] MacDonald's biographer, Kennedy of Dingwall, went even further, maintaining that the history of revivals justifies the opinion that their lasting benefits are often in inverse proportion to their emotional expression.[8] John Ross and some of his colleagues drew a similar conclusion in respect to the Manchurian awakening.

Any difference of approach, emphasis and outlook between Burns and MacDonald is best accounted for by differences of temperament, experience and maturity. It was otherwise in regard to the Manchurian revival. The differences between the Chinese leaders and the more conservative missionaries, on the one hand, and Goforth and his supporters on the other, could indeed be accounted for by irreconcilable theologies.

As the momentum of the Manchurian revival started to build, a comment by Margaret Weir, wife of the Irish Presbyterian missionary Andrew Weir, piques our interest. Mrs Weir was of the opinion that what was happening was neither spontaneous nor surprising. She wrote: 'There was nothing fortuitous about the revival .... A spiritual advance had been planned for, and prayed for, and confidently expected, but when it came, its extent and power were beyond anything ever envisaged.'[9] To make best sense of her remark we need to know something of the life of Jonathan Goforth, the beliefs he held, and the methods he adopted.

Goforth was born in 1859 to a farming family at Thorndale, in Oxford County, Ontario, Canada. He came to faith aged eighteen under the preaching of the local old-school Presbyterian minister, Rev. Lachlan Cameron. Cameron encouraged him to read Andrew Bonar's *Memoirs and Remains of Robert Murray M'Cheyne* and through this classic Goforth felt a call to the ministry. His commitment to foreign missionary work came about during his training at Knox College in Toronto, when listening to George Lesley Mackay, the first Presbyterian missionary to Formosa (Taiwan). Goforth graduated in 1887. The same year he married Rosalind Bell-Smith and the following year he was ordained a missionary to China; soon after they embarked for Shanghai, enduring a miserable passage. After language study at Chefoo, where they met John Nevius, the Goforths took up work in North Honan, but not before receiving a cautionary letter from J. Hudson Taylor of the China Inland Mission. Intent on quashing any self-confidence, Taylor warned them that Honan was 'one of the most anti-foreign provinces in China'. Adding, 'Brother, if you would enter that Province, you must go forward on your knees.'

Goforth's training at Knox Seminary coincided with a time of theological flux in the western church. The confessional Calvinism of the Westminster standards, to which the Canadian Presbyterians broadly adhered, was now under attack on two fronts. On the one hand, there was the rise of theological liberalism, sometimes called modernism, which refused to identify the Bible with the Word of God. Preferring to say that the Bible *contained* the Word of God, liberals implied that Scripture also contained what was human and fallible, but it offered no key, apart from human rationality, to understanding which was which, thus seriously undermining confidence in the Bible.

On the other hand, there was reactionary Fundamentalism. In its favour, Fundamentalism held to an unyielding belief in the Bible as the Word of God in its entirety, but against it was a readiness to abandon the old confessional doctrines for an eclectic clutter of ideas drawn from the Higher Life teaching of Wesley and Finney, a recrudescent premillennialism, and the eccentricities of John Nelson Darby and C. I. Schofield's dispensationalism. This doctrinal melange was promoted in the U.S.A. and Canada by D. L. Moody and his associates, and in Britain through the ministry of the Keswick Convention.

In this febrile atmosphere of conflicting ideas, Goforth reappraised his own convictions. His reading at the time included Jonathan Edwards' accounts of the Great Awakening in Massachusetts, but it was Charles Grandison Finney, not Edwards, who most caught his imagination. Goforth made no bones about it. He tells how in 1905 he received from a friend in India a little pamphlet culled from *Finney's Autobiography* and his *Revival Lectures* which led him to read both books in their entirety. Goforth, who at ordination had subscribed to the Westminster Confession of Faith, now devoured Finney's writings and extolled him as 'that peer of evangelists'.[10]

Goforth also believed in divine healing and the so-called 'Second Blessing', as well as embracing radical dispensationalism. He read avidly and approvingly Adoniram J. Gordon's *Ministry of the Spirit* as well as Samuel Dickey Gordon's *Quiet Talks on Power*. S. D. Gordon (no relation of A.J.'s) pressed the logic of premillennial dispensationalism to conclusions which not even

Scofield would have drawn, preposterously arguing 'that [Jesus'] dying was not God's own plan. It was a plan conceived somewhere else, and yielded to by God.'[11] This is not the place to deal with these aberrations, but we note them as influences which coloured Goforth's ministry and almost unhinged him. He admits as much. These books he said, he 'read over repeatedly', until the subject of revival had become such an obsession that his wife feared that he might have a mental breakdown. Believing Finney's theory, that any who 'wholeheartedly and unreservedly carried out God's will could have a revival', Goforth set out to discover what he came to call the 'laws of revival', determined to implement them.[12]

The notion that revivals could be generated at will and programmed into the regular life of the church links Goforth with Elizabeth Weir's assertion that the revival at Liaoyang 'had been planned for, prayed for, and confidently expected.' Not all, however, saw eye-to-eye with Elizabeth Weir. Referring to the situation in Mukden, Dr Dugald Christie agreed that all were interested in revival, believed revival was desirable in order to rouse Christians to greater zeal, and prayed for revival, but he acknowledged that when revival did come it took both himself and his colleagues utterly by surprise: 'Any general movement such as took place was far from the thoughts of any.'[13] Nor did John Ross endorse Goforth's methods or beliefs, but very carefully, pointedly but graciously, disassociated himself from them.

Having entered these important caveats, it is hard to disagree with James Webster that there were good things to say about Jonathan Goforth, not least his personal piety and commitment to doing what he believed to be the will of God, regardless of personal cost. Having heard him in 1907, Webster thought him a man with a 'breadth of vision and a sympathetic appreciation ... great and good common-sense, knowledge of the Chinese language, literature and people, simple faith, and apostolic zeal.'[14] Many of the church leaders and the missionaries appear to have agreed.

Goforth's preaching message was, said Webster, 'a simple, plain, old-fashioned one.' But it had a hard and accusatory edge designed to exploit the negative emotions of his hearers, induce in them an awareness of their sinfulness, and so convince them that they were under God's judgement from which they could only emerge through public confession and the process of revival. In a passage omitted from later editions, Webster went so far as to say that 'Mr Goforth never in any way encourages, indeed he rather represses.'[15] What lay behind this lamentable tendency was not only Finney's methodology, but also Goforth's personal experience. His visit to Korea in 1907, in company with Dr Robert Peter MacKay, the Secretary of the Foreign Missions Committee of The Presbyterian Church in Canada, brought an invitation to attend the American missionaries' prayer meeting at which Goforth felt deeply conscious of God's presence. The prayers, he said, seemed to carry him 'right up to the very Throne of God'.[16] On the walk back to their accommodation Mackay was emotionally agitated, though subdued. For most of the time he said little. Finally, his pent-up feelings exploded. Hurling a challenge at Goforth and his Honan colleagues, he exclaimed, 'What amazing power! You missionaries in Honan are nowhere near that high level.' Goforth then and there determined to see a revival in China, patterned on an impression of what he had only briefly witnessed in Korea, and by the application of Finney's methodology.

In his public ministry, Goforth set out to draw unfavourable comparisons between the revived church in Korea and the un-revived Manchurian church. The main difference, he held, was the presence of the Holy Spirit in Korea and his absence in Manchuria. According to Webster, Goforth did not preach theories of the work of the Spirit (though references to a second baptism of the Spirit are not hard to find in his account of the revival), but rather emphasised 'The holiness of God, the exceeding sinfulness and destructive nature of sin, the absolute helplessness of man without God's Holy Spirit, the possibility of keeping back the Holy Spirit from working his gracious work in and through us.'[17] The contradiction in Webster's statement is immediately apparent: how possibly could someone who is absolutely helpless without God's Holy Spirit be able to hinder the same all-powerful Spirit from working?

If Goforth did not preach theories of the Spirit's work, neither did he unfold any coherent doctrine of justification or atonement. Even if it was true, as Webster maintained, that the motif of the

Cross 'burned like a living fire in the heart of every address', little of its substance was communicated. Recalling the sting delivered to his own heart by Mackay's outburst that evening in Pyongyang, Goforth sought to demolish all joy or comfort which the Manchurian Christians might have felt, considering them deceptive and spurious. His method was to get them to see, what he seems sincerely but erroneously to have believed to be true, that by the inconsistency of their lives they had trampled on the love of God and driven him from them. His goal was to move his hearers to public confession in the hope that they would in turn influence others and so unleash a powerful emotional momentum. Goforth put it like this: 'as far as our observation has led us, we have concluded that there must first be deep conviction [of sin] among the true followers of Christ before any expectation can be entertained of moving the others.'[18]

John Ross understood this, and was disquieted by it. In words that we have already noted, by a thinly veiled, indirect criticism, he protested: 'They [the Manchurian Christians] knew they did not need to pray to God for mercy as though he were like a heathen God unwilling to grant it, for they knew that "God was beseeching them to be reconciled to him".'[19]

The matter is further complicated by Goforth's confusion over the finality of Christ's atonement. He confesses to a 'strong feeling that sins committed before conversion are under the blood of God's Holy Son and never should be confessed.' But from this he drew a bleak and unwarranted conclusion that sins subsequent to conversion were not 'under the blood' and could only be forgiven after specific and detailed confession. Moreover, sins publicly known could 'only be swept away by public confession'. Adding, 'True, this amounts to [our] crucifixion; but by our wilful disobedience we have put the Lord of Glory to an open shame, and it is the price that we must pay.'[20] Clearly, for Goforth, the price paid by Christ at Calvary was insufficient to atone for sin and it must therefore be supplemented by our own confession, either private or public. What Goforth refused to see was that, in a single stroke, he had compromised the fundamental evangelical Protestant belief that God pardons and accepts us by grace alone and that these blessings are received by faith alone.

Whatever place there may be for public confession of sin in exceptional circumstances, the Westminster Confession of Faith, to which Goforth and the Presbyterian missionaries nominally subscribed, certainly does not see audible confession as necessary to forgiveness, peace of conscience or assurance of salvation. The Shorter Catechism insists that 'Justification is an act of God's free grace, wherein he pardoneth *all* our sins, and accepteth us as righteous in his sight, *only* for the righteousness of Christ imputed to us, and received by faith *alone*.'[21] The evangelical doctrine of justification means that all a believer's sins, past, present and future, are fully pardoned on account of Christ's atoning work.

The implication is clear: Ross believed that Goforth's doctrine would subvert the teaching upon which the Manchurian church had been built. Eight years later, without any allusion to Goforth himself, but entirely relevant to his teaching, Ross concludes a chapter in *Mission Methods* with a magisterial affirmation of the entire perfection of God's plan of redemption, the Cross of Christ.

> The Cross of Christ, with its implied doctrines, satisfies the soul of the Chinese. It is the intelligent response of love to the cry of their distressed heart, which is that of an 'infant crying in the dark.' It answers their questions as to their duty to man and their relation to God. In the Cross of Christ they find an all-satisfying portion; as there they find expounded problems which Confucius refused to touch, which Buddhism and Taoism have answered so as to mislead. In religious truth, and as a guide to life, the gospel is 'all their salvation, and all their desire.' In them Christ is the 'fulness of God.'[22]

A further weakness in Goforth's preaching was his opinion that justification was a subjective experience rather than an objective legal and forensic declaration. John Murray's analogy, based on the distinction between the judge and the surgeon, is helpful here. When he performs an operation, a surgeon does something to us or in us, but that is not what the judge does: he passes a verdict concerning us. In justification God acts as a judge and his verdict on all who believe in Christ is that they are 'without condemnation'. This finding and declaration is external to us. It is not an experience we feel. Justification itself is therefore not subject to moods, nor conditional upon the performance of spiritual and moral duties. It rests solely upon the unchanging righteousness of Jesus Christ. As Murray observes, 'The purity of the gospel is bound up with the recognition of this distinction. If justification is confused with regeneration or sanctification, then the door is open for the perversion of the gospel at its centre.'[23] It is precisely this distinction which Goforth, in line with Finney, Keswick and all who propounded the Higher Life doctrine, had blurred.

It is plausible to argue that such errors arise, in part, when incredulity at the immensity of God's forgiving grace is allowed to tip over into scepticism. The question, 'Can such love be true?' has echoed down the Christian centuries. It certainly amazed Charles Wesley, who wrote:

> And can it be that I should gain
> An int'rest in the Saviour's blood?
> Died He for me, who caused His pain?
> For me, who Him to death pursued?
> Amazing love! how can it be
> That Thou, my God, should die for me?

But it is precisely at such moments that the affirmations of the Word of God must be allowed to take precedence over human emotion and logic. Such incredulity may go some way to explain Goforth's benignly intended but fundamentally harmful psychological manipulation of Manchurian Christians. But no matter what his intention was, the limitation he placed on God's readiness to forgive was a very serious error to hold, let alone advance. Goforth's error is ably and succinctly repudiated by William Still: 'Nothing so proves our guilt as the sense of condemnation which refuses to admit the possibility of mercy, and nothing so proves our blindness to the love of God as our blank unbelief of his real, complete and final forgiveness.'[24]

None of this is to deny that there were matters related to godly living that undoubtedly required to be addressed in the Manchurian church. There always are such flaws in any Christian and in every church, but the way to deal with them is not by a psychologically induced crisis experience, but through the ordinary patient, longterm, faithful ministry of the Word, carefully applied.

For all that we perceive of his theological faults, there is no reason to doubt that Goforth's sincere desire was to see Christians blessed; neither is it right to deny the authenticity and value of the revival that ensued. God is always greater than our hearts. But generosity of spirit is no justification for ignoring Goforth's unfortunate utilisation of Finney's theories of revival and his confused intertwining of justification with sanctification.[25] The truth is, that in most of the interlinked revivals of the early twentieth century the pure gold of revival was transported by very rickety conveyances. Thankfully, most influential Chinese leaders, such as Chang and Liu, maintained their distance from the world of Finney and Keswick, which mitigated the worst aberrations and allowed the revival to progress less erratically than it might otherwise have done. All of which reminds us that ultimately the spotlight must never be turned upon fallible human agents, but always upon the God of surpassing power and infinite grace, and the inestimable treasure of his gospel.

20

The Manchurian Revival: This is the Work of God

Don't go near them. Their Spirit has come down, and he is irresistible!

FROM the cross-currents swirling around Jonathan Goforth's theology and methods, we turn with relief to the events of the revival itself. One narrative of the revival is Goforth's *By My Spirit,* published in Britain by Marshall, Morgan and Scott, with a foreword by the publisher's editorial director, J. Kennedy Maclean. This brief account was written almost thirty years after the event, from memory, and evidently with less than perfect recall. With the approval of its publishers it expresses and promotes Goforth's commitment to the teachings of Finney and the Higher Life movement.

The most important contemporary account of the revival, closest to the events themselves, comes from James Webster and originated as a series of letters posted to Edinburgh to be transcribed and published by John Ross, during his 1908 furlough. It was written originally for Scottish supporters of the United Free Church's Manchurian mission. The first edition of just sixty-four pages carried the title *The Marvellous Story of the Revival in Manchuria.* It consists of Ross' preface and five brief chapters. The second and third editions, under the title *Times of Blessing in Manchuria,* were published by the Methodist Publishing house in Shanghai in 1908 and 1909. In these editions, Ross' preface, with its discrete criticism of Goforth, was supplanted by a more anodyne contribution by G. H. Bondfield, the agent of the British and Foreign Bible Society. Both of these editions include observations by the Irish Presbyterian missionaries Thomas Fulton of West Mukden, Frederick O'Neill of Fakumen, and William MacNaughtan at Hailungcheng. In 1910 an enlarged British edition was published by Marshall, Morgan and Scott, the Keswick Convention's publisher of choice, under the title *The Revival in Manchuria*. This time there was a historical introduction by Walter B. Sloan, well known as an advocate of Keswickism and as someone who shared Goforth's views.

After an introduction and warm appreciation of Jonathan Goforth himself, the ensuing chapters of Webster's first edition focus on the revival at Liaoyang, Mukden and the outstations. It ends with an assessment. The account that follows here draws primarily on Webster's and Ross' first edition, illuminated by the other editions, and on further accounts by others, including Goforth.

In Liaoyang, the meetings for Chinese New Year 1908 were held in the Wylie Memorial Church, named in honour of Rev. James Wylie who had been murdered by irregular troops at the end of the Sino-Japanese war. Right at the outset, an opportunity was given to Chang and Liu to share what they had seen and heard across the border. Both their initial and subsequent contributions to the revival are of such a magnitude that they must not be overshadowed by the work of any of the missionaries, including Jonathan Goforth. Because both men appear to have been largely unswayed by the theological crosscurrents emanating from the West, not only was their account of the Korean revival essentially objective, focussing, as it did, upon outcomes more than methods, but they also were able to stabilise the Manchurian Church after the excesses of Goforth's preaching. They were men held in the very highest regard by their missionary colleagues. T. C. Fulton, the missionary in charge of the West Church of Mukden, recorded his appreciation of Chang's ministry:

> To the coming of these two men, even more than to Mr Goforth, I attribute very much of the success of these fine meetings. I will not readily forget the first time I heard them relate the wonderful things they had seen and heard in Korea. Their manner of speaking was quiet, but their whole appearance and tone, and gesture even, were

> awe-inspiring, and they made one feel that eternal things were awfully real to them.[1]

During the first part of the week, the congregation at Liaoyang listened attentively to Goforth's lengthy addresses, and the meetings passed off uneventfully. During the latter half of the week a number responded to appeals for public confession of sin and for men or women to lead in prayer. Rev. George Douglas of the United Free Church of Scotland reported:

> There are manifestations of a profound conviction and confession of sin, accompanied by great emotion, and general pleading for mercy and forgiveness from the whole body of the people, and a sense of responsibility for the [unbelievers] around. There are abject confessions of secret idolatry, fraud, theft, adultery, opium-smoking, gambling, various forms of deceit, resistance to the Spirit, and indifference to the salvation of souls. These are made before the whole congregation, and in great distress. It has been a most awe-inspiring and humbling experience for us all. Even outsiders have been drawn into the tempest of confession and prayer, and in some cases great fear has fallen on the neighbourhood. They say: 'What has come over the Christians? Yamen torture could not draw confessions such as these from human lips, and they are respectable people enough!' 'Don't go near them,' say others; 'their Spirit has come down, and he is irresistible! You will be drawn in before you know it.'[2]

In idiomatic English, a Mukden hospital assistant called Lin Yun Sheng wrote to his former teacher, Catherine Macintyre (Ross' sister), in Haicheng to tell how unbelievers had been touched by the ministry of the Chinese evangelists:

> The effect was so great, that all the church members got roused.... They went up to Jesus one by one, cried for mercy, and owned their faults and sins. This great sight even touched the sight of outsiders. They knew their burdens were heavy enough to put them to death, but they did not know what to do. So they asked the evangelists if they could be saved. They were told, 'Jesus is not partial. He came to the world for nothing but sinners. He is only too pleased to see sinners repent, and will receive every one who cares to yield himself.' So they own their sin and become Christians immediately.[3]

Lin Yun Sheng told how Chung and Liu returned to Liaoyang to hold more meetings. The first, on Sunday, produced 'no effect whatever'. The first of two on Monday also passed off quietly, but at the second elder Liu, asking for careful attention to be paid to what was said, suddenly broke down. Lin recalled: 'He … began to weep in a very agony, looking so that no one who saw him could bear it. The room was filled with the voice of crying. Many of the [church] members and school boys owned their sins.' On Tuesday, there was some frank confession, and Wednesday was similar. Lin felt, however, that many were resisting: not giving 'their greatest burdens to OUR GRACIOUS SAVIOUR' (Lin's emphasis). Then on Thursday two outsiders arrived at the meeting. One was compelled to admit to his guilt, saying, '"I have many more sins than all the others. I am the chief bad man in the village. I used to persuade my people to go to law with others. I will not do anything like this again." He asked all the members to pray for him. So we obeyed and prayed for him. When all was finished, he said, "Ko liaopu te" (it is terrible). I hope he will soon become a Christian.' Lin was under no illusion that confession was the same as conversion: using the third person, he movingly and humbly described his own confession:

> And now I am afraid to tell you of one more who has been a Christian for a long time, but he did not do his duty. You would have been sorry for him if you had been present, for he is a friend of yours. He too owned his sins. He was sorry not only that he had sinned himself, but also because his relative sinned through him. You will deny that you have a friend like this; but you have, and he will sign his name at the end of this letter. My dear Mrs Macintyre, I hope our Great Lord will take up my heavy burden and deliver me. Will you be kind enough as to mention my name in your prayers, [so that I may] sin no more?[4]

Goforth himself barely mentions events at Liaoyang, though he recalled that a local missionary, Rev. George Douglas, likened what was happening to what he had heard from his father of the 1859 revival in Scotland. He also thought he remembered Douglas sharing with him an encouraging note which he had received from Rev. Samuel Moffet in Pyongyang, but which, in fact, was the letter brought back by Chang and Liu assuring the Liaoyang and

Mukden people of the prayers of their Korean brothers. Goforth also mentioned an 'anonymous' Chinese elder who exercised a very powerful and effective ministry after he had left; that person was, in fact, the highly regarded Chang.

From Liaoyang, Goforth travelled to Mukden, and almost immediately got himself into an altercation with his host, who, according to Goforth, denigrated the ministry of Dr MacKay, secretary of the Canadian Presbyterian Mission Board, by claiming that after hearing him at a conference in Shanghai he thought him no more than a 'windbag' with a theology 'as old as the hills'. Goforth resented this and retorted, 'I think we had better stop right here, my theology is just as old as MacKay's. In fact, it is as old as the Almighty himself.' The quarrel is interesting and may, in its own way, cast light on the infiltration of Higher Critical and liberal tendencies into the Mukden missionary circle, but without further information it is difficult to know what to make of it. Goforth's mood was not improved by his suspicion that his host's wife's absence in another city indicated her hostility to the revival, nor did he think much of his host's proposal that he should 'drop his planned addresses', and instead hold thanksgiving services. To which Goforth claimed to have replied, 'I believe that there is still much hidden sin to be uncovered…after I am through you can have all the thanksgiving meetings you like.'[5]

Goforth was a demanding guest. He complained about being disappointed in Mukden, he alleged hostility where there was probably none, and he grumbled about a failure to comply with his arbitrary stipulations. In response, it is worth noting that we would know nothing of these trivialities from those who bore the brunt of Goforth's disgruntled personality, if he had not felt the urge to justify himself in print.

The meetings at Mukden commenced on Saturday, 15th February. On Sunday about nine hundred attended morning service. It was even more remarkable to find as many at the evening service, as Chinese Christians were not accustomed to leave home after dark. This Webster attributed entirely to the influence of the Holy Spirit. At the Monday daytime service, Goforth invited the congregation to engage in public prayer 'if they felt moved by the Spirit'. An old man rose. He said he was bewildered by the expression, but he did have something to say. Directly addressing God, he unaffectedly expressed his desire to give himself wholeheartedly to the Lord forever. The sheer simplicity and utter sincerity of this request was deeply moving. Webster tellingly added, 'No manifestations followed, such as Mr Goforth longed for, but one was glad.'

That evening, however, the atmosphere became highly charged. Webster noted, 'Scores of people were praying in the most entangled fashion' and, half humorously added, 'One felt glad that it was not necessary to take down the minutes of that short sederunt. It was quite outside the limits of human interpretation. But the angel who keeps record of such proceedings was near at hand.'[6] On reflection, he noted that when the hysterical was minimal, the deep, quiet work reached its climax.

On Tuesday morning, Mr Liu, the Liaoyang deacon, gave a moving account of what he had witnessed in Korea. Next, Goforth spoke at great length, the large congregation paying full attention, with fifteen or more responding to an invitation to pray audibly and publicly. Again, Webster's observations are telling:

> The prayers were all manifestly the outpourings of hearts that had been powerfully moved. Pastor Liu [of the Dongguan congregation] has been greatly quickened. It is visible in his good old face. His son the doctor prayed to-day. He too has manifestly had a great uplift. Women prayed with great freedom, fervour, and gratitude. One was a little hysterical. But I don't think there will be much more of that. They were perhaps too much repressed in the first few days.[7]

At the evening meeting the church was three-quarters full when Liu's account of his time in Korea disquieted Webster, because he thought he 'measured everything by what he saw there'. Webster added, 'But I hope the people will not follow in a stereotyped fashion like a flock of sheep. The beautiful thing about the movement hitherto has been its… simple natural expression of the human soul touched by the Spirit.'[8]

On Wednesday morning it was Chang's turn to give a stirring address on the Korean revival. This was followed by some intense and emotional prayers; then Sung, a deposed elder, stood up, quite distraught, only to sit down again, burying his head in his hands. Finally, he rose to his feet, approached the pulpit and burst forth in a torrent of confession before falling to the ground in an agony of remorse. His confession triggered others to rush forward, throw themselves upon the ground and break forth in their own confessions. Webster attempted to reduce all this to notes, but there was such a hubbub that he was totally defeated.

As calm was restored, Sung slowly and deliberately rose to his feet once more. Removing a decorative gold bangle from his arm and a ring from his finger, he placed them on a table, disowning them as symbols of his pride and vanity, asking only that God would have mercy upon him. At that point a lone voice from the women's side was heard praying earnestly and tenderly for Sung's forgiveness. It was his wife, who all through Sung's spiritual decline had remonstrated with him and encouraged him. Totally overwhelmed, Webster commented, 'What happened thereafter that morning I cannot recall. We were like men in a dream.'[9]

On Thursday the building was full of people hungry to receive a blessing, though the mood was now calmer and better ordered, which elicited from Webster the remark, 'God be thanked for that,... elders, deacons, evangelists, members young and old, inquirers, backsliders, all are of one mind resolved...not to miss the blessing.' At one point, the whole congregation audibly prayed together at the same time, but Webster records, 'there was not the slightest discord. They were all of one mind.' At this meeting a note of renewed dedication led many to pledge land and money for the work of the gospel. Though at the time sincerely meant, many of these promises were impetuous and not always honoured.

On Friday Pastor Liu presided over a meeting where a wonderful spirit of prayer prevailed. When he asked for a few of the men to pray for himself and the elders, the whole congregation spontaneously and audibly responded. Liu had asked for prayer because he faced the difficult task of challenging backslidden Christians present in the church. This he did affectionately and gently. Affirming that church discipline would be applied where appropriate, he nevertheless longed for the day when all would be restored and united in worship and service. He then, rhetorically, asked the congregation to pray for their backslidden brothers and sisters, but the request was immediately and literally acted upon as the congregation 'set up one united cry to God, mingled with tears.' Such meetings, thought Webster, were not at all difficult to conduct. Because of the presence of the Holy Spirit, he believed they conducted themselves.

Friday was Mr Goforth's final day. Though he left, the blessing remained. Indeed it intensified. Its primary agents were Chinese. The missionaries, rightly fearful lest their participation as foreigners might hinder the work of God, had telegraphed to the Rev. Dr James Lowrie of an American Presbyterian Mission southwest of Beijing, asking him to send the Chinese pastor, Rev. Meng Chi Tseng, a good friend of Pastor Liu's, to assist at Mukden. With some difficulty, Meng was able to extricate himself from other commitments and, within the week, both he and an assistant, Elder Li, arrived in Mukden. In his first brief address, Meng told how his father had been converted when William Chalmers Burns had visited Beijing forty years earlier and how from childhood he had wanted to visit Manchuria, as 'the land beyond the barrier', as Manchuria was known, because his father considered it to be sacred because it contained the burial place of Pin Wei Liang (Burns). Meng continued:

> You are reaping today in this revival movement the fruit of the prayers of that man of God, who, just over forty years ago, began to pray for this which we now see and hear, the outpouring of the Spirit of God upon Manchuria. Even then Mr Burns, in his dreary lodging, in Newchwang, waiting patiently for the Master's call and praying while it tarried, even then he saw this day in vision, and was glad. 'God,' he said, 'will carry on his work in Manchuria. I have no fear of that.'[10]

Meng's first address was his last in the revival. The following day he fell ill and was taken to hospital, to remain there for ten days. The burden now fell on Elder Li, under whose ministry the meetings took a fresh form. Though often two or three hours long, they consisted largely of prayer. People stood to ask for prayer, both for themselves and also for friends and family. These verbal requests were often detailed, and Li struggled to make sense of some of them, mostly because the notion of 'prayer requests' was entirely novel. But he rose to the occasion, asking only that the requests be written out and handed up to the pulpit for him to read to the congregation. Webster incorporated a number of these in his letters to Ross, of which these are examples:

> Chu Ching Ho, a miserable sinner, who has been a Christian for twenty years, denied Christ and worshipped idols at the Boxer time, has been indifferent ever since. Pray for me and for my wife, who is not a Christian. Alas! I have never done anything to induce her to become one. Pray that God may have mercy upon me.[11]
>
> Hsiang Yang Sheng, a sinner without compare, who has transgressed every one of God's commandments. Pray the Lord in his infinite mercy to compassionate me. Also for my son, for many years a member, but who has drifted away, and never goes to church. Also alas! to my great sorrow my daughter-in-law and grandson are still outside. Pray to the Lord for them, and for me, that he may have mercy upon us all. I send five dollars along with this, a token of my repentance.[12]

The impression created by seven or eight hundred people simultaneously and audibly praying was unforgettable. According to Webster, there was no confusion, but a harmonious symphony of prayer was borne heavenwards in the power of the Spirit and through the intercession of the Mediator. All were impressed by the ministry of Mr Li. His humility, spiritual discernment and aptness of message fitted so perfectly the needs of the people and the time, and marked him out as one sent by God. When a lady missionary commented that he was 'the man for the hour', Webster agreed, remarking that had they 'searched China through we could not have found a man whose message could more exactly fit the psychological moment.'[13]

Mr Li's careful choice of texts meant that 'the troubled in soul were led to look to Christ', and 'The despairing got hope'. In others a sense of duty was stimulated by sermons from texts such as 'As we forgive our debtors,' 'Remember the Sabbath day, to keep it holy,' and 'Lay up for yourselves treasures in Heaven.' The congregation concentrated intently upon the Word, busily filling up their notebooks and leading Webster to conjecture that 'Mr Lee's expositions and apt illustrations will do service in many places for many days to come.'[14]

The revival was also beginning to make moral changes in the lives of those who had been blessed. The tight-fisted began to be generous. Businessmen who had kept their stores open seven days a week now observed the Lord's Day. Men hitherto timid, courageously carried the message of the revival to the outlying districts. Three lady dispensers in the hospital felt they would like to show their love to the Lord by increasing their donations to Christian work, but not wanting to act rashly asked for prayer 'that the Holy Spirit may help us in this our earnest purpose'. A wealthy young merchant pledged a regular sum of money for the men's hospital, the women's hospital, the Bible Society, and local educational and evangelistic agencies. Movingly, a very poor man humbly handed a note to the minister asking that he, the elders and the members pray the Lord to accept his black calf with the white stripe as a thank offering for the blessing he had received.

There were conversions too. A young man who had, in 1900, joined the Boxers had been in a misery of conscience ever since and cried out for mercy. The congregation prayed for him with 'unusual fervour'. Another disclosed how he had exploited the instability caused by the Boxer Rising to appropriate property and steal money. Now, deeply ashamed, he sought forgiveness. Li's ministry at Mukden surpassed all that went before, causing Webster to recognise how 'everything in the Divine working is old and everything old is new.' Indeed, he could find no better way of summarising what God was doing in Mukden than to quote words uttered one hundred and seventy years earlier by Jonathan Edwards:

> The goings of God were then seen in his Sanctuary, his tabernacles were amiable, our public assemblies were then beautiful. The congregation was alive in God's service, every one earnestly intent upon the public worship. Every hearer was eager to drink in the words of the minister as they came from his mouth.[15]

After Mukden, the revival branched out into surrounding groups of Christians which had come into existence during the great ingathering following the Sino-Japanese war of 1894. Each of these embryonic churches had its own characteristics, and each was at a different stage of development, a few progressing in the faith, but many stagnating. Their inertia, thought Webster, was mostly attributable to the inability of over-stretched missionaries to instruct, baptise and admit new converts into the membership of the church, and to nurture those young in the faith. Consequently, few had been prepared for the Boxers' ultimatum that their lives would be spared only if they denied their Lord. Weak faith found life sweet and lies cheap. Many lied to live, and after the terror had subsided returned to their homes, rebuilt their fortunes, restored their waste places, but few repented of their apostasy. Then the trials of war came again, with Russian and Japanese forces requisitioning livestock and crops, devastating fields and driving people from their homes. What was left of faith soured and Christian hope withered. Peace brought its dividends. Increasing prosperity saw the meeting places renovated and the services recommenced, though a cold formality had replaced the old ardour. Such rural outstations were ripe for revival, but the network was far too large for Elder Li to visit, even if he could have left his duties in Paotingfu for so long a period. It was decided, therefore, to organise the outstations into seven districts and appoint two or three men to work together in each. A call for volunteers found a ready response, with the number offering exactly matching the number required.

In the minds of these volunteers, some outstations were considered more desirable or promising than others, making the decision of whom to send where very fraught, and calling for the wisdom and skill of a diplomat. To resolve matters, the missionaries decided to cast lots. Each volunteer's name was written on a slip of paper and thrown into the hat of Mr Liu, the Mukden minister. The first district called was Changtan, and the first name called was of a man who really did not want to go there, but with good natured resignation, he saw the irony and uttered, 'Ai Ah! This is surely the Lord's doing.' Others followed his example, subjugating their own whims to the providence of the draw.

After the morning service on the Sunday of the fourth week of the meetings, the minister called out the names of the volunteers, inviting them to line up in front of the pulpit. A brief address, wise and encouraging, was followed by heartfelt prayer commissioning the men. On Monday evening the congregation prayed with urgency and earnestness for all the volunteers, before taking leave of each other by an emotional rendition of the valedictory hymn, 'God be with you till we meet again.' At dawn on the following Tuesday a motley collection of carts left the church bearing their occupants to all points of the compass around Mukden.

Sometime later, James Webster and Dr Liu found themselves at the village of Tuerto, thirty miles from Mukden. This village was reputed to be the least encouraging of all the outlying groups, so without a moment's hesitation, Dr Liu organised messengers to go out to invite all who were interested to come on Wednesday morning. About sixty came to hear Webster and Liu simply telling the story of the past three weeks in Mukden – nothing more. Politely, the people listened with curiosity and thoughtfulness, but when they returned in the evening, Webster and Liu thought they looked perplexed. Early on Thursday morning, as they walked together, Liu shared with Webster his misgivings about his suitability for that kind of work and regretted offering to come. Their walk brought them to a small clump of trees, where they knelt by an old willow to seek guidance. Liu's prayer was succinct and in tune with Webster's thoughts. 'Guide us,' he prayed, 'as to who shall speak, what we shall say or whether we should speak at all.' When they returned for the first gathering of the day, Webster thought Liu had been re-energised.

Liu led the meeting. After a hymn, he invited the congregation to engage in silent prayer, adding that if anyone wished to pray audibly, they might. The silence was broken by a sob from the front row, which became a brokenhearted prayer for mercy. Then a man seated at the back stood up. Making his way forward, he asked to speak, but overcome with emotion, words came only with difficulty. Gaining control, he said that he knew that he had a reputation as a good Christian, but it was not deserved. In fact, he had been very displeased when Webster and Liu had turned up the previous day because with their arrival a sense of foreboding had crept across his soul. When he heard of the revival in Mukden, rather than his anxiety being allayed, it had been heightened, and for the last hours he had dreaded his unmasking as a hypocrite. Then, falling to his knees, he sought God's pardon and the prayers of others.

The impact was electrifying. The whole congregation was moved. There followed such a flow of simultaneous prayer that it did not subside until three hours had passed. During this time Webster and Liu moved unobtrusively among the congregation seeking to help the most distressed. Here, repeating a text; there, pointing a soul to the Saviour, singing with others a verse of a hymn. Some were almost inconsolable, troubled by memories of what they had done at the Boxer time. 'Not only did I worship the idols myself,' sobbed one grief-stricken man, 'but I led my old mother to the temple and made her do the same, *and she is dead*!' He refused to be comforted.

The evening meeting saw a repetition of the morning's spontaneity. By Friday, praise was added to prayer. Gone now the dry formality. The stereotyped prayers uttered half unthinkingly for years has been replaced with vitality and freshness. These 'new petitions,' noted Webster, 'were offered with a new reverence, a new solemnity, a new humility, and a new assurance of faith, as children to a father,…in the matter of praying, as in much else, "old things have passed away, all things have become new."'[16]

Leaving Dr Liu to continue the work at Tuerto, Webster moved on to the village of Panchiapu, to meet a volunteer he had sent on ahead. Here sixty people gathered to hear the story of the revivals in Mukden and in neighbouring Tuerto. They listened politely, expressed some interest, but little more. The following morning, Webster spoke to a larger gathering. He invited prayer, and a few prayed in the old stilted traditional style. Nothing happened. Fearful that he, a foreigner, was the hindrance, Webster urged them to attend the thanksgiving meeting in Tuerto on Sunday. Many agreed to go.

That evening Webster reached Szefangtai where Dr Liu had preceded him. Some of the folk from the village had been to Tuerto and had received a blessing there and these had encouraged so many of their neighbours to attend the meeting that the place was packed when Webster arrived. Lighting the candles as dusk fell, he began. What ensued is best told in his own words:

> What a meeting that was! It needed no conducting, or very little. Occasionally it seemed well to sing a verse of a hymn, or repeat a

> divine promise, that was all. Yet there was no excitement, nothing calling for restraint.... The house was full of men and women with broken and contrite hearts, and the floor was simply watered with their tears. One had heard of such meetings. Our fathers had told us of their having been eye-witnesses to something similar, in their day, in Scotland – long ago, but we had never seen it in this fashion. It was just great, writ large. The house where we were gathered was a humble enough one, mud walled, mud floored and smoke begrimed; but it was for the moment transfigured, and became the House of God and the very Gate of Heaven.[17]

It reminded Webster of a passage from Bunyan's *Pilgrim's Progress*:

> Now I saw in my dream, that by this time the Pilgrims had entered into the country of Beulah, whose air was very sweet and pleasant. Here they continually heard the singing of birds, and every day saw new flowers appear, and heard the song of the turtle-dove in the land. In this country the sun shines both night and day. Here they were within sight of the city to which they were traveling and met some of its inhabitants – for in this land the shining ones commonly walked, because it was upon the borders of heaven.[18]

The meeting could have been interminable, but time was regulated by the candles burning out in their sockets. Then, one man brought out and lit a primitive oil lamp that gave off as much smoke as light and, by its faint light, thank-offerings were written out. The villagers were poor, but their generosity amazing.

Next morning, the Sabbath, found Webster back at Tuerto for the thanksgiving service. Telling Dr Liu how lukewarm the response had been in Panchiapu, Liu replied by expressing how disappointed he would be if those folk were to be passed over without a blessing. But there was a blessing for the Panchiapu people, for a good number of them, both men and women, had walked the ten miles to take part in the Tuerto service. Liu felt he should share his concern for Panchiapu with the congregation. As softly murmured prayers filled the room, the word 'Panchiapu' was clearly heard, repeated time and again. When this subsided, a lone voice was heard. It was that of the leading deacon of Panchiapu. Starting out with the tedious old traditional form of prayer, he suddenly realised that stereotypical prayers were lifeless husks, and let himself go. In ordinary speech he asked, 'Oh, Lord, don't leave our Panchiapu;' adding somewhat apologetically, 'there's nothing really wrong with Panchiapu, only *we are just deadly cold*.'[19]

When the meeting ended, the Panchiapu deacon and members approached Dr Liu and Webster, imploring them to return to their village and refusing to take no for an answer. Had they not seen others blessed? Had they not been blessed themselves? Now they must see their own village blessed too! So they prevailed upon Dr Liu to go back with them for three days. With Liu at Panchiapu, Webster went eight miles in the opposite direction to meet the deputies who had been at Changtan. 'They had,' said Webster, 'the bearing of men who had been at the wars and had returned victorious. It was the joy of the Seventy over again. "Lord, even the devils are subject unto us through Thy Name."'[20]

Not least among the many blessings that Webster noted was the remarkable maturing, in a very brief space of time, of the once reticent and anxious Dr Liu, who was now a deeply spiritual leader of the movement, strong and confident in the Faith. Liu gave the last address before their return to Mukden. The congregation unanimously and enthusiastically responded by spontaneously singing a hymn containing the words:

> My body, soul and spirit,
> Saviour, I give to Thee.

But for Webster, Scottish Presbyterian that he was, nothing was quite so fitting to express the mood as a psalm, and none more suitable than the Scottish Metrical version of Psalm 126.

> When Zion's bondage God turned back,
> As men that dreamed were we,
> Then filled with laughter was our mouth
> Our tongues with melody.
>
> They 'mong the heathen said the Lord,
> Great things for them hath wrought.
> The Lord hath done great things for us,
> Whence joy to us is brought.

With this anecdote Webster's first batch of letters to Ross in Edinburgh drew to an end, though he continued privately to add to his manuscript further observations, a growing collection of anecdotes, letters and other written accounts that charted the revival's movement across the country, both in the larger towns and cities, such as Liaoyang and the port of Newchwang, and the remote outstations and villages that had shared in the blessings. He recorded many varieties of religious experience, from deepest conviction of sin, where it hung in the balance whether an individual would humble themselves and confess, or whether the burden of guilt would drive them insane; to the highest forms of spiritual elation and the pure relief of forgiven sin and the rolling away of its burden; it included the joy of families united in the faith, as well as the glimpse many felt they had had of the glory of heaven and the Lamb upon the Throne.

Overall, Webster felt that those who had benefitted most from the revival, and who would in turn most benefit others, had been the Chinese evangelists. Passing through a village where three of these men had been holding meetings, Webster had wanted a word with them, but they were nowhere to be found. A person who knew, pointed to some trees at the top of a hill, adding, 'They go there to pray every morning for several hours.' To which Webster added, 'When they came down from their oratory to see me they wist not that their faces shone!'

The Holy Spirit did not discriminate on the grounds of sex, background, wealth, status or age. Women and men, young and old, poor and wealthy, noble and humble, were alike brought into a new appreciation of the gospel, granted a fresh insight into the wonder of grace, given a deeper love for Christ from which flowed a desire to serve him. Nor was it only Christians who were renewed, for there were conversions as well. But there were also disappointments; people for whom the missionaries held high hopes sometimes dismayed them.

The revival caught the interest and inspired the prayers of many, both in China and overseas, and, as always, there was a tendency on the part of those who heard accounts second or third hand to exaggerate or distort. Webster felt that no adequate assessment could be made in the first flush of excitement; it would, he thought, take decades to see the lasting fruit. Maybe a generation or more would pass before an accurate appraisal could be given of the revival's results and long-term effectiveness. It is not hard to imagine how reading these words for the first time, John Ross would be deeply moved, nod his head in approval at his colleague's cautious sagacity, and incline warmly to agree with his conclusions.

Wonderful as were the things he had seen and heard, it was clear to Webster that, without in any way discouraging a desire for revival, such awakenings were not to be seen as a normal element in the life of the Church, even if the grim realities of coldness of heart and rebellion against God were constants. Quoting from an unacknowledged source, Webster warned his readers: 'Revivals rise and fall, but the influences of worldliness and vice abide with fresh and awful persistency.'[21] So if revivals were not the normal solution to the problem, what was? The answer, thought Webster, lay in faith, the regular services of worship, the proclamation of the Word of God, and prayer. God's answer to the fallenness of this world was the inextricably intertwined mission of Christ and the mission of his church, in the power of the Spirit. Webster discouraged any tendency to luxuriate in the blessings of revival, rather he stirred up the church to fix its attention afresh on the task that remained.

> 'Look, I tell you, lift up your eyes, and see that the fields are white for harvest' (John 4:35).
>
> 'The harvest is plentiful, but the labourers are few; therefore pray earnestly to the Lord of the harvest to send out labourers into his harvest' (Matt. 9:37-38).

With the publication of a growing number of missionary memoirs and biographies, assessments of the revival of 1908 and its effects came sooner than Webster had cautioned. At a time when new and unwelcome ideas were being introduced into the Manchurian missionary community, both from the Higher Critical and liberal perspective, and from fundamentalist sources, what struck Webster was that all the one hundred and fifty Protestant missionaries in Manchuria, whether Presbyterian, Episcopal or Lutheran, were unanimous in agreeing that whatever may have been said of its human defects, the revival of 1908 was essentially a work of God's gracious Spirit.

Writing in 1933, after the death of her husband, Andrew Weir of the Irish Presbyterian mission, Margaret Weir referred to the 'limitations of the revival', but notwithstanding she held that it had 'brought a fresh conception of prayer, a new desire for fellowship with God, a deeper sense of responsibility and new joy in service.'[22] It had also boosted confidence in preaching, an earnestness in evangelism, and a greater initiative in Christian service. Nevertheless, it was true that the revival's effects were, on the whole, ephemeral and its potential largely unfulfilled. By 1911, the external manifestations, such as public confession of sin, weeping, simultaneous praying aloud, making public vows and promises, had either lapsed into a new conventionality, or had completely passed away. Some parts of the church became once more notorious for spiritual coldness and inertia.

A report commissioned by the Manchurian Presbyterian missionary conference stated that 'the net result of permanent spiritual fruit, though real and precious, has been much less than we had hoped, and the evangelistic work was specially disappointing.'[23] Numerous promises hastily made had not been kept, and many who had claimed to have been blessed had lapsed once more into their old faults. Indeed, the sudden onrush of an unsustainable warmth had made the church colder. The lesson to be learned was that a craving for the awesomely vivid, highly emotional and dramatic events of revival was unhealthy and unhelpful. These were not the main channels in which the Spirit worked: God was more often to be found in the ordinary. The compiler of the report, Andrew Weir, was aware of what he liked to call the tides of the Spirit: the constant ebb and flow of the work of God in the world. The church's best preparation for a high tide of revival, he held, was faithfulness in the ordinary work of teaching and prayer, with an awareness of need and a sense of expectancy.[24]

Weir's liberal Irish Presbyterian colleague, Frederick W. S. O'Neil, who might have been suspected of a degree of cynicism, in fact very much took the opposite view. In his highly controversial and syncretistic book, *The Quest for God in China*, published in 1925, he made a single, though very warm, reference to the revival, recounting how his friend and colleague, Rev. Ching Wen Liu of Fakumen, had, before 1908, 'given his heart to the Lord, but that outpouring of the Spirit crowned his conversion with blessing and flooded his soul with joy.'[25] In an earlier book, *The Call of the East*, O'Neil spoke of William Burns looking 'forward in vision to such a day' and adding, 'it was the best Christians who received the greatest uplift. Their eyes saw the King in his beauty. Very many changed lives date from the time of blessing in 1908.'[26]

Publishing her husband's biography some twenty-five years after the revival, Dr Christie's wife Iza, whose evangelicalism was of the broadest, warmly recollected the revival. She included in her narrative the confession of Christie's assistant, Lin Yun Sheng, adding that Christie had been one for whom 1908 had 'carried [him] back to the old stories he had heard in childhood of the Revival of 1859.'[27]

This unity, however, is disturbed by Austin Fulton (no relation of the Irish missionary T.C. Fulton) who, in his 1967 assessment of the Manchurian mission, *Through Earthquake Wind and Fire*, cast a jaundiced eye on the revival, using, in his very first mention of the word, the distancing device known colloquially as scare quotes, to cast doubt upon its authenticity. Nevertheless, even he cities with favour a comment of the United Free Church missionary, Daniel T. Robertson, that one lasting lesson of the revival was that to 'faith in one God, and joy in his mercy, was added this – that he must be served in righteousness.'[28]

Jonathan Goforth's account of the revival, written when he was over seventy, is an interesting miscellany of anecdotes, which, although it offers no analysis of the effects of 1908, by its very title, *By My Spirit,* maintains the positive consensus. This brings us back to Webster, for whom the clinching argument that the revival was a genuine work of the Spirit lay in the fact that over and over again, 'hard-headed Scotchmen, not much given to emotionalism at any time, and with a strong temperamental prejudice against religious hysteria in all its forms, were heard to say one to the other, with a sort of awe in their voice, "This is the work of God."' Among such hard-headed but soft-hearted Scots could be counted his friend and colleague John Ross.

Returning from furlough and arriving in Mukden in October 1908, Ross found that the intensity, excitement and stir of the previous months had subsided, but he appeared not to have been disappointed because the best blessings endured. In his report to the Foreign Missions Committee he was deeply grateful that:

> We received a very cordial welcome from the Christians .... The emotional side of the Revival has subsided, but the useful will remain. The people are calling a second pastor .... The Liaoyang people are also calling a pastor. Mr Webster reports: 'We have now about a dozen pastors.'
>
> The Sunday on which I arrived (25th) there were over 60 baptisms in the church by Pastor Liu. In other places I hear of many baptisms and of numbers of catechumens.
>
> I am glad to learn that the [Chinese] members in presbytery are more ready to take decided part in the ecclesiastical matters raised. No Session in Scotland carries on its work in a more business-like manner than that at Moukden.[29]

The May 1909 issue of the *Missionary Record* carried a rousing article by Ross reviewing the spiritual life and progress of the Manchurian church and calling for yet more dedicated action. It concluded with this paragraph.

> Surely the experiences of the Church of God in Manchuria within the present generation – from nothing to its present condition – calls for adoring praise, rouses the most daring hopes, and urges real effort for the conquest of the world into 'the Kingdom which is Righteousness and Peace and Joy in the Holy Ghost.'[30]

21

Peace, Perfect Peace

Peace, perfect peace, death shadowing us and ours?
Jesus has vanquished death and all its powers.
EDWARD HENRY BICKERSTETH

AS the first decade of the twentieth century approached its end, Ross, now in his late-sixties, with his health in decline, knew that time was running out. Probably acting on the advice of Dr Christie, he returned to Scotland in 1908 for a period of rest, medical consultations and discussions with the United Free Church Mission Committee concerning his future. Whether it was at this time that his terminal cancer was diagnosed is unclear. The Foreign Missions Committee considered it inadvisable for him to return. Ross, undeterred, made clear his intention to do so, offering to pay his own travelling expenses there and back if required. The committee gave way and agreed to 'sanction his going out in time to resume the Senior Theological Class in November'. In September 1909, John and Isabella and family made the long journey back to Mukden.

The Korean scholar, Dr Peter Ahrn-ho Bae, depicts this as Ross' last act of devotion to the Manchurian Church. Maybe he is right. What was certainly uppermost in Ross' mind, as in the minds of his Manchurian colleagues, was the need to reap the fruit of the revival. To minimise demands upon him, the Missionary Conference secretary, J. Miller Graham, informed the church at home and his missionary colleagues in Manchuria, that nothing should stand in the way of training Chinese pastors 'if they are to gather up the rich spiritual harvesting of the past three years'.[1]

Ross now resumed doing what he most enjoyed, equipping a body of men who would minister across Manchuria, in evangelism and the pastorate, as free as possible of dependence upon overseas missionaries. This period of service was, however, to be brief, very brief, less than six months. At the beginning of 1910, to set matters in order before his retiral from the field, he asked the Missionary Conference to appoint a successor in the Theological College. At the end of February, he was informed in a letter from Edinburgh that he had been appointed a delegate of the United Free Church to the World Missionary Conference to be held later that year. On 1st April, Frank Ashcroft, secretary to the Foreign Mission Committee, forwarded to Ross a cheque in the sum of £80 to cover his travelling expenses to Scotland, but quibbled, saying that if he took a summer break at the same time as attending the conference he would have to pay, but if it proved to be his final journey home the Committee would assume responsibility. By July, Ross, then sixty-eight-years-old, had submitted his resignation on the grounds of ill health, which 'with deep regret' the Foreign Mission Committee accepted, granting him an annual pension of £150 from the Invalided Missionaries Fund, provided he submitted a medical certificate.[2] Amongst other things, the minute paid tribute to Ross' work:

> In 1872 he was appointed missionary to China, and went to Shantung. Being impressed with the statement there was not a single Protestant Missionary in Manchuria while several Missions were carrying on work in Shantung, he crossed the Gulf of Pechili and began to preach Christ in Newchwang, where he soon had the joy of baptising converts. After a time he went to Moukden where he was the first resident Missionary to preach the Gospel. He met with much difficulty in finding a lodging, but before long he saw the fruits of his labours in souls being led to Christ. Latterly he has devoted most of his strength to training theological students, many of whom have been ordained as pastors of churches. Dr Ross has always taken a wide, statesmanlike view of the work to be accomplished, and the methods he early adopted laid the foundation on which our Manchurian Mission was built.[3]

At some point prior to 1890, Ross had purchased the Balintore estate in Easter Ross as a provision for his family after his death. The property was substantial, consisting of two farms, together with their sporting rights, a number of cottages and houses, a financial interest in the Balintore harbour, and some quarries, possibly gravel pits. By his death in 1915, he was in receipt of an income from twenty-five tenants, plus the Balintore Harbour trustees and Sir Charles Ross of Balnagowan for sporting rights. This was adequate to ensure the family's financial security for decades to come. Ross stipulated that on his death the property should be sold at full commercial value on the open market and the proceeds used to meet the terms of his will. It appears that Ross' holdings had been paid for in part by a substantial loan from his wife, who came from a family with wealthy connections. Her brother John Macfadyen was a Glasgow merchant, and a cousin, Robert F. Moffat, was a very successful businessman with a city centre office in Glasgow's Ingram Street and a prestigious home at 44 Granby Terrace, Hillhead. Both were executors of Ross' estate.[4]

Nevertheless, despite having property in the area, Ross did not choose to live the life of a laird and retire to his boyhood home; instead he purchased an Edinburgh residence at 12 Marchhall Crescent in Newington, a southern suburb. History gives us very few glimpses into the private life of the family, barely enough for us to imagine them at home in Edinburgh during much of the year but spending the summer at Balintore, strolling along the easily accessible beach, restfully enjoying the views across the Moray Firth, renewing contact with relatives and friends to regale them with tales of China. This is corroborated not only by the mundane fact that in August and September 1908, letters from the United Free Church Mission Committee were addressed to Ross at Balintore, but also borne out by a humorous anecdote picked up by James Grayson in the 1970s from another Hugh Ross of Balintore. One day, after his retiral, John Ross, so the story goes, was chatting with some local farmers but was met with blank incomprehension until his son, who was at his side, reminded him that he was speaking Chinese! As Grayson comments, even in old age Ross was so perfectly at ease with Chinese, English and Gaelic that he could not immediately distinguish which language he was speaking. He is said to have had facility in eleven different languages.[5]

In Edinburgh, Dr and Mrs Ross and their son John attended Mayfield United Free Church on the corner of Causewayside and West Mayfield, about a ten-minute walk from their home. The congregation had been founded as a Free Church of Scotland congregation in 1875 by Professor William Garden Blaikie, to serve the rapidly expanding suburb of Newington. By 1910, Mayfield had a communicant membership of around six hundred and a vibrant ministry to young people. The family found a warm welcome, being added to the roll of communicant members in January 1911. At its following meeting, Ross was associated with the Kirk Session, busily serving as an unelected elder in the congregation, visiting members in their homes in a large district, inspecting the parish's schools, and right up to the end serving on various presbytery committees.[6]

Ross shared with his minister, Rev. Lewis Davidson, a common interest in overseas missions and the church in the Highlands. In 1890 Davidson had spent a year serving the Free Church in Calcutta and visiting mission work in India, and in 1901 four months at Woollahra Presbyterian Church, Sydney, Australia. Between 1900 to 1905, he had itinerated in the Highlands, visiting many places in Inverness-shire, Ross-shire, the Black Isle and Sutherland, well known to Ross, trying to persuade conservative Highlanders to join the new United Free Church, just as Ross had earlier tried to do for the United Presbyterians, and with just about as much success because of the aversion of most Highlanders towards New College on account of the liberalism which they believed was being taught there. In 1910 Glasgow University conferred on Davidson the honorary degree of Doctor of Divinity. He intimated his resignation to the Kirk Session in November 1911 and spent the following winter at Cannes on the French Riviera, where he died on 3rd February, 1912.[7] In Davidson's absence, and until the congregation could arrange an interim moderator, Ross agreed *pro tem* to moderate the Kirk Session and undertake the minister's duty of visiting the sick of the congregation.[8]

It is likely that Davidson's successor, Ross' new minister, J. Lorimer Munro, also afforded him a large measure of satisfaction, for not only was Munro something of a scholar, but he was also of Ross' own denominational background, the United Presbyterian Church. Had he heard it, Ross would doubtless have been amused at a comment overheard after Munro's induction: 'the Union is real – a U. P. minister called to a Free Church!'[9] It was Munro who settled Ross' status as an elder. At a meeting arranged to elect a further twelve elders, the congregation was asked to formally agree with the Kirk Session's earlier decision to include Ross as one of their number.[10]

The family's return to Scotland coincided with the 1910 World Missionary Conference in Edinburgh, to which Ross had been appointed a United Free Church delegate. The conference was held between 14th and 23rd June in the United Free Church Assembly Hall, and it is regarded as perhaps the best-known ecclesiastical event ever to have taken place in Scotland and arguably the most influential. The conference was a sequel to the largely evangelical international conferences in Liverpool in 1860, London, 1888, and New York, 1900. Edinburgh 1910, however, marked a significant turning point in world Christianity. True, the conference was held on a vast scale, with some one thousand two hundred and fifteen representatives (though only fifteen Asian delegates represented the non-western world), drawn from one hundred and seventy-six largely British and North American missionary societies. Yet, unlike the earlier conferences, it represented a broader swathe of Protestant theological opinion and provided a powerful stimulus to the embryonic ecumenical movement.

Roman Catholic and Orthodox representatives had not been invited, though the organisers, open to reviewing these historic divisions, had, at the behest of High Church Anglicans, taken the contentious decision only to invite delegates of societies working among non-Christian peoples, thereby excluding most of those who conducted missionary work in South American countries. In line with this newly found sensitivity was the abandonment of John R. Mott's snappy but combative original conference watchword: 'The Evangelisation of the World in This Generation.' Instead there appeared the unmemorable and anodyne alternative: 'A Consideration of the Problems facing Missionary Societies in the Non-Christian World.' We are not told how all this went down with Ross, but he may have approved of the exclusion of the Roman Catholic Church, not least because of his strong aversion to its missionary activity in China.

Edinburgh was chosen as the location of the conference after lobbying by Rev. John Fairley Daly, secretary of the Livingstonia Mission Committee of the United Free Church of Scotland. The United Free Church also provided Joseph Houldsworth Oldham, the able Conference Secretary. Oldham's skills ensured both the smooth-running of the event and its continuing influence. Scots also played a large part in the Conference's wide-ranging enquiries into world missions and to the depth of its analysis.[11] Ross himself was a contributor.

Any detailed discussion of Edinburgh 1910 is vastly beyond our scope, but two perceptive comments are worthy of quotation. The first from Prof. Andrew Walls indicates that Edinburgh 'was a landmark in the history of mission … the high point of the Western missionary movement and the point from which it declined.'[12] The second is from Harold H. Rowdon, son of Bolivian missionaries with links to the Brethren organisation, *Echoes of Service.* Rowdon saw Edinburgh 1910 as profoundly discouraging, noting that the wide embrace of liberal ecumenism actually turned a cold shoulder towards evangelicals: 'the new ecumenism attempted to find unity through common action on the part of those who were not united on fundamental doctrines. The result was the same on the wider stage as it had been in the colleges: evangelicals began to find themselves edged out of the very movement they had commenced.'[13]

Just as Ross had been delegated to speak for the United Presbyterian Church at the London conference of 1888, so now in Edinburgh he was a representative of the United Free Church of Scotland, as well as contributing in his own right.[14] On Wednesday 15th June, he opened a question on which he was a recognised expert, a topic close to his heart: *Is it advisable to have a large Native Agency for Evangelistic Work among non-Christians dependent upon Foreign Support?*

> In the year 1872 I landed on the muddy shores of Manchuria. I discovered that there was no baptized Christian, at all events no baptized Protestant in Manchuria. … The next year there were three

men baptized in Manchuria, and these three men were taught that if it was necessary for them to believe in order to be saved, it was equally necessary for them, and obligatory on them, that they should give forth the teachings which they had received. 'Freely ye have received, freely give.' That was the motto of the first three Christian men baptized in Manchuria. Up to the present moment there have been baptized in Manchuria something like thirty thousand men and women and children. There are hundreds of thousands who have a deep interest in Christianity. There are twelve pastors supported by the native Church and several evangelists supported also by the natives. Last year the native pastor in Moukden … baptized over three hundred persons, and there was also another pastor who baptized over three hundred, and there are at least double that number in another place. Idolatry is dead in Manchuria. The temples are all crumbling into ruin …. Buddhism has not a particle of influence. These are the results largely of the preaching of the Gospel in Manchuria. By whom? I make bold to say that of those forty thousand baptized people … not more than a hundred came into the Church … by means of the foreign missionary. All that vast number of Christians already in the Church, and the hundreds of thousands who are now interested in Christianity, have been instructed entirely by the native converts. We look out among these native converts who are the best soul-winners: we pick these out and we set them apart as evangelists, and we pay them with foreign money. … To me the question here is not the question of whence the money comes; to me that is a most unimportant matter. The question is – Get all the best agents you can, native or foreign, and get them introduced into the work of the field. If the native Church is unable to do all that is necessary, send by all means the money that you have to give. Is it foreign after you have given it to Christ for his work? … If you undertake the instruction of Christian natives throughout the world, and allocate to them their work, throw upon them their responsibility of teaching their families, and their neighbours, and their countrymen, you can overtake the whole world; but without this it seems to me a physical impossibility.[15]

His mature opinions, which carried all the authority of careful thought and great experience, were cited with approbation in other Conference documents, even when they departed from traditional opinion. Whilst conventional wisdom held that it would take a minimum of ten thousand missionaries to evangelise China, not all agreed: 'some experienced missionaries incline to the opinion of the Rev. John Ross, D.D., who says: "One missionary to a quarter of a million people is an adequate proportion, if he is the kind I desiderate."'[16] The unstated proviso was that Ross' ratio could only be effective if his strategy of working indirectly through local evangelists was carefully followed. In another section of the same report, under the heading *The Superhuman Factor,* Ross was quoted as affirming the absolute indispensability of the power of God in transforming societies: 'Education ... and other intellectual and physical aids ... all these combined ... would never have evolved the Church in Manchuria.'[17]

In retirement Ross continued writing. Indeed, from 1876 up to his death, rarely two or three years passed without some fresh volume from his pen, to say nothing of numerous articles and scholarly papers. His *Mandarin Primer* had been published in 1876, the next year came *Chinese Foreign Policy* and his *Corean Primer.* 1879 saw his *History of Corea, Ancient and Modern,* the first to be written by a westerner, and the following year, *The Manchus: Their Rise and Progress.* In 1882 the Korean primer was revised as *Korean Speech, with Grammar and Vocabulary.* In 1887 his literary accomplishments reached their zenith, with his epoch-making *Yesu sŏnggyo chŏnsŏ* (the Korean New Testament), the result of ten years' painstaking work.

The Religious Tract Society published *Old Wang* in 1889. In 1897 Ross agreed to write a number of Chinese commentaries. In 1901 *The Boxers in Manchuria* came off the press, and 1908 saw his edition of Webster's revival letters: *The Marvellous Story of the Revival in Manchuria.* The following year came *The Original Religion of China,* and his final work, *The Origin of the Chinese People,* was posthumously published in 1916. Few, however, of Ross' books remained long in print. By the end of the twentieth century all were scarce, rarely found even on second-hand booksellers' shelves. His Korean New Testament had been an early casualty, supplanted by an American translation in the less accessible language of the literary elite.

In addition to his writing, despite facing limitations due to increasing ill-health, in the period between returning home in

1910 up to November 1914, Ross continued to preach and raise support for the Foreign Missions Board, both in churches near to his Edinburgh home, such as in Whitburn and Blackburn in West Lothian, at St Andrew's Church, Falkirk, and Rev. T. W. Paterson's congregation at Mid Calder, as well as further away, in places such as Selkirk, Irvine, Hamilton and Auchterarder, Falkland and Freuchie. He also addressed students at Glasgow University and, if he was to be spared, felt inclined to accept an invitation to deliver a series of lectures on Chinese language and culture at Cambridge University.

It was not to be. By the summer of 1915 Ross was terminally ill with cancer of the colon. He was moved into The Royal Scottish Nursing Home in Torphichen Street, Edinburgh, where he was cared for by the matron, Miss Middleton, and her competent nurses. The end came on Saturday, August 7th, 1915, when, at a quarter past five in the morning, attended by Mr Frank E. Jardine, later President of the Royal College of Surgeons of Edinburgh, John Ross suffered fatal heart failure.[18] In the seventy-fourth year of his life, John Ross' soul, as The Shorter Catechism so beautifully puts it, was at that moment made perfect in holiness and passed immediately into glory. His body, being still united to Christ, was a few days later reverently laid in Newington cemetery, a short walk from his home, where it continues to rest until the resurrection. The inscription on the cold grey granite headstone is as frugal in details as the man was reticent in life:

In loving memory
of
Rev. John Ross, D.D.,
for over forty years missionary
of the U. F. Church in Manchuria,
China.

On the plinth are the three opening words of Bickersteth's glorious hymn: 'Peace, perfect peace.' The stone also commemorates the price Ross paid to engage in missionary service: the loss of his first wife, Mary Ann, and four children of his second marriage: Hugh, Findlay, Jackie, and Cathie Jane, all buried far away at Newchwang.

A formal commemorative minute of the Foreign Mission Committee of the United Free Church of Scotland acknowledged that by the time of Ross' death there was in Manchuria, as direct result of his efforts, 'a great mission, which now includes three colleges, two hospitals, seven congregations, eighteen outstations, and a Christian community of four thousand, two hundred and forty-two souls.' There had also come into being in Korea, a country he visited but once, a large and flourishing church.

Another heartfelt obituary in *The Record of the Home and Foreign Mission Work of the United Free Church of Scotland*, by his friend James Webster, gave thanks to God for 'power as a preacher of the Gospel to non-Christians; … lucid expositions of Scripture to believers; … missionary statesmanship; … keen desire and effort to realise a Church united, evangelical, self-administrating and self-supporting.'[19]

Writing in the *Chinese Recorder and Missionary Journal*, James W. Inglis, his Mukden colleague and successor at the Theological Hall, paid tribute to the 'qualities of the pioneer, the power to endure solitude and isolation, the capacity of turning out a great mass work …. He commanded respect by his power of rapid decision in thought and action, and by his wide-ranging grasp of the problems of the time … his colleagues cherish his memory, as of one whose whole mind and heart were devoted to China.'[20]

Twenty years later, writing for the Church of Scotland's *Life and Work* magazine, Mrs Iza Christie, widow of the Mukden doctor, Dugald Christie, looked back to the church in China and Korea and could say that 'its marked advance in self-government, in self-support, in independence of decision, is the natural outcome of the principles laid down by John Ross, and carried out consistently by him and others to establish the Kingdom of God.'[21]

The *Congregational Notes* of Mayfield United Free Church also marked his passing, noting that 'When the life of Dr Ross is written, the story of how he sent the Gospel into Korea, will be recognised as one of the most thrilling chapters in the history of Mission enterprise.' Then with an allusion to *The Pilgrim's Progress*, the reader was exhorted: 'May … we, looking upward, realise the triumph in this passing of a dedicated soul, and hear the trumpets sounding for him on the other side.'[22]

Mayfield Kirk Session gives us a rare and therefore valuable insight into the warmth and Christ-likeness of John Ross' character, engrossing in its minutes their deep sympathy for Mrs Ross and her children and a very affectionate tribute to John Ross' loving, diligent and energetic service as an elder:

> He was affectionate and faithful in his oversight of the people under his immediate care while the whole membership benefited by his counsel and example. The Prayer meeting was enriched by his presence and devotions, and every one of the Home Mission Agencies of the Congregation received his warm sympathy and active help .... Dr Ross was loved and trusted by all his colleagues. They looked up to him .... They recognised that he [discharged his duties] because of the excellent spirit that was in him – a spirit [generous] yet discrete, a spirit full of charity and peace, a spirit of wonderful patience, the patience of hope. All this suggested the Master, whom till the very end of his days he served. It is therefore a happy memory of a Christian life crowned with labours of love, that remains an inspiration to his brethren.[23]

All that Ross was and did was God's work, of course. He had been enabled by God's power, and so to him be all the glory. But he had accomplished it through John Ross and his stewardship of the many gifts entrusted to him: vision, pioneering effort, skilful translation, well organised Bible and Christian literature distribution, the conscientious training and motivating of Chinese and Korean evangelists, and five years' humble service as an elder in an Edinburgh congregation.

22

The Hope of the Reaper

He gave his best to China, and he gave it all ungrudgingly. He sowed unsparingly and he reaped abundantly. To few is given the joy of seeing the fruit of one's labours in the measure granted to him.

James Webster

EVEN for a Scottish Highlander, John Ross was self-effacing and reticent in the extreme, which, as we have so often had to say, makes it exceptionally difficult for readers in another age to know the real man, share his thoughts, understand his moods or empathise with his emotions. Little or nothing of himself is found in his own writings. No diaries or personal letters appear to have survived. It was left to his colleagues on the Mayfield Kirk Session, but especially his close friend James Webster, to lift a corner of the curtain to allow us a glimpse of what they saw and knew.[1] In his obituary article in the *Missionary Record*, entitled *The Maker of the Manchurian Mission*, Webster saw Ross' death as a watershed: 'It will never be the same to some of us, now that Dr Ross has gone. Manchuria has become one of the Church's most precious missionary heritages, and she owes it in very large measure to Dr Ross. It is not too much to say that he made the Manchurian Mission.'

Webster goes on to tell how on arriving at Chefoo in August 1872, Ross thought the area quite well enough served by missionaries, so that he and his new bride Mary Ann could turn their attention to the unevangelised twenty millions of Manchuria. The bleak, forlorn and depressing appearance of Newchwang in October 1872 might have deterred many, but not him, for whom appearance counted little, for he was going 'to look for men and not to search for scenery.' And, despite the emotional upheaval of the birth of his son and Mary Ann's death so soon after, he found the men for whom he searched. The first was Old Wang, then Liu and Chang, the first pastors of Mukden and Tieling, and by 1882 some fifty converted men could call Ross their spiritual father, bringing him 'intense joy'.

His was a disciplined life: regularly preaching to the unconverted, showing patience with rowdy hecklers, systematically teaching new converts, and always doing so with unfailing respect, courtesy and tact. Webster 'never once saw him lose his self-control', even in the face of severe provocation. Invariably busy, he made time for research in a 'stuffy study replete with Chinese tomes and Korean manuscripts'. Keen to see for himself the conversions reported by his Korean colporteurs and undeterred by winter's cold, Ross set out with Webster for the Yalu valleys, cheerfully facing heavy falls of snow, crossing high mountains, forcing their way through blocked passes and dangerous ravines. Warnings of bears and tigers and bandits might send his Chinese companions scurrying to safety, but he went on undeterred. Safely in the valleys, meeting new Korean Christians, Ross spared neither a moment of time nor an atom of energy. Day after day, often all day and far into the night, he preached to an eager and untiring audience: 'his vision was being fulfilled before his eyes. His soul glowed with the joy of the reaper.'

Then there was his missionary statesmanship, especially his wise resolution of the comity problem between the Presbyterian Church of Ireland and the United Presbyterians by the formation of a single Manchurian Church, self-supporting, self-governing and self-propagating, served by missionaries of both churches united in a single missionary conference. After referring to Ross' academic honours and church accolades, Webster concludes: 'the enduring memorial of his devoted and fruitful life … was the Church of Jesus Christ in Manchuria, of which he dreamed, for which he laboured and prayed, and which he lived to see realised.'

Webster makes, however, a very curious omission: there is no mention of the Theological Hall at Mukden, nor of Ross' part as founder, teacher or Principal. Why did Webster draw a veil over this institution? Indeed, why did his successor, J. W. Inglis, in his *Chinese Recorder* obituary of Ross, refer to it with but a single cursory comment? Had the Hall already become an embarrassment, a bone of contention as the missionaries were drawn into an acrimonious debate over liberal theology, cultural syncretism, scientific evolution, Higher Criticism and the authority of the Bible?

The story of liberalism in the Scottish churches has been told repeatedly from many perspectives, making it necessary here only to sketch in briefest outline a few salient features. In the Free Church of Scotland, the question became publicly notorious in 1876 with accusations made in the Aberdeen Presbytery about an article on the Bible in the *Encyclopaedia Britannica* which had been contributed by William Robertson Smith, Professor of Hebrew at the Free Church College in Aberdeen. It was alleged Robertson Smith had treated the sacred Scriptures in an 'irreverent, if not heretical' manner. Naturally, he rebutted these allegations, asserting his belief in the inspiration and authority of all the canonical books of Scripture. But that didn't satisfy his critics and the case rumbled on until May 1881, when, on a vote of three hundred and ninety-four to two hundred and thirty-one, the General Assembly found against him and removed him from his post on the grounds that his writings – a second very contentious article had been published subsequently – cast 'grave doubt on the historical truth and divine inspiration of several books of Scripture'.[2] The Free Church Assembly's action may indeed have resisted the progress of Higher Criticism in the church, but it had not halted it.

In the United Presbyterian Church the mood was more tolerant. The Synod of 1879 had passed a Declaratory Act giving office bearers latitude in interpreting the Westminster Confession of Faith's teaching on predestination, divine election, the extent of human sinfulness and what the Confession might mean by the six days of creation. In 1892, in order to accommodate a hoped-for union with the United Presbyterians, the more liberal party in the Free Church pushed back and managed to persuade the General

Assembly to pass a similar act allowing differences of opinion on all points of doctrine in the Confession of Faith which did not enter into the elusive and undefined 'substance of the Reformed Faith'.

Neither Declaratory Act resulted in wholesale abandonment of the old evangelicalism, but both allowed for a speculative openness that led many to embrace what was euphemistically termed 'evangelical liberalism'. Such theological imprecision was the price that the Free Church's Dr Robert Rainy and his pro-union associates were happy to pay for the formation of a United Free Church in 1900. Little wonder then that when New College came under United Free control the liberal inclinations of scholars such as George Adam Smith and Marcus Dods went unchecked. It is also unsurprising that similar ideas were introduced into missionary colleges overseas. Which, of course, begs the question of John Ross' view of criticism and the liberal agenda. An answer is found in his *Mission Methods*. There Ross writes:

> At no stage in their spiritual history has Criticism of the Bible, in the ordinary acceptation of the term, been submitted to the Christians in Manchuria. Criticism has been of great service to the Church of Christ when its efforts have been directed to discover, by its constructive action, the full and real contents of Scripture. Its value is purely academic in its combative and destructive moods. Then it is interested only, or mainly, in grammatical, philological, or chronological discussions. One critic of note declared he could by imagination and common-sense discover the proper text of Isaiah. Imagination comes in handily pretty often. Common-sense is not so generally manifest, the office of modern criticism seems to be to satisfy the intellect, but it leaves the sore heart of man unaffected and untended. It cannot alter the needs of man. It cannot, and does not attempt to satisfy the yearnings of his soul. It cannot answer his heart's anguished cry for light. It has not made the way of salvation any clearer. It has not made the person of the Saviour any dearer. Yet these matters, connected with the soul-need of man, are what the missionary has to consider, With these he is to employ his strength, his wisdom, his devotion, and his time .... Enough now for all our energy to convey, for Chinese intelligence to receive, the grand unchanged moral principles of the Book, with its wholly satisfactory replies to the deepest and most perplexing questionings of the soul, which press for solution wherever

> man is found. ... The teaching of the Church in Manchuria has been directed to an exposition of the set of doctrines which the Apostle Paul sums up under the name of 'the Cross of Christ.'[3]

What Ross had in mind when he wrote 'Criticism has been of great service to the Church of Christ' were the benefits of so-called Lower Criticism, the reverent and constructive attempt by scholars to reconstruct, from an increasing availability of early biblical manuscripts, the most reliable text of Scripture. What he warned against was Higher Criticism's speculative theories, which he too sanguinely believed would shortly be doomed to obsolescence: 'Much of what is novel and popular now will soon become antiquated and forgotten; while the eager researches [of scholars] will divulge further information to upset, to modify, and to guide critical theories at present prominent.'[4] If only!

Ross outspokenly condemned Higher Criticism as the 'combative and destructive moods' of liberal scholars who preferred 'imagination and common-sense' to the internal evidence of the dates, identity, location, intention and meaning of the Bible's various human authors. Over against the inherent weaknesses of criticism, Ross saw Holy Scripture's enduring and unfailing testimony to Christ and his Cross. What he said in 1888 to the London Missionary Conference described what he had always believed and continued to believe: the only way to win China was the old way:

> by the 'glorious Gospel of the blessed God' preached freely to the people. Christian friends, suppose all of you were scientific men and women, I would say here ... that 'I am not ashamed of the Gospel of Jesus, for it is the power of God unto salvation' to the Chinaman as it is to you here in London.

It seems safe to say that, unlike some of his colleagues who were won over to a more liberal perspective, Ross' theological position at the end of his life was essentially what it had been at the outset of his missionary career: conservative, Calvinistic and evangelical. Not only did he not hold the new methods of western theological science himself, but he also refused to expose his Chinese students to them. In an important passage in *Mission Methods* he explains his early method of instruction and why it changed:

> At the beginning of the mission, when catechumens were few, we met for an hour every day for the study of Scripture and the exposition of Christian duty. ... A course of theology was supposed to be the proper mode of feeding these babes. The doctrine of faith, as embodied in the Epistles to the Romans and Galatians, was carefully, systematically, day after day ... expounded. That was the first and the last class called upon to undergo the training of a formal theological course. This kind of teaching is not well adapted to the Chinese mind, which requires, to appreciate it, a good deal of experience and preparatory instruction. The theological difficulties which have arisen in the West regarding the nature of faith, its mode of operation, and its precise value in the system of grace, are quite unknown to the Chinese, who do not understand why such difficulties should exist. The habit of mind which raised the difficulties is wholly alien to the Chinese. There are the plain facts of the Gospels. There are the clear statements of the Epistles. When the Chinaman becomes a believer, he believes these. To believe is 'just to believe,' to take as true and to act on the statements as true. There is only one kind of belief possible.[5]

Some have considered Ross' method of instruction unfortunate because it inadvertently left his students exposed when the liberal onslaught eventually came. Chinese scholar, Michael M, has said: 'Scripture requires and history demonstrated that the Chinese church leaders needed as much training in doctrine as their Western counterparts, whatever the perceived difference in "the Chinese mind" may have been.'[6]

The story of the Theological Hall over the decades after Ross is one of decay and decline, with the theological slide commencing almost immediately he was out of the way. Ross' successor was Rev. James W. Inglis, who had been at the Hall with Ross and T. C. Fulton since 1902.[7] Inglis also worked part-time with the Christian Literature Society for China. By the beginning of the twentieth century, the society's policy was ambivalent over doctrinal matters, inviting liberals, as well as conservatives, to submit manuscripts for publication.[8] Difficult as it is to determine where Inglis precisely stood in the theological spectrum, it is not without significance that in its 1923 report the Christian Literature Society commended two books to Chinese theological students: Inglis' *Christ Not Mythical* (1910) and Prof. David Smith Cairns' *The Reasonableness of the*

Christian Faith (1920).[9] Cairns' liberalism is well attested.[10] How closely Inglis' thought was aligned to Cairns is hard to say, but, had he been so inclined, he was well enough placed to have resisted the implications of having his book juxtaposed with Cairns' as recommended volumes.

The spirit of openness and tolerance, evinced by the Christian Literature Society, was also characteristic of the United Free Church. After the departure of the ultra-conservative Free Presbyterians in 1893, the refusal of the Free Church constitutionalists to join the 1900 union, and decades of bitter ecclesiastical contention, few in the United Free Church were of a mind to pass judgement on theological liberalism in their own colleges in Scotland, let alone one on the other side of the world. It was not so in Ireland. The United Free Church's partner in Manchuria, the Presbyterian Church in Ireland, was a largely rural, conservative and evangelical church; in it, there was a small, but growing and vociferous group who welcomed theological innovation. These people were clustered around the Assembly's College in Belfast or involved in the denominational bureaucracy. Tension between the two factions was increasing.

In 1899, Rev. Thomas Crosby Fulton, minister of Mukden's West Church, had been appointed by the Irish Church as the Old Testament lecturer at the Mukden Theological Hall, and after Ross' retiral he continued in that role.[11] Fulton had a sterling reputation as an evangelist and church planter, baptising over a thousand converts between 1897 and 1899.[12] How open he was to liberalism and Higher Criticism is hard to discern, but some of his Irish colleagues most certainly were.

The Rev. Andrew Weir, for one, didn't believe in the verbal inspiration of the Bible, let alone subscribe to the doctrine of the Westminster Confession of Faith, which he thought outdated, inadequate or plain wrong.[13] In working for Chinese ecumenism, Weir advocated union around what he called 'the essential spirit-filled [note lower case] vitality of the Faith once delivered to the Saints', but certainly not the Westminster or any other existing confession. Weir was not alone. There was also the provocative Fred W. S. O'Neill, who, according to his grandson, was not only 'on the liberal side' but 'enjoyed … arousing controversy'.[14]

On the other side, among the more conservative Irish missionaries, were members of the Gillespie family from Co. Down. Rev. William H. Gillespie had gone out in 1892, followed four years later by his sister Annie. Brief though her acquaintance with the Mukden Hall was – she died after six months in the country – it was sufficient to detect liberal teaching. At the time, their brother John, a medical doctor, was planning to join them, but because of what she saw as erroneous teaching, Annie advised him to stay at home. Disregarding her advice, John with his new wife, Catherine Hunter, arrived in 1900 and soon discovered the liberal tendencies of some of their colleagues. They stuck it out for six years before returning to Ireland. The Gillespies all held strictly to the Westminster Confession.[15]

Another concerned Irish missionary was Rev. James McCammon. Appointed to the teaching staff of the Hall by the Irish Presbyterians in 1914, McCammon became increasingly disenchanted and resigned. He set up the independent Newchwang Bible Institute, an alternative scheme for training prospective ministers of the Manchurian Church.

How far the theological inclinations of the Hall and the Missionary Conference had shifted after Ross' departure, may be seen by the reaction – or lack of it – to a highly contentious paper presented by Frederick O'Neill in 1913. It was published without challenge in the *Chinese Recorder* but when reprinted in *The Witness,* a fortnightly Belfast religious paper, it immediately attracted controversy. A formal complaint was made to the Mission Board by Rev. James Hunter, a relative and one-time minister of the Gillespies. Hunter tabled detailed objections to O'Neill's syncretistic ideas, which, he contended, were more aligned with pantheism than with Christianity.[16] In the event, the dispute fizzled out: the Board, not wanting to alienate evangelical supporters, suppressed dissent; whilst Hunter, on hearing of the death of one of O'Neill's children, let the matter drop. Hunter's complaint was substantial and not easily brushed away. It helped fuel an ensuing battle with liberalism, which in 1927 resulted in the secession of Hunter and his followers, and their formation of the Irish Evangelical Church.[17]

Not only did the Theological Hall miss Ross' leadership, but his missionary strategy, the creation of a self-governing church, was also frustrated. By 1912, neither the Irish nor the Scottish churches had enacted the provisions necessary to grant the Manchurian Presbyterian Church full legislative independence. Impatience was growing in the Chinese church and the danger of schism loomed. The Missionary Conference, taking matters into its own hands, advised the church to carry on as if the decisions had already been taken, though it would be another decade before the home churches caught up.[18] Despite adequate financial support in Scotland and Ireland for the Theological Hall, it struggled throughout the 1920s to fulfil its vision. This was reflected in the 1931 Principal's report to the Missionary Conference, which acknowledged inadequate attention being paid to the spiritual life of the students, insufficient preparation of evangelists and pastors, deficient training for the organisation of Sunday Schools, and poor library facilities.[19]

That same year the Japanese occupied Manchuria, imposing tight control on the college, and requiring both official registration and the intrusion of government appointees as board members and lecturers. After the 1939–45 war, the Irish missionary, Dr H. K. Johnston, who had suffered internment in Japan, reported that the college's teaching staff was depleted, its student registrations low, and money was scarce. The outlook was bleak.[20]

The death in 1949 of Rev. J. W. Findlay, the college's Principal, more or less coincided with Mao Zedong's declaration of the creation of the People's Republic of China. An initial period of liberty led in 1953 to a union with Yanjing Theological Seminary, but in 1958 Mao's Great Leap Forward suppressed Christianity, closed colleges and church buildings, and required pastors and teachers to undertake what the government termed 'productive work'. In 1982, two years after the death of Mao, Deng Xiaoping allowed some churches and colleges to re-open. The college now became Northeast Theological Seminary, relocated to an eight-storey building in Shenyang City, as Mukden had become known, and in 1996 moved onto a large campus in a scenically impressive location.[21]

Today, the seminary claims to have four hundred students taught by twenty-three full-time and ten part-time teachers, and since 1982 has had seventeen hundred graduates. Its website reveals its link to the liberal pro-government National Christian Council of China and offers access to two Chinese Bible versions, a downloadable Bible app, and a mobile app for the church magazine *Tian Feng* (*Heavenly Wind*), the organ of the Three-Self Patriotic Movement (TSPM) of the Protestant Churches of China.

It is tempting to ask whether the present Three-Self Patriotic Movement, whose name is so redolent of John Ross' thought, is, somehow, a vestige of his influence. Given the direction it has taken, most commentators deny that it is. Writing in 1961, Leslie Lyall, in his *Come Wind, Come Weather,* had no doubt that the Three-Self Patriotic Movement was far removed from the original Three-Selfs principle. Through a process of so-called 'sinofication', its primary purpose had been to establish the religious, cultural and political dominance of the Chinese Communist Party over the church and to sever relations with overseas churches. Far from encouraging independence, this policy in fact made the church entirely dependent upon a totalitarian state.[22] And yet for all that, the very fact that it is called the Three-Self Patriotic Movement is surely an involuntary hat-tip to Ross and his colleagues, whose advocacy so grounded these principles in the minds even of opponents of the authentic gospel that they have resurfaced, if only as a parody of the original.

The Three-Selfs doctrine is necessarily alive among China's unregistered churches. These congregations are served by pastors and attended by members vulnerable to arbitrary arrest and incarceration, the demolition of their meeting places, the confiscation of Bibles, and the removal of the visible symbols of their faith. Frequently referred to as the house-church movement, many of these non-conforming congregations are courageous bastions of Biblical radicalism, willing to suffer the loss of all things, even life itself to remain faithful to Christ. It is claimed that here are to be found Korean Christians using their business connections as channels for the gospel. Their aversion to Communism leading them to join unregistered churches, connecting them to their own prayerfully supportive network of congregations in South Korea.[23]

It would appear that the entirely Chinese Shenyang Dongguan Church, though a government approved Three-Self Patriotic congregation, has not lost sight of John Ross' mission and there is evidence that his memory is still honoured, and his work commemorated. When Prof. James Grayson visited the church in the mid-nineteen eighties, he saw the place, on the wall above the pulpit, where a plaque commemorating Ross was once displayed. This was removed during the Cultural Revolution but reinstated some years later.[24] If the plaque had been taken into safekeeping, as seems probable, then this was done at some considerable personal risk, thus demonstrating the esteem in which Ross was still held, more than seventy-five years after his death.

Around 2015, there appeared slight signs of a thawing in the relationship between some of the Three Selfs Patriotic Movement churches and some of the unregistered churches, leading to hope for closer cooperation.[25] But in 2016, President Xi Jinping represented Christianity as a threat to state security, warning that China 'must resolutely guard against overseas infiltrations via religious means'.[26] Among other crackdowns, 2019 saw the arrest of two hundred elders, pastors and deacons of the unregistered Early Rain Covenant Church. Their outspoken Pastor Wang Yi was imprisoned for nine years for 'inciting to subvert state power'. This was the most severe anti-Christian penalty for over a decade. China watchers now fear a deteriorating situation with renewed persecution under Xi, citing as evidence 'digital authoritarianism' with 'half-a-billion digital surveillance cameras linked to the social-security system, giving authorities the power immediately to deduct welfare or pension payments from so-called offenders.'[27]

Against this bleak outlook the Apostle Paul might well have interjected the words, 'But God!' And so too might have John Ross, who lived to see the Chinese church survive the violent persecutions of his day and thrive. Incontrovertibly, the Chinese church continues to grow. Millions profess faith in Christ. More go to church on Sunday in China than in Europe. Under a headline that reads, 'Protestant Christianity is booming in China: President Xi does not approve,' *The Economist* claimed in September 2020 that official Chinese figures, always inclined to underestimate, now admit the existence of thirty-eight million Protestants and ten to twelve million Catholics.[28] The reality may be very many more. Some allege that Christians now outnumber members of the Communist Party.[29]

Our story began with a death, that of William Chalmers Burns in a hovel in Newchwang. It has ended with a death, that of the man who, under God's blessing, was to a very large degree the answer to Burns' prayers and the fulfilment of his prediction that 'God will carry on the good work'. Of that, neither had any doubt. Burns saw little fruit: Ross much. Such is the inscrutable economy of God. Yet both stories taken together illustrate to a degree of perfection our Lord's teaching that 'unless a grain of wheat falls into the earth and dies, it remains alone; but if it dies, it bears much fruit.'

The recurring Scriptural motif of life springing out of death and bearing a great harvest in the most alien of environments is seen supremely in the death and resurrection of Jesus Christ and the redemption of the world. It has also been repeated in microcosm throughout the history of the church's international mission. The story of the Manchurian and Korean churches is evidence that Christian faith and the life of the Spirit refuses to be suppressed, even though periods of stagnation and barrenness, declension and faithlessness, repression and violent persecution may come. Spiritual life must reproduce. It cannot do otherwise. The seed is potent. The germ of life is dynamic. But first it must be bruised and buried and die before fresh green shoots emerge and mature into a great harvest.

For the church in China, as elsewhere, this perspective provides the necessary corrective to the twin dangers of unbelieving pessimism and exaggerated triumphalism. Like the wider Chinese church, the Manchurian church flourished after the fierce persecution of the 1900 Boxer uprising. Though weakened by the self-inflicted wounds of theological liberalism, it survived Japanese occupation. A further harvest followed the suppression of religion during Mao's Great Leap Forward. Today, despite heavy-handed government policy, the degree of church growth in China is such that the church is outrunning itself and cannot keep up with an adequate supply of trained leaders and resources.

Not only is the church in China growing, but there are faint signs that it may be doing so in North Korea, a place reputed to be the hardest in the world in which to be a Christian. It would not be surprising: south of the border between North and South Korea the Protestant Christian community accounts for forty-five percent of all religious believers, or twenty percent of the total population. The answer to all who wonder why the gospel should prove so irrepressible is to be found in the words of Scripture, echoed daily in the prayers of the church, vigorously affirmed by a dying missionary, and lived out in the life of John Ross. They are those articulated in the Lord's Prayer whose origin is in 1 Chronicles 29.11:

> Yours, O Lord, is the greatness and the power and the glory and the victory and the majesty, for all that is in the heavens and in the earth is yours. Yours is the kingdom, O Lord, and you are exalted as head above all.

The last lines of Henry Grattan Guinness' sonnet commemorating William Chalmers Burns serve as an appropriate conclusion to the story of John Ross of Manchuria and Korea (the first word may be altered to suit either case):

> China, I breathe for thee a brother's prayer,
> Unnumbered are thy millions. Father, hear
> The groans we cannot. Oh, Thine arm make bare,
> And reap the harvest of salvation there.
> The fulness of the Gentiles, like a sea
> Immense, oh, God, be gathered unto Thee.
> Then Israel save, and with His saintly train,
> Send us Immanuel over all to reign.

Who's Who?

These biographical notes may help readers identify some of the key people in the story of John Ross, and/or differentiate between those with similar names. For further information on those marked with an asterisk,* see entries in such dictionaries as *Biographical Dictionary of Christian Missions*, *Dictionary of Scottish Church History and Theology*, *Oxford Dictionary of National Biography*, *Fasti of the United Free Church of Scotland,* or the online *Biographical Dictionary of Chinese Christianity.*

Allen, Roland* (1868–1947). Born in Bristol, England. Anglican priest, missionary, influential missionary strategist and constructive critic of the church, author. Allen's important views on radical indigenous, spontaneously expanding, self-supporting, self-propagating, and self-governing churches only gained a significant following after his death. His thought, closely allied to that of John Ross, found expression in his writings, especially the following (all available in modern editions): *Missionary Methods. St Paul's or Ours?* (Cambridge: Lutterworth Press, 2006); *The Ministry of the Spirit. Selected Writings* (Cambridge: Lutterworth Press, 2006); *The Spontaneous Expansion of the Church and the Causes which Hinder it* (Cambridge: Lutterworth Press, 2006). Allen died in Nairobi, Kenya, in 1947.

Arthington, Robert* (1823–1900). Born in Leeds, England. Reclusive evangelical premillennialist millionaire and shrewd investor, mission donor and philanthropist. Motivated by a pre-millennial reading of Scripture prophecy, he believed that the spread of Christianity would hasten the Second Coming of Christ.

On inheriting a fortune of £200,000 on the death of his Quaker father in 1846, Arthington, who became a Baptist, but never held office in a church or a missionary society, invested successfully, and contributed generously to the evangelistic work of the Baptist Missionary Society (BMS), the London Missionary Society (LMS) and other missionary and philanthropic work. He funded the translation and printing of John Ross' Korean New Testament. Generous towards others, he was parsimonious towards himself, gaining the soubriquet 'The Miser of Headingley.' See: Brian Stanley, 'The Legacy of Robert Arthington' in *International Bulletin of Missionary Research*, October 1998. Arthington died in 1900 at Teignmouth, England.

Blair, William Newton* (1876–1970). Born Salina, Kansas, USA. American missionary to Korea. Blair and his wife Edith arrived in Pyongyang, Korea, in 1901 as missionaries under the Presbyterian Board of Missions. He was present at and closely involved in the Korean Revival of 1907. After long service, Blair, with his second wife Katharine, returned to the USA in 1940 and retired in 1947. He died in Duarte, California, USA, in 1970. His account of the revival is published in Bruce F. Hunt, *The Korean Pentecost* (Edinburgh: Banner of Truth Trust, 1977).

Burns, William Chalmers* (1815–1868). Born in Duns, Scotland. Missionary to China, pioneer of Manchuria, translator. After brilliant academic success at Aberdeen and Glasgow Universities, Burns was licensed in 1839 by the Church of Scotland Presbytery of Glasgow. After his conversion in 1832 he allied himself with a group of young evangelicals which included the Bonar brothers and Robert M. M'Cheyne. In 1839, Burns agreed to become *locum* at St. Peter's in Dundee during M'Cheyne's absence in the Holy Land. Here he experienced revival, and also in the same year at his father's church in Kilsyth. At the Disruption in 1843 he joined the Free Church of Scotland. In 1844 he went to Canada, returning two years later to become a minister of the English Presbyterian Church. He went to China, first serving the expatriate community of the Free Church of Scotland of Hong Kong, whilst learning Chinese and familiarising himself with Chinese history and culture, then at

Amoy, where he began translating *The Pilgrim's Progress*. In 1855, Burns was in Shanghai and courageously agreed to try to reach the headquarters of the Taiping rebels in Nanjing to discern the nature of their links with Christianity. Unsuccessful in achieving this objective, he nevertheless distributed large quantities of Christian literature on his travels. Between December 1855 and July 1856 he worked alongside James Hudson Taylor, sixteen years his junior. Each influenced the other: Burns followed Taylor in adopting Chinese dress and culture, Taylor found Burns' godliness inspiring. In 1867 Burns left for Newchwang, but soon developed a chest infection from which he did not recover. He died in Newchwang on April 4, 1868 and is buried there. See: Islay Burns, *Memoir of Rev. Wm. C. Burns: Missionary to China from the English Presbyterian Church* (London: James Nisbet, 1870).

Chang-shun a.k.a. Blind Chang (c.1849–1900). 'The Apostle of Manchuria,' Christian teacher, evangelist and martyr. Chang came to Christian faith in 1886 after visiting Mukden hospital in great poverty, ill-health and blindness. To test the reality of his faith the missionaries sent him home to Tai-ping-gow unbaptised, but promised to visit at a future date. On arrival in October 1886, James Webster found not only Chang ready for baptism, but a company of believers and enquirers. Webster baptised nine, including Chang, who became the nucleus of a church. Acting as an unpaid evangelist, Chang relocated to a village one hundred miles further east, where it was hoped he would continue in his fruitful ministry for 'many years to come'. He did, until in 1900, during the Boxer Uprising, he had to be hidden away in the Valley of Peace. Considering the safety of others more important than his own suffering, he delivered himself up. The Boxers, filled with superstitious dread, declined at first to kill him, but after a few days' detention, Chang was hacked to death, his body burned and his ashes scattered. Some years later the government erected a monument to his memory.

Christie, Dugald* (1855–1936). Born in Kingshouse, Glencoe, Scotland, Christie became a medical missionary in Mukden, Manchuria. Converted during D. L. Moody's Glasgow mission of 1874, Christie, in preparation for a career as a medical missionary with the Free

Church of Scotland, studied medicine at Edinburgh University and gained valuable practical experience in connection with the Edinburgh Medical Missionary Society. In 1882, Christie married Elizabeth Hastie Smith, and within a few months departed for Mukden, Manchuria, with the United Presbyterian Church. Christie believed that medical care was no adjunct to missions but integral. After only two years he opened Manchuria's first hospital at Mukden (with free treatment), and later a medical school run on the highest professional standards, offering a five-year medical course. Elizabeth died in 1888. In 1892 Christie married the missionary Elizabeth (Iza) Inglis (1865–1962). He died in Edinburgh, Scotland, in 1936, and is buried with his second wife at the Grange cemetery in Edinburgh.

Fulton, Thomas Crosby (1855–1942). Born in Carnmoney, Co. Antrim, Northern Ireland. Fulton was educated at Queens College, Belfast, BA 1882, Royal University of Ireland, Belfast, MA, and a theological course at Assembly's College, Belfast. Ordained by the Templepatrick Presbytery of the Presbyterian Church in Ireland in 1884. Sailed to China in 1885. Appointed Irish Presbyterian lecturer at Mukden Theological Hall. Awarded Doctor of Divinity by Irish Presbyterian Theological Faculty in 1913. He retired from China in 1941 and died the following year in Belfast.

Goforth, Jonathan* (1859–1936). Born in Thorndale in Ontario, Canada, Goforth became a well-known Presbyterian missionary evangelist and revivalist, author and speaker. During his theological education at Knox College, Toronto, where he also volunteered at the Toronto City Mission, he met and married artist, Rosalind Bell-Smith, in 1887, departing for North Honan in 1888. In 1905, Goforth wholeheartedly embraced the revivalist teaching of Charles G. Finney. On a visit to Korea in 1907, he witnessed the revival in Pyongyang and returned to Manchuria bent on commencing a similar awakening by utilising Finney's methodology. In 1908 a revival occurred in Manchuria, in which Goforth played a part, but whilst the Scottish and Irish missionaries warmed to Goforth as a person, appreciating his prayerful and diligent spirit, they generally eschewed his theology and methods, of which Ross and others were publicly tactfully critical. Later Goforth contested the influx of liberal ('modernist') theology in Canadian Presbyterian circles in China, parted company with his former colleagues in the Honan Presbytery, and was later refused financial support by the Canadian Presbyterian Church. Worn out by sustained travel and work, in 1929 Goforth was laid aside for several months, but spent the time recalling and dictating revival stories which were later published as *By My Spirit*. The Goforths returned to Canada in 1934. On October 7, 1936, at Wallaceburg, Ontario, after a demanding day's ministry, he fell asleep and never woke up.

Gützlaff, Karl Friedrich August* (1803–1851). Born in Pyritz, Pomerania, he was a linguist, interpreter, translator, evangelist and ardent advocate of missions to China. Gützlaff's father was a master tailor, the family were Lutheran pietists. He proved to be a brilliant student, but at seventeen was too old to enter university in the usual manner. Showing significant initiative he threw a poem into the carriage of King Frederick William of Prussia, appealing for help. The king sent him to Johannes Jaenicke's missionary institute in Berlin. Deciding to be a missionary to the Chinese, he made three journeys along the Chinese coast between 1830 and 1833 as an interpreter on British ships involved in the nefarious opium trade. In 1833, at significant risk to life and well-being, he entered China as an independent missionary, remaining until 1839, when his position became untenable on the outbreak of the First Opium War. He then took up a position as Chinese-language secretary in the British diplomatic service. Gützlaff translated the Bible into Chinese and parts into Thai, as well as the Gospel and Epistles of John into Japanese. His involvement in the formation of the Chinese Evangelization Society (CES), as well as his missionary methods and personal example inspired Hudson Taylor and influenced the policy of the China Inland Mission. Some consider Gützlaff as naive, if not culpable, both in regard to bogus converts who fraudulently exploited him and his own compromising connections with the opium trade. He died in 1851 in Hong Kong, China.

Hardie, Robert Alexander (1865–1949). Born in Haldimand, Ontario, Canada. Physician and Methodist missionary in Korea. In 1890, after medical studies at the Toronto School of Medicine,

Hardie with his wife and two-year-old daughter departed for Korea. An unsettled decade ensued. In less than three years the family lived in five different cities, including Nagasaki in Japan. In 1896 the Hardies furloughed in Canada, with Robert returning alone to Wonsan in October 1897. In 1898 he joined the American Southern Methodist Episcopal Church, who sent him to Songdo in the north. He returned to Seoul in 1899, less than a year later. In 1900 he returned to Wonsan, was reunited with his family, and remained there until 1909. In August 1903 he attended Mary Culler White's prayer meeting in Wonsan in low mood and depressed spirits. Disappointed by his lack of success, he audibly confessed in prayer what he understood as his failures. The six missionaries present were greatly moved by his frankness. Later, on hearing of this, some Korean Christians, to whom public loss of face was culturally disastrous, were greatly moved and adopted the practice in often emotional gatherings. In 1907, Hardie's influence upon the American Presbyterian missionaries in Pyongyang, especially Lee and Blair, led to public confession of sin being accepted as a normal phenomenon accompanying revival. In the 1908 Manchurian revival, public confession became integral to Jonathan Goforth's method. While not condemning public confession *per se,* John Ross and some of his colleagues cautioned against any manipulation of emotions to obtain it. Hardie died in 1949 at Lansing, Michigan, USA.

Hudson Taylor, James* (1832–1905). Native of Barnsley, England. Pioneer missionary, founder of China Inland Mission (CIM), advocate of indigenous missions and proponent of faith missions. Brought up in a Christian home, at fifteen he commenced to learn accountancy. Converted at the age of seventeen, he dedicated his life to missionary service in China. He prepared by avidly reading books about China, familiarising himself with the Mandarin language, studying Latin, biblical Hebrew and Greek, and undertaking a course in medicine at the Royal London Hospital in London. In 1853 he joined the Chinese Evangelization Society (CES) and arrived in Shanghai, China, in March 1854. In 1855 he scandalised fellow missionaries by adopting Chinese dress and habits. The financial collapse of the CES left him penniless. He resigned and lived on unsolicited donations and other provisions, given, he ardently believed, in answer to prayer. This experience of 'living by faith' later became key to the operating principles of CIM. Taylor married Maria Dyer in 1858. His poor health necessitated their return to the UK in 1860, where he resumed medical training, qualifying in 1862 as a Member of the Royal College of Surgeons and in midwifery. In 1866 he formed the nondenominational CIM. After asking supporters to pray for twenty-four 'willing, skillful labourers', the Taylors departed for China with their children and the team of new workers. In time, CIM workers established a Christian presence in each of China's twelve provinces. By 1895, CIM missionaries accounted for over half the Protestant missionary force in China. In the Boxer uprising seventy-nine CIM missionaries and children were killed. Taylor's refusal of any reparation impressed Chinese leaders and softened attitudes towards Christianity. At the time of his death in 1905, the CIM had eight hundred and twenty-five missionaries in all twelve Chinese provinces (hence the prayer for twenty-four workers, two for each), more than three hundred mission stations, over five hundred local Chinese helpers, through whom it was thought some twenty-five thousand Chinese people had become Christians. Taylor died in 1905 at Changsha, China.

Henderson, John of Park* (1780–1867). Christian philanthropist. Henderson was born in Bo'ness, Scotland, becoming a successful merchant and an ardent member of the United Presbyterian Church (UPC). He gave generously to his church's activities at home and overseas (he built the Religious Institution rooms in St George's Place, Glasgow, and the Virginia Street offices of the UPC's Mission Board), as well as funding a number of religious publications and the Evangelical Alliance. He was a staunch advocate of Sunday as a day of worship and rest, once spending £4,000 to send a periodical to every railway worker in the country in the hope of convincing them that Sunday railway journeys were wrong. In 1850 he founded The Henderson Prize at Glasgow University for essays on a subject prescribed by the Faculty of Divinity, which in every third year at least must relate to the divine authority, practical value and influence of the Sabbath. He supported Dr William Parker's work in China which laid foundations for the United Presbyterian missions in the country. Henderson's contributions to missions and other causes are believed to have been in the order of £30,000 or more each year. He died at his home at Park, Scotland, in 1867.

Hunter, Dr Joseph Molyneaux (1833–1884). Born in Belfast, Ireland. Medical doctor, and pioneer Irish Presbyterian missionary to China. Converted in boyhood, Hunter described himself as a 'wild youth' until he settled down in his late teens to live a consistent Christian life, taking every opportunity of telling others about Christ. He studied at Queen's College (later University) in Belfast and at Edinburgh University, Scotland, receiving the Diplomas of Royal Colleges of Physicians and Surgeons in Edinburgh. Following service as a ship's surgeon, he and his wife Elizabeth Jayne Smyth arrived in China in 1869 to succeed the recently deceased William C. Burns. The Hunters were among the first Irish Presbyterian missionaries to Manchuria. Renowned for his hardihood and courage, Hunter itinerated widely in Manchuria, sometimes travelling over two thousand miles selling Gospels, providing medical aid and propagating the gospel. After fifteen years unbroken service, in 1884 he decided to return to Ireland for furlough, but died at sea, aged fifty-one years-old. See: R. H. Boyd, *Waymakers in Manchuria* (Belfast: Foreign Missions Office, 1940); F. W. S. O'Neil, *The Call of the East: Sketches from the History of the Irish Presbyterian Church Mission to Manchuria, 1869–1919* (London: James Clark, 1919).

Inglis, James William (1861–1943). Born in Johnstone, Scotland. Missionary, theological lecturer, Principal of Mukden Theological Hall, author. Only son of Rev. James Inglis (UPC, Johnstone) and Frances Wordley, he was the brother of Elizabeth (Iza) Christie. Educated at Paisley Grammar School, Glasgow Academy, and Glasgow University, M. A. 1881, Edinburgh United Presbyterian Theological Hall, University of Leipzig, 1885. Ordained UPC Presbytery of Edinburgh in 1890. Married Caroline Margaret Napier, 1900. Publications in Chinese, *inter alia*: *Christianity and the Modern Mind*, Shanghai, 1916; *Christ Not Mythical*, Shanghai, 1926. *Commentary on St. Luke,*

Shanghai; *Commentary on Acts,* Shanghai, 1925; *Commentary on Colossians,* Shanghai, 1929. Publications in English, *inter alia*: *Christ Not Mythical*, 1926; *The Nestorian Share in Buddhist Translation*, Shanghai, 1917; *Blind Chang*, Edinburgh, 1901. Died, 16 January 1943 in Edinburgh.

Lee, Graham (1861–1917). Born in Rock Island, Illinois, USA. Pioneer American Presbyterian missionary to Pyongyang, Korea. Lee's academic successes included a Bachelor of Arts degree from Princeton in 1889, followed by courses at Hartford Theological Seminary (1889–1890) and a doctorate from McCormick Theological Seminary (1891–1892). He was ordained by the Rock River Presbytery (PCUSA) in 1892, departing the same year for Korea. After eighteen years missionary service, including making a significant contribution during the 1907 revival, Lee's health failed and he returned to the USA, becoming minister of Concord Presbyterian Church (PCUSA), California. He died at Gilroy, California, in 1917, aged 58 years.

Liu Chuen-yao (Pastor Liu). Disciple of Blind Chang, evangelist and first pastor of Dongguan Church, Mukden, which was founded by Ross in 1889. After his return to Mukden in 1881, Ross recognised Liu's gifts and Christian character and trained him for further usefulness. Liu was one of the first deacons to be elected by popular ballot and ordained in Mukden. In 1896 he was ordained pastor of Dongguan Church. Supported by his wife, Liu maintained a faithful testimony, surviving the sufferings of the Boxer persecution to continue as the senior minister of Manchurian Presbyterians.

Liu the deacon and silversmith accompanied missionary Rev. James Wylie to seek help after an attack on the mission by Manchurian irregulars on their way to fight in the First Sino-Japanese in 1884. Putting his own safety at risk, Lui remained with Wylie when he was fatally wounded.

Liu the evangelist, who with Chang, a licentiate for the ministry, was sent to Korea by the Manchurian Presbytery to report on the revival of 1907.

Dr Liu, son of Pastor Liu, a medical doctor and church deacon. Although by nature retiring and modest, Liu had a significant role during the Manchurian revival of 1908. One of Dr Christie's assistants at the hospital, he afterwards took up medical practice in the city of Mukden. He is not to be confused with another Mukden doctor, Dr Liu T'ung-lun (c.1893–1986).

MacGill, Hamilton Montgomerie* (1807–1880). Born at Catrine, Ayrshire, Scotland. Minister of the United Presbyterian Church, Home and Foreign Missions secretary, and hymnologist. The youngest son of Thomas Macgill. From 1827 Hamilton MacGill was educated at Glasgow University (which conferred upon him the degree of D.D. in 1870) and from 1831 at the Divinity Hall of the United Secession church in Glasgow. He was licensed by the presbytery of Kilmarnock in March 1836 and ordained and inducted minister of Duke Street Church, Glasgow, in February 1837. In 1840 he departed with a number of the Duke Street congregation to establish a new church in Montrose Street. In 1858 he became Home Mission Secretary of the United Presbyterian Church, and in 1868 Foreign Mission Secretary, editing *The Missionary Record of the United Presbyterian Church*. Having supervised John Ross' work in home mission, he saw his great potential as a foreign missionary and energetically recruited him for China. As a member of the Hymnal Committee of the United Presbyterian Church (1870–76) he contributed to the Presbyterian Hymnal (1876). MacGill was notable for his highly regarded translations of Greek and Latin hymns, publishing a collection as *Songs of the Christian Creed and Life* (1879). He died on June 3, 1880, at Paris, while on his way to the South of France to restore his health.

Macintyre, John (1837–1905). Born on the banks of Loch Lomond at Luss, Scotland. Minister and missionary of the United Presbyterian Church, John Ross' brother-in-law and colleague. John Macintyre was born into a family of ministers. His grandfather, Rev. Hugh Macintyre D.D., was a minister at Loanends UPC, Co. Antrim. His father was minister of Largs UPC, and in 1880 his uncle Isaac was inducted as second minister of Portree UPC, before emigrating in 1886 to Tasmania. John Macintyre was educated at Paisley, the University of Heidelberg, and the UPC Theological Hall, Edinburgh. After experience at Thread Street UPC, Paisley, he was ordained in 1865 and inducted to the UPC charge of Baillieston, Glasgow. Appointed missionary to China in 1871, Macintyre moved to Manchuria in 1874, working in Haicheng and Newchwang. In 1876 he married Catherine Ross, the sister of John Ross, whose infant son Drummond she had come to care for on the death of Ross' wife, Mary Ann Ross in 1873. Macintyre was closely involved with Ross in itinerant evangelistic and church planting work, as well as recruiting Koreans to assist in the translation of the New Testament. One of the first worshipping groups of Koreans met in Macintyre's home in Mukden and from there crossed the border to evangelise Korea. See: Robert Small, *History of the Congregations of the United Presbyterian Church, from 1733 to 1900* (Edinburgh: David M. Small, 1904); Mrs Duncan M'Laren, *Missions of the United Presbyterian Church: The Story of our Manchurian Mission* (Edinburgh: Office of the United Presbyterian Church, 1896). Macintyre died in 1905 at Beidaihe, China.

Nevius, John Livingstone* (1829–1893). A native of Ovid, New York, USA. Presbyterian missionary and mission strategist. Of Dutch descent, Nevius was educated at Union College, Schenectady, and Princeton Seminary, graduating B.D. in 1853. Before leaving seminary, he offered himself for missionary service to Presbyterian Board of Foreign Missions, and after marrying Helen Coan set out for China in September 1853. Arriving in Shanghai, they met several pioneer missionaries, including Hudson Taylor, before moving to Ningbo. A diligent student of Chinese, Nevius chose not to follow Hudson Taylor or W. C. Burns in adopting Chinese dress, and at home he lived in a western manner, which he believed did not hinder his missionary work. Relocated to Shandong Province in 1861, and then ten years later to Yantai (Chefoo). There they built a large house and raised American fruit trees on a semi-commercial basis. Always hospitable to others, they were nevertheless controversial, with some considering their standard of living to be extravagant. From 1872 to 1881 Nevius itinerated around sixty preaching points, some as far as three hundred miles from Yantai, which, it was said, he managed with 'painstaking care, patience, and skill.'

In 1885 Nevius published *The Planting and Development of Missionary Churches* and the following year *Methods of Missions Work.* At a conference of missionaries held in Shanghai in 1890 he presented the essence of these works in a paper which laid the foundations for what became known as the 'Nevius Method'. After the conference, on his way home to Chefoo, he stopped briefly in Korea to meet some American missionaries who wholeheartedly adopted his method for their work. The Nevius Method, which was not unique, included gospel preaching and the development of indigenous churches built on the Three Selfs Principle, Bible teaching and memorization, the alleviation of poverty, and cooperation with other missionary bodies or, at the least, sensible comity agreements. Nevius died in 1893 at his home in Chefoo, China.

Ross, Alexander* (1834–1925). Architect. Ross was educated in Inverness at The Royal Academy and Dr Bell's Academy, gaining practical experience with a building firm before entering his father's architect practice. In 1853, aged nineteen, he set up his own architectural practice. His firm designed a wide variety of buildings, including many Highland churches, large and small, for, *inter alia*, the Roman Catholic Church, Scottish Episcopalian Church, the Church of Scotland, the Free Church of Scotland, the United Presbyterian Church and the United Free Church, including the Chapelhill UP church. Ross was an Episcopalian and a political conservative, with many public service and business interests in Inverness. He died in 1925 at Inverness, Scotland, and was buried there at Tomnahurich cemetery with full Masonic rites. He was not a relation of John Ross.

Ross, Catherine (1852–1926). Born in Balintore, Scotland. John Ross' sister. Catherine came out to Newchwang in 1874 to care for baby Drummond, following the death of Mary Ann Ross the previous year. Catherine married Ross' colleague John Macintyre at Newchwang in 1876, with Ross conducting the ceremony. She survived her husband by twenty-one years, remaining in China for the rest of her life, dying in 1926 in her seventy-third year at Haicheng, S. Manchuria.

Ross, Mary Ann, née Stewart (1846–1873). John Ross' first wife. They married 26th March 1872 at her home, Larkfield, Ferry Road, Leith. Died 31 March, 1873 at Newchwang, interred beside the grave of William Chalmers Burns. Her only child was:

Ross, Drummond Stewart (1873–1944), born at Newchwang in 1873. After his mother's death, he was cared for by his aunt Catherine. After her marriage to John Macintyre in 1876 he was brought up in their home. At some point he settled in South Africa and became a teacher in a government school at Worcester, Cape Province. In 1910, he married twenty-year-old Florence Jane Huggins at St Mark's, Cambridge, East London. The couple had two children, Florence Marion and Margaret Sybil. In 1914, Drummond joined the South African Field Ambulance Corps, with the artillery rank of Gunner. After training at Royal Army Medical Corps in Twezeldown, Surrey, England, the corps was shipped to Alexandria, Egypt. In 1917, he was transferred to the newly formed Labour Corps with the rank of Second Lieutenant and was the same year promoted to Lieutenant in the Chinese Labour Corps, whose recruiting hub was Weihai in Shandong Province. Drummond served without great distinction, receiving the three campaign medals, the 1914 Star, the British War Medal and The Victory Medal. He was demobilised in 1920, returned to Worcester and resumed teaching. On retirement he and Florence removed to Cape Town, taking up residence in the appropriately named Balintore Road, Rondebosch, in the district of Wynberg; they named their home 'Hame.' Drummond died on 7 April, 1944, at 'Hame' and was buried in Plumstead Cemetery, Cape Town. Florence survived him by thirty years, dying aged 85 on 29 August 1975 at Stellenbosch.

Ross, Isabella Strapp née Macfadyen (1852–1930). Second wife of John Ross. Born at Paisley, Renfrewshire, Scotland on 11 August 1852, daughter of Findlay Macfadyen and Margaret Lang Killoch. Married John Ross in Glasgow on 24th February, 1881. There were eight children, four of whom died in infancy: Hugh (b./d. 1883), Findlay (b./d. 1884), John (Jackie) (b./d. 1888) and Catherine (Cathy) Jane (b./d. 1889), all are buried at Newchwang, Manchuria. Their four surviving children, all born at Mukden, Manchuria, were:

Margaret Pritty (1884–1956). She married Henry McClure Anderson, architect at Tientsin (Tianjin), China, where he entered a partnership with Edwin Cook as Cook & Anderson. Anderson died, aged 65, in the British American Nursing Home in Tientsin on 10 August 1942. He is remembered as the planner of Tiestsin's Wudadao (Five Great Avenues), consisting of over two hundred and thirty buildings in an eclectic mix of European styles in a prime location in the British concession.

John Herbert (1891–1951). Graduated M.A. (1913) University of Edinburgh, then studied at New College, Edinburgh. Student assistant at Edinburgh Dalry, 1915–1916. War service with Royal Army Medical Corps in Far East Russia, 1918–19. Ordained and inducted Laurieston United Free Church, Falkirk (1920–25); in 1925, he was inducted to Renwick United Free Church, Great Hamilton St., Glasgow. Married Marion Muir Morton, 1926. Died 1951 and buried in New Eastwood Cemetery, Glasgow.

Findlay Macfadyen (1893–1918). Ross' youngest son. Educated at George Watson's College, Edinburgh. Served in France as a Lieutenant in the 1st/9th Battalion Royal Scots. Killed in action on 1st August 1918. Buried in Raperie British Cemetery, Villemontoire, France. At his mother's request, his headstone bears the same inscription as his father's: 'Peace Perfect Peace.' Awarded posthumous Military Cross.

Isabella Sutherland (b. 1902–d. 1961). In 1927 she married Rev. Robert Ritchie Watt; they had a daughter, Sheena Isabella. Robert Watt was born 1893, was educated at Comrie Primary School, Crieff Morrison's Academy and the University of Edinburgh M.A. (1919). During the First World War he served in H. M. Forces in Gallipoli, Egypt, Salonika and France (1914–18). He returned to study at New College (1919–20) and was ordained for Foreign Mission service by United Free Presbytery of Auchterarder in 1922 before sailing for the Gold Coast (Ghana). From the union of the United Free Church and the Church of Scotland in 1929 he served as a missionary with the Church of Scotland, was inducted in 1946 to Fenwick Parish

Church, Fenwick, Ayrshire, and died in 1953 in the manse there. Isabella died in the Edinburgh Royal Infirmary, 14 July, 1961.

Thomas, Robert Jermain (1840–1866). Missionary martyr to Korea. Born at Rhayader, Radnorshire, Wales, where his father was a Congregational minister. He began lay preaching at the age of fifteen. In 1856 he was a teacher at Oundle, Northamptonshire, and graduated from New College, University of London in 1863. He was ordained, married and departed to China under the auspices of the London Missionary Society in 1863. Resigned LMS 1864. Visited Korea in 1865. The following year he joined the American ship *General Sherman* as an interpreter. Thomas was killed when the ship was attacked. He is regarded as the first Protestant martyr in Korea. In 1931, 'The Robert Jermain Thomas Memorial Church' was built near the spot where he died.

Underwood, Horace Grant* (1859–1926). Born in London, UK, his family emigrated to the USA in 1872. A graduate of New York University and New Brunswick Theological Seminary, he became a Presbyterian missionary, educator, and translator, dedicating his life to developing Christianity in Korea. Underwood's older brother, John T. Underwood, was an entrepreneur with the family business, Underwood Typewriter Co., based in New York, whose wealth helped to finance his brother's missionary endeavours. He died in 1926 in Atlantic City, New Jersey.

Wang Ching-ming a.k.a. Wang the Illustrious or 'Old' Wang (c.1840–1885). Born in Pekin. Under Ross' tutelage, Wang became the founder of Christianity in Manchuria. He died in Mukden in 1885. See John Ross, *Old Wang: The First Chinese Evangelist in Manchuria* (London: Religious Tract Society, 1889).

Webster, James* (1854–1923). Born at Marnoch, Scotland. United Free Church of Scotland missionary to Manchuria. Friend and colleague of John Ross. Studied at the University of Glasgow, the Free Church College, Glasgow, and New College, Edinburgh. Webster was ordained by the Free Church Presbytery of Edinburgh in 1882. He married Elizabeth Hamilton Scott (1853–1922) the same year and together they went straight to Manchuria. He took up work in Mukden in 1885 and visited the Kando valleys with Ross. He established the work in the area around Tiehling. He returned to Scotland for furlough in 1893. He was active during the Revival of 1908 and wrote the letters which Ross transcribed and published as *The Marvellous Story of the Revival in Manchuria*. After thirty years' service in Manchuria, he returned to Scotland and was appointed UFCS joint Foreign Mission Secretary in 1910. Webster died on 24 June 1923, of gangrenous cholecystitis (gangrene of the gallbladder) at his home, 19 Drumsheugh Gardens, Edinburgh.

White, Mary Culler (1875–1973). Born in Perry, Georgia, the daughter of George H. and Emma Culler White. Mary was educated in Hawkinsville and Wesleyan College, graduating in 1891. She taught in Hawkinsville for seven years after which she completed a course at Scarritt College and offered herself to the Methodist Foreign Mission. She served in China from 1901 to 1943, when, after internment by the Japanese, she was repatriated to the USA and forbidden to return. It was in her home in 1903 that fellow missionary Robert Hardie made an emotional public confession of sin, something that was to become typical of the revivals in Korea in 1907 and in Manchuria in 1908. When White died in 1973 a grave was opened in Evergreen Cemetery, Perry, Georgia, as a temporary resting place for her ashes before their return to China, where they were scattered.

Williamson, Alexander* (1829–1890). Born in Falkirk, Scotland. Missionary to China, translator and traveller, senior colleague of John Ross. Williamson commenced missionary service in China with the London Missionary Society (LMS), arriving in Shanghai with his wife Isabelle in 1855. After only two years, ill health caused him to return to Scotland where he remained for a further six. In 1863 he returned to China as the first overseas agent of the National Bible Society of Scotland, travelling extensively in north China, Mongolia, and Manchuria to distribute the Bible and preach. In 1867, Williamson, who had provided Robert Jermain Thomas with Bibles for Korea, travelled to Corean Gate, and was able to sell Christian books to Korean merchants. Williamson's letter enthusiastically advocating the spiritual needs of Manchuria and

Korea led to the United Presbyterian Church agreeing to John and Mary Ann Ross' settlement in Newchwang. In 1871 Williamson and his wife returned to Manchuria. In 1874 he became an agent of the United Presbyterian Mission, and remained in Yantai. He returned to Scotland in 1883 to recuperate his health, and while there founded a Book and Tract Society for China (later known as the Society for Diffusion of Christian and General Knowledge among the Chinese). In 1886 the Williamsons returned to Shanghai, China, where Isabelle died. Williamson himself died four years later, in Yantai; he was sixty-one years of age.

Geographical Note and Place Names

Manchuria

'The region of the Manchus,' the area of modern China, within the provinces of Heilongjiang, Jilin, and Liaoning. The area in which much of the main narrative of this account took place, formerly within the Chinese Empire, bordering Inner Mongolia on the west, Korea on the south-east, Russia on the east, and China to the south-west and the north. Manchuria was disputed territory, with Russia, Japan and Korea variously making claims to sovereignty over larger or smaller areas. It is a modern name, possibly first used by the Japanese cartographer Takahashi Kageyasu (1785–1829), then commonly adopted by Europeans, but not used by the Chinese themselves, who generally deprecate the name. The name is now almost obsolete.

Chinese Names

When quoting original sources, the text generally adheres to the spelling of Chinese names found in those sources. Otherwise for the sake of consistency the old missionary spelling of names, as in the left column, is adopted. To assist location on modern maps, the name now commonly in use is given in the right-hand column. The place names listed are not a complete list. It has not been possible to check the names of some of the small villages. Unchanged names are not listed.

Newchwang .... Yingkou
Amoy .... Xiamen
Canton .... Guangdong

Ningpo	Ningbo
Chefoo	Yantai
Chosen	Zhoushan
Foochow	Fuzhou
Fukien	Fujian
Hankow	Hankou
Tientsin	Tianjin
Nanking	Nanjing
Suchow	Suzhou
Shantung	Shandong
Ch'ing-Chou-Fu	Qing Zhou
Gulf of Peichihli (Pechili)	Bohai Sea
Fengwhangchung	Fenghuang
Kando	Jiandao
Mukden (also Moukden, Mookden)	Shenyang
Liaoyong	Liaoyang
Shuang-cheng-pu	Shuangcheng
Shan-si	Shanxi
Pei-Tai-Ho	Beidaihe
Liao-Tung	Liaodong
Chin-chou	Jinzhou
Szefangtai	Siping

Korean Names

South Korean place names are given in their pre-2000 form. North Korean place names are unaltered.

Notes

Chapter 1: William Burns: The Spiritual Father

NOTES TO PAGES 11-13

1. Islay Burns, *Memoir of Rev. Wm. C. Burns: Missionary to China from the English Presbyterian Church* (London: James Nisbet, 1870), p. 347.

2. Ibid., p. 37.

3. Ibid., p. 352.

Chapter 2: Heir to a Goodly Heritage

NOTES TO PAGES 17-25

1. Lewis Rose Nigg, 'County of Ross and Cromarty' in *The New Statistical Account of Scotland* (Edinburgh and London, W. Blackwood and Sons. 1845), Vol. 6, p. 21.

2. John Ross' death certificate gives his father's occupation as master tailor.

3. See Eric Richards, *The Highland Clearances: People, Landlords and Rural Turmoil* (Edinburgh: Birlinn, 1988), pp. 138, 149-51.

4. James Thomson, *The Value and Importance of Scottish Fisheries* (London: Smith, Elder, 1849), pp. 173-74.

5. Rose, *New Statistical Account*, p. 31.

6. Hugh Miller, *Scenes and Legends of the North of Scotland: Or, the Traditional History of Cromarty* (Edinburgh: Adam and Charles Black, 1835), p. 269.

7. Miller, pp. 184, 205.

8. Donald Sage, *Memorabilia Domestica: Or Parish Life in the North of Scotland* (Wick: W. Rae, 1889), p. 12.

9. John Noble, *Religious Life in Ross* (Inverness: Northern Counties Newspaper and Printing and Publishing Company, 1909), p. 163. Cf. John Gillies, *Historical Collections of Accounts of Revival* (rpt. Edinburgh: Banner of Truth Trust, 1981), p. 453.

10. John Kennedy, *Days of the Fathers in Ross-shire*, p. 14.

11. Ibid., p. 16.

12. Noble, p. 87

13. Ibid., p.88.

14. Richards, *The Highland Clearances*, p. 99.

15. For the history of the Nigg United Presbyterian congregation, see Robert Small, *History of the Congregations of the United Presbyterian Church, 1733–1900* (Edinburgh: David M. Small, 1904), pp. 622-57.

Chapter 3: STUDENT AND HOME MISSIONARY

NOTES TO PAGES 32-49

1. James A. Skinner, *The First Schools in the Seaboard Villages* at https://www.seaboardhistory.com/gallery/hilton-of-cadboll-school/the-first-schools-in-the-seaboard-villages-written-by-dr-j-a-skinner-march-2014/ Accessed 1 February 2022.

2. *New Statistical Account*, vol. XIV, p. 293.

3. *NSAS*, vol. XIV, p. 31.

4. Skinner, *The First Schools in the Seaboard Villages.*

5. Cf. John Alexander Lamb, *Fasti of the United Free Church of Scotland* (Edinburgh: Oliver and Boyd, 1956), p. 531.

6. Robert H. W. Shepherd, *Lovedale, South Africa: The Story of a Century, 1841–1941* (Lovedale: Lovedale Press, n.d.), p. 92.

7. James Buchan, *The Expendable Mary Slessor* (Edinburgh: St Andrew Press, 1980), p. 25.

8. John Brown, *Analytical Exposition of the Epistle of St. Paul the Apostle to the Romans* (Edinburgh: William Oliphant and Co, 1857), p. 301.

9. Glasgow University Matriculation Albums, Sessions, 1862–63, 1864–5, 1866–67.

10. Proceedings of the Synod of the United Presbyterian Church, Appendix, p. 151.

11. Ibid., p. 152.

12. John Murdoch, *Highlander*, 7 June, 1873, p. 8, cited by Allan W. MacColl, *Land, Faith and the Crofting Community: Christianity and Social Criticism in the Highlands of Scotland 1843–1893* (Edinburgh: Edinburgh University Press, 2006), p. 90.

13. Robert Small, *A History of the Congregations of the United Presbyterian Church, 1733–1900* (Edinburgh: David Small, 1904), vol. II, p. 167.

14. Robert Hay, 'Improvement not Clearance: A factor's instructions to his ground officers on the Isle of Lismore, 1831–46,' in *Review of Scottish Culture* 22: pp. 99-119.

15. Margaret A. Miller, *MacDougall McCallum Heritage Foundation Scholarship Report 2013*, at https://www.macdougallmccallumheritagefoundation.com/2013-scholarship-recipient-1 Accessed 12 January, 2022.

16. An allusion to Hosea 6:4, where the morning cloud is transient.

17. Proceedings of the Synod of the United Presbyterian Church, 1870, Appendix, p. 156

18. Ibid., p. 157.

19. C. H. MacGill (ed.) *Memories of the Rev. Dr Hamilton M. MacGill (*Edinburgh, Andrew Eliot, 1880), pp. 91-92.

20. Minute Book of the United Presbyterian Foreign Mission Board, p. 365 (22 April 1870). A circular letter from MacGill to a small group of members of the Foreign Mission Board, namely, William Watson, Forres; James Scott, Inverness; George Robson, Inverness; Dr G. Johnson, Edinburgh; Andrew Mitchell Esq. Glasgow.

21. Letter from MacGill to Ross, 25 July, 1870.

22. Proceedings of the Synod of the United Presbyterian Church, 1870, p. 375.

23. Minute Book of the United Presbyterian Foreign Mission Board, p. 972 (2nd February 1872).

24. The house is mentioned in the list of Lost Scottish Villas at http://www.slch.org.uk/list.html (Accessed 17th April, 2022).

25. Though Larkfield is shown as Mary Ann's normal residence on the marriage registration document, it is possible that her father did not own the property. *Scotland: Owners of Lands and Heritages*, 1872–73 Return, lists Drummond Brothers as the owners of the three-acre property named Larkfield at Trinity, Ferry Road, Leith, which had at the time the substantial gross annual value for rateable purposes of £111.

26. I am very grateful to Emeritus Professor Donald Meek for drawing my attention to the marriage registration document in *Marriages in the District of Port of Leith in the County of Edinburgh*, 1872, p. 19, no. 37.

27. Obituary by John James Bonar (Greenock) in *The Free Church Monthly*, January 1, 1880, p. 16.

28. Hew Scott, *Fasti Ecclesiae Scoticanae* (Edinburgh, Oliver and Boyd, 1915), vol. I, p. 153.

29. Anon. 'Newhaveners of History: The Rev. Dr James Fairbairn' in *The Bow Tow* (Newsletter of Newhaven Heritage Centre), Issue 4, January–March, 2015, p. 4.

30. David O. Hill and Robert Adamson, *The Pastor's Visit*, accession number: PGP HA 293, Scottish National Portrait Gallery.

31. Minute Book of the United Presbyterian Foreign Mission Board, p. 276 (12 April 1872).

Chapter 4: Go West, Young Man

NOTES TO PAGES 53-57

1. *Minutes of the Foreign Missions Board of the United Presbyterian Church*, 29 July 1872, pp. 267-68. Cf. letter MacGill to Ross, 12 April 1872.

2. Mark Twain, *Roughing It* (1872, New York: Penguin Classics, 1985).

3. Helen Hunt Jackson, *Bits of Travel at Home* (Boston: Roberts Brothers, 1878), pp. 3ff.

Chapter 5: Opium and Missionaries

NOTES TO PAGES 59-73

1. See, e.g. Andrew Porter, 'David Cameron in China: ministers refuse calls to remove poppies,' in *The Telegraph*, 10 November 2010 at https://www.telegraph.co.uk/news/politics/david-cameron/8121570/David-Cameron-in-China-ministers-refuse-calls-to-remove-poppies.html Accessed 19 January, 2022.

2. Neil Connor, 'China media continues to laud Xi's visit and UK ties,' in *The Telegraph*, 23 October 2015 at https://www.telegraph.co.uk/news/worldnews/asia/china/11949941/China-media continues-to-laud-Xis-visit-and-UK-ties.html Accessed 19 January 2022.

3. J. H. Bavinck, *Introduction to the Science of Missions* (Philadelphia: Presbyterian and Reformed Publishing Co., 1960), p. 81.

4. Andrew Robinson, 'Why the Poppy Remains all the Rage,' in *The Lancet*, vol. 388, December 10, 2016, p. 16.

5. For Chatterton's death, see Nick Groom, 'The Death of Chatterton' in *From Gothic to Romantic: Thomas Chatterton's Bristol*, ed. Alistair Heys (Bristol: Redcliffe Press, 2005), pp.116-25.

6. Christopher D. Sneller, 'Take away your opium and your missionaries: The Opium Wars (1839–60) and the Chinese National Psyche,' in *Transmission*, Autumn 2012, pp. 20-22.

7. For the USA's involvement in the opium trade, see Jacques M. Downs, 'American Merchants and the China Opium Trade, 1800–1840,' in *The Business History Review* 42, no. 4 (1968): pp. 418-42.

8. Letter from Captain Elliot to Viscount Palmerston, November 16th 1839, received March 27th 1840, in *Additional Papers Relating to China: Presented to both Houses of Parliament by Command of Her Majesty 1840*, p. 5.

9. War with China – Adjourned Debate, Hansard, 8 April 1840, vol. 53, cc749-837.

10. Theodore Walbrond (ed), *Letters and Journals of James, Eighth Earl of Elgin* (London, J. Murray, 1872), p. 385.

11. Gladstone's Diary, cited by Austin Ramzy, 'How Britain Went to War With China Over Opium' in *The New York Times*, 3rd July, 2018, at https://www.nytimes.com/2018/07/03/world/asia/opium-war-book-china-britain.html retrieved 6th March 2019.

12. *United Presbyterian Missionary Record*, 1st January 1874, p. 17. For the Sassoons and their part in the opium trade, see: M. Mayer, 'Bagdadi Jewish merchants in Shanghai and the Opium trade,' in *Jewish Culture and History* vol. 2.1 (1999), pp. 58-71; Jonathan Kauffman, *Kings of Shanghai: The Rival Jewish Dynasties That Helped Create Modern China* (London: Abacus, 2021); Joseph Sassoon, *The Global Merchants: The Enterprise and Extravagance of the Sassoon Dynasty* (London: Allen Lane, 2022).

13. Arnobious, 'Against the Heathen (Book II),' in *Ante-Nicene Fathers*, Vol. 6.X. Ed. Alexander Roberts, James Donaldson, and A. Cleveland Coxe (Edinburgh: T & T Clark, 1887), pp. 70-77.

14. S. Frederick Starr, *Lost Enlightenment: Central Asia's Golden Age from the Arab Conquest to Tamerlane* (Princeton: Princeton University Press, 2013), p. 452.

15. Marco Polo, *The Travels of Marco Polo the Venetian* (London: J. M. Dent, 1908), p. 15.

16. R. G. Tiedemann, 'China and its Neighbours,' in Adrian Hasting (ed.), *A World History of Christianity* (Grand Rapids: W. B. Eerdmans, 1999), p. 384.

17. Anon., *Chinese Imprints and a Screen*, Catalogue 1491 (London: Maggs Bros. Ltd., 2017), p. 25.

18. John Ross, *Chinese Foreign Policy* (Shanghai: 1877), p. 19.

19. J. Beeching, *The Chinese Opium Wars* (London: Hutchinson, 1975), p. 61, cited by Christopher D. Sneller, '"Take Away Your Opium and Your Missionaries": The Opium Wars (1839–60) and the Chinese National Psyche,' in *Bible In Transmission*, Winter 2012, pp. 20-22.

20. Charles Taylor, *Five Years in China: With Some Account of the Great Rebellion and a Description of St. Helena* (New York: Derby and Jackson, 1860), p. 51.

Chapter 6: In Chefoo

NOTES TO PAGES 59-73

1. Frances Wood, *No Dogs and Not Many Chinese: Treaty Port Life in China 1843–1943* (London: John Murray, 1998).

2. Ed. Arnold Wright, *Twentieth Century Impressions of Hongkong, Shanghai, and other Treaty Ports of China: Their History, People, Commerce, Industry, and Resources* (London: Lloyds Greater Britain Publishing Company Limited, 1908), pp. 767ff.

3. *The Sydney Gazette and New South Wales Advertiser*, Thursday 22 January, 1837, p. 3. https://trove.nla.gov.au/newspaper/article/2211547# – accessed 18th April 2019.

4. *Proceedings of the Old Bailey*, https://www.oldbaileyonline.org/browse.jsp?id=t18541127-30&div=t18541127-30&terms=Tierney#highlight – accessed 18 April 2019.

5. Cf. https://archiveshub.jisc.ac.uk/search/archives/9047e110-3230-3431-9ee8-67db25153c9b – accessed 19 April, 2019.

6. Changyu Pioneer Wine Company, 18th July 1896, an employment contract for Baron Max von Babo with Thio Tiauw Siat [Cheong Fatt Tze] to superintend production at the latter's winery. Sold at auction by Christies, London, 16 January 2014. https://www.christies.com/lotfinder/Lot/wine-in-china-changyu-pioneer-wine-5762524-details.aspx – accessed 18 April, 2019.

7. Diplomatic and Consular Report. China. *Report for the years 1903–05 on the Trade of Chefoo, No. 3729 Annual Series* (London: His Majesty's Stationery Office, 1906), p. 4.

8. Mildred Cable, *China: Her Life and People* (London: University of London Press, 1946), p. 129.

9. Norman H. Cliff, 'Building the Protestant Church in Shandong, China,' in *International Bulletin of Missionary Research,* April 1998, pp. 62-68. Cf. Xiuhua Wang, *Explaining Christianity in China: Why a Foreign Religion has Taken Root in Unfertile Ground,* Master of Arts thesis for Department of Sociology, Graduate School, Baylor University, 2015.

10. Mrs Duncan M'Laren, *The Story of our Manchurian Mission* (Edinburgh: Office of the United Presbyterian Church, 1896), pp. 11ff.

11. T. B. Ray, *Southern Baptists in China* (Richmond, VA: Foreign Mission Board Southern Baptist Convention, n.d.) pp. 7f.; cf. 'Early Southern Baptist China Missions' in William Cathcart (ed.), *The Baptist Encyclopedia* (Philadelphia: Louis H. Everts, 1881), at http://baptisthistoryhomepage.com/china.sb.early.missions.html – accessed 19 April 2019.

12. Cf. Brian Stanley, 'Richard, Timothy' in ed. Gerald H. Anderson, *Biographical Dictionary of Christian Missions* (Grand Rapids: William Eerdmans, 1998), p. 576.

13. *United Presbyterian Missionary Record*, 1st July 1873, p. 571.

14. *United Presbyterian Missionary Record*, 1st August 1873, p. 606.

15. *Minutes of the Foreign Missions Board of the United Presbyterian Church,* 26th November, 1872, p. 172.

16. In February 1869, responding to William Burns' wish, the Presbyterian Church in Ireland sent a medical doctor, Dr Joseph Hunter, and a missionary minister, Rev. Hugh Waddell, as their first missionaries to Manchuria. Cf. Austin Fulton, *Through Earthquake, Wind and Fire,* (Edinburgh: St Andrew Press, 1967), p. 31.

17. *Minutes of the Foreign Missions Board of the United Presbyterian Church*, 25 March 1873, pp. 219-20.

Chapter 7: The Valley of the Shadow

notes to pages 85-91

1. *United Presbyterian Missionary Record,* June 2nd, 1873, p. 572.

2. *United Presbyterian Missionary Record,* 1st August 1873, pp. 605f.

3. Ibid., p. 606.

4. James H. Grayson, 'A Spark in North East Asia: A Personal Hagiography of a Scottish Missionary to Manchuria: John Ross (1842–1915)' in Clyde Binfield (ed.) *Sainthood Revisioned: Studies in Hagiography and Biography* (Sheffield: Sheffield Academic Press, 1995), p.97.

5. *United Presbyterian Missionary Record,* 1st August 1873, p. 606.

6. John Ross, 'History of the Manchurian Mission,' in *The Chinese Recorder and Missionary Journal*, VXIII, no. 7, July 1887, pp. 255-63.

7. *United Presbyterian Missionary Record,* 1st August 1873, p. 607.

8. *United Presbyterian Missionary Record*, 1st November 1873, p. 670.

9. Ibid., p. 671.

Chapter 8: WANG CHING-MING: THE CHINESE AGENT

NOTES TO PAGES 94-103

1. For Stewart's initiative, see T. Jack Thompson, *Touching the Heart: Xhosa Missionaries to Malawi, 1876–1888* (Pretoria: University of South Africa, 2000).

2. Max Warren, *To Apply the Gospel: Selections from the Writings of Henry Venn* (Grand Rapids: W. B. Eerdmans, 1971), p. 23.

3. For Wang's life and ministry, see John Ross, *Old Wang: The First Chinese Evangelist in Manchuria* (London: Religious Tract Society, 1889).

4. *United Presbyterian Missionary Record*, 2nd November, 1874, p. 306.

5. Ross, *Old Wang*, p. 11.

6. Ibid., p. 114.

Chapter 9: ADVANCE TO MUKDEN

NOTES TO PAGES 108-112

1. For Dr Joseph M. Hunter, his colleagues and work, see Robert Higginson Boyd, *Waymakers in Manchuria: The Story of the Irish Presbyterian Pioneer Missionaries to Manchuria* (Belfast, Foreign Mission Office, Church House, 1940); and Austin Fulton, *Through Earthquake, Wind and Fire: Church and Mission in Manchuria 1867–1950* (Edinburgh: The Saint Andrew Press, 1967).

2. *United Presbyterian Missionary Record,* 1st January, 1874, p. 17.

3. Ross, *Old Wang*, p. 44.

4. Mrs Duncan M'Laren of St Oswald's, Oswald Road, Grange, Edinburgh, was the Honorary Secretary of the United Presbyterian Edinburgh Zenana Society and a member of the committee of the Hill Murray Mission to the Blind and Illiterate Sighted in Northern China, of which John Ross' colleague, James Webster, was chairman.

5. *United Presbyterian Missionary Record,* 1st August 1874, pp. 243f.

6. M'Laren, *Story,* p. 117.

Chapter 10: PROGRESS IN MUKDEN AND BEYOND

NOTES TO PAGES 114-128

1. M'Laren, *Story,* p. 37.

2. Ross, *Old Wang*, pp. 47-48.

3. Ibid., p. 54.

4. Elizabeth Inglis Christie, *Dugald Christie of Manchuria: Pioneer and Medical Missionary* (London: James Clarke, 1932), pp. 9-27.

5. The Evangelical Union Church were also known as the 'Morisonions', after James Morison, a prominent preacher of Arminianism and founder of the denomination subsequent to his suspension from the United Secession Church in 1841. For Morison, see *Dictionary of Scottish Church History and Theology*, pp. 607f.

6. For Mukden medical work, see Christie, *Dugald Christie of Manchuria.*

7. Fulton, *Through Earthquake, Wind and Fire,* pp. 32-35.

8. Christie, *Dugald Christie of Manchuria*, pp. 52 ff.

9. Ibid., p. 52.

10. Frederica Gordon-Cumming, *The Inventor of the Numeral-type for China* (London: Downey & Co., 1898), p. 79.

11. Ibid., p. 83.

12. Ibid., p. 79.

13. Christie, *Dugald Christie of Manchuria*, pp. 146-47.

Chapter 11: KOREA: RECONNAISSANCE

NOTES TO PAGES 134-145

1. Alexander Williamson, *Journeys in North China, Manchuria, and Eastern Mongolia: With Some Account of Corea* (London: Smith, Elder & Co, 1870), vol. 2, p. 299.

2. Ibid., p. 327.

3. Ibid., p. 326.

4. Official Korean Government reports (Kojong Archives) and US Government *Report on the Murder of the Officers, Crew and Passengers of the American Schooner General Sherman at the Ping Yang River, Corea* at: https://web.archive.org/web/20071019185740/http://www.kimsoft.com/2002/sherman-0.htm. For a Korean account of the incident, see Professor Han Gyu Mu, *The General Sherman Incident of 1866 and Rev. Thomas' Martyrdom* at https://web.archive.org/web/20070930020145/http://www.kimsoft.com/2000/sherman2.htm – accessed 7 January, 2022.

5. John Ross, *History of Corea: Ancient and Modern; with Description of Manners and Customs, Language and Geography*, (Paisley: J. & R. Parlane, 1891), p. 294.

6. For Robert Jermain Thomas, see Alexander Wylie, *Memorials of Protestant Missionaries to the Chinese: Giving a List of Their Publications, and Obituary Notices of the Deceased* (Shanghai: American Presbyterian Mission Press, 1867), pp. 267-268; George Paik (Nak-chun Paek), *The History of Protestant Missions in Korea, 1832-1910*, (Seoul: Yonsei University Press, 1987); Sebastian C. H. Kim and Kirsteen Kim, *A History of Korean Christianity* (Cambridge: Cambridge University Press, 2015), pp. 55, 84, 132, 256.

7. See Brian Stanley, 'The Legacy of Robert Arthington' in *International Bulletin of Missionary Research*, 22, no. 4 (October 1998): pp. 166-71.

8. John Ross, 'Visit to the Corean Gate,' in *Chinese Record and Missionary Journal*, (Nov. Dec. 1875), pp. 471-72.

9. John Ross, 'The Corean Version of the New Testament: How I Came to Make It,' in *United Presbyterian Missionary Record*, May 1, 1883, pp. 206-07

10. Peter Ahn-Ho Bae, *The Three-Self Principle and the Mission Method of John Ross: A Study in the Formation of the Early Korean Presbyterian Church, 1874–1893.* PhD Thesis for King's College, University of Aberdeen, 2001, pp. 136 ff.

11. Ross, 'The Corean Version.'

Chapter 12: The Trials of Bible Translation and Publishing

notes to pages 149-159

1. James S. Sinclair, 'A Series of Lectures on the Declaratory Act (1892)' in Macpherson A. (ed.) *History of the Free Presbyterian Church of Scotland 1893–1970* (Glasgow: Publications Committee, Free Presbyterian Church of Scotland, n.d.), p. 404.

2. Emeritus Professor James Grayson of the School of East Asian Studies at the University of Sheffield, personal communication, 9 April, 2022.

3. *UCLA Online Archive Korean Christianity* at http://koreanchristianity.cdh.ucla.edu/sources/books/ – accessed 14 April, 2022.

4. Pawel Kida, 'Korean parts of speech viewed by western scholars from 1832 till 1890' in *Asia and Africa in the Changing World: The XXVIII international conference on historiography and source studies of Asia and Africa* (St Petersburg: St Petersburg State University, Faculty of Asian and African Studies, 215), pp. 218ff.

5. John Ross, 'The Christian Dawn in Korea,' in *The Missionary Review of the World,* Princeton, volume 3, April 1890, p. 247.

6. Ross to the BFBS, 23 June, 1880, in 'The Korean Work from China, The British and Foreign Bible Society, "The Editorial Correspondence Books, Inward, The British and Foreign Bible Society, 1880–1897,"' in *The Historical Materials of the Korean Bible Society*, vol. 1, transcribed and edited by Sung-Deuk Oak (Seoul: The Korean Bible Society, 2002, no pagination). Cf. John Ross, 'Christian Dawn in Korea,' pp. 241-48.

7. Sung Il Choi. *John Ross (1842–1915) and the Korean Protestant Church: The First Korean Bible and Its Relation to the Protestant Origins in Korea*. Ph.D. thesis, University of Edinburgh, 1992, p. 11.

8. Choi, *John Ross,* p. 120.

9. Kim and Kim, *History,* pp. 57-58. Cf. Sung-Deuk Oak, 'Competing Chinese Names for God: The Chinese Term Question and Its Influence upon Korea,' in *Journal of Korean Religions* 3, no. 2 (2012): pp. 102-06.

10. Choi, *John Ross,* p. 105.

11. Ibid., p. 103.

12. Oak, *Historical Materials,* 18 February, 1880.

13. Ibid., 10th May, 1880.

14. Choi, *John Ross,* p. 150.

15. Kim & Kim, *History,* p. 57.

16. Choi, *John Ross,* p. 150.

17. Writing to his counterpart in the BFBS, Slowan forwarded the committee's minutes of a meeting at which Ross' attitude and behaviour in prosecuting an application for further funding had been discussed. Ross, dissatisfied with the slow progress of the talks, had withdrawn his application, only to reinstate it shortly afterwards. Moreover, disappointed with the NBSS' offer of help, he did not disclose to Slowan or the committee that he had approached the BFBS with a view to placing his translations in their hands. That the NBSS was deeply disappointed by this goes without saying. Though it was said. The committee's minutes recorded that the Korean translations were the work of Scottish missionaries in the service of a Scottish Church, and that the first portions of their translation had been published with the assistance of the Scottish Society, and, by implication, with Scottish money, all of which help was still available. The minute adds that the committee could not but regret being deprived of the privilege of completing the publication of the Korean New Testament. Nevertheless, it respected Ross' ability and earnestness, and deplored any misunderstanding which had led him to withdraw from cooperating with them. The minute recorded the committee's hope that if Ross would work 'along with other competent translators' it would be prepared to proceed with the publication of his version of the New Testament, if not as a complete work – as he insisted – then at least in instalments, as they had done in publishing the Gospels of Luke and John. To the committee's minutes, Slowan appended his personal comment as a warning of what the BFBS officials could expect.

18. Oak, *Historical Materials,* July 28, 1882.

19. Ibid., September 21, 1882.

20. Ibid., March 24, 1882.

21. Choi, *John Ross,* p. 146.

22. Oak, *Historical Materials,* Sept. 21, 1882.

23. Choi, *Historical Materials,* p. 148.

24. Choi, *Historical Materials,* p. 236. Cf. W. D. Reynolds, 'Early Bible Translations,' in *Korean Mission Field,* Vol 26, September 1930, pp. 185-89.

25. Choi, *John Ross,* pp. 168-69.

26. Richard Rutt, 'Concerning the New Testament of the Korean Bible,' in *Technical Papers for the Bible Translator,* Vol. 15, No. 2, April 1964, p. 82.

27. Kim and Kim, *History,* p. 67.

Chapter 13: The Korean Valleys

NOTES TO PAGES 164-170

1. Ross, *Christian Dawn,* p. 243.

2. Ibid., p. 244.

3. Ibid., p. 254.

4. Ibid, pp. 254, 244.

5. Kim & Kim, *History*, pp. 10-11.

6. Ross, *Christian Dawn,* p. 246.

Chapter 14: The First Korean Churches

NOTES TO PAGES 171-181

1. *Peep of Day* can be found at: https://archive.org/details/peepofdayorserie00mort/page/n15/mode/2up Accessed 10 January 2022.

2. Cf. Bae, *The Three-Self Principle*, pp. 136ff.

3. John Nevius, *Methods of Missionary Work* (New York: New York, Foreign mission library, 1886). For a brief introduction, see Everett N. Hunt, 'The Legacy of John Livingston Nevius,' in *International Bulletin of Missionary Research*, July 1991, pp. 120-24.

4. Lamin Sanneh in the foreword to the 2006 edition of D. M. Paton (ed.), *The Ministry of the Spirit: Selected Writings of Roland Allen* (Cambridge: Lutterworth Press: 2006), p. xvi.

5. Hubert J. B. Allen, *Roland Allen: Pioneer, Priest and Prophet* (Cincinnati: Forward Movement Publications, 1995), p. vii.

6. James W. Inglis, 'In Memoriam,' in *Chinese Recorder and Missionary Journal,* XVIII, no. 1, January 1916, pp. 49-51.

7. H. J. B. Allen, *Roland Allen*, pp. 60-61.

8. Kim and Kim, *History*, p. 58.

9. Ross, *Christian Dawn*, p. 247.

10. Kim and Kim, *History*, p. 58.

11. Horace Grant Underwood, *The Call of Korea: Political, Social, Religious* (New York: Fleming H. Revel, 1908), pp. 137f.

12. Choi, *John Ross,* p. 259.

13. Roy E. Shearer, *Wildfire: Church Growth in Korea* (Grand Rapids: William B. Eerdmans, 1966), p. 41.

14. Horace Grant Underwood, 'Today from Korea,' *The Missionary Review of the World* (November 1893), p. 816.

15. Shearer, *Wildfire*, p. 44.

16. L. George Paik, *The History of Protestant Missions in Korea, 1832–1910* (Pyongyang: Union Christian College Press, 1929), p. 45. Cf. Kim and Kim, *History*, p. 59.

17. John R. Mott, et. al, *Report of Commission I: Carrying the Gospel to All the Non-Christian World* (Edinburgh: Oliphant, Anderson and Ferrier, 1910), p. 333.

Chapter 15: Death and Resurrection

NOTES TO PAGES 183-189

1. Christie, *Dugald Christie.* p. 75.

2. F. W. S. O'Neil, *The Call of the East: Sketches from the History of the Irish Mission to Manchuria, 1869–1919* (London: James Clark, 1919), p. 31.

3. M'Laren, *Story,* p.108.

4. John Ross' letter to Senatus of the University of Glasgow, 1894, https://www.universitystory.gla.ac.uk/image/?id=UGSP02843&o=&start=&max=&l=R&biog=WH9276&type=P&p=2 – accessed 11 January, 2022.

5. M'Laren, *Story,* p. 111.

6. O'Neil, *The Call of the East,* p. 33.

7. Christie, *Dugald Christie,* pp. 83-84.

8. Ross, *Mission Methods,* pp. 125-26.

Chapter 16: The Blood of Christians is Seed

NOTES TO PAGES 192-205

1. Ross, 'The Situation in China' in MRUPC, 1, Sept. 1900, pp. 205-06.

2. Ross, *Mission Methods,* pp. 60-61.

3. R. G. Tiedemann, 'Baptism of Fire: China's Christians and the Boxer Uprising of 1900,' in *International Bulletin of Missionary Research,* 2000, vol. 24.1, pp. 7-12.

4. R. H. Boyd, *Waymakers in Manchuria* (Belfast: The Foreign Mission Office, 1940), p. 189.

5. Christie, *Dugald Christie,* p. 88.

6. Ross, *Missionary Methods,* pp. 202-03.

7. Christie, *Ten Years in Manchuria: a Story of Medical Mission work in Moukden,* 1883–1893, written in 1895, five years before the Boxer trouble, mentions Ross on pages 8, 13 and 68. Christie's *Thirty years in Moukden, 1883–1913, Being the Experiences and Recollections of Dugald Christie* (1914), edited by his wife, has three mentions of Ross' name. Iza Christie's biography of her husband, *Dugald Christie of Manchuria: Pioneer and Medical Missionary: the Story of a Life with a Purpose* (c.1932) has five references, one of which uncritically refers to Ross sharing with her husband an ordeal during the Russo-Japanese war of 1904. But see Mrs Dugald Christie, 'Pioneers: Rev. John Ross, Manchuria' in *Life and Work: The Record of the Church of Scotland,* (5) 1934, pp. 76-78.

8. J. Miller Graham, *East of the Barrier, or, Sidelights on the Manchuria Mission* (New York, Fleming H. Revel, 1902), pp. 179-80.

9. Dugald Christie (ed. Iza Christie), *Thirty years in Moukden, 1883–1913: Being the Experiences and Recollections of Dugald Christie* (London: Constable, 1914), pp. 121-22.

10. Christie, *Dugald Christie,* p. 92.

11. Graham, *East of the Barrier,* pp. 223-24

12. Fulton, *Through Earthquake, Wind and Fire,* p. 342.

13. A. E. Glover, *A Thousand Miles of Miracles: A Personal Record of God's Delivering Power from the Hands of the Imperial Boxers of Shan-si* (London: Hodder and Stoughton, 1904), p. 340.

14. Ross, *Mission Methods*, p. 172.

15. Graham, *East of the Barrier*, pp. 225-26.

16. Cf. Christie, *Thirty Years*, p. 162.

17. Russian and Japanese soldiers committed appalling atrocities, as did the French and Germans. Indeed, in words that would come back to haunt Germany in two world wars, Kaiser Wilhelm II belligerently urged on his soldiers by reminding them of how a thousand years earlier 'the Huns under their King Attila made a name for themselves', adding, 'may the name German be affirmed by you in such a way in China.' Nor were American and British troops innocent of the indiscriminate killing of Chinese of both sexes and all ages. Cf. Robert Leonhard, *The China Relief Expedition: Joint Coalition Warfare in China Summer 1900*, essay at https://www.jhuapl.edu/Content/documents/ China%20ReliefSm.pdf, p. 60.

18. Roland Allen, *The Siege of the Peking Legations, Being the Diary of the Rev. Roland Allen* (London: Smith Elder, 1901), p. 297.

19. Choi, *John Ross*, p. 242, cf. *Missionary Record of the United Free Church* for 1902, p. 18.

Chapter 17: The Maturing of the Manchurian Church

NOTES TO PAGES 207-222

1. Alfred Costain, *The Life of Dr Arthur Jackson of Manchuria* (London: Hodder and Stoughton, 1911), p. 72.

2. 'Respectfully presented by the Presbyterian Church of Manchuria of the right religion of Jesus to the Presbyterian mother Church in Scotland to set forth the praise of the Lord …' (Cf. M'Laren, *Story*, p. 113).

3. Ross, 'Appeal on Behalf of the Suffering Manchurian Christians,' in MRUFC, 1901, p. 105.

4. Leopold Guy Francis Brooke, *An Eye-witness in Manchuria* (London: Everleigh Nash, 1905), p. 233.

5. J. W. Inglis, 'Manchuria,' in Marshall Broomhall (ed.), *The Chinese Empire: A General and Missionary Survey* (London: Marshall, Morgan and Scott, 1907), p. 313. Inglis was a missionary with the United Presbyterian Church, and the brother of Iza Christie, wife of Dr Dugald Christie.

6. Broomhall, *The Chinese Empire*, p. 317.

7. Ross, *Missionary Methods*, p. 5.

8. Christie, *Dugald Christie*, p. 83.

9. Ross, *Missionary Methods*, p. 116.

10. Ross, Ibid., p. 125.

11. Ross, Ibid., pp. 130-31.

12. Costain, *The Life of Dr Arthur Jackson*, p.11.

13. M'Laren, *Story*, p. 73.

14. M'Laren, Ibid., p. 75.

15. M'Laren, Ibid., p. 91.

16. M'Laren, Ibid, p. 83.

17. Costain, *The Life of Dr Arthur Jackson*, p. 71.

18. M'Laren, *Story*, p. 113.

19. Ross, *Missionary Methods*, p. 101.

20. Ross, Ibid., p. 138.

21. Bae, *The Three-Self Principle*, p.106.

22. *United Presbyterian Missionary Record*, 2 November, 1874, p. 307.

23. John Ross, 'Notes on Manchuria,' in T*he Chinese Recorder and Missionary Journal*, VI, no. 3 (May-June 1875), p. 215.

24. J. G. Barker and S. Le Marchant Moore, 'A Contribution to the Flora of Northern China,' in *The Linnean Society Journal*, XVII (1879), pp. 375-90.

25. E. Bretschneider, *The History of European Botanical Discoveries in China* (London: Sampson, Low, Marston and Company, 1898), vol. I, pp. 703-05.

26. John Ross, 'Visit to the Corean Gate' in *Chinese Recorder and Missionary Journal*, 5 (1875), pp. 471-72.

Chapter 18: Revival in Korea

notes to pages 226-246

1. Kenneth Scott Latourette, *The History of the Expansion of Christianity*, Vol 6 (Exeter: Paternoster Press, 1971), p. 418.

2. A fine summary of Appenzeller's missionary contribution is Edward Poitras, 'The Legacy of Henry G. Appenzeller,' in *Bulletin of International Missionary Research*, October 1994, pp. 177-80.

3. Kim and Kim, *History*, p. 67.

4. Andrea Kwon, 'The Legacy of Mary Scranton,' in International Bulletin of Mission Research, 2018, 42 (2): pp. 162-70.

5. Roy E. Shearer, *Wildfire: Church Growth in Korea* (Grand Rapids: William B. Eerdmans, 1966), p. 169.

6. Ibid., p. 174.

7. Cited by Shearer, *Wildfire*, p. 174.

8. Edward Poitras, 'Appenzeller, Henry Gerhard,' in Gerald Anderson (ed.), *Biographical Dictionary of Christian Missions* (Grand Rapids: William B. Eerdmans, 1998), p. 26.

9. Shearer, *Wildfire*, p. 164.

10. William N. Blair and Bruce F. Hunt, *The Korean Pentecost* (Edinburgh: Banner of Truth Trust, 1977), p. 34.

11. Ibid., p. 73.

12. Ibid., *Korean Pentecost*, p. 74.

13. Kim and Kim, *History*, p. 93.

14. R. A. Hardie, 'God's Touch in the Great Revival,' *Korea Mission Field*, Vol. 10 (January, 1914), p. 22, cited by Jung-Sook Lee, 'Reconsidering Mary Culler White's Visit to Wonsan in 1903,' in *Torch Trinity Journal*, Torch Trinity Graduate University, Seoul, vol. 10, no.1, 2000, pp. 75-94.

15. Laura MacDonald, *'Minister of the Gospel and Doctor of Medicine': The Canadian Presbyterian Medical Mission to Korea 1898–1923*, MA thesis, Queen's University, Kingston, Ontario, Canada. February, 2000.

16. M. C. Fenwick, 'From Our Missionary' in *The Canadian College Missionary,* vol. 6, No. 5 (May 1896), p. 68. Cited by Chil-Sung Kim in *The Role of Robert Alexander Hardie in the Korean Great Revival and the Subsequent Development of Korean Protestant Christianity,* Ph.D. thesis for Asbury Theological Seminary, Wilmore, Kentucky, 2012.

17. Chil-Sung Kim, *Role of Robert Hardie*, p.28.

18. R. A. Hardie, 'From Our Missionary (Gensan, August 6, 1895),' in CCM, Vol. 5, No. 7 (October 1895), pp. 106-07. Cf. Frederick James Glover, *Dispatches from the Wilderness: A History of the Canadian Missionaries and Korean Protestants in Northern Korea and Manchuria, 1893–1928,* Ph.D. dissertation, University of Calgary, 2018, p. 71.

19. Chil-Sung Kim, *Role of Robert Hardie*, p. 84.

20. Samuel G. Craig (ed.), B. B. Warfield, *Studies in Perfectionism* (Nutley, NJ: Presbyterian and Reformed Publishing, 1958).

21. See J. I. Packer, *Keep in Step with the Spirit* (Leicester: Inter-Varsity Press, 1984) pp. 150f.

22. L. H. Underwood, *Fifteen Years among the Top-Knots or Life in Korea* (New York: American Tract Society, 1908).

23. Twenty-Sixth Annual Report of the Woman's Foreign Missionary Society, Methodist Episcopal Church, South, for 1903–04 (Publishing House of the Methodist Episcopal Church, South, 1904), p. 27. Cited in Jung-Sook Lee, 'Reconsidering Mary Culler White's Visit to Wonsan in 1903' in *Journal of the Church History Society in Korea* (No. 21, October 2007) at http://www.ttgst.ac.kr/upload/ttgst_resources13/20124-222.pdf

24. Jonathan Goforth, *When the Spirit's Fire Swept Korea* (Grand Rapids: Zondervan, 1943), p. 7.

25. L. H. Underwood, *Fifteen Years,* p. 427.

26. Indisputably, for all its theological flaws, the Keswick Convention was very effective at mobilising Christians for missionary service. Writing in 1914, Walter B. Sloan could say that he personally knew over sixty missionaries who claimed that it was at Keswick that they received a missionary call, or had been stimulated by hearing the various missionaries who spoke there. Dr Eugene Stock

held that there was 'not a mission field which is not indebted to Keswick for one or more of its labourers – in some cases several of them' (Cf. Walter B. Sloan [1914], 'The Influence of the Keswick Convention on Missionary Work,' in *International Review of Mission*, No. 3: pp. 708-20.

27. L. H. Underwood, *Fifteen Years*, p. 336.

28. As a student, Torrey had been influenced both by Finney's writing and the theological liberalism he encountered when a university student in Germany. He renounced liberalism after hearing Moody, going on to contribute essays to *The Fundamentals*. He appreciated the diametrically opposed C. G. Finney and C. H. Spurgeon, was critical of dispensationalists, holding to the possibility of miracles today, though he had an aversion to preaching on divine healing after an altercation with the boorish and eccentric John Alexander Dowie. At the point at which he comes into this story, he was superintendent of the Moody Bible Institute and had, in 1901, edited and published *How to Promote and Conduct a Successful Revival.*

29. Blair and Hunt, *Korean Pentecost*, p. 77.

30. William N. Blair in *Korean Pentecost* misspells both Hardie (Hardy) and Johnstone (Johnson).

31. Walter B. Sloan in James Webster, *The Revival in Manchuria* (London: Morgan and Scott, 1910), p. 4.

32. Graham Lee, 'How the Spirit Came to Pyeng Yang,' in *Chinese Recorder*, March, 1907, pp. 172-76.

33. See Kim and Kim, *History*, p. 94.

34. Lee, *How the Spirit Came*, p. 176.

35. Blair & Hunt, *Korean Pentecost*, p. 87.

36. Underwood, *Fifteen Years*, p. 347.

37. Kim and Kim, *History*, p. 95.

38. Jonathan Goforth, *By My Spirit* (London: Marshal Morgan and Scott, n.d.), p. 184. For the seven hundred and fifty-six new communicants, see Underwood, *Fifteen Years*, p. 350.

39. James E. Adams, *Annual Personal Report to the Board of Foreign Missions of the Presbyterian Church of the USA* (Taegu, Korea, 1910–11).

40. Shearer, *Wildfire*, p. 56.

41. For the sufferings of the Korean Church, see Blair & Hunt, *Korean Pentecost*, pp. 97-156.

Chapter 19: The Manchurian Revival: Characters and Crosscurrents

NOTES TO PAGES 249-261

1. Margaret Weir, *Andrew Weir of Manchuria* (London: James Clark, n.d), p. 109.

2. Blair and Hunt, *Korean Pentecost*, p. 87; Webster, *Revival* (1910), pp. 97 and 116; Weir, *Andrew Weir*, p. 111; F. W. S. O'Neil, *The Quest for God in China* (London: George Allen and Unwin, 1925), p. 247.

3. John Ross (ed), James Webster, *The Marvellous Story of the Revival in Manchuria* (Edinburgh: Oliphant Anderson and Ferrier, 1908), pp. 7-12.

4. Boyd, *Waymakers*, p. 194.

5. Weir, *Andrew Weir*, p.111-12.

6. Burns, *Memoir of Rev. Wm. C. Burns*, p. 105.

7. John Kennedy, *The Apostle of the North: The Life and Labours of Rev. Dr John M'Donald* (London: T. Nelson, 1866), p. 226.

8. Ibid., p. 236.

9. Weir, *Andrew Weir*, p. 108.

10. Goforth, *By My Spirit*, p. 180.

11. S. D. Gordon, *Quiet Talks About Jesus* (Cincinnati: Jennings and Graham, 1906) p. 114.

12. Goforth, *By My Spirit*, p. 24.

13. D. Christie, *Thirty Years in Moukden*, p. 209.

14. Webster, *The Revival in Manchuria* (1910), p. 50.

15. Webster, *Times of Blessing* (1909), p. 8.

16. Goforth, *By My Spirit*, p. 29.

17. Webster, *The Revival in Manchuria* (1910), pp. 51-52.

18. Goforth, *By My Spirit*, p. 18.

19. Ross, preface to Webster, *The Marvellous Story of the Revival in Manchuria* (Edinburgh: Oliphant, Anderson and Ferrier, 1908), p. 11.

20. Goforth, *By My Spirit*, pp. 18-19.

21. Westminster Shorter Catechism Q/A 33 (author's emphasis).

22. Ross, *Mission Methods*, p. 90. The quotation 'all their salvation, and all their desire' is from 2 Samuel 23:5.

23. John Murray, *Redemption Accomplished and Applied* (Edinburgh: Banner of Truth Trust, 1961), p. 121.

24. William Still, D. C Searle and S. B Ferguson (eds.), *The Collected Writings of William Still: volume III, Theological Studies in Genesis and Romans* (Tain: Rutherford House and Christian Focus Publications, 2000), pp. 210-11.

25. Some of these issues, as they relate to North America, have been explored by Iain H. Murray, *Revival And Revivalism* (Edinburgh: Banner of Truth Trust, 1994); and in the context of the United Kingdom by David W. Bebbington and David Ceri Jones (eds), *Evangelicalism and Fundamentalism in the United Kingdom during the Twentieth Century* (Oxford: Oxford University Press, 2013).

Chapter 20: The Manchurian Revival: 'This is the Work of God'
notes to pages 265-282

1. Webster, *The Revival in Manchuria*, pp. 63f.

2. Webster, *Times of Blessing*, p. 37.

3. Ibid., p. 35.

4. Ibid., pp. 35-36.

5. Goforth, *By My Spirit*, p. 36.

6. Webster, *Marvellous Story*, p. 30.

7. Ibid., p. 31.

8. Ibid., p. 32.

9. Ibid., p. 35.

10. Ibid., p. 38.

11. Ibid., p. 41.

12. Webster, *Times of Blessing*, pp. 15-16.

13. Webster, *Marvellous Story*, p. 43.

14. Webster, *Times of Blessing*, p. 17.

15. Webster, *Marvellous Story*, p. 44, citing Edwards' *A Faithful Narrative of the Surprising Work of God in the Conversion of Many Hundred Souls in Northampton* (Boston: James Loring, 1831), p. 24., republished in *The Works of Jonathan Edwards*, volume 1 (Edinburgh: Banner of Truth Trust), p. 347.

16. Webster, *Marvellous Story*, p. 54.

17. Webster, *Times of Blessing*, p. 24.

18. Ibid., p. 25.

19. Ibid., p. 26.

20. Ibid., p. 26.

21. Ibid., p. 78.

22. Weir, *Andrew Weir*, p. 109.

23. Ibid., p. 110.

24. Ibid., p. 112.

25. Frederick W. S. O'Neil, *The Quest for God in China* (London: George Allen and Unwin, 1925), p. 247.

26. Frederick W. S. O'Neil, *The Call of the East: Sketches from the History of the Irish Mission to Manchuria 1869–1919* (London: James Clark, 1919), p. 65.

27. Iza Christie, *Dugald Christie*, p. 117.

28. Fulton, *Through Earthquake, Wind and Fire*, pp. 39, 51 and 89.

29. John Ross, 'Manchuria: Good Items from Moukden,' in *MRUFCS*, January 1909, p. 16.

30. John Ross, 'Manchuria: Spiritual Life and Progress' in *MRUFCS*, May 1909, p. 214.

Chapter 21: Peace, Perfect Peace

NOTES TO PAGES 286-295

1. Bae, *The Three-Self Principle*, p. 106.

2. *Minutes of the Foreign Mission Committee of the United Free Church* for 1910, no. 1639 and no. 1763.

3. *Minutes of the Foreign Mission Committee of the United Free Church* for 1910, no. 1763.

4. For Ross' Balintore property holding see: Valuation Rolls VR011500060-/208, Ross and Cromarty Country, pp. 208, 202, 240 of 430, 1915. As required in Ross' will, most of the Balintore properties appear to have been disposed of shortly after his death in 1915. The Valuation Rolls for 1920 shows the Easter Balintore farm still in the name of John Ross, but probably this refers to his eldest son, John Herbert.

5. Grayson, *Legacy*, p. 170.

6. Minutes of Mayfield United Free Church Kirk Session, 1905-15, pp. 138-41; 162-63; 311-12.

7. Ed. J. A. R. Moffat, *Mayfield 100: 1875–1975* (Edinburgh: Publications Committee Mayfield Church, 1975).

8. Minutes of Mayfield United Free Church Kirk Session, pp. 171-79.

9. Moffat, *Mayfield.*

10. Minutes of Mayfield United Free Church Kirk Session, pp. 247-48.

11. Kenneth R. Ross, 'Edinburgh 1910: Scottish roots and contemporary challenges,' in *Theology in Scotland* XVII.I (2010): pp. 5-21.

12. Andrew F. Walls, *The Cross-Cultural Process in Christian History: Studies in the Transmission and Appropriation of Faith* (Edinburgh: T&T Clark, 2002), p. 53.

13. Harold H. Rowdon, 'Edinburgh 1910, Evangelicals and the Ecumenical Movement,' in *Vox Evangelica* 5 (1967): pp. 49-71.

14. James Johnson (ed.), *Report of the Centenary Conference on Protestant Mission of the World*, (London: James Nisbet, 1889), pp. 235-38, 255.

15. World Mission Conference, 1910, *Report of Commission 1: Carrying the Gospel to all the Non-Christian World*, (Edinburgh: Anderson & Ferrier, 1919), pp. 429-31.

16. Ibid. p. 103.

17. Ibid., p. 358.

18. Death certificate: *Statutory registers Deaths 685/1 434.* 1915, Deaths in the District of St George in the City of Edinburgh, pp. 145, 434.

19. James Webster, 'The Maker of the Manchurian Mission: An Appreciation of the late Rev. John Ross D.D. in *The Record of the Home and Foreign Mission Work of the United Free Church of Scotland*, no.177, September 1915, pp. 394-97.

20. James W. Inglis, 'In Memoriam – The Rev. John Ross D.D.,' in *Chinese Recorder and Missionary Journal*, XVII., no. 1, January 1916, pp. 49-51.

21. Mrs Dugald Christie, 'Pioneers: The Rev. John Ross, Manchuria,' in *Life and Work*, 5, 1934, pp. 76-78.

22. Anon, *Mayfield United Free Church Congregational Notes*, 3 October, 1915, pp. 1-2.

23. Minutes of Mayfield United Free Church Kirk Session, 29th September, 1915.

Chapter 22: The Hope of the Reaper

NOTES TO PAGES 297-308

1. James Webster, 'The Maker of the Manchurian Mission,' in *The Missionary Record of the United Free Church*, September 1915: vol.15, issue 177.

2. *The Proceedings of the General Assembly of the Free Church of Scotland* (1881), pp. 316-18.

3. Ross, *Missionary Methods*, p. 82.

4. Ibid., p. 83.

5. Ibid., pp. 80-81.

6. Michael M., 'A Brief History of Western Presbyterian and Reformed Mission to China,' in Bruce P. Baugus (ed.), *China's Reforming Churches: Mission, Polity, and Ministry in the Next Christendom* (Grand Rapids: Reformation Heritage Books, 2014), Kindle location 946.

7. Minutes of the Foreign Mission Committee of the United Free Church of Scotland, 22nd March 1910, p. 264.

8. The thirty-fourth Annual Report of the Christian Literature Society for China, for the year ending September 30, 1921, p. 21.

9. The thirty-ninth Annual Report of the Christian Literature Society for China, for the year ending September 30, 1926, p. 31.

10. Marlene Finlayson, 'Theology and Ecumenism after Edinburgh 1910,' in David Fergusson, Mark W. Elliott (eds), *The History of Scottish Theology, Volume III, The Long Twentieth Century* (Oxford: Oxford University Press, 2019), p. 71.

11. Manchuria Mission Council Minutes, 24 October 1911.

12. William Palmer Addley, *A Study of the Birth and Development of the Overseas Missions of the Presbyterian Church in Ireland up to 1910*, Ph.D. thesis for the Queen's University, Belfast, 1995, p. 231.

13. Weir, *Andrew Weir*, p. 117.

14. Mark O'Neill, *Frederick: The Life of my Missionary Grandfather in Manchuria* (Hong Kong: Joint Publishing, 2012), p. 154.

15. Weir, *Andrew Weir*, pp. 158-59. W. J. Grier, *The Origin and Witness of the Irish Evangelical Church* (Belfast: Evangelical Bookshop, n.d.), pp. 18ff. William Addley, *Rev. James Hunter of Knock* (Belfast: Presbyterian Historical Society of Ireland, 2018), pp. 66-67.

16. Addley, *Rev. James Hunter*, p. 67.

17. Fulton, *Through Earthquake, Wind and Fire*, p. 366; cf. Addley, *Rev. James Hunter*, p. 67.

18. Ibid., pp. 56-58.

19. Ibid., p. 61.

20. Ibid., p. 220.

21. Cf. *http://en.ccctspm.org* (information dated 25 Sept. 2017), accessed 11 January, 2022.

22. Leslie Lyall, *Come Wind, Come Weather* (London: Hodder and Stoughton, 1961).

23. Kim and Kim, *History*, p. 310.

24. Personal communication.

25. Brent Fulton, 'China: A Tale of Two Churches?' in Bruce P. Baugus (ed.), *China's Reforming Churches: Mission, Polity, and Ministry in the Next Christendom* (Grand Rapids: Reformation Heritage Books, 2014), Kindle location 3796.

26. 'China's Xi warns against religious infiltration from abroad,' Associated Press, April 24, 2016.

27. Rebecca Paveley, 'Persecution of Christians predicted to worsen in China,' *Church Times*, 19th February 2021.

28. 'Protestant Christianity is booming in China: President Xi does not approve,' 15 September, 2020, at https://www.economist.com/graphic-detail/2020/09/15/protestant-christianity-is-booming-in-china – accessed 5 February 2022.

29. Steven W. Mosher, 'Why the Crackdown? Christians Now Outnumber Communists in China.' 24 November, 2014, at https://aleteia.org/2014/11/24/why-the-crackdown-christians-now-outnumber-communists-in-china/ – accessed 5 February, 2022.

Bibliography

Manuscript Sources

Acts of the General Assembly of the Free Church of Scotland (1881).

Epistle from the Manchurian Presbytery to United Presbyterian Church (1888).

Editorial Correspondence Books of the British and Foreign Bible Society (1880–1897).

Letter Books of the Foreign Mission Committee of the United Presbyterian Church.

Minute-books of the Foreign Mission Committee of the United Presbyterian Church.

Proceedings of the Synod of the United Presbyterian Church (1870).

Government Records, Parliamentary Sources and Legal Records

China, No.1 (1872) *Correspondence Respecting the Circular of the Chinese Government of February 9, 1871, Relating to Missionaries.*

Diplomatic and Consular Report. China. *Report for the years 1903–05 on the Trade of Chefoo, No. 3729 Annual Series* (London: His Majesty's Stationery Office, 1906).

Letter: Captain Elliot to Viscount Palmerston, Nov. 16th, 1839, received March 27th, 1840, in *Additional Papers Relating to China: Presented to Both Houses of Parliament by Command of Her Majesty 1840.*

Official Korean Government reports (Kojong Archives).

Proceedings of the Old Bailey.

Records Relating to Property Interests in Chefoo, China, held by Fergusson & Co.

United States Government *Report on the Murder of the Officers, Crew and Passengers of the American Schooner General Sherman at the Ping Yang River, Corea.*

War with China – Adjourned Debate, *Hansard,* 8 April 1840, vol 53.

Newspapers and Journals

Canadian College Missionary Report.

Highlander.

International Bulletin of Missionary Research.

International Review of Mission.

Korea Mission Field.

Keswick Week.

Life of Faith.

Missionary Record of the United Presbyterian Church.

Missionary Review of the World.

New York Times.

Missionary Record of the Home and Foreign Mission Work of the United Free Church of Scotland.

Sydney Gazette and New South Wales Advertiser.

Technical Papers for the Bible Translator.

Torch Trinity Journal.

Articles

Peter Bush, 'The Rev. R. P. MacKay: Pietist as Denominational Executive,' paper for the Canadian Society of Presbyterian History.

A. Chow, 'Jonathan Chao and "Return Mission": The Case of the Calvinist Revival in China,' in *Mission Studies* 36.3.

Norman H. Cliff, 'Building the Protestant Church in Shandong, China' in *International Bulletin of Missionary Research,* April 1998.

Neil Connor, 'China media continues to laud Xi's visit and UK ties,' in *The Telegraph*, 23 October 2015.

D. S. Crawford, 'Mukden Medical College (1911–1949): an outpost of Edinburgh medicine in northeast China. Part 1: 1882–1917; building the foundations and opening the College' in *Journal of the Royal College of Physicians of Edinburgh*, Volume 36: Issue 1: 2006.

James H. Grayson, 'John Ross and Cultural Encounter: Translating Christianity in an East Asian Context,' in *Studies in Church History*, 06/2017, Vol.53.

James H. Grayson, 'The Legacy of John Ross' in *The International Bulletin of Missionary Research*, October 1999.

James H. Grayson, 'A Spark in North East Asia: A Personal Hagiography of a Scottish Missionary to Manchuria: John Ross (1842–1915)' in Clyde Binfield (ed.) *Sainthood Revisioned: Studies in Hagiography and Biography* (Sheffield: Sheffield Academic Press, 1995).

R. A. Hardie, 'God's Touch in the Great Revival,' in *Korea Mission Field,* vol. 10, Seoul (January 1914).

Jeanette Hardage, 'The Legacy of Mary Slessor' in *The International Bulletin of Missionary Research*, Vol. 26, issue: 4, October 2002.

Robert Hay, 'Improvement not Clearance: A factor's instructions to his ground officers on the Isle of Lismore, 1831–46' in *Review of Scottish Culture,* vol. 22.

Everett N. Hunt, 'The Legacy of John Livingston Nevius,' in *International Bulletin of Missionary Research*, July 1991.

David W. Kim, 'From Manchuria to the Korean Peninsula: The Scottish Impact in Late Nineteenth Century Korea,' in David W. Kim (ed.) *Religious Transformation in Modern Asia* (Brill: 2015).

Kirsteen and Ko Hoon Kim, 'Who Brought the Gospel to Korea?' in *Christianity Today,* February 2018.

Jung-Sook Lee, 'Reconsidering Mary Culler White's Visit to Wonsan in 1903,' in Torch Trinity Journal, Torch Trinity Graduate University, Seoul, vol. 10, no.1, 2000.

James McCammon, 'Newchwang Bible School in Manchuria,' in *Christianity Today,* November 1936.

Sung-Deuk Oak, 'Competing Chinese Names for God: The Chinese Term Question and Its Influence upon Korea,' in *Journal of Korean Religions* 3, no. 2 (2012), pp. 89-115.

Rebecca Paveley, 'Persecution of Christians predicted to worsen in China,' *Church Times*, 19 February 2021.

Andrew Porter, 'David Cameron in China: ministers refuse calls to remove poppies,' in *The Telegraph*, 10 November 2010.

Austin Ramzy, 'How Britain Went to War with China Over Opium,' in *The New York Times*, 3 July, 2018.

Andrew Robinson, 'Why the Poppy Remains all the Rage' in *The Lancet*, vol. 388, December 10, 2016.

Kenneth R. Ross, 'Edinburgh 1910: Scottish roots and contemporary challenges' in *Theology in Scotland* XVII.I (2010).

Harold H. Rowdon, 'Edinburgh 1910, Evangelicals and the Ecumenical Movement,' in *Vox Evangelica* 5 (1967).

Richard Rutt, 'Concerning the New Testament of the Korean Bible,' in *Technical Papers for the Bible Translator,* Vol. 15, No. 2, April 1964.

Bill Sewell, 'Missions to Manchuria', in *Canadian Journal of History,* vol. 54, issue 1-2, 2019.

Christopher D. Sneller, 'Take Away Your Opium and Your Missionaries,' in *Bible In Transmission*, Winter 2012.

Brian Stanley, 'The Legacy of Robert Arthington,' in *International Bulletin of Missionary Research*, October 1998.

R. G. Tiedemann, 'Baptism of Fire: China's Christians and the Boxer Uprising of 1900,' in *International Bulletin of Missionary Research*, 2000, vol. 24.1.

Horace Grant Underwood, 'Today from Korea,' in *The Missionary Review of the World*, November 1893.

A. F. Walls, 'William Robertson Smith and The Missionary Movement,' in William Johnstone, *William Robertson Smith: Essays in Reassessment* (Sheffield: Sheffield Academic Press, 1995).

Yuanchong Wang, 'Revisiting the Forgotten Border gate: Fenghuang Gate, and the Emergence of the Modern Sino-Korean Borderline, 1636–1876,' in eds. Cathcart, Green and Denny, *Decoding the Sino-North Korean Borderlands* (Amsterdam: Amsterdam University Press B.V. 2021).

James Webster, 'The Maker of the Manchurian Mission,' in *The Missionary Record of the United Free Church*, September 1915.

Academic Theses

William Palmer Addley, *A study of the birth and development of the overseas missions of the Presbyterian Church in Ireland up to 1910,* Ph.D. thesis for the Queen's University, Belfast, 1995.

Peter Ahn-Ho Bae, *The Three-Self Principle and the Mission Method of John Ross: a Study on the Formation of the Early Korean Presbyterian Church (1874–1893),* Ph.D. Diss. University of Aberdeen, 2001.

Sung-il Choi, *'John Ross (1842–1915) and the Korean Protestant Church: The First Korean Bible and its Relation to the Protestant Origins in Korea.'* Ph.D. Diss. Edinburgh University, 1992.

Frederick J. Glover, *'Dispatches from the Wilderness: A History of the Canadian Missionaries and Korean Protestants in Northern Korea and Manchuria, 1893–1928,'* Ph.D. dissertation, University of Calgary, 2018.

Chil Sung Kim, *'The Role of Robert Hardie in the Korean Great Revival and the Subsequent Development of Korean Protestant Christianity,'* PhD diss., Asbury Theological College, Wilmore, Kentucky, 2012.

Laura MacDonald, *'Minister of the Gospel and Doctor of Medicine'*: The *Canadian Presbyterian Medical Mission to Korea 1898–1923,* MA thesis, Queen's University, Kingston, Ontario, Canada. February 2000.

Sung-Deuk Oak, *The Historical Materials of the Korean Bible Society.* Vol.1, The Korean Bible Society, Seoul, 2002.

Hyung Shin Park, *Presbyterian Missionaries in Southern Manchuria, 1867–1931: Religion, Society and Politics,* Ph.D. Dissertation for the Graduate Theological Union, Berkeley, California, 2008.

Xiuhua Wang, *Explaining Christianity in China: Why a Foreign Religion has Taken Root in Unfertile Ground,* Master of Arts thesis for Department of Sociology, Graduate School, Baylor University, 2015.

Printed Sources

Primary

James E. Adams, *Annual Personal Report to the Board of Foreign Missions of the Presbyterian Church of the USA* (Taegu, Korea, 1910–11).

Marshall Broomhall, *The Chinese Empire: A General and Missionary Survey* (London: Marshall, Morgan and Scott, 1907).

William N. Blair and Bruce F. Hunt, *The Korean Pentecost* (Edinburgh : Banner of Truth Trust, 1977).

Lord Brooke, *An Eye-witness in Manchuria* (London: Everleigh Nash, 1905).

Islay Burns, *Memoir of Rev. Wm. C. Burns: Missionary to China from the English Presbyterian Church* (London: James Nisbet, 1870).

Dugald Christie (ed. Iza Christie), *Thirty years in Moukden, 1883–1913: Being the Experiences and Recollections of Dugald Christie* (London: Constable, 1914).

Dugald Christie (ed. Iza Christie), *Ten Years in Manchuria: A Story of the Medical Mission Work in Moukden: 1883–1893* (Paisley: J. and R. Parlane, n.d).

Iza Inglis Christie, *Dugald Christie of Manchuria, Pioneer and Medical Missionary. The Story of a Life with a Purpose* (London: James Clarke, 1932).

Iza Inglis Christie, *Jackson of Mukden* (London: Hodder and Stoughton, 1923).

Alfred Costain, *The Life of Dr Arthur Jackson of Manchuria* (London: Hodder and Stoughton, 1911).

William Gibson, *Not Weary in Well-Doing, or, the Life and Work of Mrs Helen Lockhart Gibson* (Edinburgh: John Menzies and Co. 1888).

A. E. Glover, *A Thousand Miles of Miracles: A Personal Record of God's Delivering Power from the Hands of the Imperial Boxers of Shan-si* (London: Hodder and Stoughton, 1904).

Jonathan Goforth, *By My Spirit,* (London: Marshall, Morgan and Scott, n.d.).

Jonathan Goforth, *When the Spirit's Fire Swept Korea* (Grand Rapids: Zondervan, 1943).

Rosalind Goforth, *Goforth of China* (London: Marshall, Morgan and Scott, 1937).

S. D. Gordon, *Quiet Talks About Jesus* (Cincinnati: Jennings and Graham, 1906).

Helen Hunt Jackson, *Bits of Travel at Home* (Boston: Roberts Brothers, 1878).

James Johnson, *Report of the Centenary Conference on Protestant Mission of the World* (London: James Nisbet, 1889).

John Kennedy, *Days of the Fathers in Ross-shire* (Inverness: Northern Chronicle, 1897).

John Kennedy, *The Apostle of the North. The life and labours of the Rev. Dr M'Donald* (London: Nelson, 1866).

William MacKelvie, *Annals and Statistics of the United Presbyterian Church* (Edinburgh: Oliphant and A. Elliot, and Glasgow: D. Robertson, 1873).

Mrs Duncan M'Laren, *Missions of the United Presbyterian Church: The Story of our Manchurian Mission* (Edinburgh: Office of the United Presbyterian Church, 1896).

C. H. MacGill (ed.), *Memories of the Rev. Dr Hamilton M. MacGill (*Edinburgh: Andrew Elliot, 1880).

Hamilton M. MacGill, *Conference on Missions held in 1860 at Liverpool* (London: James Nisbet, 1860).

J. Graham Miller, *East of the Barrier, or, Sidelights on the Manchuria Mission* (New York, Fleming H. Revel, 1902).

John R. Mott, et. al., *Report of Commission I: Carrying the Gospel to All the Non-Christian World* (Edinburgh: Oliphant, Anderson and Ferrier, 1910).

John Noble, *Religious Life in Ross* (Inverness: Northern Counties Newspaper and Printing and Publishing Company, 1909).

Sung-Deuk Oak (ed), *The Historical Materials of the Korean Bible Society*, (Seoul: The Korean Bible Society, 2002).

F. W. S. O'Neil, *The Call of the East: Sketches of the History of the Irish Mission to Manchuria, 1869–1919.* (London: James Clarke, 1919).

F. W. S. O'Neil, *The Quest for God in China* (London: George Allen and Unwin, 1925).

Hyung-shin Park, *The Rev. John Ross: A Primary Sourcebook* (Seoul: Institute of the History of Christianity in Korea, 2019), two volumes.

Timothy Richard, *Forty-Five Years in China: Reminiscences* (London: T. Fisher Unwin, 1916).

John Ross, *Chinese Foreign Policy* (Shanghai: 1877).

John Ross, *Old Wang: The First Chinese Evangelist in Manchuria* (London: Religious Tract Society, 1889).

John Ross, *Missionary Methods in Manchuria* (Edinburgh: Oliphant, Anderson and Ferrier, 1903).

John Ross, *The History of Corea Ancient and Modern with Description of Manner and Customs, Language and Geography* (London: Eliot Stock, 1891).

John Ross, 'The Corean Version of the New Testament: How I Came to Make It,' in *United Presbyterian Missionary Record*, May 1883.

John Ross, 'The Christian Dawn in Korea' in *The Missionary Review of the World*, April 1890.

Donald Sage, *Memorabilia Domestica: Or Parish Life in the North of Scotland* (Wick: W. Rae, 1889).

Robert Small, *History of the Congregations of the United Presbyterian Church, 1733–1900* (Edinburgh: David M. Small, 1904).

Charles Taylor, *Five Years in China: With Some Account of the Great Rebellion and a Description of St. Helena* (New York: Derby and Jackson, 1860).

Horace Grant Underwood, *The Call of Korea: Political, Social, Religious* (New York: Fleming H. Revel, 1908).

L. H. Underwood, *Fifteen Years among the Top-Knots or Life in Korea* (New York: American Tract Society, 1904).

James Webster ed., John Ross, *The Marvellous Story of the Revival in Manchuria* (Edinburgh: Oliphant, Anderson and Ferrier, 1908).

James Webster, *Times of Blessing in Manchuria: Letters from Mukden to the Church at Home from February 17–April 30, 1908* (Shanghai: Methodist Publishing House, 1909).

James Webster, *The Revival in Manchuria* (London: Morgan & Scott, 1910).

Elizabeth Weir, *Andrew Weir of Manchuria* (London: James Clark, n.d).

Alexander Williamson, *Journeys in North China, Manchuria, and Eastern Mongolia; with some Account of Corea* (London: Smith, Elder & Co., 1870).

Alexander Wylie, *Memorials of Protestant Missionaries to the Chinese: Giving a List of Their Publications, and Obituary Notices of the Deceased* (Shanghai: American Presbyterian Mission Press, 1867).

Secondary

Bill Addley, *Rev. James Hunter of Knock* (Belfast: Presbyterian Historical Society of Ireland, 2018).

Hubert J. B. Allen, *Roland Allen: Pioneer, Priest and Prophet* (Cincinnati: Forward Movement Publications, 1995).

Roland Allen, *Missionary Methods: St. Paul's or Ours?* (London: R. Scott, 1912).

Roland Allen, *The Spontaneous Expansion of the Church: And Causes that Hinder It* (London: The World Dominion Press, 1927).

Roland Allen, *The Ministry of the Spirit: Selected Writings*, (ed). D. M. Paton (Cambridge: Lutterworth Press: 2006).

Roland Allen, *The Siege of the Peking Legations, Being the Diary of the Rev. Roland Allen* (London: Smith Elder, 1901).

Anon., *Chinese Imprints and a Screen*, Catalogue 1491, (London: Maggs Bros. Ltd., 2017).

Arnobius, 'Against the Heathen (Book II),' in *Ante-Nicene Fathers*, Vol. 6.X. Ed. Alexander Roberts, James Donaldson, and A. Cleveland Coxe (Edinburgh: T & T Clark, 1887).

Bruce P. Baugus, *China's Reforming Churches: Mission, Polity, and Ministry in the Next Christendom* (Grand Rapids: Reformation Heritage Books, 2014).

J. H. Bavinck, *Introduction to the Science of Missions* (Philadelphia: Presbyterian and Reformed Publishing Co., 1960).

David W. Bebbington and David Ceri Jones (eds), *Evangelicalism and Fundamentalism in the United Kingdom during the Twentieth Century* (Oxford: Oxford University Press, 2013).

J. Beeching, *The Chinese Opium Wars* (London: Hutchinson, 1975).

Robert Higginson Boyd, *Waymakers in Manchuria: The Story of the Irish Presbyterian Pioneer Missionaries to Manchuria* (Belfast, Foreign Mission Office, Church House, 1940).

William N. Blair and Bruce F. Hunt, *The Korean Pentecost and the Sufferings Which Followed* (Edinburgh: Banner of Truth Trust, 1977).

James Buchan, *The Expendable Mary Slessor* (Edinburgh: St Andrew Press, 1980).

Mildred Cable, *China: Her Life and People* (London: University of London Press, 1946).

Austin Fulton, *Through Earthquake Wind and Fire: Church and Mission in Manchuria 1867–1950,* (Edinburgh: The Saint Andrew Press, 1967).

William Perry Fogg, *Round the World: Letters from Japan, China, India, and Egypt* (Cleveland, 1872).

W. J. Grier, *The Origin and Witness of the Irish Evangelical Church* (Belfast: Evangelical Bookshop, n.d.).

John Gillies, *Historical Collections of Accounts of Revival* (rpt. Edinburgh: Banner of Truth Trust, 1981).

Alistair Heys (ed.), *From Gothic to Romantic: Thomas Chatterton's Bristol,* (Bristol: Redcliffe Press, 2005).

Hewat, *Vision and Achievement, 1796–1956: A History of the Foreign Missions of the Churches united in the Church of Scotland* (London: Thomas Nelson and Sons, 1960).

J. C. Keyte, *In China Now: China's Need and the Christian Contribution* (London: Livingstone Press, 1923).

Sebastian C. H. and Kirsteen Kim, *A History of Korean Christianity* (Cambridge: Cambridge University Press, 2015).

K. S. Latourette, *Christianity in a Revolutionary Age, Volume 3* (Exeter: Paternoster Press, 1970).

K. S. Latourette, *A History of the Expansion of Christianity, Volume 6.* (Exeter: Paternoster Press, 1971).

Leslie Lyall, *Come Wind, Come Weather* (London: Hodder and Stoughton, 1961).

Wonsuk Ma and Kyo Seong Ahn (eds), *Korean Church, God's Mission, Global Christianity* – Regnum Edinburgh Centenary Series, Volume 26 (Oxford: Regnum Books International, 2015).

Allan W. MacColl**,** *Land, Faith and the Crofting Community: Christianity and Social Criticism in the Highlands of Scotland 1843–1893.* Scottish Historical Review Monographs (Edinburgh: Edinburgh University Press, 2006).

Lesley A. Orr Macdonald, *A Unique and Glorious Mission: Women and Presbyterianism in Scotland, 1830–1930* (Edinburgh: John Donald, 2000).

Kenneth Macfarlane, *The Rev. John Ross D.D. Remembered: 1842–1925* (Logie Secretarial Services, 1995).

Alexander Macpherson (ed.), *History of the Free Presbyterian Church of Scotland 1893–1970* (Glasgow: Publications Committee, Free Presbyterian Church of Scotland, n.d.).

J. A. R. Moffat (ed), *Mayfield 100, 1875–1975* (Edinburgh: Publications Committee Mayfield Church, 1975).

Favell Lee Mortimer, *Peep of Day* (London: T. Hatchard, 1851).

Iain H. Murray, *Revival and Revivalism: The Making and Marring of American Evangelicalism, 1750–1858* (Edinburgh: Banner of Truth Trust, 1994).

John Murray, *Redemption Accomplished and Applied* (Edinburgh: Banner of Truth Trust, 1961).

J. I. Packer, *Keep in Step with the Spirit* (Leicester: Inter-Varsity Press, 1984).

George Paik, *The History of Protestant Missions in Korea, 1832–1910* (Pyongyang: Union Christian College Press, 1927).

Marco Polo, *Il Milione* (English translation – *The Travels of Marco Polo, the Venetian*, London: J. M. Dent, 1908).

T. B. Ray, *Southern Baptists in China* (Richmond, VA: Foreign Mission Board Southern Baptist Convention, n.d.).

Lewis Rose, 'County of Ross and Cromarty' in *The New Statistical Account of Scotland* (Edinburgh and London, W. Blackwood and Sons, 1845), Vol. 6.

Eric Richards, *The Highland Clearances: People, Landlords and Rural Turmoil* (Edinburgh: Birlinn, 1988).

Roy E., Shearer, *Wildfire: Church Growth in Korea* (Grand Rapids: William B. Eerdmans, 1966).

Robert H. W. Shepherd, *Lovedale, South Africa: The Story of a Century, 1841–1941* (Lovedale: Lovedale Press, n.d).

D. C. Searle and S. B. Ferguson, *The Collected Writings of William Still: volume III, Theological Studies in Genesis and Romans* (Tain: Rutherford House and Christian Focus Publications, 2000).

S. Frederick Starr, *Lost Enlightenment: Central Asia's Golden Age from the Arab Conquest to Tamerlane* (Princeton: Princeton University Press, 2013).

R. G. Tiedemann, 'China and its Neighbors,' in ed. Adrian Hasting, *A World History of Christianity* (Grand Rapids: W. B. Eerdmans, 1999).

James Thomson, *The Value and Importance of Scottish Fisheries* (London: Smith, Elder, 1849).

Mark Twain, *Roughing It* (1872, New York: Penguin Classics, 1985).

Jules Verne, *Around the World in Eight Days* (London: Sampson Low, Marston, Low, & Searle, 1873).

Andrew F. Walls, *The Cross-Cultural Process in Christian History: Studies in the Transmission and Appropriation of Faith* (Edinburgh: T&T Clark, 2002).

B. B. Warfield, *Studies in Perfectionism* (Nutley, NJ: Presbyterian and Reformed Publishing, 1958).

Max Warren (ed.), *To Apply the Gospel: Selections from the Writings of Henry Venn* (Grand Rapids: W. B. Eerdmans, 1971).

Frances Wood, *No Dogs and Not Many Chinese: Treaty Port Life in China 1843–1943*, (London: John Murray, 1998).

Arnold Wright (ed.), *Twentieth Century Impressions of Hongkong, Shanghai, and other Treaty Ports of China: Their History, People, Commerce, Industry, and Resources* (London: Lloyds Greater Britain Publishing Company Limited, 1908).

Index

C

Christian Focus Publications

Our mission statement –

STAYING FAITHFUL

In dependence upon God we seek to impact the world through literature faithful to His infallible Word, the Bible. Our aim is to ensure that the Lord Jesus Christ is presented as the only hope to obtain forgiveness of sin, live a useful life and look forward to heaven with Him.

Our books are published in four imprints:

CHRISTIAN FOCUS

Popular works including biographies, commentaries, basic doctrine and Christian living.

CHRISTIAN HERITAGE

Books representing some of the best material from the rich heritage of the church.

MENTOR

Books written at a level suitable for Bible College and seminary students, pastors, and other serious readers. The imprint includes commentaries, doctrinal studies, examination of current issues and church history.

CF4•K

Children's books for quality Bible teaching and for all age groups: Sunday school curriculum, puzzle and activity books; personal and family devotional titles, biographies and inspirational stories – because you are never too young to know Jesus!

Christian Focus Publications Ltd,
Geanies House, Fearn, Ross-shire,
IV20 1TW, Scotland, United Kingdom.
www.christianfocus.com